When Will the Illuminati Crash the Stock Market?

Other Books by Soul Esprit

The Great Deception
The Coming of Wisdom
Fools Paradise
Seven Who Dared
The Criminal Fraternity
Genesis 1:29 Diet
Fractal Trading
The Globalist's Agenda
Everything is a Test

Book Ordering Information at End of Book

All praise, honor, and glory be to God –
the LORD God Almighty, the Lord Jesus Christ

When Will the Illuminati Crash the Stock Market?

An Insider's Look at the Elite Satanic Luciferians
Who Dictate the Rise and Fall of Global Economies

Soul Esprit

Servant of the Lord Jesus Christ

NarrowGate Publishing

***When* Will the Illuminati Crash the Stock Market?**

Published by NarrowGate Publishing

All Scripture verses quoted are from the Authorized 1611 King James Bible.

Illustrations on the following pages by *DDees.com*:
27, 61, 80, 87, 93, 103, 107, 111, 114, 126, 128, 143, 184, 187

ISBN: 978-0-9841279-0-0

Library of Congress Control Number: 2009931805

Second Edition 2014

CONTENTS

And it shall come to pass in that day, saith the LORD, that there shall be the noise of a cry from the fish gate, and an howling from the second, and a great crashing from the hills. Howl, ye inhabitants of Maktesh, for all the merchant people are cut down; all they that bear silver are cut off. And it shall come to pass at that time, that I will search Jerusalem with candles, and punish the men that are settled on their lees: that say in their heart, The LORD will not do good, neither will he do evil. Therefore their goods shall become a booty, and their houses a desolation: they shall also build houses, but not inhabit them; and they shall plant vineyards, but not drink the wine thereof. The great day of the LORD is near, it is near, and hasteth greatly, even the voice of the day of the LORD: the mighty man shall cry there bitterly. That day is a day of wrath, a day of trouble and distress, a day of darkness and gloominess, a day of clouds and thick darkness, A day of the trumpet and alarm against the fenced cities, and against the high towers. And I will bring distress upon men, that they shall walk like blind men, because they have sinned against the LORD: and their blood shall be poured out as dust, and their flesh as the dung. Neither their silver nor their gold shall be able to deliver them in the day of the LORD's wrath; but the whole land shall be devoured by the fire of his jealousy; for he shall make even a speedy riddance of all them that dwell in the land.

– Zephaniah 1:10–18

PREFACE

This stock market forecast and future historical timeline is not intended as prophesy in the Biblical sense of the word, but is based upon correlations between the Books of Genesis, Daniel, Revelation, and reoccurring cycles evident in the implicit order of God's natural design. Neither is it speculation, but a certainty, subject to only minor revision dependent upon the unfolding of world events which shape the emergent result. The conclusions to follow are derived from objective criterion with a proven high degree of reliability.

Many who read this book will disbelieve the imminence and accuracy of the timeline and its global implications; most will not acknowledge the aftermath consequences until the Crash event is well underway or completed. The government-controlled media will attempt to discredit the author's conclusions with the disinformation label, "Conspiracy Theory" (ref. Appendix E).

It is also realized by the author that, in the interim since he began organizing information into book form (1992), the illiteracy rate of the American public has exponentially increased (less than 4 percent of Americans read a book per year). A new generation has spawned during this brief interlude; fewer are able to read truthful information such as this volume, and consequently, are limited to visual media – TV, videos, Hollywood films – most of which are government controlled, and therefore distort or suppress the truth. By young adulthood the average individual is so thoroughly brain-washed with government media *programming,* they have lost any critical thinking ability and are *incapable* of recognizing the truth should they encounter it. Additionally, their brains have become a battlefield for deploying civilian biochemical warfare agents such as vaccines, MSG, Aspartame, Fluoride, Chemtrails/HAARP, and the atmospheric electromagnetic pollution that surrounds us. The result is an alteration of normal brain wave function; a severing of their conscious mind from objective reality. Just as they remain blissfully unaware of the Illuminati's mind-numbing Chemtrails being sprayed upon them *daily* from the sky above (since 1998), plainly visible overhead: ("Huh … what'er *chemtrails*?"); likewise, the mind-controlled and chemically lobotomized will remain oblivious to the clear and present warning issued in this timely work: ("Huh … *what* stock market crash?"). Ecclesiastes 9:5 states: *The dead know not anything.*

The American people, increasingly illiterate by government design, have for decades been systematically rendered truth adverse by government-controlled public schools, government-controlled "churches," television *programming,* and government-controlled media. Consequently, they are no longer sufficiently cognizant to form an independent opinion; the social engineering "thought masters" have formed and packaged it for them. Regardless of any truth that may leak through the scripted press, the public will remain transfixed before a big screen monitor in order to receive their daily dose of "mind think." For them, truth is television; lies are the truth. They will uncritically believe and parrot anything they see or hear on TV. Because they hate the truth (The Truth is Jesus Christ; John: 14:6), an *entire nation* has become terminally ignorant to the point where they now call evil, good; and good, evil. Isaiah 5:20: *Woe unto them who call evil good, and good evil; that put darkness for light, and light for darkness; that put bitter for sweet, and sweet for bitter*! Because the wickedness of man has increased to the level where the American people no longer feel outrage over injustice; a nation so unrighteous they will not stand against even the most egregious government atrocities; because they hate the Kingdom of God and love the government of Satan, *therefore,* God is about to judge America and the rest of the world. This book specifies when that Final Judgment is likely to occur ... *and none of the wicked shall understand; but the wise shall understand* (Daniel 12:10).

Only the few Elect Remnant of *True* Christians throughout the world will believe the truth, and they *will* defend it with their very lives, because they shall experience in *this present generation* that which is spoken of in the Bible: the time of Great Tribulation (Matthew 24:29-31). Only a *True* Christian believes the Word of God and understands there is no "Pre-Tribulation Rapture": ... *we must through much tribulation enter into the kingdom of God* (Acts 14:22). *He that endureth to the end shall be saved* (Matthew 10:22; 24:13; Mark 13:13). *He that overcometh, and keepeth my works until the end, to him will I give power over the nations* ... (Revelation 2:26).

Until the end: ... *hold fast, and repent* (Revelation 3:3).

– Soul Esprit
December 17, 2003

INTRODUCTION

"Some even believe we are part of a secret cabal working against the best interests of the United States, characterizing my family and me as 'internationalists' and of conspiring with others around the world to build a more integrated global political and economic structure – one world, if you will. If that is the charge, I stand guilty, and I am proud of it."

– David Rockefeller
from his autobiography, "Memoirs", pg. 405

It was a typical day in October of 1929 when the Governor of New York, Franklin Delano Roosevelt, invited England's Prime Minister, Winston Churchill, to New York City. There was nothing unusual about that particular day, everything seemed normal while they reclined in the plush rear seat of a black Rolls Royce chauffeured limousine. The two world leaders must have gazed out the side window, at the thronging masses of pedestrians lining the sidewalks; the working class men and women ... whom they were about to *financially ruin.*

The infamous stock market crash of 1929 was no mere accident. Even though modern historians all agree that the greatest economic tragedy in American history was caused by an excess of over leveraged stock purchases, there were other causal factors which served to exacerbate the ominous credit bubble.

In the carnival atmosphere of the *Roaring Twenties*, Wall Street was the center of international attention; it was the place where you could make a fortune, establish your mark for future generations. It seemed like everyone was "playing the market"; not only the traditional well-healed savvy investor, but also the common man – blue collar factory workers, farmers, anyone with an extra dollar to invest in a "sure bet." It seemed like everyone put their money in the stock market, ready to take a gamble; and if they had no cash money to invest, they borrowed it from the commercial banks, loaned to them at up to 90 percent the value of their home or family farm. They borrowed on *margin*, mortgaging the free and clear assets of their future posterity. Everyone was confident in the economy; it was stable, the world was at peace, there were no wars looming on the horizon. Everyone made money picking winning stocks, companies whose earnings never seemed to decline. Yes, it seemed like *everyone* was in the stock market, and *everyone* was a winner; even the proverbial street corner shoe shine boy was a self-proclaimed stock market expert. But, as history reveals – everyone *was wrong*! (Except the *insiders*.) In a matter of hours, sometimes minutes, everything was lost – their entire life savings, their house, their future.

Like all world leaders today, both FDR and Churchill were Luciferians: Satan-worshipping sorcerers, descendants from generational Illuminati bloodlines. Roosevelt was a high-ranking 33 degree Freemason; Churchill, a Druid witch. Together with Hitler and Stalin, who were also practicing disciples of Lucifer (aka Satan, the Devil), they were the "front men" of their day, mere figurehead puppets dancing on a string pulled by their invisible Illuminati masters. Yet, they all knew it was going to happen, for there exists a hierarchy of councils: secret and semi-secret societies, both above and below the *Round Table world supra-government* (referred to by its subordinates as "The Council"). Those positioned in the upper echelon of the hierarchy were political insiders privy to the plan to crash the U.S. economy, devaluate the dollar, and plunge

America into an economic depression that would be followed by their *planned* World War II. These world leaders had previously been made aware of what their superiors (primarily the international Rothschild banking cartel) intended to do, and they were expected to follow orders that were part of a long-term scheme euphemistically known in occult circles as, "The Plan". It has been the objective of this transnational shadow government to destroy the world's *cash economy* and replace it with a *cashless* electronic system that would eliminate nation-state sovereignty and bring all countries under dictatorial control of a worldwide totalitarian Police State government regime. In addition to the stock market crash and WW II, The Plan also called for more government-created crisis (later disingenuously labeled by the Illuminati-controlled media as "terrorism") and, in the early part of the twenty-first century, a third world war and emergence of a *global government* dictatorship to control and enslave the entire population of the world.

Roosevelt and Churchill were merely following a pre-planned script. Serving as media mouthpieces to manipulate and control the masses through the supragovernment-owned media, they *were not* the ultimate authority deciding the fate of Western Civilization. That earthly rule was vested in the hands of only a few men (and women) positioned near the top of the Illuminati pyramid of power – apparently invisible – yet comprising an eminently powerful closed group of generational witches and Satanists; individuals who, in obedience to their fallen angel leader – Satan/Lucifer/the Devil – routinely sacrifice living human beings to appease the insatiable blood lust of their underworld lord and master. (*This* is reality. TV, Hollywood, and the evening news are the *fantasy*.) Recognizable faces performing unspeakably wicked deeds for their unseen leader is what is required of them in order to maintain their dominion and control over the human population of the entire planet. Blood rituals, human child sacrifice, transmutated otherworldly creatures without conscious or a soul – these are the entities who run the world. By such spiritual means they gain incalculable multi-generational wealth and strategic advantage over the world's people. (The battle is never as it seems, but is *entirely* spiritual. Ephesians 6:12.) Those who truly rule the world are the men behind the political puppets; multi-generations of diabolical men and their offspring who control the American federal government, and all earthly governments, *to this very day.*

The stock market crash of 1929 was no mere accident. (Neither was America's *second* supra-government planned "terrorist act": the 1941 Japanese bombing of Pearl Harbor.) The early 1930's engineered meltdown of the American economy would cause reverberations throughout the globe; and in America, chaos, confusion and desperation among the suddenly impoverished multitudes of frightened men and women who would demand *a Solution.* As always, the international world controllers had a ready made "Solution" to the "Problem" which *they* created. The Luciferian globalists presented to the American people a *welcomed remedy* by utilizing their traditional approach for bringing about social change: the Hegelian Dialectic: Thesis – Antithesis – Synthesis; Crisis – Reaction – Solution; Stock Market Crash – Economic Depression and WW II – New Deal and restructuring of European power balance. This has always been the globalist's standard modus operandi for creating *change.* (The "change" much proclaimed by current Illuminati-appointed figurehead, U.S. President Barack Obama, was not meant as change in a positive constructive sense, but rather, change in terms of loss of liberty, economic devastation, and a global Police State dictatorship.) It is a formula which they have perfected and utilized repeatedly throughout modern world history. The Dialectic Principle worked back then, and it also worked during September 11, 2001; the gullible American people never questioning the *disinformation* created by the Illuminati-controlled media.

Here is how the Dialectic Principle works: First, they (the transnational Luciferian shadow government) create a *crisis.* Then, in response to the expected *reaction* of the terrified masses, they fabricate media propaganda to justify government intervention, offering a *solution* that seems plausible to the undiscerning public. In so doing, they pass legislation by Executive Order (circumventing Congress and the vote of the people) to bring the world closer to an oppressive global government. Desired result: The people *love* their enslavement. After all, "the government" saved them from "The Terrorists."

Wars and insurrections, Pearl Harbor/WWII, crashing radio-controlled jet airliners into the New York World Trade Towers on September 11 (and blaming it on the Arabs), the *fake* "War on Terrorism," the globalist's oil and opium "wars" in the Middle East – all of these merely serve as stepping stones for Satan's millennial scheme to bring all of mankind into servitude to him *through human government.* As U.S. General Smedley Butler wrote in his 1935 classic book, *War is a Racket*: "Wars are really a continuous stream of coordinated acts of terrorism, related to money and power instigated by the people who will benefit from the war and its expected end result. War is an instrument to expand economic power by destroying the national institutions and intelligent people of the victimized nation." The Devil's faithful servants in positions of power, such as all past U.S. Presidents since Woodrow Wilson (except Kennedy), have been Illuminati pawns, mere "sock puppets" who shamelessly advocated loss of U.S. sovereignty and Constitutionally guaranteed freedoms by an encroaching Police State control grid that will soon reduce human liberty to the size of a microchip. It is the same infamous agenda first introduced into the common vernacular by Illuminatus spokesperson, George Herbert Walker Bush, when publicly referring over 100 times to a *"New World Order."*

In this present modern era, the reliable Hegelian formula consists of the following planned events: First: *Create a Crisis*: Collapse the World Trade Center Towers, and then the U.S. Stock Market. Second*: Formulate the Reaction*: Take away the people's rights to life, liberty and the pursuit of happiness by passing unconstitutional legislation such as Homeland Security and the Patriot Acts, anti-

Second Amendment gun confiscation laws, abolish First Amendment free speech, and other Police State tactics "to protect you from the terrorists." Third: *Offer the Solution:* Microchip everyone on earth in order to track and enslave the world's people by an interlocking surveillance control grid, a computerized global dictatorship (*even more* protection from the "terrorists"). In various forms, this basic approach has proven effective for the Luciferians throughout world history. This formula has been remarkably consistent, therefore, ascertaining what they will do next is highly predictable.

The Hegelian Dialectic is commonly practiced throughout the Illuminati crime syndicate. For example, one of the many criminal government front groups – the IRS (i.e. Federal Mafia) – threatens: "Pay us *protection money* (unconstitutional personal income taxes to fund government criminal activities) or we'll throw you in prison and devastate you and your family." Another organized crime element – the scripted controlled media – smiles and says: "Believe our propaganda lies (e.g. 'We're at war with *Iraq* because *Arabs* attacked the Twin Towers and so you need to be protected from further acts of government-staged terrorism by forfeiting your Constitutional rights – for your own protection, of course') and we'll allow you to be our microchipped mind-controlled slave. T*hen* we'll throw you in prison and devastate you and your family." (Levying a federal income tax upon citizen's personal income is *illegal*, as determined by a Supreme Court decision ruling that it violates the 16th Amendment to the U.S. Constitution. The legal provision allowing for a personal income tax was *never ratified* into law! Therefore, income taxes are nothing more than *extortion payments* – coercion at the implicit point of a gun/imprisonment – and which you *Constitutionally do not owe.* One hundred percent of coerced tax revenue goes to a nongovernmental private bank, The Federal Reserve, to *pay interest* on money it loaned to the U.S. federal government. Not one cent of citizen's personal income taxes ever goes toward government public services; it all goes to finance the Illuminati's war machine and their New World Order global terrorism and depopulation campaign. Your extorted tax "pay-offs" are therefore funding your own destruction.)

Although the stock market collapse of 1929 was *apparently* caused by over-margined consumer borrowing, on another level, all that was required to deflate the rapidly expanding credit bubble was the creation of a panic-causing rumor – nothing substantial or having any basis in corporate solvency – only a rumor, *one lie* to strike sudden fear into the heart of Wall Street and precipitate a massive sell off of stock shares by the major New York City brokerage houses, whose principals *were also* Illuminati insiders. Once Wall Street's tenuous stability was disturbed, panic selling by the insiders produced a domino effect, and, with no available interested buyers, stock prices exponentially plummeted. (As a reward for his "cooperation," Churchill was reimbursed for his massive stock market losses by Bernard Baruch of Goldman Sachs brokerage firm.)

This was the superficial mechanics of the crashing U.S. economy that created a four year economic Depression in America and required *25 years* for GNP productivity to recover. It was all part of a longer range multi-generational plan to create a global economy for sustaining a global international dictatorship. Yet, there is a more subtle understanding to the apparent causes of the sudden calamitous stock market crash that ravaged the United States economy in a matter of months, served as a prelude to World War II, and ushered in the Presidency of *newly promoted Illuminist*, Franklin Delano Roosevelt.

BACK OF U.S. ONE DOLLAR BILL SHOWING THE FRONT AND REVERSE SIDES OF THE GREAT SEAL OF THE UNITED STATES

The two circular objects on either side of the word, "ONE," are not the official Seal of the United States, but of the Illuminati Freemasons in 1782.

The Illuminati globalists who designed the art work for the U.S. paper currency (proposed by Secretary of Agriculture/ Vice President Henry Wallace in 1935 during the Presidency of Franklin Roosevelt, a 33 degree Luciferian Freemason) did not intend for the phrase "IN GOD WE TRUST" to mean the Holy God of the Christian Bible. Instead, they intended it to mean their unholy "god," Lucifer, also known as Satan, the Devil. Likewise, whenever they refer to "Christ," they do not mean Jesus Christ of Nazareth – God in the flesh – but their coming New World Order planetary leader, "Antichrist."

In the center of the dollar bill, in the largest type, is the word, "ONE," denoting the Luciferian's "ONE WORLD." Their plan is to create ONE world currency, ONE global religion, and ONE world government; divesting all nations of independent sovereignty, under the dictatorial rule of a *United Nations* (UN) headed by ONE individual (Antichrist), a global political leader indwelled by the spirit of their unholy god, Lucifer.

The image on the right (front side of the Great Seal) shows a scroll in the Luciferian Masonic eagle's beak that bears the cryptic

Latin phrase, *E Pluribus Unum*, which translates into the English, "Out of many, One." Again, this decades old crypto-code signifies their plans for global unification, i.e. "Out of many nations one supra-national government will emerge." The "eagle" is actually an occult "Phoenix" arising from the ashes of the destroyed presently existing political and economic "Old" World Order. Look closely to discover the prevalence of the numerical count of "13": the number of arrows held in its talons (13), number of leaves on the olive branch (13), number of berries on the olive branch (13), number of vertical stripes on the shield (13), stars above the Phoenix bird (13), letters in the Latin phrase *E Pluribus Unum* (13).

Now examine the left image (reverse side of the Great Seal) and count the levels of brick comprising the Illuminati pyramid (13), and also the number of letters in the Latin phrase *Annuit Coeptis* (13). All this Luciferian numerology is *by design*, and is intended to convey occult significance to be understood only by those initiated into Masonic Witchcraft rituals. (Note: Masonic Luciferians read from right to left. Nearly everything they do is backward and upside down. Hence, the reverse side of the Great Seal is on the left side of the dollar bill, and the front of the Seal is on the right side.) Contrary to explanations offered to the general public by Masonic disinformation sources, the multiple 13's were not meant as referring to the original 13 colonies established by the English Monarchy. Author, Barry Smith, in his book, *Final Notice*, states: "There are 13 families or groups heading up the World Government plan. These families are portrayed as the 13 layers of blocks found on the strange seal on the reverse side of the US $1 bill." Fritz Springmeier, in his volume, *Bloodlines of the Illuminati*, reports from information provided to him by defected insiders, naming and identifying these 13 families as comprising the global Illuminati. The Roman numerals inscribed on the bottom layer of blocks is MDCCLXXVI which equals 1776, the official year the Illuminati is *said* to have been founded. This is also the date for the drafting of the U.S. Constitution, which was merely a symbolic gesture. (Contrary to popular opinion, the Illuminati was not established in

1776 by Adam Weishaupt, a Bavarian Jesuit priest, but its origin can be traced back at least 4000 years to the pagan Babylonian Mystery Religions of Sumeria, Egypt and Mesopotamia. ref. Revelation 17:5.) In truth, this numerical series is actually a code for the number of the Beast 666 (ref. Revelation 13:18):

MDCCLXXVI
DC - LX - VI
6 6 6

Information disseminated on the Internet regarding the meaning of the symbols, colors, and Latin phrases that were used to create the Great Seal is *disinformation* – i.e. falsehoods intended to deceive the uninformed public. To a Masonic Luciferian, words, phrases and symbols often have double and triple meanings, and are meant to convey the *exact opposite* implied by their common usage.

TRANSLATION OF LATIN INTO ENGLISH ON REVERSE SIDE OF THE GREAT SEAL OF THE UNITED STATES AND BACK SIDE OF THE U.S. ONE DOLLAR BILL

Annuit Coeptis

Announcing Our Endeavor

... Novus Ordo Seclorum

... **of a** New Secular (worldly/unGodly) Order

New World Order

CHAPTER 1

PERFECT ORDER IN APPARENT CHAOS

An historical price chart of the Dow Jones Industrial Average (DJIA/DOW) Stock Index is a graphic representation of America's economic growth, which officially began at the inception of the New York Stock Exchange in 1792. Upon cursory examination, one notices the long-term slope of the price line gradually moving upward over time, occasionally disrupted by sudden brief periods of decline that soon quickly recover, and which are followed by a continuation of the former trend. To the astute observer there exists an uniformity in what appears as regular cycles of advance and regress. This regularity can be compared to a series of ascending stair steps.

Examining the price data in shorter time intervals reveals periods of steep and prolonged stock market devaluations. These declines represent price movements which correspond to varying degrees of crashes throughout American history, such as transpired in 1929, and later, in 1987, 1998, 2001, 2008 and 2010. Although these abrupt losses were considered extreme at the time of their occurrence, in the overall long-term chart of the DJIA (logarithmic scale), they are of little consequence, appearing as mere blips on the screen of centuries-long historical price data. In fact, when viewing a graphic illustration of the long-term steadily advancing U.S. economy (logarithmic scale), if one were not aware these panic-driven "mini-crashes" had occurred, it would be difficult to ascertain that anything "unusual" had taken place.

All naturally occurring phenomenon exhibit an *ordered structure*, a repeatable form based on identical subunits making up the whole. This "self similarity" appears to be God's preferred way of structuring physical systems and of organizing the material universe into a stable and *ordered configuration*, one that can quickly adapt to *predicable chaos*. (In this context, the terms "ordered" and "chaos" are metaphors describing interaction taking place in a higher dimensional realm. These words can be associated with the absolute concepts of good and evil which directly correlate with God and with Lucifer/Satan the Devil, respectively. The LORD God, the Lord Jesus Christ, Creator of the universe, are the God of perfection, order and righteousness. Lucifer/Satan, the corrupted angel created by God, is the epitome of imperfection, disorder, chaos, confusion and unrighteousness. Since the fall of mankind in the Garden of Eden, he has been granted by God the authority to rule over those who desire to serve him. ref. Luke 4:5,6. It is *they* who are primarily responsible for creating chaos in today's world. These Scriptural truths should be kept in mind when considering the implications of spiritually charged words used in a material sense.)

God's perfect order is evident in all of His creation, on every scale: from the subatomic atom to mega-clusters of galaxies. Throughout the seemingly infinite universe there exists certain mathematical relationships characteristic of physical systems; a design evident, for example, in minute electron orbitals or the universe of planetary and galactic systems. The distinguishing features of God's perfect order can be directly observed in the repeatable patterned sequence of the outline of a leaf, silhouette of a tree, mountain range, or an aerial view of a shoreline. It can also be seen in a population growth curve: the natural life cycle of growth, maturation and death. When a graphic representation is made of energy dissipating physical systems, a similar pattern emerges. For instance, a shock wave, voice print, or an oscilloscope tracing of a heart beat. Each of the above shows a characteristic upward advancing energy pulse terminating in a peak, which soon abruptly declines to approximately the initial level. This is a typical bell-shaped curve well known to science, and illustrates a pattern common to all time-dependent phenomena. To the untrained eye there may seem to be no discernible design evident in the previously mentioned examples, yet, hidden within the apparent chaos is a subtle order manifested at every level, even to the minutest degree.

It has often been said that "history repeats itself." Since natural laws created by God operate on a reoccurring cycle, there is built-in reliability for predicting the subsequent design pattern of any naturally occurring system. Consequently, it is possible to determine, often with amazing precision, the eventual completion of an incomplete cycle. Since most natural time-dependent occurrences exhibit basically the same intrinsic design character when plotted graphically, once that character is understood, it becomes possible to anticipate the subsequent time-related outcome of future events.

When illustrated graphically, an economic cycle, such as demonstrated by the DJIA, is a representation of a standard growth curve, and is similar in design to the other periodic functions previously mentioned. Price oscillations in a broad-based market represent the sum total future aspirations and fears of a large number of individual investors; the graphic price data is a visual illustration of the collective opinions of the divergent group from which it was compiled. Price movements are therefore not a meaningless chaotic jumble, but rather, a concise summary of *mass human expectations* regarding the future. It is highly organized information with an implicit order and underlying meaning.

In conclusion, identifying where a market's price is located at any point in its long-term cycle provides an unique perspective of its future course. To illustrate the past, present, *and future* of a particular market economy, one needs to first recognize the implicit order evident in the apparent random chaos created by the collective investing public. This can be seen in the DJIA, as well as other large stock indexes, such as any of the Standard & Poor's Indices (S&P 500, 400, 100). Although volumes of economic data are collected and analyzed by economists seeking to describe the future production, management and distribution of American and global resources, such a tedious approach has not only proven to be inaccurate, but is also unnecessary. This is because *fundamental data* is always incomplete, often subjective, and therefore leads to erroneous conclusions. Consequently, the approach taken by economists and other modern-day soothsayers hoping to foretell the future is inadequate for describing the destiny of the U.S. economy. This daunting task is greatly simplified by an understanding of the intricate design of God's perfectly ordered universe.

CHAPTER 2

IMMINENT WORLD MONETARY COLLAPSE

For the vision is yet for an appointed time, but at the end it shall speak, and not lie: though it tarry, wait for it; because it will surely come, it will not tarry.

– Habukkuk 2:3

... they have seduced my people, saying Peace; and there was no peace ...

– Ezekiel 13:10

The Creator of the universe: The LORD God/I AM/Almighty God/JEHOVAH, Jesus Christ, said: I *am Alpha and Omega, the beginning and the end* (Revelation 1:8; 21:6; 22:13; Genesis 17:1; Exodus 3:14; 6:2,3; 15:3). God is "outside" of time; beyond the physical dimension. He is not His creation. Whatever He speaks, He creates; it comes into a state of being by means of His *spoken* Word. God *spoke* the entire universe into existence (Genesis 1:1-27). He literally created it by His *Word*, which is *Jesus Christ* (Revelation 19:13; Ephesians 3:9; Colossians 1:13-16; Revelation 4:11). He knows the future because He has already spoken it, and thus, created it. God's *written* Word, the *1611 King James Bible*, is the spoken Word of God (Jesus Christ) in *written* form. It is His prophesy to mankind, and has existed since *before* the beginning of time (John 1:1-3). Therefore, whatever His written Word says, has *already* been created, and therefore, *must* come to pass.

Since God has determined what is to occur, nothing happens by chance or accident. In the realm of infinity where God inhabits, that which is to occur has *already* occurred. It is a timeless dimension, where everything that can be known is already known by God. Thus, in the infinite mind of God, history is predetermined. Ecclesiastes 1:9: *The thing that hath been, it is that which shall be; and that which is done is that which shall be done: and there is no new thing under the sun.* In the affairs of mere mortals, God knows the course of future events.

Applying God's implicit design to an historical record of the DJIA reveals this Stock Index has been reliable for accurately predicting the future direction of the U.S. economy, and has correspondingly provided a high degree of predictability for anticipating the political and social conditions to follow. Repeatable cycles are evident in all time frames: from one minute intervals to periods spanning centuries of price data. The long-term economic cycles coincide with business expansion and contraction, and with few understood exceptions, the basic design character remains constant throughout boom times and depressions, inflationary and deflationary periods, wars and recessions. Does this design pattern preexist, or is it shaped by the historical events themselves? Both, the progress of civilizations and the destiny of the individual human soul are bound by time in a timeless dimension ruled by the will of Almighty God (Matthew 6:10; Luke 11:2). Ultimately, *God's will be done.* (Human free will decisions were made, but an omniscient God already knew what those decisions would be, and therefore, in an infinite sense, the outcome was predetermined.)

Apparent chaos found in the natural world is subject to an underlying order and predetermination. Future world events are unfolding according to God's intrinsic laws. Large Stock Indices, such as the DJIA, as a visual representation of the U.S. economy, have historically provided a predictable graphic illustration of American industry: past, present *and future.* Therefore, the forces governing financial markets are *not* random unpredictable chaos, but *are expected* to occur predicated on certain design parameters, and God establishes the parameters. Since the Creator of the universe, Jesus

Christ, is not a God of confusion, but of order, therefore, the ultimate future emergent design is knowable. In much the same manner, the corresponding historical events can also be ascertained *in advance* (e.g. crashing global stock markets can only be *the result* of a major international financial crisis). To the mind of mortal man, the world seems chaotic; but to the eternal God Who is *Alpha and* Omega, the Beginning and the End – knowing the start *and* completion of all things – the course of human endeavors is proceeding exactly according to *His Plan*, not "The Plan" of a Luciferian cult of psychotic rich men calling themselves "Illuminati," the "Illuminated Ones." (If only they had a sense of humor. But God surely does. Psalm 2:4.) In more recent economic history, the DOW has become a "Consumer Confidence Index" having little or no relevance to the true state of the U.S. economy. For at least the last 30 years, and especially since 2003, the Illuminati have utilized the DJIA stock index to create a false and misleading impression of stability and economic growth of corporate America. Like the NASDAQ, S&P, and other large Indices, the Dow Jones Industrial Average is *insider manipulated* by the supra-national government to generate massive profits for themselves, but also for the purpose of pacifying the American people. The last thing the globalists want is for a stampeding herd of angry television-watching zombies to suddenly awaken from a mind-controlled stupor and become aware of the steep drop-off toward which they have been herded. Since the aftermath of September 11, 2001, these other Indices, in not demonstrating the artificial "strength" of the DJIA, have provided a more accurate assessment of a hopelessly floundering U.S. economy.

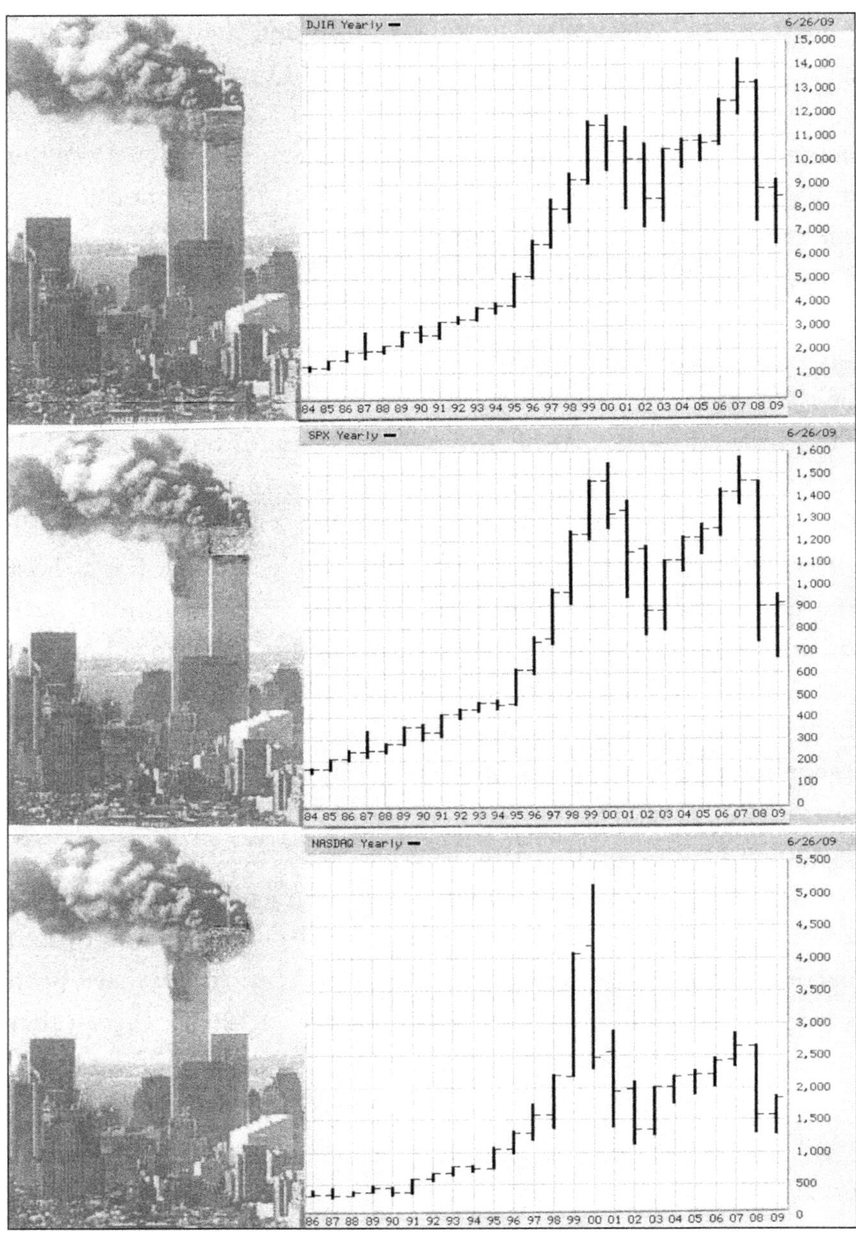

9/11 collapsing NYC Trade Towers compared to price charts of DJIA, S&P, NASDAQ

In the two years following the Illuminati's aborted crash of late October 2005, the DJIA diverged from all other stock indices, making new all-time highs in 2006 and 2007, while the other economic barometers continued to struggle below their previous 2000 high levels. (The S&P 500 temporarily made a new high in 2007, but closed the year below its 2000 peak.) Clearly, the world controllers were fattening the sheep for the slaughter (ref. *Preface* and *Chapter 6*).

Chaos Theory predicts a widely divergent outcome when initial parameters are altered. This is called the Butterfly Effect. Any *fundamental* approach to anticipating future economic trends is radically altered by even *minute changes* to the initial conditions. This can be seen, for example, by the limited accuracy of weather forecasting, where small changes in the initial conditions produce large changes in the outcome of long-term events. Therefore, a static, rather than a dynamic approach, is inherently limited and will produce inaccurate results. For this reason it is mere speculation for economists to forecast the future course of economic events, since constantly changing conditions insures the initial state will "spontaneously shift" to yield wrong conclusions. Typically, their opinions prove to be incorrect, and, at best, are bad advice. To the dismay and confusion of many, the upward or downward movement of financial markets, and the U.S. stock market in particular, is not always a direct function of external events. There is often no observable relationship between political or economic news and the subsequent direction in which the market will react. This is because these events are not the *antecedent*, but rather, the *consequence* of a pre-existing determination established by the rule of God, not by the rule of men.

Summarizing: U.S. stock Indices are graphic representations of the hopes and financial deliberations of a large group of investors speculating on the future of the American economy. Price movements can be affected by international events. The Index price level is a resultant of human emotions en masse: greed and fear. When illustrated graphically, these emotions form a quantifiable pattern configured by God's unchanging natural laws. Consequently, collective human decisions are predictable because stock Indices will follow essentially the same pattern as other naturally occurring time-dependent phenomenon. Since the U.S. stock market is a major economic indicator reflecting the overall performance of American industry, and because all the world's economies have become interdependent, therefore, to accurately forecast the future of the *global economy* one need only apply to the DJIA an understanding of the operation of God's intrinsic design.

When considering the configuration study described above, at this present juncture the probability has approached certainty that the American economy will soon experience a severe and prolonged stock market devaluation. This will be a degree of severity exceeding any previous financial disaster in U.S. or world history. The collapse will occur in stages, and will ultimately exceed in magnitude the devastating crash of 1929, with all the accompanying dire social, political, and economic repercussions.

Because all the world's economies have become interlinked, when the U.S. stock market crashes, *so too* will the economies of other nations. This will provide an opportunity for the Illuminati globalists to use the pre-planned economic disaster to install their long awaited dictatorial world government, the so-called New World Order. Their talking head political puppets – Presidents, Prime Ministers, Heads of State – will convincingly present to the dazed and confused public a ready made "Solution" to the crisis which they (the talking head political puppets) promoted. As occurred on 9/11, future government-staged acts of terrorism are planned to occur and have been carefully calculated to bring the American people and the entire world population under the direct control of an *international oligarchy dictatorship* that will covertly steal away their rights and freedoms, while promising them safety from the "*terrorists*," which, obviously, is the international supra-government itself. Insider, Dr. Johannes B. Koeppl, former German defense ministry official and advisor to NATO, had this to say: "The interests behind the Bush Administration, such as the CFR, The Trilateral Commission – founded by Brzezinski for David Rockefeller – and the Bilderberger Group, have prepared for and are now moving to implement open world dictatorship within the next five years. They are not fighting against terrorists. They are fighting against citizens."

Out of the planned chaos and confusion of a world rapidly being consumed by the flames of bank failures, collapse of the real estate industry, mass unemployment, home loss, middle class poverty, socialist-regulated health care; there will emerge from the smoldering ashes, the Illuminati's "savior," their rising star, their firebird *Phoenix,* the one whom they have long anticipated: *Antichrist.* Seated atop the very pinnacle of the global Masonic pyramid of Luciferian world control, he will be indwelled with the full power of Satan to deceive and destroy the masses desperate for a world political leader, a "savior," a "messiah." The long awaited impostor will promise to *fix the Problem* by offering *the Solution.* As the ultimate politician, this diabolical deceiver will restructure and unite world economies by means of a global cashless currency: an electronic transfer system of credits and debits that will render paper money and all other forms of monetary exchange – *including gold and silver coin and bullion* – non-redeemable, and therefore, obsolete. (Citizen ownership of precious metals and gem stones will be prohibited by the new government, declared illegal, and *without any redemptive value.* Bartering on the underground "black market" will subject such participants to "contraband laws." Government-empowered citizen spies and the threat of a life sentence in a FEMA Death Camp will discourage circumventing the cashless global tracking system.) At some point after the U.S. and global stock market collapse, the only acceptable form of currency exchange will be a microchip implant in the right hand – positioned beneath the webbing skin between thumb and index finger; or in the forehead. (Invisible spiritual Mark, i.e. *agreement* with the Beast government and *submission to its dictates* also qualifies as allegiance to the Antichrist, and will subject such individuals to the same penalty as those who receive a physically embedded microchip, i.e. eternity in hell.) Revelation 13:16-17: *And he causeth all, both small and great, rich and poor, free and bond, to receive a mark in their right hand, or in their forehead. And that no man might buy or sell, save he that had the mark, or the name of the beast, or the number of his name.* Those refusing to be injected (marked) with this subdermal microchip will be unable to buy or sell in the newly restructured *global economy* of the Luciferian New World Order (NWO) global dictatorship.

Today, the U.S. federal government, having violated the Constitution and Bill of Rights, is *illegitimate.* All its unconstitutional laws and decrees are rendered null and void. Unrighteous human civil government *is the Beast* spoken of in the books of Daniel and Revelation. The modern-day government of America – at all levels (Federal, State, County), as well as all foreign national governments – are the embodiment of Satan's kingdom on earth. They *are* the image of the Beast (Revelation 13:14-17). The New World Order is the "savior" of all those who serve the human government kingdom of Satan. Ostensibly a political construct, in truth, it is a *spiritual system* designed to enslave the souls of men.

By official edict, the ruling elite International Hierarchy will legislate death via starvation or internment in a FEMA prison for those (God's people and other resisters of legal unrighteousness) who refuse to comply and receive a surgical implant of the Beast's microchip. All who submit to the demands of their Criminal Fraternity overlord masters, affirming the unrighteous decrees of an ungodly illegitimate authority, obeying /serving (worshipping) the image of the Beast: human civil government; instead of the God of heaven: the Lord Jesus Christ; and allowing themselves to be "chipped," are promised a special place in the burning Lake of Fire ... *for ever and ever* (Revelation 14:9-11; Daniel 3:1-7; Revelation 13:4, 16:2, 19:20, 20:4).

Although God has granted the temporary *ruler of the world,* Satan, through his earthly kingdom of human government (Matthew

4:8,9; Luke 4:5,6; Revelation 11:15), the authority to persecute all the world's people during this concluding chapter of mankind's history, it is *God Almighty* Who determines the ultimate future course of humankind. And, while the Illuminati globalists continue working tirelessly behind the scenes – plundering, plotting, and planning to trigger the greatest economic fiasco ever – their diabolical machinations are nevertheless transparent and subject to the time schedule of the *Ruler of the Universe.*

The Crash event will proceed according to God's timing; it will follow *His Plan* and *His design.* Even though Satan's people believe themselves to be in control of deciding the future destiny of mankind, they can do *absolutely nothing* unless God *allows them* to do it.

CHAPTER 3

THE GLOBALIST'S AGENDA

"For we are opposed around the world by a monolithic and ruthless conspiracy that relies primarily on covert means for expanding its sphere of influence – on infiltration instead of invasion, on subversion instead of elections, on intimidation instead of free choice, on guerrillas by night instead of armies by day. It is a system which has conscripted vast human and material resources into the building of a tightly knit, highly efficient machine that combines military, diplomatic, intelligence, economic, scientific and political operations. Its preparations are concealed, not published. Its mistakes are buried, not headlined. Its dissenters are silenced, not praised. No expenditure is questioned, no rumor is printed, no secret is revealed. It conducts the Cold War, in short, with a war-time discipline no democracy would ever hope or wish to match.... I am asking your help with the tremendous task of informing and alerting the American people, confident that with your help man will be what he was born to be, free and independent."

– Former U.S. President John F. Kennedy, April 27, 1961

"The high office of President has been used to foment a plot to destroy the American's freedom, and before I leave office I must inform the citizen of his plight." – JFK, shortly before he was assassinated

"The illegal we do immediately. The unconstitutional takes a little longer."

– Henry Kissinger
former Nazi Third Reich / Illuminati foreign relations agent
World Affairs Council Press Conference, April 19, 1994

The term, "Globalist," as used in the context of this book, refers to a network of individuals from Illuminati crime "families" (referred to by their members as "The Family," or "The Fathers") that wield immense power and influence worldwide, and who, by virtue of their vast multi-generational wealth, control all national governments. (The political figurehead leaders of the pivotal nations: Britain, America, Israel, serve as their media mouthpiece.) All are part of multi-billionaire dynasties, and at least two generational crime dynasties own and control assets valued in the trillions of dollars. These are the top level Luciferians of the world; Satan-directed individuals who strive diligently to reduce the world population by their Agenda figure of 98 percent. (That goal will not be achieved because Matthew 24:22 requires the return of Jesus Christ before the Illuminati eradicates all life on planet Earth. *And except those days should be shortened, there should no flesh be saved: but for the elect's sake those days shall be shortened.*)

They instigate wars and finance both sides of the conflict; plan and carry out acts of staged terrorism, then blame it on an innocent target group; cause social upheavals, pitting one race against another to bring about their desired end. They determine global political policies and create weapons of mass destruction to use on the citizens of countries whom they plan to overthrow. They force "socialized medicine" (e.g. "Obama's" Health Care Bill) upon a U.S. population whom they have made sick and diseased, intending to eliminate the "unfit" – the elderly, disabled, and chronically ill. They institute school programs which indoctrinate five and six year old children in how to have safe sex, and teach them that same sex marriage and homosexuality are normal and good. They tell elementary school children to report their parents to authorities, and prepare them for Martial Law city lockdown quarantines by simulated mock school shootings: mind-control conditioning them using Soviet-style drills (e.g. pointing a loaded pistol at their head to terrorize them to accept gun control laws). Their "Death Education" program instructs students in how to commit suicide. (Columbine High School was a CIA MK-Ultra mind-control beta-test project.) They indoctrinate children with Hollywood witchcraft (e.g. Harry Potter films and books) and anti-Christian school curriculum, and give them Prosac and Ritilin to mask the brain damage caused by their Lead/Aluminum/Mercury vaccines. They cultivate and harvest illegal drugs: the Middle East poppy fields to manufacture heroin; the cocoa in South America to make cocaine. Through federal organizations – CIA, FBI and BATF – several of the crime families, most notably, the Bushes, direct the world narcotics trade, distributing drugs in America's cities and school yards, while declaring a phony "War on Drugs," imprisoning their street competition with life sentences for possessing a few ounces of marijuana. They add one of the most toxic of all substances known to man – Mercury – to common processed food ingredients like corn syrup (high fructose corn syrup found in soft drinks, bread, and thousands of other processed food items), and through any of their fascist business enterprises, such as McDonald's, manufacture deadly Cadmium-tainted children's food and beverage containers which damage a child's developing brain. The global elite own and control the legal counterpart of the illegal drug trade – pharmaceutical companies – which creates over the counter and prescription drug dependency among the general population whom they have systematically poisoned and transferred diseases via lethal components present in municipal drinking water, processed packaged "food," the Chemtrailed atmosphere, and mass inoculations with vaccines (e.g. "Flu Shots"). They write the medical school text books that teach doctors how to be "drug dealers," middlemen between the Illuminati pharmaceutical drug companies and a drugged citizenry in desperate need of a "fix." They determine the acceptable daily 10 news stories to be repeated on all the alphabet evening news networks, which they own and control. They Chemtrail poison the air, genetically modify the food, and put tranquilizers (Fluoride and Lithium) in the municipal drinking water supply to create a drugged population made too feeble-minded and apathetic to rise up and oppose them. By means of the Chemtrail atmospheric aerosol spray operation they are altering the human genome – the Genetic Code for mankind – and spread autoimmune stealth diseases like flesh-eating Morgellons, Lupus, Cancer, and Chronic Fatigue Syndrome to billions of people all over the globe. They put brain destroying Sodium fluoride in baby formulas to lower IQ's and cause incurable Autism. They manufacture infant nursing bottles from a type of plastic (Bisphenol A) which causes early onset of puberty in girls (by age 3-7), and feminizes and delays the onset of puberty in boys, making them sterile and passive/non-resistive as adults. By Illuminati-decreed government mandate, brain-damaging anti-psychotic drugs (Lithium, Prosac, Zoloft, Paxil, Xanax, Dista, etc.) are required to be given to healthy elementary school children. They (the Rockefellers) created "Women's Lib" to double the Illuminati's tax revenues and sever the cohesive family unit; alienate the children, take them from the home; State-operated schools becoming their new caretaker for indoctrinating them into the Globalist's Satanic Agenda. They build FEMA Concentration Camps ("Re-education Centers") all across America and the world; death camps to imprison those who speak out against their Orwellian tyranny or who refuse to be inoculated with their disease-transferring vaccinations. They genetically modify plants to irrevocably produce indigestible hybrid species which disable cellular metabolism in humans and animals. They crossbreed unrelated animal species, contaminating animal and human genetics; inserting animal DNA into humans, human DNA into animals to create grossly deformed creatures never before seen. They determine eugenic "public health" policies: partial birth abortion (murdering a live human being at up to 9 months pregnancy; crushing the infant's skull outside the womb). They decree mandatory forced vaccinations containing toxic heavy metal components and disease-causing microorganisms. They control the food industry so that all processed packaged foods contain the neurotoxins MSG, Aspartame, and bioengineered chemical substances known to degrade and destroy human and animal health. They create money out of nothing, print currency for the cost of a small piece of paper, then sell it to their privately owned "federal" banks at face value, while charging the unsuspecting public daily compounded interest on borrow funds. They ignore the U.S. Constitution, stage terrorist attacks, orchestrate public shootings, then enact anti-Second Amendment gun confiscation laws to take away the citizen's guns which could be used to defend themselves from government predators, and call it "Gun Control." They federalized all U.S. police departments, use the army and marines against the citizenry, nullifying Constitutional Law and States Rights jurisdiction. They appoint their own Communist regime into high political office, replacing those who uphold the Constitution, and empower figureheads such as State Governors and U.S. Presidents, while staging mock elections to fool the public into thinking they have a choice in a "no party system." They establish dictatorships and dethrone kings; they daily set the price of Gold; they crash economies.

AGENDA 21

"What is needed is an organization that governs the world."

–Joseph Ratzinger, Pope Benedict XVI, 2009

During the Rio de Janeiro Earth Summit in 1992, some of the above criminal acts against humanity were codified in a document known as Agenda 21 (Agenda for the 21st Century). Presented in environmental-sounding terminology, speaking of superficially noble causes such as "Sustainable Development" and "Rewilding of America," the true objective of this globalist's plan was to reduce the world population to a "more manageable" number of inhabitants, somewhere between 1 billion and 3 billion poverty-stricken peasants. The current estimate for the world population is

7 billion; their goal is to reduce that level by at least 80 - 90 percent, i.e. 1.4 billion - 700 million, and possibly by as much as 98 percent (140 million). Population reduction, people control, government land grabs, are the *real* objectives of the Globalist's Agenda 21.

Key Illuminati front men present at the "Earth Summit" – the usual Washington D.C fraternity of socially acceptable criminals – created the "Earth Charter" in the form of a massive government document, some forty chapters in length, detailing the various ways and means by which the Luciferians intend to terrorize and enslave the peoples of the world in a surveillance matrix grid that will abolish personal privacy, Constitutional freedoms, and ownership of private property. Many of the focal issues described in Agenda 21 are topics that will be discussed in the succeeding chapters of this book, and are relevant to the thesis of precisely anticipating a worldwide economic crash and its resultant consequences. Some examples of the technologies that are already being implemented for controlling the masses and preparing them to accept, and even welcome, a global dictatorship are the following: Chemtrails, electromagnetic pulsed energy transmissions (e.g. microwave towers, HAARP), disease-causing and nervous system destroying vaccines, gene altering genetically modified (GM) processed packaged foods, genetically modified biological organisms (GMO's), Fluoride and Lithium added to municipal drinking water supplies, ubiquitous surveillance cameras on every street corner, RFID national ID biometrics cards and Mark of the Beast human implantable microchips. This is not describing 1940's Nazi Germany, and neither is it science fiction fantasy, but hard reality, and it is currently happening i*n America today.* These few examples are only the start of the Hitlerian nightmare planned for a U.S. population of 325 million people by the unrelenting assault of the Illuminati Global Hierarchy.

According to the original Earth Charter document, Agenda 21 "is a comprehensive plan of action to be taken globally, nationally and locally by organizations of the United Nations System,

Governments, and Major Groups in every area in which humans impact on the environment." Environmentalism is one of the main "false flag" rallying points used by government usurpers for creating a spurious sense of urgency and catastrophic alarm among the masses that have been made terrorist-phobic by a series of government-staged crisis. The clear and stated objective of Satan's people (all those functioning within the broad banner of human civil government) is to implement further "controls" by cataloguing the entire global population in a planetary data bank in order for them to be more effectively monitored and eliminated. Since the 1960's, globalism and environmentalism ("Mother Earth Gaia Worship") have been used by the world's political/financial elite as the poster child for justifying the creation of their long awaited world slave state. Environmentalism, the so-called "Green Movement," and viewing the Earth as a "nurturing mother" or "living being," are commonly held beliefs of *Witchcraft*, thus further confirming the agenda of the world controllers as being strictly of a spiritual *demonic nature* expressed in political jargon. To the mind-controlled masses, the Globalist's Agenda has a beneficent humanitarian appeal.

Agenda 21 is the globalist's blueprint for bringing the world under the rule of their Antichrist world leader. It is part of "The Plan" which past Luciferians have painstakingly hoped to one day implement, but lacked the necessary means of controlling the entire world population. In today's computerized microchip age, they finally have that means.

Satan has always used deception and infiltration to control human beings: it worked in the Garden of Eden; it worked in Nazi Germany; it is working now in today's New World Order America. His willing human servants are easily deceived by causes which superficially appear to be necessary and beneficial. The God-rejecting masses reject the truth and believe the lie; they love their slavery. As Adolph Hitler stated: "1935 will go down in history for the first time a civilized nation has full gun registration. Our streets will be safer, our police more efficient, and the world will follow our lead into the future." *The masses applauded him.* Immediately afterward, the Third Reich took over and enslaved the entire population of Germany. In today's Gestapo Police State NWO America, Hitler's prediction has come true: gun registration and subsequent confiscation of citizen's firearms is among the globalist's top priority. No guns; no resistance.

Near the pinnacle of the occult pyramidal structure of the world's power elite are positioned the *Illuminati*, select individuals from perhaps as few as 13 multi-generational crime families who acquired their vast wealth and global influence by causing death, disease, famines, wars and destruction. They made an agreement with death, a binding blood pact with the literal Devil himself. Their agenda is Agenda 21: *World Domination;* their modus operandi is Ordo Ab Chao: *Order out of Chaos.* They create the chaos, then control *both sides* of the conflict, infiltrating every countermovement, government, media, education, and the financial banking system. In the words of globalist Zionist, Theodor Herzl, "We will lead every revolution against us." For millennium, their diabolical ancestors have planned the takeover and subjugation of the entire human race. It is their all-consuming passion, one for which, as stated by JFK, "no expenditure is questioned," and which has, in fact, been a lucrative source for generating their astronomical wealth. (JFK was actually one of "them" but harbored ideals conflicting with the Illuminati majority, and consequently, like Abraham Lincoln, was assassinated.) Exactly why they generationally propagate their evil deeds is somewhat of a mystery. This chapter will attempt to address their rationale in the most concise manner possible for a work of this length, for entire volumes have been written about them; the evil which they have perpetuated against humankind is *Legion.*

Why do they do it? ... There are two answers: the apparent answer and the correct answer. For most people today, the former will suffice, but for readers of this book who are interested in knowing the truth, the latter is preferred. The apparent reason for their insatiable will to deceive and destroy is because they want more power and control. Yet, they already own all the world's natural resources and control wealth in excess of what they could utilize in a thousand lifetimes. Therefore, amassing money and its consequent power is not their primary motivation for destroying life on planet Earth. (Anytime they want more money, all they have to do is fire up the ole' printing press and make a few extra hundred billion.) Ostensibly, the world's criminal elite have an unquenchable thirst for attaining personal power and control, and not merely over the world's resources or economically, but over *all of mankind.* And it does not stop there, since the spiritually demented do not simply want to control people, they want to literally *own them.* They want complete and *total* power and domination over other physical bodies. "Power is in tearing human minds to pieces and putting them together again in new shapes of your own choosing," said the inquisitor in Orwell's novel, *1984*, to an accused 'resister of the Party' as he lay strapped upon a medical examination table, drugged and tortured with electroshock. "We shall squeeze you empty, and then we shall fill you with ourselves," proclaimed the cold-blooded interrogator, echoing the desires of his monstrous real-life modern day equivalents. "The more the Party is powerful, the less it will be tolerant: the weaker the opposition, the tighter the despotism." These insightful statements cogently describe the morbid wishes of Satan's government people and their tireless efforts to induce or suppress an impotent response from the terror-stricken chemically-lobotomized public (ref. *The Criminal Fraternity: Servants of the Lie*).

Human civil government thrives on presumed ownership and control of people, places and things. It forms a parasitic relationship with unique human beings when redefining individual souls as their "subjects," "citizens," "human resources," faceless entities, mere commodities to be exploited for its own personal gain. Governments boldly change God-given rights into "privileges"; usurping title to land, home, automobile, and new born infants (government-issued Birth Certificate). They desire to own it all – everything – the land, the people, even individual's private thoughts (media mind-control programming). And to prove their "ownership" they are now planning for everyone to be identified by a physically implanted microchip that will enable Satan's government people to track "their property" anywhere "it" goes; and which can function as the sole means of currency exchange, turned on and off to suit the desire of the "property" owners. Satan's servants in government produce nothing, and like parasitic leeches, subsist off the life blood of those who are the true produces in any society, but who desire a king to rule over them. Rejecting the only true King, Jesus Christ, the God-rejecting masses want a corrupt human king as their surrogate ruler. *"Give us a king to judge us like all the nations,"* demanded the crowd of Israelites in 1 Samuel 8:6. When God gave them their heart's desire, the substitute king was only too willing to oppress, usurp, and destroy them. *This* is the inherent nature of all human governments (1 Samuel 8:6-22). Human civil government is the global elite's favored tool for feasting on the masses. As Thomas Jefferson once stated: "When the people fear the government, there is tyranny; but when the government fears the people, there is liberty." Today, as in other times throughout human history, the people are *absolutely terrified* by the government.

Governments consist of the *vilest* men (Psalm 12:8), who are *the basest of men* (Daniel 4:17); *men of high degree*, who *are a lie* ((Psalm 62:9). These are "Satan's people," his loyal servants who daily bow before their lord and master (Daniel 3:3,7), which is disguised in many forms, and in aggregate creates the Image of the Beast (Revelation 13:14,15; 14:9,10). All those associated with human government are merely dancing puppets on a string, headpiece filled with straw. By contrast, God's people bow to *no one*, except Jesus Christ (Daniel 3:12,18).

Servants of the only true and righteous God, Jesus Christ, are not part of the kingdom of Satan, therefore, unrighteous human government has no rightful jurisdiction over them. God's people are *exempt* from the oppressive rule of Satan's government people, who have legal spiritual jurisdiction *only* over their own kindred-spirited kind. *He suffered no man to do them wrong: yea, he reproved kings for their sakes. Saying, Touch not mine anointed, and do my prophets no harm* (*1* Chronicles 16:21-22).

At the bottom of the pyramidal-shaped Luciferian power hierarchy, the lower degree Freemasonry "worker bees" (Secular Humanism, York Rite/Scottish Rite Freemasonry, etc.); consisting of police, attorneys, judges, certain influential professionals and business interests, and various other Masonic wards of the state, are controlled by high-ranking politicians at the federal and supra-federal level (e.g. ruling members of the CFR, Bilderberg Group, B'nai B'rith, Grand Orient) which are controlled by a number of exceptionally wealthy international crime families (Pilgrim Society, Round Table Groups, Committee of 300) that, through their fascist corporate/political enterprises (includes the Federal Reserve banking system), control all the governments of the world. Near the capstone of the Illuminati pyramid (Council of 33), the major global crime families (Council of 13) are controlled by leaders of the old surviving European Monarchies, known as the "Black Nobility." Above them is an unnamed "Council of 3" operating in the vicinity of Southern Belgium. Individuals such as these are the *real global* leaders. Those portrayed in the media as world decision makers are merely front men/women, "window dressing," stuffed suits positioned before cameras to appear as if they were in charge, but who are in fact there to take the spotlight off their Illuminati bosses which direct world-impacting decisions from behind the scenes. Situated at the very pinnacle of the capstone, controlling all those positioned in the lower strata, sits Lucifer/Satan/the Devil (ref. hierarchy depicted on front cover of this book).

Yet, the *true* and *correct reason* for why these diabolical men (and women) do heinous generational evil against humanity is quite another matter, one that involves an awareness and wisdom of the multi-dimensional nature of the spiritual realm. Not mystical, as parroted by New Agers and others of like-minded persuasion; not esoteric, as understood by the New Ager's sister occultists: Freemasons, Wiccan witches/Satanists (i.e. "Luciferians," some of whom are at large in your neighborhood as political or spiritual leaders of the community). True wisdom comes only from the 1611 King James Bible. It is far more than merely a "book," for it is the literal spoken Word of God in perfect written form, which has *existed since before the beginning of time*: John 1:1-3 (Jesus Christ is the *spoken living Word of God*; He always existed in a timeless dimension. Therefore, His *written living Word of God*, the 1611 KJV, always existed.) As the original source of all truth and understanding, the 1611 King James Bible is the definitive meaning of the word, "spiritual." For example, Luke 4:5-8: *And the devil, taking him up into an high mountain, showed unto him all the kingdoms of the world in a moment of time. And the devil said unto him, All this power will I give thee, and the glory of them: for that is delivered unto me; and to whomsoever I will give it. If thou therefore wilt worship me, all this shall be thine. And Jesus answered and said unto him, Get thee behind me, Satan: for it is written, Thou shalt worship the Lord thy God, and him only shalt thou serve.* Notice Jesus did not refute that it is *Satan* who owns and controls all the "kingdoms of the world" (i.e. governments). *This* – not CNN, FOX News, or MSNBC – is the truth. From a single passage of Holy Scripture it is clear why the rich men of the world seek to rule over mankind. Simply stated: They are carrying out the desire of the one whom they worship and serve – Satan, the Devil, also known as *Lucifer.* Thus, the globalists and their underlings are known as "Luciferians." As for the *real reason* why they commit heinous atrocities against the individual and collective mankind: *Satan demands of them to make human blood sacrifices to him*; desecrate the image of God, shed innocent blood; *to steal, and to kill, and to destroy* (John 10:10). This is what *all* human governments do, and whether or not individual bureaucrats are consciously aware of it, they do it for their master, Lucifer/Satan.

It is no coincidence that all of the world's major political players, as well as nearly all the captains of industry, members of semi-secret societies such as the CFR, Bilderbergers, Trilateral Commission, etc.; and the world's high-level religious leaders, including modern Protestantism and the Vatican/Jesuits/Knights of Malta; privately, covertly, enthusiastically serve Satan/Lucifer as the god of this world. (At their core level, all organized religions are controlled by the Luciferian Hierarchy. *True* Christianity is the only exception, and exists apart from organized *man-made* religions, *including* Professing/pseudo-Christianity. As the only *God-made* religion, True Christianity is solely controlled by Almighty God Jesus Christ.) Politicians in Washington D.C., and in all countries throughout the world, share the *same demonic spirit* as their lord and master. Their mission is identical to that of their father, Satan: *to kill, steal, and destroy.* Without hardly any opposition resistance from a sheep-like narcoleptic public, they have descended into the lowest abyss of human depravity. As unabashed Servants of the Lie, they will do whatever their chief commander, Satan, demands of them in order to maintain his throne at the top of the Illuminati all-seeing eye pyramid of power (ref. *Introduction*: back side of one dollar bill). More than anything, Satan desires to overthrow God's Kingdom and destroy all human beings and all life on planet Earth. In particular, he revels in the suffering, torture, desecration and death of the image of God: *Children.* Hence, the Globalist's Agenda targets infants and young children. Human/child sacrifice on the bloody altars of the world's political and financial elite is a primary goal of all politicians, at all levels of government.

Among the above, only David Rockefeller can be considered "Illuminati", and is the third tier down from the top of the satanic pyramid (Lucifer - European Black Nobility/Rothschilds - Rockefellers). All the rest are mere "power brokers" with no political decision-making authority. Ritual child sacrifices are routinely performed to appease their master, Satan.

Some of the most demented members of any society can be found occupying positions within government – at all levels: supra-national, federal, State, local. A disproportional large majority are serial killers, pedophiles, homosexual sadists, sociopathic psychopaths who delight in speaking lies and participating in the destruction of life – human life in particular. The political and financial elite have a long well established history of tormenting and decimating mankind; the so-called "nobility" of this world are known for their perverse interest in desecrating innocent human beings, especially children and virgin humanity, as exemplified by the following historical figures:

✦ In the late-sixteenth century, Countess Erzebet (Elizabeth) Bathory of Hungary, known as "The Blood Countess," over a course of years, tortured for weeks and months at a time – and bleed to death – 650 unmarried peasant girls whom she abducted and kept in her castle dungeon. She epitomized the political spirit by living off the life blood of tortured humanity. The Blood Countess hoped to revitalize her fading youth by daily bathing in the still warm blood of her virgin victims. Like all those in a position to exercise power over others weaker than themselves, she made full use of her legal carte blanche exemption from prosecution by the corrupt political system she represented. The Countess was never convicted of any crimes, but was eventually sentenced in a "show trial" (to make it look official) and subsequently confined to house arrest in her castle, while her accomplices received the death sentence. Not once during her 4 year confinement prior to her death did she utter a word of remorse for the unspeakable crimes she had committed. Throughout the time of her reign of terror she was in full control of her reasoning facilities, was well-educated, intelligent, and could speak 3 languages. As a direct parallel to modern blood-lusting globalist vampires, the Blood Countess sacrificed the girls in satanic rituals. Like today's D.C. political elite, she and her staff were avid practitioners of witchcraft and Satanism, and were not clinically insane, but rather, *demon-possessed.*

Countess Bathory carried on the tradition of what human governments have always done: torture and cold-blooded murder of the poor and defenseless is a way of life for those intoxicated with power. Corpses of kidnapped young peasant girls were found buried in and around her Castle, their bodies full of holes from chunks of their flesh torn out with red hot tongs; some were still alive. Creating wars, aborting 60 million babies in the U.S. alone; using "slow kill" methods to murder billions with vaccines; poisoned food, poisoned air and poisoned water; today's global elite continue the debased tradition of their sadistic ancestors. It's not just "bad breeding"; it's a "spiritual thing."

✦ Vlad III "The Impaler" of Walachia, prototype for Bram Stoker's Count Dracula, cultivated human sacrifice to the point of nauseating battle-hardened soldiers of Alexander the Great's army as they marched into Romania on a mission of conquest. So mortified by the sight of thousands of naked human corpses impaled on long sharpened poles lining the roads and byways, they turned back and aborted their military campaign. In similar fashion to the Blood Countess and all political despots throughout world history, Vlad The Impaler considered human life to be of trivial consequence, merely a source of personal amusement. Ultimately, most everyone who served under his tyrannical rule ended up skewered on a pole. The rank and file bureaucrats of today's U.S. government terrorist regime should heed the precedent, for *they too* shall one day meet with a similar fate at the hands of their Illuminati masters. Satan's government people will eventually come to the realization that none of them are safe from the aftershock of the tyranny which they created or allowed to proliferate. Regardless of position, *all* of them *are expendable.*

The above two examples are by no means extraordinary, and pale in comparison to crimes committed against humanity in more recent times by mass murders and serial killers with names like Pol Pot (2-3 million), Hitler (2-6 million), Stalin (20 million), Mao Tse-tung (40-70 million), Rumsfeld/Cheney/ Bush crime families (tens of millions), and the global genocide network consisting of the Rockefeller and Rothschild Dynasties (presently, hundreds of millions; eventually, billions).

The upper-level globalists pipe the tune, and their lackey politicians, supported by the Illuminati-controlled media, dance to it.

Their minor objectives are seemingly endless: constant wars, staged acts of terrorism, engineered crisis, unconstitutional laws to take away citizen's rights and fund the Globalist's Agenda; legislation to permit abortions, break up the family, promote homosexuality, remove the Christian God of Heaven from the social and cultural milieu. Their unbridled madness goes on and on ... Aluminum/Mercury vaccines to create brain-damaged Autistic children, FDA-approved mind and body destroying drugs and antibiotics to give people incurable diseases (Cancer has been curable since the 1920's: ref. Otto Warburg, awarded the Noble Prize for discovering that cancer cannot exist in an oxygen environment.), genetically engineered terminator crop seeds and microorganisms, genetically modified carcinogenic food, fluoridated water, Chemtrail air, mind-controlling microwave HAARP frequencies ... the list continues to grow. Political tyrants have at their command a myriad number of ways to *steal, kill, and destroy* in fulfillment of the will of their diabolical leader, Lucifer/Satan. *This* is their raison d'être; they live to usurp, murder and maim. Satan's government people are sociopathic/psychopathic serial killers who either consciously choose to do evil or cannot distinguish between good and evil. Satan's people derive a perverse sense of pleasure and fulfillment by inflicting pain and witnessing the suffering and death of others, especially infants and small children, the poor, and those too weak or ignorant to defend themselves. Acting as the global version of the school yard bully, in reality they are cowards at heart; consciousless remorseless fiends; freakish spiritually/genetically-altered quasi-human/demon hybrids (ref. Chapter 5/*Supernature*). They truly are the *serpent seed of Satan* (Genesis 3:13; Genesis 6:4; Daniel 2:43; 2 Corinthians 11:3; 2 Peter 2:14; John 8:44). The mind-controlled public worships political figureheads as gods and saviors, and the television-zombified masses vote and cheer them on: "Our government wouldn't do *that*! They care about us!" But the truth is: "Your government" intensely despises you and wants to obliterate you from off the face of this earth! Only, you have been physically, cognitively, and spiritually damaged so that you are unable to realize it. Criminally insane personalities gravitate to occupy positions within government; they desire to become part of a system that reflects their own psychopathology. As delusional and deceptive "charming psychopaths," Satan's government people can appear charismatic, refined, dignified, articulate, eloquent even, while they stare out at you from the illuminated all-seeing eye in your living room ... and kill you with a disarming smile.

The mass delusion of worshiping government leaders is entrenched into the cultural ethos of a thought-controlled society, and the reality of that true state of affairs never enters their mind. Government does not want to eradicate illegal drugs; it wants to proliferate the usage of illegal drugs among the general population, especially the youth. Government leaders do not want to protect citizens from criminals and from terrorists; *they* are the criminals and terrorists. They do not want a physically, mentally and spiritually healthy society; they want a sick and diseased society that is cognitively disabled and anesthetized, easily controlled, rejects the only true living God (Jesus Christ), and without question follows their counterfeit "antichrist," which is the *government bureaucracy.* They do not want a peaceful society, and are not interested in making the world a better place in which to live; they want chaos, mass destruction and death; they want human sacrifice in order to gain spiritual power for dominating and controlling the masses. The world's financial/political elite are not feverishly striving for global government for the purpose of establishing world peace, but rather for the objective of erasing all national boarders in order to further consolidate their political and economic power base. Causing destruction and carnage; born to lie (Psalm 58:3), they want power to deceive, manipulate, rule over, and destroy humankind. They realize that in order to obtain that power they must appease, by human blood sacrifice (genocidal wars, manufactured diseases, suicidal and genocidal medical practices, fabricated crisis, etc.), the one whom they serve – their leader, their master, the father of lies. John 8:44:

Ye are of your father the devil, and the lusts of your father ye will do. He was a murderer from the beginning, and abode not in the truth, because there is no truth in him. When he speaketh a lie, he speaketh of his own: for he is a liar, and the father of it.

Once you, the reader, discover who is behind all the conflict in the world, and their mindset and political agenda, everything that is presently transpiring globally will begin to make perfect sense.

It has been reported that certain members of the Rothschild Illuminati crime dynasty of Europe set a place at their dinner table for Lucifer, the Devil. Occasionally he makes a guest appearance, dressed in a tuxedo: charismatic, refined, dignified, articulate, eloquent even. As are all "charming psychopaths," he is a liar, the progenitor and father of lies; he is *the consummate politician*. Predictably, the Rothschild global genocide crime syndicate owns and controls a large percentage of the world's corporations and natural resources (estimated at 50 percent). Like their U.S. counterpart, the Rockefeller global genocide crime cartel, they are *multi-trillionaires*. Satan offers handsome rewards for the generational evil done by these two supremely wicked bloodlines.

THE DEMONIC AGENDA

... they shall mingle themselves with the seed of men ...

– Daniel 2:43

UFO's - ET's - New Age - Eastern Mysticism - Globalism - New World Order. What do these terms all have in common? The upper echelon world leaders, human-demon hybrids whose physical/spiritual genetic material – i.e. *seed of men* – has been *mingled* with that of fallen demonic angels, believe they are acquiring their information on how to control and destroy mankind from ancient advanced beings which they think are from another planet or hyperspace dimensional realm. The political/financial elite's assumed source of information and direction may sound like a comical farce, but this is what these *modern primitives* actually believe! (The reader must be a Holy Spirit indwelled True Christian in order to comprehend the truth reality of human-demon hybridization.) "ET's" communicate with them on a regular basis – directly or telepathically; they have conversations with what they think are interdimensional beings, "space people," "extraterrestrials" physically manifesting as human-like creatures; "greys," various reptilian forms, "reptoids," or some other futuristic expression of "highly advanced space aliens" which typically hail from a parallel universe or exotic galactic locales such as Zeta Reticuli (nonexistent) or the Pleiades (a visible six-star cluster in the Taurus Constellation). This is considered carefully guarded information within a closed circle of generational Illuminati witches and Satanists. They truly believe it. Of course, they are all totally mad.

Those individuals of some prominence outside this occult inner circle who report similar personal experiences and seek a public forum in which to "spread the word" may otherwise be considered lucid, stable, accomplished individuals – i.e. they have established credibility in another field of endeavor and their opinions are accepted as believable and trustworthy. They may be lower tier NWO operatives not directly involved in politics, or they may have been pre-programmed by CIA mind-control techniques and thus appear to be seemingly in opposition to government, the New World Order, mind-control of the masses, or anything else having to do with globalism and the Globalist's Agenda. They convincingly act as if they are "citizen advocates" and simply wish to "educate and warn the people" (ref. Chapter 8/Project Mockingbird). Such individuals feel obligated (by "the aliens") to deliver "an important message to the world." As self-appointed prophets, they may have had a "spiritual awakening experience" that was life changing and started them on a journey of evangelizing the world with the Demonic Agenda – i.e. during one or more specific events in their life they suddenly became indwelled with demons. Oftentimes, they forsake their former career and devote full-time energy and resources to writing books or speaking before small groups of people all over the world, encouraging them to spread the message which they have received from the enlightened "space aliens" regarding the future destiny of mankind ... and that message is always the same:

a. Denial of the Deity of Jesus Christ: He was a "wonderful teacher," like Buddha, Mohammad, Confucius. Or, no historical record exists that He ever lived. God is an impersonal energy force, a cosmic vibration, oneness. All is one; you are God (Eastern Pantheism); you are "a god" (Mormonism).

b. You have untapped unlimited potential, lived before in another lifetime (reincarnation), and can "create your own reality."

c. Earth was "seeded" by beings arriving from another planet in deep space; highly advanced civilizations have previously existed on Earth (Atlantis, Lemuria); the Earth is hundreds of thousands, even millions, of years old.

d. The "space aliens" are a race of highly evolved humanoid creatures with superior intelligence and advanced technology: "See our UFO space craft?" ... "We are here to help you so that you do not destroy yourselves."

e. Truth is relative. Denial of the absolute truth of the Bible. Adamant rejection of all religions, and a special loathing for True Christianity. (i.e. "Religion" = the Christian God.)

f. The Picean Age is ended and we are about to start the Age of Aquarius, the New Age of enlightenment and evolved mankind, which only the spiritually adept will survive. Humans must unite as one. All those who cannot receive this message (i.e. True Christians) are to be eliminated.

g. There is no God, no good or evil; only energy and love (not a selfless concern for the welfare of others, but rather, self-centered New Age Yuppy love.) Humans are merely a manifestation of condensed light, a hologram, materialized energy. We evolved, created ourselves, and will live forever.

h. This information needs to immediately reach as many Earth people as possible because a great planetary consciousness awakening/Paradigm Shift is about to commence.

All of the foregoing statements are patented falsehoods, calculated deceits, simplistic lies. Anyone yet retaining an intact mind can discern that the obvious intent of the "ET's" is to discredit the Christian God and His Holy Word: Jesus Christ/1611 King James Bible. They are not interested in dealing with the Globalist's Agenda, because it is also *their* agenda. They did not presumably travel thousands or even millions of Light Years across intergalactic space to help mankind survive destruction, but to teach them the false Eastern Philosophy that Jesus Christ is not God and the Bible is not true. (And they didn't travel anywhere, but were always "here.") Their major focus is an indirect attack upon any vestige of True Christianity that may yet survive in a world about to be engulfed in the flames of God's righteous Judgment. (Only item "h" has a ring of familiarity to it – i.e. there *is* an imminent planetary awakening, but it is *not* what the "ET's are advertising.) Their true objective is clear: "Believe our lies (which you cannot realize are lies because you have denied the truth/Truth and have therefore been given over [by God] to a lying spirit – i.e. *us* [2 Thessalonians 2:10-12]), and work tirelessly to convince others that our lies are truth (you are now *our slave* and have no choice but to obey us), so that we can harvest as many human souls as will join hands together when we all march confidently forward into the future world – 'a kinder, gentler' New World Order world – emerging from the flames of global destruction … and into the pit of a burning hell fire … together … for all of eternity."

Obviously, "aliens," "ET's," "Greys," "UFO's," "reptilians," etc. are *masquerading demons.* This conclusion is easily derived, especially in consideration of the fact that "extraterrestrials" precisely fit the description of *fallen angels* that is provided in the Bible (Genesis 3:1-5; Isaiah 14:29; 2 Corinthians 11:14). The "space messengers are here" *lie* is intended for the spiritually damned. The spiritually alive know them as demons/devils, and their message as transparent deception. Demonic spirit beings can assume any material or nonmaterial form, including that of a "flying saucer," for the purpose of deceiving those who are spiritually naïve or deliberate enemies of the truth. Anyone who believes a lie, God has given over to the ET demons *for destruction* (2 Thessalonians 2:10-12). The truth-adverse either knowingly or unwittingly signed a binding "Spiritual Contract" authorizing the demons to have authority and control over their mind and emotions, and sometimes even their physical body ("alien abductions"). Hence, those taken captive by the great deception naively believe that "alien entities" are who they claim to be. Those choosing to serve the lie are dead while they live – spiritually dead; there is no life, or truth, in them. Their trust in masquerading harbingers of hope for a dawning New Age of Aquarius is hope in the burning lake of hell fire and brimstone prophesied in Revelation 21:8: ... and *all liars, shall have their part in the lake which burneth with fire and brimstone: which is the second death.* When the Illuminati world controllers are ready to activate Project Blue Beam – staging a fake "alien invasion" using computerized holographic technology – the spiritually deceived will drop to their knees worshipping their "other-worldly" saviors whom they have trusted will deliver them from the government-created terror. But, the perverse irony is they will be playing directly into the hands of a cruel and sadistic master that has taken them captive.

Verbally command "aliens," "ET's," "Greys," "UFO's," hauntings, etc. in the name of Jesus Christ, then watch them suddenly disappear! Luke 10:19,20: *Behold, I give unto you power to tread on serpents and scorpions, and over all the power of the enemy: and nothing shall by any means hurt you. Notwithstanding in this rejoice not, that the spirits are subject unto you; but rather rejoice, because your names are written in heaven.*

The Demonic Agenda is the "alien version" of the Illuminati's Globalist's Agenda. They were both written by the same author: Lucifer/Satan/the Devil. Many will be deceive by it. 2 Timothy 3:7: *Ever learning, and never able to come to the knowledge of the truth.* Daniel 12:10: ... *the wicked shall do wickedly: and none of the wicked shall understand....*

Only God's people can know the truth: ... *but the wise shall understand* (Daniel 12:10). *For there shall arise false Christs, and false prophets, and shall show great signs and wonders; insomuch that, if it were possible, they shall deceive the very elect (*Matthew 24:24).

i.e. It is *not possible* to deceive the Elect.

CHAPTER 4

THE SIGNIFICANCE OF CHEMTRAILS

... I will cover the sun with a cloud, and the moon shall not give her light.
– Ezekiel 32:7

... the sun and the moon shall be dark, and the stars shall withdraw their shining ... The sun shall be turned into darkness, and the moon into blood, before the great and terrible day of the LORD come. – Joel 2:10,31

And he opened the bottomless pit; and there arose a smoke out of the pit as a smoke out of a great furnace; and the sun and the air were darkened by reason of the smoke of the pit. – Revelation 9:2

One of the quickest ways to determine an individual's spiritual allegiance is to ask a simple question: "Have you noticed the Chemtrails in the sky?" This inquiry is not intended to ascertain their level of awareness or pool of general knowledge, but rather is a definitive test for *their love of the Truth* (John 14:6), or lack thereof (2 Thessalonians 2:10-12).

Keep in mind that the supra-government International Hierarchy has *daily* been visibly dumping into the air mega-tons of mile-wide swaths of white Aluminum dioxide embedded with radioactive Barium and other toxic heavy metals, virulent mutated pathogens, stealth viruses, and never before seen strains of bioengineered diseases, for *more than 16 years!* This is being done *globally*, and is a billion dollar a day operation. Surely, by now, anyone who is even minimally aware would have observed the multitudes of unmarked jets in the sky (this author has sighted as many as 10 simultaneously overhead), flying at right angles to each other, at the same altitude (in violation of FAA regulations), laying down long white trails of poisonous Chemtrail emissions that persist throughout the day, spread out to cover the entire visible sky, and occlude the sun. (Common jet aircraft exhaust forms when water vapor crystallizes at freezing temperatures in the upper atmosphere. These condensation trails, so-called "Contrails," dissipate and vanish within about 60 seconds.) It seems reasonable to assume that a thinking person would have at some point over the last 16 years asked them self, "What are all those planes doing up there?" or "What are all those persistent white streaks in the sky?" Likewise, any rational person of average intelligence would have mentioned the alarmingly rigorous air traffic and spewed effluent seen overhead to their family, friends, work associates, church pastor. Mentally intact sentient beings would have surely questioned such strange and unusual phenomenon, and even become outraged by the obvious attack from the sky above ... but that has not been the case. And the following are the reasons why:

The first point of departure from a reality-based perception of the world begins with one word: *Television*. If you are still watching "TV" you are being *mind-controlled and programmed* – without any conscious awareness of it. Your subconscious mind, your thoughts, your actions, are not fully your own; and what is more, you have no awareness they are not your own. The luminous eye strategically positioned in your home has proven to be the most efficient brain-washing machine ever devised by Satan for captivating the heart, mind, and soul of the last three generations of hapless humans. By means of the chromosome-damaging ionizing radiation-emitting Cathode Ray Tube (CRT television screen) or LCD or Plasma screen, one's locus of awareness can be transposed to anywhere the globalist world controllers wish to divert it. Watching TV is a form of *hypnotic induction* that invokes a trance state which facilitates the programmed implantation of messages into the subconscious mind of the viewer. Within 20 seconds of passively observing an active TV monitor one's brain wave function downgrades to a lower frequency sleep-like Alpha State of electrical activity and awareness; an hypnotic stupor of basal consciousness that renders the individual highly susceptible to suggestion and unable on a subconscious level to distinguish between material reality and induced fantasy. "The victim of mind-manipulation does not know that he is a victim. To him the walls of his prison are invisible, and he believes himself to be free. That he is not free is apparent only to other people. His servitude is strictly objective," wrote Aldous Huxley in 1958. (The author of the famous novel, *Brave New World*, Huxley was an Illuminati insider.) Further, the content of modern television *programming* has been carefully *crafted* to indoctrinate the viewer into a passive acceptance of the globalist's objectives. As a result, an entire world culture is unconsciously absorbing the values and belief system of Hollywood actors playing roles and conforming to the Globalist's Satanic Agenda. Television has now been *weaponized*, transformed into a tool for destruction of traditional Christian family values, and for widespread public indoctrination into the Luciferian's demonic belief system. Today, anyone who believes in the true purpose behind Chemtrails, or of an emerging global government dictatorship, poisoning of the food supply, the dangers of vaccinating children or fluoridating municipal drinking water supplies, is portrayed on television and in the news media as a "Conspiracy Theorist." A public which accepts labeling those who expose lies and deceit as "kooks" is proof that TV mind-control programming is indeed effective. Isaiah 5:20: *Woe unto them that call evil good, and good evil; that put darkness for light, and light for darkness; that put bitter for sweet, and sweet for bitter!* (ref. Appendix E).

Invisible television electromagnetic radiation, beamed in the 1-100 Hertz range, is known for inducing people to become docile, compliant, well behaved subjects of the globalist's *Brave New World/*

New World Order. Vlf (Very low frequency) and Elf (Extremely low frequency) wavelengths in this range can also induce a state of confusion, frustration, rage, paranoia, visions, nightmares, and other altered states of mind which the Luciferians may find useful to facilitate their various agendas. This mind manipulating radiation is being emitted from the TV screen, and is also directly transmitted to the human brain via HAARP (High Altitude Active Auroral Research Program) microwave frequencies propagated through the atmospheric electrochemically conductive *plasma medium* (nanoparticulate Aluminum and Barium) created by Chemtrail planes. (In North America, the major HAARP microwave array, consisting of 360 antennas that can generate up to 1 billion Watts of electromagnetic energy, is located in Gakona, Alaska, a vast wilderness area in the Southeast portion of the State.) The highest output of Vlf/Elf HAARP mind-controlling transmissions was registered on September 11, 2001, during the NYC World Trade Center Illuminati-staged political maneuver, and on each succeeding anniversary of that bold assault on the rights and liberties of the American public. The reason for this periodic intensified energy transmission is to induce an altered state of consciousness – apathy, lack of concern, lethargy – in the minds of the already docile dumbed-down American people. At a time when the nation was reported to be "under siege" (by the supra-government of the Illuminati), when there was a "federal ban" on all air traffic for nearly two weeks following the shadow government's demolition of the Twin Towers, Chemtrail planes were daily seen crisscrossing the sky with city wide swaths of expanding Aluminum dioxide and Barium sulfate. (Aluminum and Barium are electrically conductive metals that enhance the efficiency of HAARP transmissions to control weather and the human mind. They are also known to be neurodegenerative and carcinogenic agents.) And even more amazing, *no one seemed to notice*! Or, if some noticed, they *didn't care.* Apathy and complacency are characteristic symptoms of drinking fluoridated water, ingesting Lithium and Mercury doped foods and beverages, and cognitive impairment from HAARP-generated frequencies.

Chemtrails spread out to create a contiguous plasma grid for transmitting pulsed HAARP microwaves directly to the electrochemically conductive Aluminum/Barium contaminated brains of every person on earth. Specific low frequency transmissions delivered to the cerebral cortex adversely influences an individual's ability to think clearly and rationally. For example: the inability to accurately perceive one's environment ("huh, what'er chemtrails?"), evaluate, question, feel outrage over injustice. In effect, television electromagnetic emissions and Chemtrail/HAARP microwave frequencies create *zombies:* mindless creatures who will only respond as they are *programmed* to respond; not think, but feel what they are *told to feel.* If a rational individual – for instance, one still retaining an intact mind and the wisdom and foresight to have thrown the trance inducing TV into the garbage dumpster years ago – presents irrefutable evidence proving the existence, purpose and dangers of Chemtrails to a zombified television watcher, such a walking dead person will not only elicit ignorance of the facts, but will do so with some degree of cognitive dissonance (confusion); i.e. you can point at the planes and lingering Chemtrails in the sky above, but it will not fully register in their semi-conscious mind. Further, the more they are pressed to recognize the obvious, the more frustrated and vehement they will become. "Those are just regular planes up there." ... "They're all goin' to the same destination." ... "The government wouldn't do that to us." (These are actual responses that people made to the author upon being asked about Chemtrails seen in the sky above.) If the issue is forced, physical attack is likely to ensue. When the first martyr, Stephen, confronted the religious leaders of that day – the Pharisaic Jews – with the truth that they were guilty of the murder of their Messiah, God in the flesh/Jesus Christ, and that their fathers killed all the prophets, they not only became irrationally indignant, but actually *bit him,* i.e. they *literally* gnawed on him with their teeth! (Acts 7:54). Haters of the truth are typically struck with sudden madness upon being told the truth: *Then they cried out with a loud voice, and stopped their ears, and ran upon him with one accord.* (v.57). Lastly, they stoned him to death (v.58). When confronted with an inconvenient truth, mind-controlled zombies often become enraged unthinking beasts. Their conscious mind has developed a blind spot, which, in Orwellian *newspeak* is called "Crimestop." Knowing the truth, or even *thinking* the truth, is forbidden, and dangerous. In a country that once boasted of a First Amendment right to free speech, publicly speaking the truth is called "Hate Crime." In today's America, the Orwellian "Thought Police" have arrived.

So, therefore, we have the first cause for Chemtrail denial: *Government mind-control induced by the family television set and HAARP-generated mind-control frequencies.*

The second explanation for why hardly anyone, out of a U.S. population of 325 million people, is even in the slightest degree aware or disturbed by what Chemtrails portend, is that, for most people, ignorance truly is bliss. They *do not want to know* about anything that is not relevant to their usual routine of work, TV, food, sleep. Like laboratory rats in a cage, as long as they are fed and comfortable, they have no need to learn or experience anything new. The Illuminati pejoratively refers to them as "Useless Eaters." (Regarding this one issue, the Illuminati might be correct. But unlike the Illuminati, the author does not believe they should be exterminated.) They simply do not wish to know – even knowledge beneficial for them – how to safeguard their health, for example. They do not want to be confused with facts. They want to avoid "negative" thoughts or hearing anything that might disturb them out of their "Useless Eater Comfort Zone." This mindset is characteristic of the American middle class (smug affluent "Yuppies") who believe in "the system," and who's "god" is *government.* They will reject any truth that does not support their *newspeak mentality.* In spite of all the evidence to the contrary, they yet believe today's communist-hijacked U.S. government is legitimate, and maintain that Chemtrails do not exist, vaccines are safe and necessary, and "there's no need to worry" as the world implodes all around them. They are a living cliché: "Life is good," they all chirp in unison, like a flock of caged parakeets. The yuppy middle-class, soon to be extinguished and merged with the poverty-stricken lower class upon collapse of the U.S. economy, have a 1960's Beetle's Eastern mysticism "all you need is love" (self-centered love) New Age mentality. Placidly co-existing under the shadow of their legal criminal overlords, with government-controlled media propaganda bombarding them on every side, they prefer to vicariously live out their lives by watching other people on TV, and are content to be experimental test subjects in a taxpayer-funded government mind-control experiment. Truth-haters delight in not knowing the real and present dangers of the current world political/economic crisis. (They get all the "truth" they can handle from watching the controlled media evening news.) It is a comfort for them not to have to think; no sense of responsibility, no obligation to act, no moral conscious. Willful ignorance is the preferred mode of an intellectual coward; the truth is unsettling, unimportant. They do not know, and neither do they want to know – even when meticulously told the truth, they simply have no interest in it and fail to see any relevance the truth may hold for their daily lives. Therefore, a book such as this will have little appeal to them. Proverb 1:22: ... *fools hate knowledge.* However, willful ignorance and cowardice *does* have a downside: Revelation 21:8: *But the fearful, and unbelieving ... and all liars, shall have their part in the lake which burneth with fire and brimstone: which is the second death.*

This author has personally witnessed *Professing* Christians (ref. Appendix G) – in one case, a church "Pastor" – who, when glaringly obvious broad white streaks of Chemtrail plumes were being simultaneously ejected from behind several planes directly overhead, *refused to even look up*! His degree of cowardice was truly astounding. Clearly, he had no love of the Truth (Jesus Christ). Yet, his lack of appropriate response was not an exception, but rather, is a general rule. In fact, over a sixteen year period, the author has encountered almost no one who will *even acknowledge* this government "in-your-face" terrorism against the people. As few as 2 people among more than a hundred that were asked the above question answered in the affirmative. Could those who deny the obvious – some of whom professed to be "Christian" – have any love for the truth? Obviously, in this age of media deception, the truth has become irrelevant. 2 Thessalonians 2:10-12: *And with all deceivableness of unrighteousness in them that perish; because they received not the love of the truth, that they might be saved. And for this cause God shall send them strong delusion, that they should believe a lie: That they might all be damned who believed not the truth, but had pleasure in unrighteousness.* This Scripture establishes that the seeming inability to perceive the truth, or to openly acknowledge it once it has been revealed, is a consequence of an individual's *unrighteousness*. Because of their *opposition to the truth*, they are deceived. Such pathetic individuals are cursed by God, Who sends them a *strong delusion* (*a curse*). Unless they repent of their unrighteous deeds and believe the gospel of Jesus Christ, their eternal destiny has already been determined. In the interim, they will strive in the meaningless pursuit of money, until *abruptly encountering* a *Twilight Zone* reality: *Up ahead, there's a sign post that reads*: *Lake of Fire*! The Chemtrail Denial Syndrome is symptomatic of a deeper underlying spiritual problem.

The third group of "Chemtrail-challenged" are those seemingly blind to the reality of what is being done to them on a daily basis from the skies above, yet, not because they are cerebrally numbed by television and HAARP mind-control frequencies, or because they are too self-absorbed, lazy, and truth adverse to care; but because their minds are *bound by demons*. For all the atheists, agnostics, witches, New Agers and pseudo-Christians reading this – yes, there *really are* such entities as *demons*. They are *demonic angels*, not angels of God. The Bible calls them *devils*. Demons/devils are not some diffuse impersonal "energy" or "force"; they are not a state of mind, but are distinct personalities of disembodied spirits that will lodge within any convenient residence: house, statue (ref. Appendix

G), or other inanimate object; yet their preferred abode is *within* the physical body, mind, and spirit of human beings. They like to disguise themselves as witch's nature spirits, earth deities, fairies, gnomes, elves, or forest pixies. Devils enjoy similar anonymity as ghosts, hauntings, and things that go "bump" in the night. Demons are also fond of impersonating the New Ager's "angels" (demonic angels), ascended masters, higher self, avatars, spirit guides, "good witch"/bad witch, channeled personalities (e.g. Edgar Cayce), UFO's, aliens, and little "greys" (from the planet Fruit Cake). They can appear as reptilians, orbs of light, or whatever else they have to be in order to appeal to the preferences of their targeted host. Impersonators *par excellence*, they are truly masters of disguise and deceit. Both the Old and New Testament are replete with accounts of these disembodied spirits, malevolent *demonic angels* who defected along with Lucifer in an ongoing rebellion against God to deceive and destroy mankind. They are among the type spoken of in the Bible: the *fallen angels* who united (spiritual genetically; Luke 1:34-37) with earth women to create a race of giants. Genesis 6:4: *There were giants in the earth in those days; and also after that, when the sons of God came in unto the daughters of men, and they bare children to them, the same became mighty men which were of old, men of renown.* As stated by God's inerrant Word, their offspring survives to this present time (*... and also after that*); i.e. they still exist in today's modern world. Based upon the discussion in a previous chapter, where can there can be found dense concentrations of these *human-demon hybrids*?

As was the case with the first Christian martyr, Stephen – an illustration of the madness of crowds – so too, any Jesus Christ-centered seeker of the Truth should expect to be "bitten" by those who despise hearing the truth about Chemtrails. (But if you *really* want to see madness in action, observe the crazed response to speaking the truth of the 1611 King James Bible, especially to *Professing* Christians.) There is very little point in attempting to reason with a demon-indwelled individual; you may think you are talking to the person, but you are not. The voice you hear is being directed by a disembodied spirit, or more likely, spirits, which have taken up residence within that person's mind and physical being. (Typically, however, it is not a full-time occupation, since these malevolent bodiless spirits come and go at will. A classic example of this can be seen in the characteristic abrupt mood transformation of an alcoholic.) It is not in the occupying demons' best interest to allow their captive human slave to hear the truth, or to focus on it, or even so much as momentarily consider it, since doing so could result in being "evicted" from their "home." A significant portion of the daily walk of Jesus Christ during his earthly 3 year ministry involved casting out devils/demons. Being God Himself, they instantly recognized Who He was, and in the case of the Gadarene madman, a *Legion* of spirit comrades – about 2000 of them – pleaded to be relocated into a herd of swine foraging in a nearby field. (The Hebrew word, *Legion*, means 2000 in number.) As the true account proceeds, the vanquished devils immediately caused the pigs to become struck with *sudden madness,* suicidal when they ran headlong over a steep cliff into the sea and drowned (Mark 5:1-15; Luke 8:26-35). Such is the destiny of all those afflicted with "unclean spirits," who refuse to repent of their unrighteous works. (Demons are granted by God a *spiritual legal right* to afflict those harboring unrepentant sin: idolatry, unforgiveness, sexual immorality, occult involvement – these are only some of the "spiritual rights" by which malevolent spirits have authorized access into a person's soul being.)

But what has this to do with Chemtrails? Most people who are unable to perceive the obvious, or, that are unwilling to acknowledge what is clearly evident, are either being Vlf/Elf mind-controlled, or are selfish uncaring spiritually lazy cowards, as previously described. Their minds are either electrochemically manipulated through the atmospheric medium or via government media propaganda; or, they may simply prefer being willfully ignorant. But there is yet a third possibility, and that is *demonic mind control.* In that case, spiritual blindness is not caused by an external electromagnetic source, psychologically engineered propaganda, or by any lack of intestinal fortitude, but rather, is due to a literal *spiritual* causal factor. A substantial percentage of people in today's *revived neopagan American culture* (at least 40 percent) are afflicted by this third cause. It is no laughing matter they are literally *warehousing demons*. In fact, many individuals today are *infested* with them.

The fourth and final group of Chemtrail perceptually deficient comprises perhaps the largest percentage of those who are truth adverse. These are victims of the Globalist's Agenda biochemical warfare assault upon the world's food and water supply. Sadly, because of the planned destruction of their mind by the calculated use of Fluoride and Lithium added to their drinking water; as well as packaged processed foods containing MSG, Aspartame, genetic modification; Chemtrail air, and vaccines; they cannot recognize what the NWO Luciferians are doing to them. Because they have been genetically and chemically *lobotomized*, their mind is rendered unresponsive to normal stimuli that would elicit curiosity, anger, outrage in a healthy individual. By globalist design, their intelligence has been compromised to such a degree they are incapable of recognizing the obvious; their brain neural network has suffered extensive organic impairment of its synaptic junctions; brain electrical activity has been significantly reduced, lowering their level of cognitive awareness. Most people today are not fully conscious, and are essentially asleep, a mere shadow of the human spirit that once existed among the general population. Lobotomized sheeple (people that exhibit the docile characteristics of sheep) will smile while boarding a government bus en route to a FEMA Concentration Camp, where they will be separated from their family, housed in prison-like conditions, and summarily executed. Their mind disabled from grasping the reality of what is being done to them, they care nothing about the Globalist's Agenda ... as they are taken captive, and go silently into the night.

"Well then shouldn't we all just drink the fluoride water and eat the doped food and breathe the poisoned air, so we'll be numb and won't know what's being done to us?" This was an actual response from a college-degreed Secondary School teacher (her silent husband cowering behind her), in a classic demonstration of typical middle class New Ager Yuppyism, upon being informed by the author about Chemtrails/HAARP, Vaccines, GM/GMO's, Aspartame, MSG, Fluoride, and the New World Order Martial Law citizen imprisonment agenda; leaving no doubt whatsoever as to why the international Luciferians encounter zero resistance to their planned mass murders and global tyranny. *Cowards* are the *first* to be cast into the Lake of Fire (ref. Revelation 21:8). "The truth must be told. The hottest places in hell are reserved for those who in a period of moral crisis maintained their neutrality. There comes a time when silence is betrayal." – Martin Luther King, Jr.

There exists research in the social science literature suggesting that most people do not look up. Typically, they maintain a downward aspect to their viewing range, restricting their field of vision to the area between the ground and about eye level. Is this bizarre behavior a deliberate strategy to avoid being reminded of the righteous judgment of God in the heavens above? Or, is it a convenient way to evade observation of today's atmospheric takeover by the globalist elite? With continuous daily Chemtrailing since 1998, why has virtually no one spoken out against this lethally toxic assault on public health? There has been no official statement or ban from the EPA; not a word of protest from the "green movement," Greenpeace, etc. When Congressman Dennis Kucinich of Ohio (presently a Senator), proposed a Bill to Congress in 2001 (Space Preservation Act, HR 2977) banning all atmospheric weapons testing and bioagents used against civilian populations, specifically mentioning *Chemtrails*, his Bill was struck down and the word "Chemtrails" was omitted from the public record and also from the version of the Bill he re-introduced in 2002 as HR 3616, and again in 2003 as HR 3657. A media blackout of this degree could only be mandated by an international ruling body, i.e. the Illuminati supra-government. Those few individuals that have penetrated the aerosol spray secret operation or defected from the global genocide Chemtrail project affirm that it is one of the most secretive government programs in existence today. Incidentally, politician Kucinich never again publicly spoke a word about Chemtrails, and was subsequently nominated (appointed by his Illuminati handlers) to "campaign" for the highest office in the land – "President" – i.e. Illuminati frontman. (A reward for his silence?) Like all members of *The Criminal Fraternity*, he does what he is told. "There is a power so organized in America, so subtle, so watchful, so pervasive, so interlocked that you better not speak about it above a whisper when you speak in condemnation of it," wrote former U.S. President Woodrow Wilson. This particular Illuminati-appointee was effectively used by his controlling Rothschild overlords to establish an unconstitutional centralized banking system in America – the Federal Reserve (second Plank of Karl Marx's Communist Manifesto) – which controls the U.S. federal government, and who was instrumental in the creation of the unconstitutional Internal Revenue Service by passage of the Underwood Act of 1913.

The worldwide Chemtrail people-spraying campaign is a visible barometer for testing who does and does not love the truth. Those who fail to recognize and acknowledge Chemtrails for the significant role they play in the coming global Police State prophesied in the Books of Daniel, the gospels, Revelation, and in other prophesies throughout Scripture, will, upon their soon demise, have fulfilled their own eternal destiny: ... *hell hath enlarged herself* (Isaiah 5:14). Anyone who refuses to oppose Chemtrails, or who steadfastly denies their existence or significance, has denied the truth. Those who deny the truth, have denied *The* Truth: Jesus Christ (John 14:6). Such a person, especially if claiming to be "a Christian," is a hypocrite, *is not* Saved, and has proven them self to be an impostor; they are merely a *Professing* Christian masquerading as a *True* Christian. Simply stated, they are *a liar.* Believing a lie is the same as speaking a lie. There are no liars or spiritual cowards in the kingdom of heaven – all of them eternally reside in hell. Revelation 21:8: *But the fearful, and unbelieving ... and all liars, shall have their part in the lake which burneth with fire and brimstone: which is the second death.*

After attempting to inform and forewarn people about Chemtrails and other forms of government mind/body destruction, such as vaccinating children, the author's conclusion is counsel received from the wisest of the wise: *Let them alone: they be blind leaders of the blind. And if the blind lead the blind, both shall fall into the ditch* (Matthew 15:14). *Perverse disputings of men of corrupt minds, and destitute of the truth, supposing that gain is godliness: from such withdraw thyself* (1 Timothy 6:5). *Ever learning, and never able to come to the knowledge of the truth* (2 Timothy 3:7).

They don't want the truth? ... The Word of God advises to *leave them alone.* Let them believe lies. *He* will deal with them.

CHEMTRAIL SECRECY

The preceding four reasons explaining why Chemtrails are an unknown phenomenon among the general public explains how the ongoing biological warfare conspiracy can remain "hidden in plain view." Yet, the *news media* also plays a major role in maintaining the citizenry in a state of perpetual ignorance. The supra-government Illuminati has banned all media outlets (television, newspapers, magazines) from uttering or printing a word about the existence of Chemtrails and their Orwellian implications. Any serious attempt to make the spray operation known in the mainstream media are immediately squelched.

Illustrating this effect on a microcosmic level, during a recent incident when the author arrived at a Walmart store to pick up processed film of photographs he took of Chemtrial skies (ref. 2010 photo collage), he was informed by the sales clerk that the film had been "lost." After the store employee made several phone calls to ascertain the possible whereabouts of the purloined photos, the author was advised to return the next day to pick up the processed film. Upon arrival the following day, a new clerk was behind the counter in the photo department, an individual never before seen by the author, and who produced an envelope package containing processed film, but it was not the author's film. Subsequently, when a swarm of store personnel suddenly converged upon the author to stage an altercation, and he *invoked the name of Jesus* Christ (realizing their unprovoked attack was spiritually contrived and initiated on a higher level of command and control – both, spiritually and temporally), their threatening posture immediately escalated to *invoking the police.* A concerted (failed) effort was then launched to have the author arrested on nonexistent charges. The original photos were never recovered. Walmart is a pilot New World Order citizen surveillance prototype; Chemtrails are a top secret black budget Illuminati project. Those attempting to expose this conspiracy of silence should expect confrontations directed from "central headquarters."

Postscript: Several months have now transpired since the Walmart episode. As this book is being prepared to go to print, it has become public knowledge that Walmart employees are instructed by their superiors in the Illuminati network to report any "suspicious activity" among store patrons. Having sent out for processing undeveloped film of New World Order Chemtrailing, the author qualified as "suspicious," "a threat." (Satan's government people always consider the truth to be "a threat.") Therefore, the author's above analysis of the bizarre incident was correct, thus confirming that Walmart is indeed a New World Order prototype used by the global crime syndicate for "beta-testing" citizen surveillance.

"In-your-face" Chemtrails are a top secret high-level black ops Illuminati project that is *not* to be reported on. In every Walmart store there is at least one government operative acting as an employee shill. In this case, the "unfamiliar clerk" was later identified as the *store pharmacist.* In Greek, pharmacy means "*sorcery.*" Therefore, the government Cointelpro agent hoping to entrap the author with false charges that would result in arrest and incarceration, was, of course, a *witch/sorcerer.* Despite Satan's best efforts, a second set of photographs were filmed by the author and processed elsewhere. Further ramifications are discussed at the end of this chapter.

A National Epidemic of Willful Ignorance, Government Mind Control, or *Spiritual Blindness?*

... and none of the wicked shall understand; but the wise shall understand.

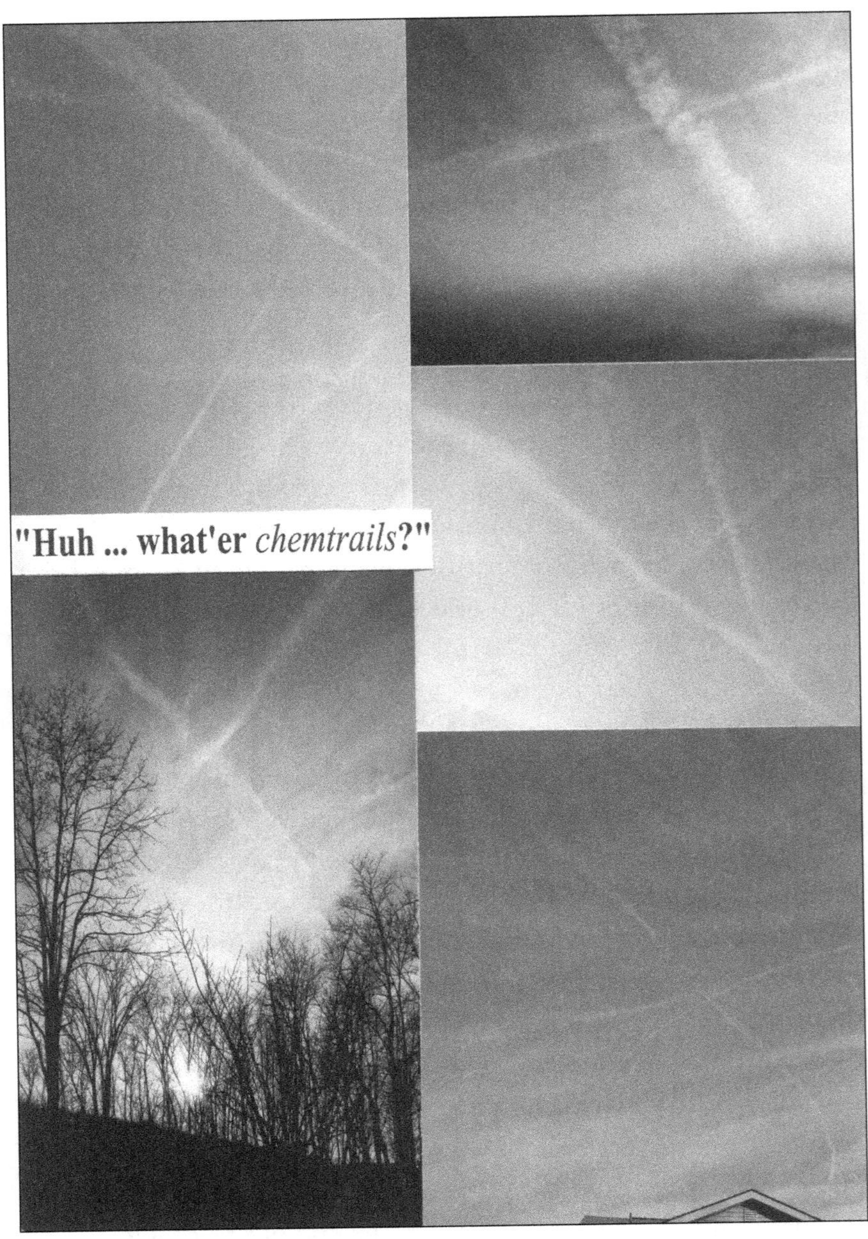

These are photographs of Chemtrail skies in 2008, taken 5 years after those on the previous page. For the following pages, note the progressive increase in volume and intensity over periods of just 1 year. Cell phone towers and MSG/Aspartame fast food restaurants enhance the effects of the global mind-numbing campaign that is escalating in preparation for the worldwide economic collapse. From 2003-2008, atmospheric electro-conductivity resulting from output of HAARP Vlf/Elf mind-control frequencies *doubled* each year, a 32 fold increase.

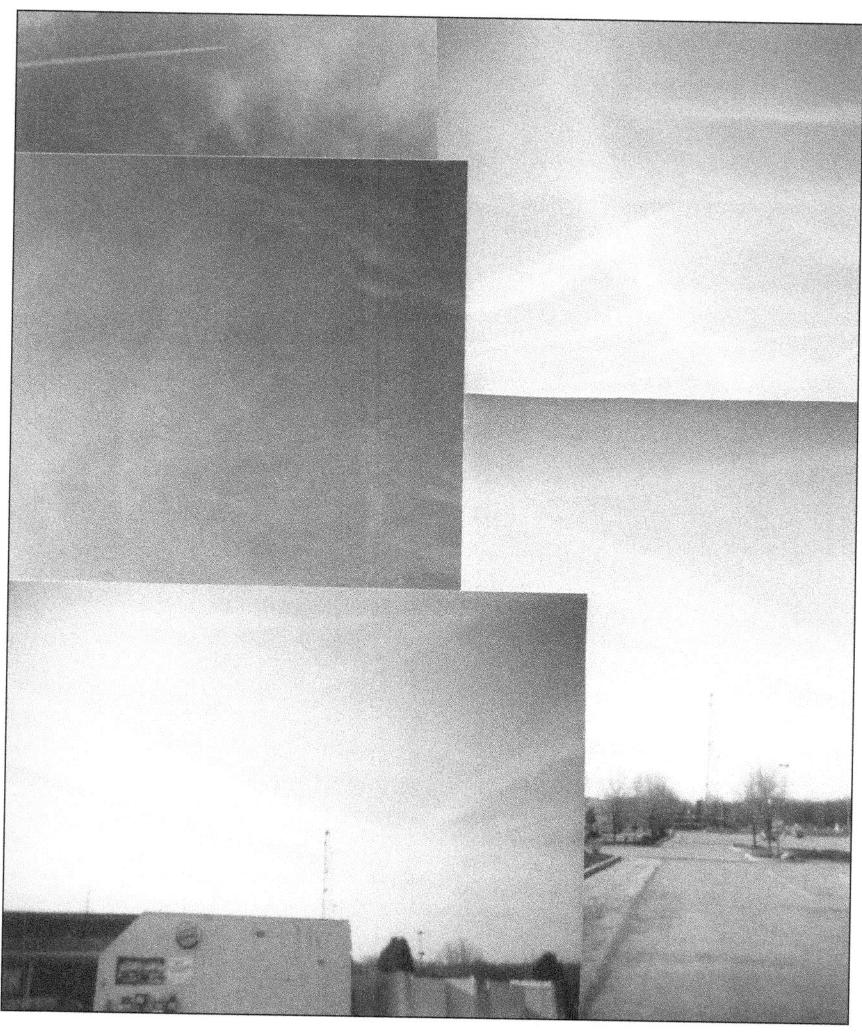

Chemtrails 2009: The atmospheric plasma medium through which Alaskan microwave frequency transmitter (HAARP) propagates energy – to control the weather, and people. See all those silent white planes up there? Notice the hazy skies lately? Any chronic respiratory ailments? Irregular heartbeat? Digestive problems? Thank Big Brother, now in *your* neighborhood ... and no one suspects anything is *wrong*.

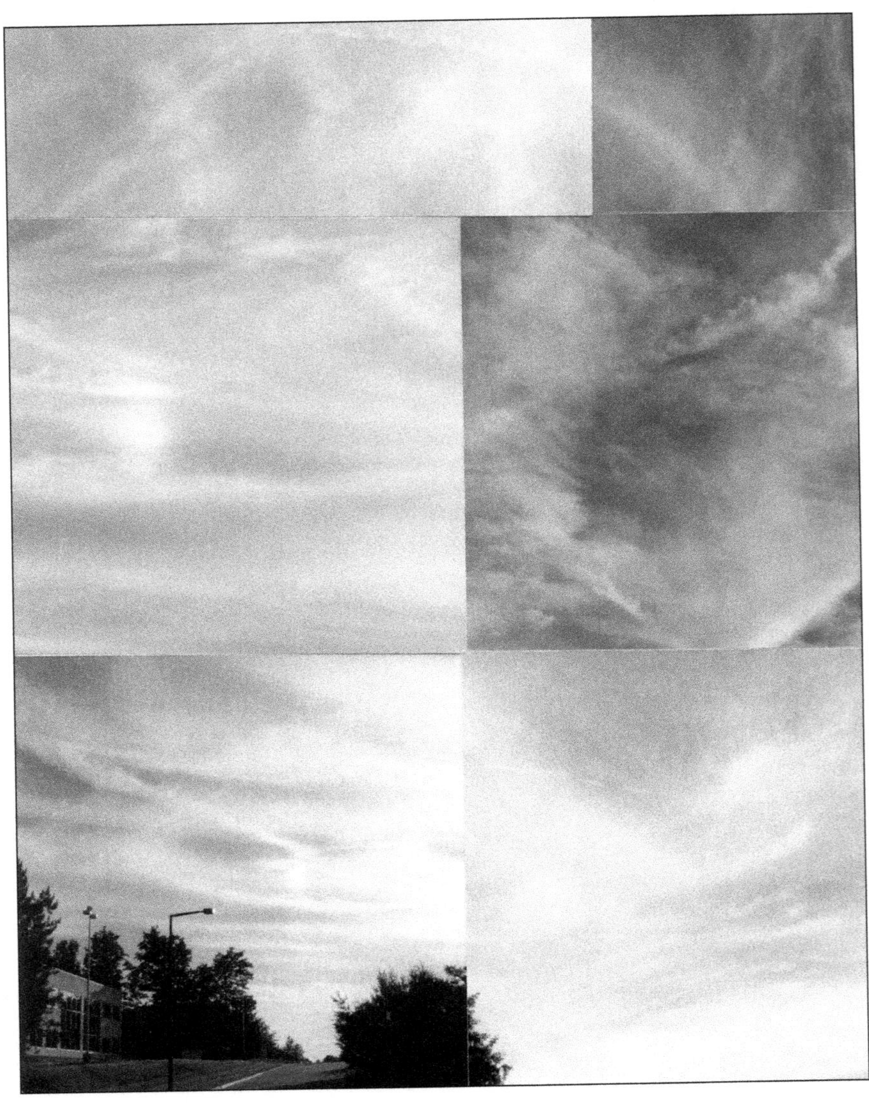

Chemtrails 2010: The Chemtrail composition is changing over time. More virulent bioengineered strains of bacteria, viruses, and fungi; presence of self-replicating *polymer nanofibers* acting as a substrate vehicle for skin penetrating biochemical warfare components associated with *Morgellan's Disease*. Chemtrails are the fulfillment of Matthew 24:7 endtime prophesy: ... *there shall be* ... *pestilences* ...

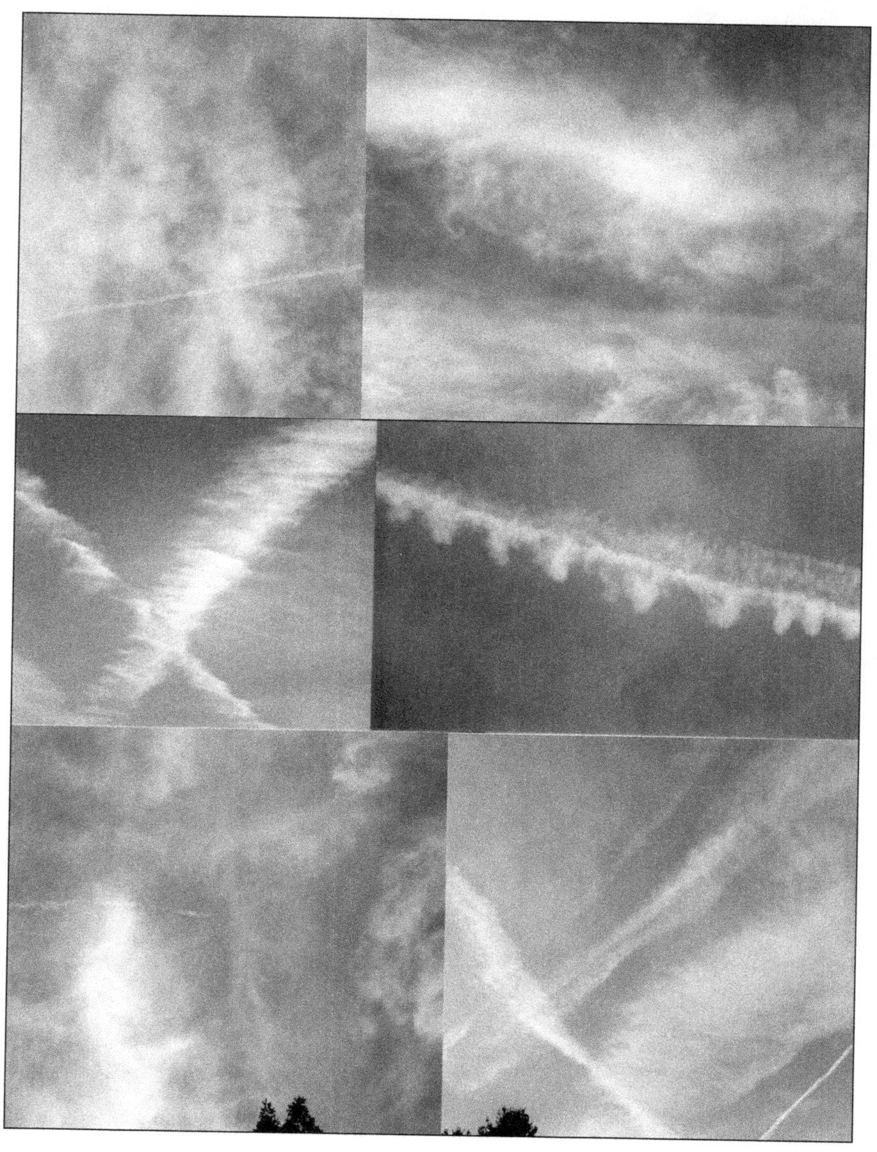

These are what normal cloud formations look like. They are distinctively different from the artificial "cloud cover" created by Chemtrails.

Normal cloud formations in a haze of *persistent* residual Chemtrails. Jet aircraft "Contrails," the result of turbo exhaust water droplets condensing at high altitude lower temperatures, typically begin to dissipate within about a minute.

Chemtrails are technically known as "Operation Cloverleaf" or "Operation Raindance." On February 20, 2010, the government-controlled media attempted to confuse the public with disinformation when acknowledging the existence of Chemtrails, and is now referring to them by the more scientific-sounding and benign term, "Geoengineering." (The terms, "Chemtrails" and "Geoengineering" are still barred from usage in UN documents.) Like most supra-government "Black Operations," the Illuminati global aerosol spray campaign serves a multifaceted agenda. Since 1998, soon after a speech made by Edward Teller (physicist who worked on the Manhattan Project that created the Atomic Bomb which destroyed Hiroshima and Nagasaki), microfine particles of elemental Aluminum, invisible to the naked eye, have been detected in the atmosphere. Teller spoke to fellow globalists at a closed Bilderberg meeting where he described the possibility of seeding the troposphere with nanoparticle-size metallic Aluminum that would serve as an electrically conductive medium for the propagation of directed microwave electromagnetic pulses generated by Bernard Eastlund's patented HAARP microwave technology. Since then, the "Dr. Strangelove" mad eugenicists have been mass inoculating – by breathed air – an unsuspecting world population with a changeable Chemtrail concoction of weaponized nanoparticles, bioengineered bacterial and viral pathogens, and toxic heavy metals. This global genocide project is funded and directed by one or more of the Illuminati crime families, including major funding from the Rockefellers and the Bill Gates Foundation. (The Rockefeller crime syndicate, originators of global depopulation genocide policies, also fund and promote Planned Parenthood, the abortion industry, and own and control the pharmaceutical and biotechnology industries which create the components present in Chemtrails and vaccines.) The billion dollar per day spraying of the world's people pays for itself by increased citizen expenditure for Rockefeller pharmaceutical drugs, antibiotics, and vaccines to "treat" symptoms of Chemtrail exposure. Invisible airborne particles saturate the air, inoculating the human and animal population with disease; breathed nano-sized Aluminum crosses the blood-brain barrier and lodges in the microglial cells of the cerebral cortex. The water soluble radioactive Barium component of Chemtrails dissolves in open water systems and ground water aquifers. Both of these elements are known to change reproductive genetics and create neurodegenerative disorders (e.g. Alzheimer's, Parkinson's, Autism). They transform individual human brains into walking antennas for receiving directed electronic pulses from HAARP microwave generators strategically positioned throughout the world. (This effect will become more fully integrated when combined with a human implantable subdermal microchip with GPS capability.) The news media is under strict Illuminati orders not to truthfully report the global mind-control genocidal spray operation, and the general public is too dumbed-down to care. Those few with knowledge of Chemtrails "aren't talking."

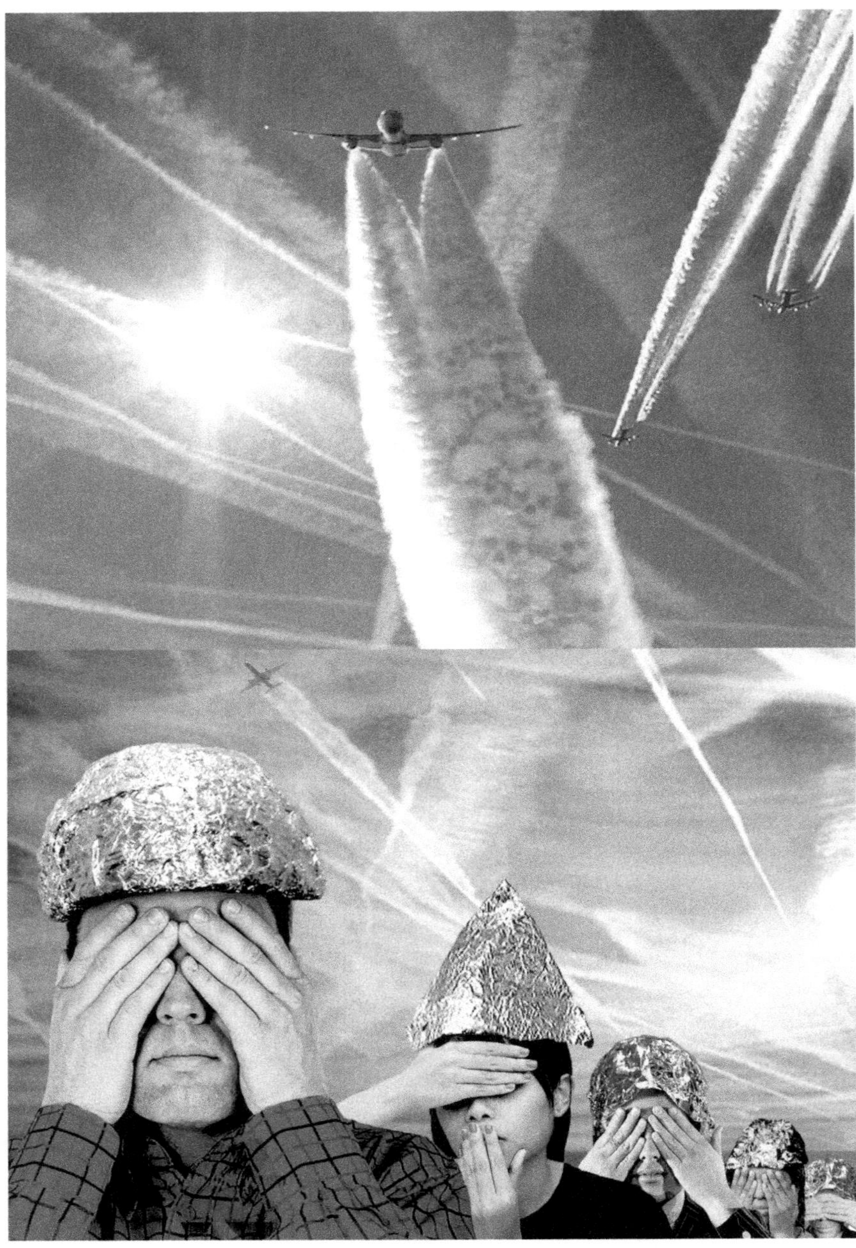

The chemically-electronically controlled public "sees no evil, hears no evil, speaks no evil."

Billions of people all over the globe are daily being sprayed from the sky above; the lower atmosphere is completely saturated with invisible microfine particles of elemental Aluminum, Barium, and other toxic elements that are ingested by every air-breathing creature on Earth, and – what is even more disturbing – hardly anyone knows about it … or wants to know.

FOUR ASPECTS OF CHEMTRAIL "OPERATION CLOVERLEAF"

1) *Mass Genocide, Global Depopulation, Eugenics*

   Give people diseases upon breathing the man-made polymer nanofibers and micro-particulate radioactive toxic heavy metal pathogenic effluent spewed by Chemtrail planes. The synthetic nanofibers act as a delivery system for transporting disease-causing pathogens, and have an affinity for binding with Chemtrail toxic metals such as Barium, Aluminum, Cadmium, and Thorium. The radioactive isotopic forms of certain Chemtrail constituents (e.g. Barium and Thorium) can change the genetic structure of somatic and sex chromosomes and thus alter the human Genetic Code. The cationic synthetic fibers are *self-replicating*, reproducing and growing *within the intracellular tissue of the human body*, especially the abdominal area. Under microscopic examination, the fibers often appear as a tangle of spider web-like material that upon higher magnification resembles a spiritually significant chain of dragon or wolf heads. One of Chemtrail's main biological vectors is *Mycoplasm,* a disease-causing fungus. Principal metal components (Aluminum, Barium) are neurodegenerative, interfering with the function of brain neurotransmitters and the neural network: nerve cell body and associated dendrites and synaptic junctions. Brain glial cells (astrocytes and microglia), upon contract with even nanomolar concentrations of these toxic metals, elicit an enhanced inflammatory response, a prolonged sickness reaction triggered by the immune system, the short-term health consequences of which can be even more devastating than contracting any of the various Chemtrail diseases. Diagnosis of Parkinson's, Alzheimer's, Autism, and other neurodegenerative disorders can be directly attributed to the presence of elemental *Aluminum* in brain tissue. This pathogenicity maximizes global genocide by synergistically enhancing adverse health effects, for example, when Aluminum (Chemtrails) combines with Mercury (vaccines) and Fluoride (municipal drinking water). Some independent researchers have speculated that certain chemical constituents of Chemtrails are necessary to activate autoimmune stealth diseases transmitted by vaccines. Other known Chemtrail components are Strontium 90 (a waste product from nuclear reactors), Sulfur hexafluoride (a suffocating gas), Titanium (systemic nerve poison), Arsenic, Lead, Mercury, Uranium – all are highly toxic to humans and have been detected in the Chemtrail witch's brew. The component Chemtrail mixture frequently changes as the mad globalists test new ways to inoculate and contaminate their human targets. For example, human excrement has been identified in ground samples of Chemtrails collected throughout the world. Currently, there is some evidence to suggest the presence of "nanobots," self-assembling miniature robots that enter a human or animal host and take over or disrupt the function of bodily processes. Another major component of spewed Chemtrails is Ethylene dibromide (JP8 Jet Fuel), which is a known carcinogen. This lethal chemical component created the *rainbow* image seen in the previous third page of Chemtrail photos (2009). Commonly known as a "sun dog," it is literally an "oil slick" in the sky.

Ever since commencement of the Chemtrail poisoning of the world population, hospital emergency admissions in America for upper respiratory aliments have skyrocketed. Even the Center for Disease Control in Atlanta Georgia (an Illuminati genocide front) has reported a corresponding rise in sickness and disease that began soon after Chemtrail spraying was initiated. Typical symptomologies of Chemtrail exposure are: upper respiratory illness, pneumonia, lung congestion and chronic dry cough with repeated attempts to expel phlegm (Mycoplasma candida fungus), chronic low grade flu-like symptoms without a fever, nausea, stiffness in back of the neck (spinal meningitis virus), gastrointestinal disturbances and a bloated sensation in the stomach after consuming even small amounts of food (replicating polymer fibers expanding within the intracellular tissue of the abdominal wall), arthritis joint pain and stiffness, full body systemic weakness (Chronic Fatigue Syndrome), and other previously mentioned debilitating and toxic effects. Extending the morbid list of Chemtrail induced illnesses is Morgellons Disease, typified by the self-replicating polymer nanofibers erupting through ulcerated lesions in the skin and from bodily orifices. Oils present on the skin epidermis break down the plasticized fibers into fragments which are then absorbed directly through the skin to enter the bloodstream. Created in mad eugenics laboratories (primarily Monsanto), it is infectious and spreads to all family members, including pets. (To see the tiny polymer fibers, rinse your mouth with a small amount of red wine, then spit it back into a glass.)

The concentration of nanofibers in the ambient surface air at ground level is empirically calculated by the author to range between a minimum of 1 fiber per cubic yard and 1 fiber per cubic inch, depending upon factors such as wind, drift rate, frequency of atmospheric spraying, and proximity to last dumping of Chemtrails. For more on the Chemtrail composition, reference author's book, *Genesis 1:29 Diet.*

Since the reality of Chemtrails has finally been admitted by the criminal U.S. government, the mad globalists have proposed spraying 10-20 million metric tons of particulate Aluminum per year into the atmosphere for the stated goal of "cooling the planet." An obvious falsehood, Chemtrail artificial cloud cover *traps* lower frequency infrared light waves and *heats* the earth's lower atmosphere, thus, daily global Chemtrail spraying creates a *localized increase* of so-called "global warming." Red China is the only nation that has not cooperated with the Illuminati gangster eugenicists, and has reportedly prohibited the Chemtrail doping of their skies. There is no Chemtrail spray activity over Washington, D.C., District of Criminals.

Breathed nano-size particles cross the blood-brain barrier to lodge in the microglial cells of the cerebral cortex, causing brain inflammation and neurodegenerative disorders. The Acetic acid lower PH from drinking apple cider vinegar neutralizes alkaline Chemtrail Barium. For those who wish to reduce their inhalation exposure to Chemtrails, it is advised to wear a double thickness particle/dust mask (2 masks, non-asbestos/non-latex) whenever venturing outdoors, especially on heavy "spray days" preceding a storm front and on the day following a rain shower. It is also recommended to dress in a long sleeve shirt, hat, and full leg covering to prevent absorption of skin penetrating polymer fibers. The best course of action is to seal your windows and doors and remain inside as much as possible; a HEPA filter air purifier in every room. An antidote for the Mycoplasm fungus component of Chemtrails is the antifungal herb *Turmeric*. A general antidote and disease preventative for a broad spectrum of Chemtrail afflictions can be made with the following natural ingredients: Add to a 10-12 ounce glass jar a 1/8 teaspoon measure of the following: crushed oregano, sea salt, echinachia, garlic powder, turmeric powder, crushed basil leaves. Fill the jar with distilled water. Take small sips throughout the day. Repeat 3-5 times per week. Fasting before taking the Chemtrail Antidote is most efficacious. (This mixture can also be used as a safe and effective medium for brushing your teeth.) A cure for Chemtrail Bronchial congestion: Mixture of 1 part oil of oregano and 3 parts olive oil. Place several drops from an eyedropper under the tongue. Inhale slowly to draw vapor into lungs. (For pets, Dip Q-tip into oil of oregano. Rub onto paws.) Drinking large amounts of *distilled water* will electrochemically bind the water molecule components of hydrogen and oxygen with toxic metals and other foreign matter to remove them from the body. An average size adult male should consume at least a gallon of *distilled* water daily (stored in a *glass* container, not plastic) to purify bodily tissues and organs of the Chemtrail metallic components. Tap water, or water that has been filtered by Reverse Osmosis or any other filtration method, *does not* provide this crucial benefit. Do not believe the disinformation claiming distilled water leaches minerals from the body, etc. The purest form of water possible, drinking it is the single most effective action that can be taken to improve and maintain good health.

2) *Weather Modification*

HAARP electromagnetic energy heats up the ionosphere to affect the weather. The microwave frequency energy waves interact with metallic Chemtrail components present in the atmosphere to electrostatically control weather fronts and to redirect the ten major jet streams located over the Northern and Southern Hemispheres of the globe. These massive air flows can also be manipulated by Tesla Scalar Technology (created by HAARP) which can propagate powerful Longitudinal Electromagnetic Waves to create, enhance, and direct natural disasters such as tornados, hurricanes, earthquakes, volcanic eruptions (above and undersea), tsunamis, droughts, floods. By Illuminati design, these environmental catastrophes are being created or enhanced to produce crisis situations as a pretext for more government intervention and control over civilian populations; causing regional chaos by destruction of agricultural crops and food shortages, forced evacuations and concomitant dependency upon the government for life-sustaining needs, and for the soon declaration of a Martial Law National State of Emergency that will suspend and *officially* nullify the U.S. Constitution. (Unofficially, the Constitution and Bill of Rights have *already* been nullified.) In this manner, the Illuminati-controlled government offers "The Solution" to "The Crisis" which *they* created. And their "Solution," as always, is more control over the people; take away their God-given and Constitutional rights; make them dependent upon an illegitimate Antichrist government for their physical needs.

Scalar Electromagnetics, generated by the HAARP weather modification project, as well as from other electromagnetic (EM) directed sources located throughout the world, are also being utilized to manipulate high and low pressure zones that can influence the weather and form storm fronts. Intensified Chemtrail spraying typically occurs in advance of an approaching weather system – created or enhanced by HAARP/Scalar EM waves – in order for rain to lower the nano-particulate pathogenic mixture to ground level, where these poisons are breathed by people and animals, and can drain into open and subterranean bodies of water, thus further contaminating rural and urban drinking water supplies.

3) ***Military Applications*: "Star Wars" space weaponry using HAARP/Tesla Scalar Electromagnetics/Chemtrail ionic plasma interaction.**

During the globalist's 1990-1991 Gulf War, the Chemtrail spray operation was part of the U.S. military arsenal of "bio-weapons testing" that was used on Iraqi soldiers, civilians, and American soldiers. HAARP performed perfectly, inducing a state of confusion, hallucinations and terror among the Iraqis located in the vicinity of the war zone staged military theater; the "enemy" subsequently surrendered without any confrontation. For 16 years, Chemtrails in conjunction with HAARP, have induced similar psychological effects on civilian populations worldwide as the output of electromagnetic mind-control frequencies escalates on a yearly basis. (The world population is becoming increasingly zombified.)

Nikola Tesla rediscovered Scalar Waves after they were first identified by James Clerk Maxwell, who devised a set of mathematical equations that were the basis for Einstein's Relativity Theory. Maxwell and Tesla realized that the vacuum of space is filled with a mysterious kind of energy that radiates as Longitudinal Waves from any dipole source (cell mitochondria, battery, magnet, celestial body in space, entire galaxies and clusters of galaxies). Tesla is credited with inventing a device which extracts from the atmosphere this inexhaustible source of free energy, and that propagates as Scalar Longitudinal Waves. The Soviet Union is believed to have created weapons of mass destruction using this powerful Longitudinal Wave technology which is capable of penetrating through the earth and can create natural disasters such as earthquakes, volcanic eruptions, tsunamis, tornados, hurricanes. This weaponized technology can be directed at civilian populations and rogue nations that refuse to cooperate with the globalist's plans for abolishing their national sovereignty to establish the Illuminati's NWO international Police State control matrix.

There are recent reports from all over the world: Asia, Europe, Africa, North America, of *millions* of dead birds falling from the sky en masse. This is not caused by a "Bird Flu epidemic" (as proposed by the controlled media), but is likely to be the direct result of Chemtrails/HAARP. The birds have inhaled electrochemically conductive nanoparticulate Aluminum and Barium, thus, when HAARP is activated and directed to a localized area, the birds are instantaneously "zapped" by pulsed microwaves. Likewise, massive fish die-offs in the oceans and lakes.

4) *Mind Control*

HAARP propagates microwave frequencies in the critical 1-100 HZ range that affects human cognitive function and can induce an hypnotic state (10 HZ). Powerful bursts of directed microwave radiation are being transmitted to large areas of the country (for example, Eastern United States) and impacts both humans and animals. Modified behavioral responses range from apathy to indiscriminate rage. Induced effects include: visions, voice hallucinations, confusion, "mind fog" or the inability to think clearly, disintegration of the reasoning faculty; loss of ability to differentiate between truth and falsehood, reality and fantasy – as exemplified by, for example, uncritical acceptance of anything the government-controlled media broadcasts on the television evening news: "... another Arab terrorist was arrested today in connection with the September 11, 2001 Twin Towers attack ...." But the truth is: *The government did it* (ref. Appendix E). A physically/psychologically traumatized or electrochemically controlled individual is characterized by eliciting a high degree of compliance, passivity, unquestioned *acceptance and obedience* to illegitimate authority or anything disseminated by the government-controlled media. A mind-controlled subject lacks any of the characteristics of an alert intact mind. Such a thought-controlled individual has no critical thinking capability: no truth discernment, no curiosity, no inquisitiveness, no deductive reasoning ability, no outrage over injustice, and will rigorously defend falsehoods of which they have no knowledge. The "Sheeple" are uninterested and unconcerned about legislation intended to take away their God-given and Constitutional rights and abolish the middle class in America, transforming the U.S. into a third world nation (NAFTA/Open Borders, Patriot Acts 1, 2; Homeland Security), and are without any moral convictions regarding unjust laws (Hate Crime Bill, Gun Control Laws, Gay Rights, abortion, etc). A controlled mind *will not* resist tyranny; such a person will comply with any demands to surrender their freedoms. (They will even put on their own handcuffs.) Zombification of the American and global population is further exemplified by citizen's gross ignorance and emphatic denial of the most overt threat to their health and personal liberty by a transnational shadow government which has declared war upon the world's people, spraying them like pestiferous insects. Lack of awareness or denial of the true objectives of Chemtrails are proof that most people today are being Vlf and Elf mind-controlled.

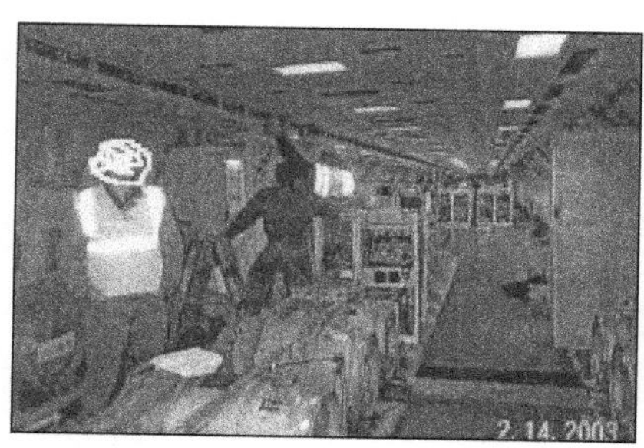

Interior of a Chemtrail plane, showing tanks of chemical/biological warfare agents.

Chemtrail planes are unmarked, all white, fly at a rapid speed at high altitude without making any sound detectable at ground level, and are retrofitted with spray apparatus that spews the pathogenic particulate mixture from beneath the wings. (Most commercial airliners also add the Chemtrail poisons to their jet fuel.) The planes are primarily C-130-135 cargo carriers departing and returning to refuel from key U.S. military bases, as well as major commercial airports throughout the world. Executives and maintenance personnel from all the commercial airlines are cooperating with the international terrorist government in systematically poisoning the world population, and remain silent while death is being sprayed into the air. Those in the industry that have discovered the retrofitted spray apparatus on refueling commercial airliners have been silenced or murdered. (During refueling, commercial Chemtrial planes are replenished with their load of toxic poisons by "Honey Trucks," which simultaneously dispose of the human waste on board while refilling spray tanks. No one suspects it.) In America, the Bechtel Corporation, one of the largest defense contracting companies in the world, is in charge of planning Chemtrail flight schedules and arranging daily flight patterns to optimize spray dispersal and track drift rates with Global Positioning Satellites. Evergreen Air (Evergreen International), located at Pinal Airpark, Marana,

Arizona, has been a CIA/NSA secret facility for over four decades. It is at this government front that planes are modified for use as a Chemtrail delivery system. There are several other military facilities throughout the country acting as a base for regional Chemtrail operations, such as Wright-Patterson Air Force Base in Dayton, Ohio. Each region of the country has a central processing location.

Satanic symbols formed by the intersection of two or more Chemtrails are commonly seen in the sky. A pentagram, also known as a Bathomet or Goat Head of Mendes, is the triangular-shaped symbol displayed in the Frontispiece of this book (opposite the Title Page). Created by Chemtrails, and shown below, it was photographed directly above the author's residence on the day preceding an earlier book edition. This was *not* a "coincidence."

Death inducing Chemtrails are a sacrificial offering to Lucifer, whom the globalists serve.

Large X's formed by Chemtrails are commonplace in the sky above, and are the means by which satellites track the rate of Chemtrail aerosol dispersal (ref. first and fourth pages of previous Chemtrail photo collage). The letter "X" is also one of the symbols which signifies Satan/Lucifer/the Devil. Satanic symbols in the sky are a visual means for the transnational government crime syndicate to covertly communicate affirmation of their diabolical agenda among themselves, while at the same time conveying allegiance to their lord and master, Satan, *the prince of the power of the air* (Ephesians 2:2). Similarly, high-ranking U.S. government officials are often seen in the media wearing a particular shade of blue tie. This color of blue is from ancient Babylonian culture, signifies Semiramis/Astoroth/Astarte/Isis/Diana goddess worship (i.e. worship of demons/devils), and is a visible means by which Satan's criminal elite signal their allegiance to his Babylonian Mystery Religion Illuminati witchcraft New World Order global government (Revelation 17:5). Further implications of the mystery religion blue-colored tie suggests they are "tied to," united with, in support of, Satan's image of the Beast: i.e. *global government* and the soon to be revealed *Antichrist* world dictator (Revelation 13:14,15;19:20). In their demon-indwelled genocidal madness, the world's political/financial elite are merely simple-minded modern primitives.

Wherefore seeing we are compassed about with so great a cloud of witnesses ... (Hebrews 12:1). Can the reader discern the hooded robed figure seated in the clouds of the 2010 Chemtrail photo collage shown on the next page? Look closely at the bright area in the lower left photograph on that page, reproduced below. Who is the most likely identity? (Hint: Ephesians 2:2).

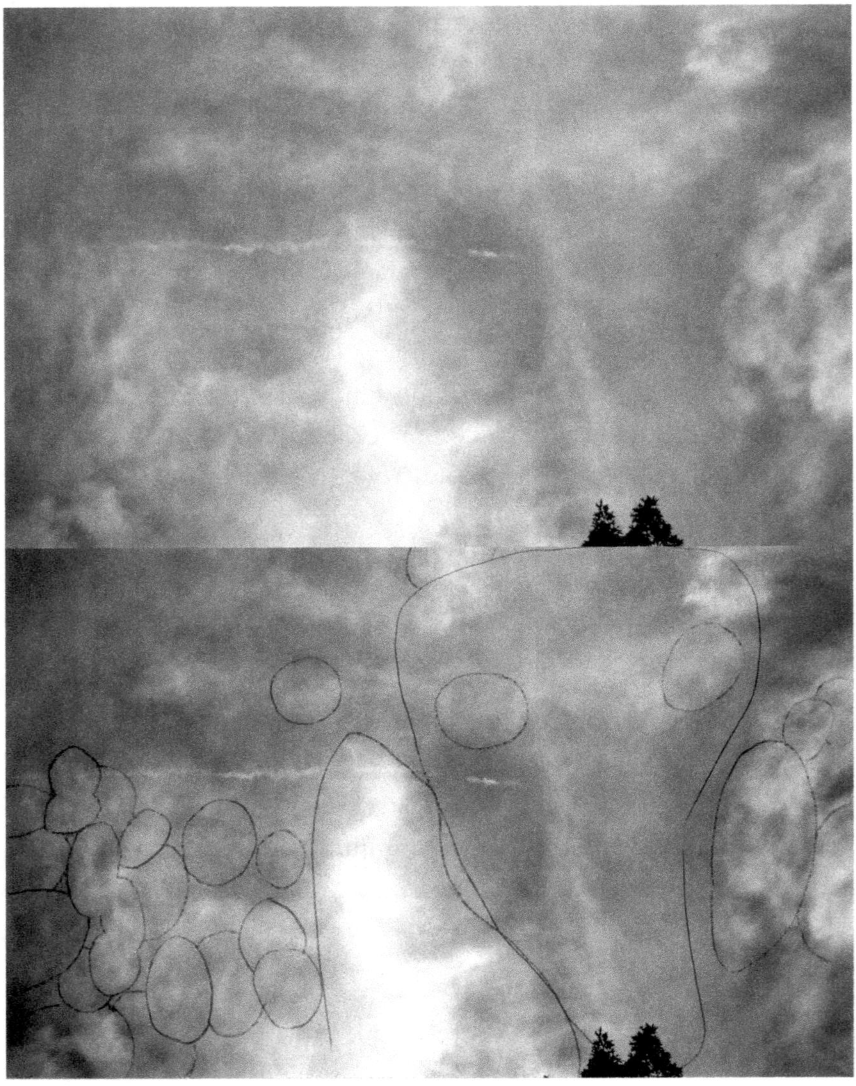

This photograph of Chemtrails is the same as that previously referenced. Upon close inspection, the author discovered at least 30 embedded images. (Still more are evident in a superimposed multiple layering effect.) The mathematical probability of this occurring by chance in a single photo is greater than 2 billion to 1.

God allowed the Walmart incident to occur so the first set of photographs would be confiscated in order for the second set to serve as a witness to the stark spiritual reality behind the modern phenomena of chemically poisoning the Earth and its inhabitants. This single photo alone should make it obvious to anyone that *death* is the only objective behind the Chemtrail global aerosol campaign.

Throughout all of human history, the more God's people are persecuted the more their testimony to the truth spreads and proliferates. Satan meant the aborted Walmart entrapment for evil, but God meant it for *good* (Romans 8:28). Therefore, speak out against the injustice, tyranny, and oppression caused by Satan's people, and do not be afraid of the consequences. You will one day be Judged according to your every word and action, or lack thereof (Matthew 12:36). Sins of commission/sins of omission incur the wrath of God. Therefore, take heed to what you say and do … or fail to say and do. Accusers are present; witnesses are watching.

Postscript: In the same 2010 photo collage as the previous image, the upper left photo reveals two human faces, showing clearly defined features, located just above the horizontal Chemtrail. Can there be any doubt that we are immersed in a transdimensional reality, which, for the most part, remains completely hidden? Yet, it was inadvertently revealed by the global mad eugenics and human eradication program known as "Chemtrails."

What the author believes we are seeing in these two photographs is the next higher dimension manifesting in the material realm. These images are registering in Chemtrails because they are a spiritually-charged medium, having Biblical prophetic significance for the present endtimes.

CHAPTER 5

VACCINES, MSG, ASPARTAME, FLUORIDE, GM/GMO's, NEWS MEDIA

Doth not wisdom cry? and understanding put forth her voice? … But he that sinneth against me wrongeth his own soul: all they that hate me love death.

– Proverb 8:1,36

And wisdom and knowledge shall be the stability of thy times …

– Isaiah 33:6

"A truth's initial commotion is directly proportional to how deeply the lie was believed. When a well-packaged web of lies has been sold gradually to the masses over generations, the truth will seem utterly preposterous and its speaker a raving lunatic." – Dresden James

"A false conclusion, once arrived at and widely accepted is not dislodged easily, and the less it is understood, the more tenaciously it is held."

– Cantor's Law of Preservation of Ignorance

"In a time of universal deceit, telling the truth is a revolutionary act."

– George Orwell, (Eric Blair)
author of the dystopian novel, *1984*

Whenever attempting to get to the truth of a matter, it is never a good idea to go to the party or parties which have a vested interest in maintaining a certain position. *For the love of money is the root of all evil* (2 Timothy 6:10), and people do indeed lie.

There *is no* "controversy" over the vaccine issue – it was "they" who promoted that term to leave open the possibility that anything can be true, no matter how absurd. Do you believe 9/11 was carried out by "Arab terrorists" led by a little guy in a rag hat hiding out in a cave somewhere? ... The government-owned media ministers of propaganda say it's so. Is Mercury and Lead good for a child's developing brain? ... That's what the Illuminati-controlled U.S. government has told you to believe about vaccines. Do you *really* think there is a "two party system" in America, and that your "vote" will change anything? If so, this chapter will seem like a "revolutionary act"... but only for those who are under the spell of "universal deceit."

VACCINES

"I found that the whole vaccine business was indeed a gigantic hoax ... you'll kill far more children than would have died from natural infections."

– Dr. Kalokerinos, MD

"The AMA, AAPeds, CDC, FDA, Dept of HHS, pharmaceutical companies, and the US Congress have all maintained that there is absolutely no autism/vaccination connection, and the onset of Autism around the time of an MMR [Measles, Mumps, Rubella vaccine] is "purely coincidental."

– Dr. Sherri Tenpenny

Especially over the last 100 years, the supra-government International Hierarchy has been working diligently to create new ways to murder and maim the entire world population. Two world wars and continuous bloodshed in political skirmishes around the globe are not sufficient to satisfy their lust for human carnage. More death and escalating loss of human life is needed to appease their blood-lusting master. Genetics gone mad, genocidal eugenics, creating pandemics, spreading global disease – these are integral means for achieving their depopulation objective and ultimate goal of total world domination.

They bioengineered the AIDS virus and injected it into unsuspecting Africans during the early 1980's under the guise of a public health "disease preventative." Today, thanks to the Illuminati-controlled World Health Organization, fifty percent of the African continent is afflicted with AIDS, and the other half are carriers for the disease. Many millions have died as a result, and in the near future tens of millions more will suffer horrible AIDS-related deaths. Closer to home, in America, the CDC is now calling for 233 vaccinations between birth and 25 years of age, each vaccine containing 5 mg of toxic Mercury (just 1 mg of Mercury is sufficient to cause permanent cognitive disability). The same smiling serial killers mandated that new born infants and school-aged children be inoculated with over 100 vaccine injections (22 in the first year; as many as 9 in a single office visit) containing a brain destroying concoction of Aluminum, Mercury, Arsenic, Lead, live cancer cells, MSG, bioengineered disease-causing bacteria, squalene (Gulf War Syndrome), formaldehyde (embalming fluid), live viruses, and other ingredients to insure that the present and all future generations of children are plagued with lifelong incurable diseases and maintained at the cognitive level of drooling idiots. Administered by your often well-meaning, but *amazingly ignorant*, pediatrician or general practitioner MD, this massive biowarfare assault upon Americans and citizens of other countries throughout the world continues to go unchallenged by a public *made apathetic* and targeted for extinction. It's all about "population control," and they want to control *YOU.*

The planned government-mandated attack upon your baby is intensified during a child's first 2 years of life; compulsory vaccines timed for when the infant's brain is experiencing the most rapid growth phase. It is at this point the Illuminati shadow government makes it a mandatory requirement that children receive the greatest number of vaccines (shots). Through government inoculations, infants are injected with more than 51 vaccines by 6 months of age, are required to be injected with 23 viruses before age five, and many more vaccine injections (nearly 200) mandatory within the next few years. Your doctor will tell you the viruses are "killed, non-living," but that is only a half-truth (i.e. a lie). These pathogenic disease-causing viruses are *still capable of transferring disease* after a process to weaken (attenuate) them. Further, the *viruses mutate* within the human body, creating even more virulent (extremely harmful, deadly) strains of the original virus. Therefore, vaccinations are literally transferring diseases to your children, which you trusted the doctor-approved "shots" were protecting them against! Vaccine-injected viruses reside in every cell of the body and pass through the blood-brain barrier where they accumulate in higher concentrations in brain tissue. The brain's long-term *sickness response* to vaccines is a consequence of toxic metals, biochemical warfare food additives such as MSG and Aspartame, and viral and bacterial components in vaccines which produce *neurotoxins*. The Thimerosal Mercury component of vaccines *cannot be excreted by the body*; it is retained in the somatic tissue where higher concentrations continually accumulate. The resultant neurological dysfunction in children and infants manifests as Encephalitis, Autism, Sudden Infant Death Syndrome (SIDS), Attention Deficit Disorder (ADD/ADHD), and many other diseases of "unknown origin." (If your infant or young child cries uncontrollably, it is likely due to *brain inflammation* resulting from constant activation of the brain's immune system: *immunoexcitotoxicity* caused by vaccine heavy metal toxicity.) A *synergistic toxicity* effect occurs when Mercury, Fluoride, Lithium, MSG, Aspartame, or other excitotoxins are present in combination in the brain. (The term "excitotoxins" was created by Dr. John Olney; "immunoexcitotoxicity" was coined by Dr. Russell Blaylock.) Neurodegenerative diseases such as MS, Polio, and Cerebral Palsy, are only some of the common manifestations of heavy metal toxicity and neurotoxins produced by bacteria present in the vaccine "witch's brew" administered to new born infants, toddlers, school aged children, the unsuspecting public, and pets.

Vaccines trigger autoimmune diseases. Antigenic components present in the vaccine injection cause a long-term autoimmune response where the body's own immune system attacks vital organs such as the pancreas and bone marrow, thus creating diseases like cancer, diabetes and leukemia in a formerly healthy individual. There exists a direct causal relationship between the administration of a vaccine and a diagnosis of many kinds of cancer later in life. After receiving a vaccine, the body's heightened *immune response* can be life threatening. This may be a delayed reaction, manifesting after 2 years or longer, or it can be immediate.

The elderly contaminated with a yearly dose of "Flu shots" (pneumococcal and meningiococcal viruses) have been given a lethal concentration of disease viruses (as many as 20), as well as pathogenic bacteria, and Aluminum and Mercury, stored in the microglia cells of their brain. The ensuing death among the elderly which sometimes occurs shortly after receiving a yearly "Flu shot" is never attributed to the actual cause: the Flu Vaccine! Likewise, Parkinson's, Alzheimer's, and other neurological diseases are seldom attributed to the *real* causal factor: *Vaccines*! But your doctor doesn't know that. Public health authorities and physician societies such as the AMA (American Murder Association) *rabidly insist* that the elderly must receive their "yearly Flu shot." Why the urgency to inject the elderly? It is because the elderly and the very young are a *target population* for global genocide. Don't believe the confident pontifications of your duped MD. He/she only does what the AMA dictates. Look closely at the eugenicist's lips: they lie when they're moving. Proverb 17:4: *A wicked doer giveth heed to false lips; and a liar giveth ear to a naughty tongue.* Over the last 30 years, the number of elderly who believe the obfuscation of these habitual pathological liars has increased 300 percent.

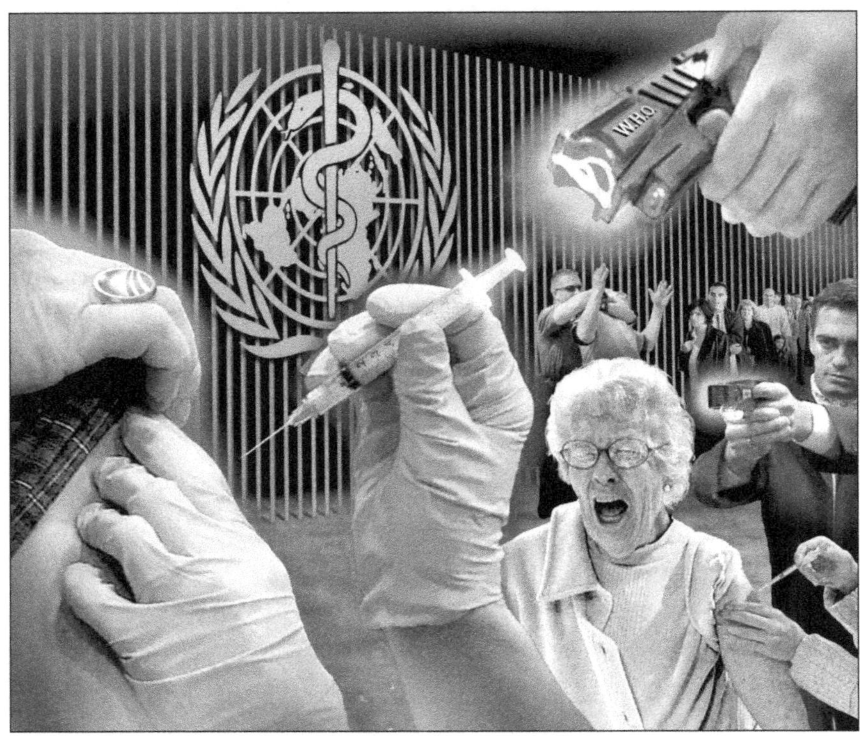

Elderly "Mom and Pop" are a primary target group of the global eugenicists.

Vaccines increase the level of inflammatory brain cell destructive *cytokines* in the brain, which overactivates the brain's immune system to trigger *major depression*. This is one of the primary reasons why the elderly are so often diagnosed with depression, suicidal, and perhaps even homicidal tendencies.

Vaccine ingredients produce heavy metal toxicity, especially Mercury and Aluminum, which directly causes Alzheimer's, Parkinson's, ALS (Lou Guering's Disease), Huntington's Disease, Gulf War Syndrome, and a myriad of other degenerative diseases of the Central Nervous System. Among children, these vaccine components produce Autism and learning disabilities. (Currently, 1 child in 6 has a learning disability. There is *no incidence* of learning disabilities or Autism among the Amish, who *refuse* vaccines.) The presence of Aluminum (Al3+) increases the toxicity of Mercury.

There is a further synergistic effect when combining vaccine components such as Aluminum and Mercury with the Hydroflurosilicic acid added to municipal drinking water supplies, the Glutamate present in MSG foods and beverages, and the Aspartic Acid component of Aspartame. In utilizing neurodegenerative elements of vaccines to enhance the effect of other engineered biowarfare agents, the Illuminati psychopaths knew *exactly* what they were doing.

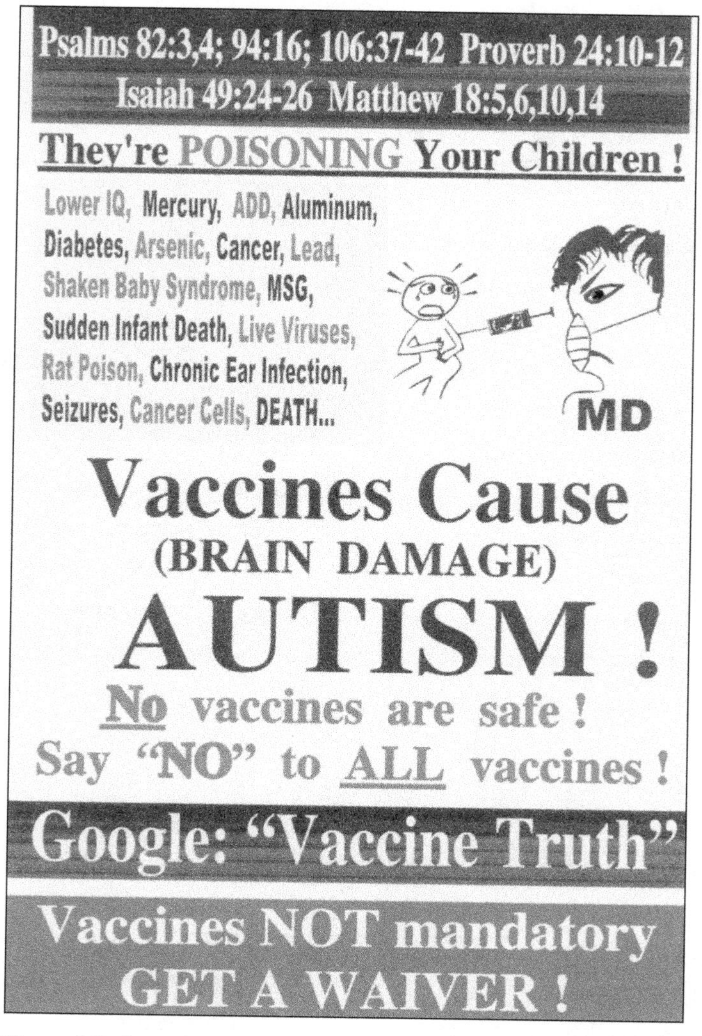

The public is authorized to make copies for mass distribution.
(Flyer or 2' x 3' Poster)

All childhood and world epidemic diseases were *already* in the late stages of decline – virtually eradicated (> 90% decline from the peak) – when vaccinations first became mandatory in the early 1950's. Therefore, vaccines had *nothing* to do with eliminating so-called "pandemics." Forced inoculations were, and continue to be, strictly a government depopulation campaign.

Vaccines are clearly genocide. Nearly every disease that is vaccinated against *rarely* occurs in America. Vaccinating for prevention of a disease with an incident rate of < 1/100,000 is a figure typical of epidemiological data. Yet, vaccines kill or maim tens of thousands per 100,000! Hepatitis B, for example, is only known to occur among certain "high risk" groups such as IV drug users and prostitutes. So why are new born infants injected with a lethal dose of the Hepatitis virus within an hour after birth? Why?... to create permanent *physiological and cognitive damage, cause brain inflammation from the excitotoxic effects of a vaccine, induce brain cell death and cerebral dysfunction from vaccine toxic components, and to transfer the disease* – that's why. More than 22,000 reports of hospitalizations and injuries, including 300 deaths following Hepatitis B vaccinations, have been reported since 1996 to the government's vaccine Adverse Event Reporting System (The Eagle Forum, Spring 2000, pg. 1). Nearly 20,000 times more children die or are permanently damaged from vaccines than from the diseases they are being vaccinated to prevent. The mad globalists are now manufacturing disease-causing vaccines to "protect" against problems created by their disease-causing vaccines! Mandatory forced Mercury vaccine inoculations are one of their preferred *population control weapons* to kill off, dumb-down, and weaken the world population.

The effect of receiving repeated vaccines is *cumulative.* Thimerosal (Ethyl mercury), as well as other lethal vaccine components previously mentioned, accumulate in brain tissue during the rapid growth years of a child's brain development. Excitotoxins, such as Mercury, are known to damage DNA, and to *instantaneously* destroy brain cells and synaptic connections *upon contact.* The Aluminum constituent of vaccines short circuits nerve impulse transmissions in the brain neural network, causing learning disability cognitive dysfunctions such as Attention Deficit Disorder (ADD) and Autism. Aluminum interferes with cellular and metabolic processes of the nervous system; it creates a condition known as "Itchy Nodules," where children itch for 4 years because of the Aluminum present in the injected vaccine. Women vaccinated during pregnancy produce children with a higher incidence of schizophrenia.

The Department of Defense classifies Mercury as a hazardous waste product that is lethal to humans when swallowed, inhaled, or absorbed through the skin. The Environmental Protection Agency acknowledges that factory emissions of this toxic element "can damage the brain and nervous system, and is especially dangerous to fetuses and small children." Yet, the Center for Disease Control (CDC) claims Mercury is harmless and can be injected into your child's body! The Swine Flu vaccine contains 25,000% the amount of Mercury considered "safe." High levels of Mercury are present in a common processed food ingredient, Corn Syrup (high fructose corn syrup), and packaged "fruit cup" sold at your supermarket, as well as in many other food items.

INCIDENCE OF AUTISM AMONG THE U.S. POPULATION

2010: **1 in 60**
2009: 1 in 67
2008: 1 in 91
2004: 1 in 150
1991: 1 in 2500
1980: 1 in 10,000
1970: 1 in 50,000

There has been a greater than 4100% increase in Autism from 1991 to the present. When compared to 1980, the 2010 figure rose by nearly 17,000%; since 1970 it has escalated 83,000%. This data directly corresponds with government mandated vaccinations.

The science supporting the vaccine theory – that a weakened form of a disease-causing pathogen induces the immune system to manufacture antibodies to fight against it and thereby confers immunity from contracting a disease – is a *false and misleading conclusion* selected from research that has more in common with witchcraft than it does objective science. This is especially true in today's genocide-driven New World Order, where the intent of the globalists is to destroy life, not to preserve it. Conflict of interest typifies the standard mode of *government-funded* "vaccine research" where scientists on the government payroll are financed by government-controlled pharmaceutical companies. Both, the government and pharmaceutical companies, have the same goal: *Global Genocide.*

Vaccines are one of the finest examples of faulty science combined with an unlimited federal budget for government-sponsored propaganda supporting terrorism against its "own people." In 2005, the federal government approved $7.2 billion to fund "Operation Bioshield," a massive vaccination campaign to "protect" citizens from "future pandemics" which the government *plans to create*! (In truth, the $7.2 billion protects vaccine companies from liability arising from the damage caused by their vaccines. A document signed by the Secretary of Health and Human Services, and approved by President Obama, exempts Federal officials and pharmaceutical companies from liability lawsuits resulting from vaccines.) Not since Darwin spun his politically-motivated evolutionary fables (long since discredited by respected scientists) has disinformation so effectively brainwashed the world population. Americans, especially, are susceptible to being manipulated by the government-controlled media, partially because they have been "mass medicated" by drinking lithium/fluoride tap water (Lithium is a tranquillizer; ingesting fluoride creates apathy and significantly reduces intelligence.), and partly because they have no love of the truth/Truth. In consideration of the fact that *vaccines do not prevent or inhibit any disease*, but actually *cause the disease they are vaccinating against, as well as creating other diseases and physiological/cognitive dysfunctions*, it is truly astonishing how an entire American culture implicitly trusts someone wearing a white lab coat when ordering their little children to "hold out your arm." It is unconscionable when a mother or father never questions that Hepatitis B, for example, is an *unknown* disease among new born infants, yet will allow their baby to be injected with a lethal dose of Mercury/Aluminum/Lead/live cancer cells/bioengineered viruses immediately after birth. Soon, perhaps within minutes, when their infant is convulsing with seizures, the dazed and confused parents still don't "get it." The "good doctor" is on hand to explain: "It's only a reaction to the vaccine," and assure them: "Not to worry." But then, months later, the child is diagnosed with Autism, irreversible neurological damage to the brain ... and nobody has a clue how it could have occurred! Typically, severely Autistic children pull out their hair, bang their head against the wall; repeating the same meaningless motions for hours at a time. It is heart-rendering to observe such a child, one who will never develop beyond an IQ of 70, requires a lifetime of special education and medications – which *enhance* Autism (in the U.S. over 100 million doses of Prosac were issued in 2008: 1 person in 3) – imprisoned in a mind that cannot communicate with the outside world, except through frustrated attempts to speak: agonizing grunts, squeals, and nonsense syllables. Their complex of emotions and needs are more likely to be expressed as rage, prolonged fits of crying and self-inflicted wounds, the daily routine for a vaccine-damaged Autistic child. "Milder" consequences of vaccination are no less disconcerting: ADD/ADHD life-long learning disabilities limits any potential a child could have realized if he or she had not been vaccinated and was allowed to develop normally. (Note: a newborn infant of the author's brother was given the Hepatitis B vaccine after birth while still in the hospital, and immediately thereafter pathetically convulsed with seizures. The child was brain damaged and cognitively impaired by a single shot of a vaccine. The infant's father, who works in the medical field, ignored the author's cautionary advice, and to this day *continues vaccinating all his children with brain stunting, disease-causing doses of vaccines.* Such a recalcitrant level of ignorance is not uncommon among today's truth-rejecting media brainwashed society.) And the doctor ... was just "following orders": a federally mandated protocol passed down from the global Luciferian eugenicists. Additionally, there was an ulterior motive for "doctor" to destroy the mind and body of a new born infant; an incentive to bypass any moral conscious: as part of the criminal government mandatory hospital immunization policy, his employer, the hospital, received a government subsidy "kickback" of $100 for each innocent child vaccinated with life long disease. But vegetative Autism with its attendant lower IQ and ADD learning disabilities are not the only consequences of vaccinating your children. The sporadic intense high-pitched shrieking cry of a disease-inoculated child is the result of suffering from the effects of vaccine-induced *brain inflammation*. Food allergies, asthma, eczema, crib death (Sudden Infant Death, Shaken Baby Syndrome), MS, Chronic Ear Infection, cancer, diabetes, male sterility, female infertility, chronic illnesses, Cerebral Palsy, are only some of the resultant consequences of vaccinating a developing human being. *Death* is also on the list.

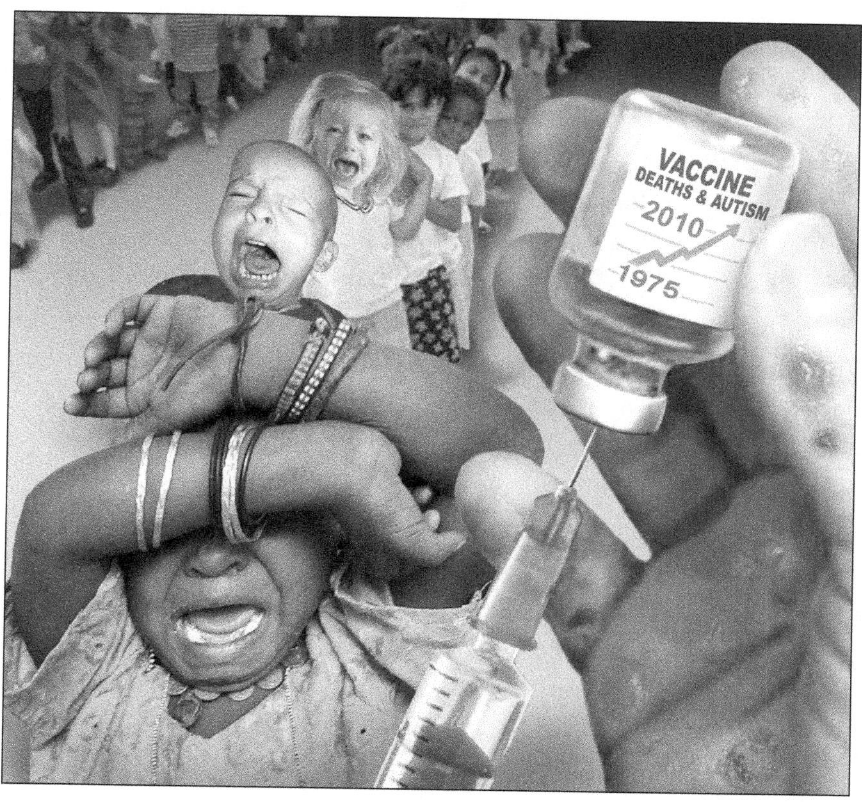

Got Autism? Be sure to thank *your doctor.*

VACCINES ARE *DISEASE INNOCULATIONS*

Nearly all known cases of polio were caused by the polio vaccine. The polio epidemic of the 1940's and 1950's has been directly linked to tonsillectomies of the 1930's (tonsils are part of the immune system and are integral in manufacturing antibodies against the polio virus). By globalist's design, a polio epidemic in Nigeria was caused by the polio vaccine. In America, during the early 1950's, the Simian Monkey Virus (SVI-SV40) contaminated 100 million doses of polio vaccines with live cancer cells and indestructible amoeba cysts (Acanthamoeba, known to transmit the brain-consuming disease meningoencephalitis). *By intentional design*, this vaccine was administered to children, and today, the cancer rate in America is over 50 percent. Among the Amish, a religious sect with strict beliefs prohibiting vaccinations, Autism is only found among the few Amish children who were vaccinated. Any truthful graph charting the history of vaccinations versus the decline of the disease (e.g. Polio, Malaria, Small pox, Yellow Fever, Cholera, etc.) will show that the disease was already in an advanced state of remission *long before* vaccines were initiated – i.e. vaccines had no positive effect whatsoever upon eradication of the disease. The decline was strictly a function of improved sanitation, clean water, better nutrition, and healthier living conditions.

Your doctor *will not* tell you the truth about vaccines because he/she is a coward and fears losing his/her AMA license to practice medicine, or *can not* tell you the truth about vaccines, due to deliberate ignorance or greed (80 percent of a pediatrician's income comes from vaccines). Doctors take their marching orders from their master, the America Murder Association (AMA). Your doctor will not tell you vaccines are a politically motivated genocide program, or about vaccine exemptions, or the alternative natural means available to treat the detrimental consequences of having vaccinated your children. (e.g. Dr. Rashid Buttar developed a simple procedure that detoxifies metals and effectively removes Mercury from the body of Autistic children.) Your pediatrician or GP/MD is funded and supported by a supra-government owned and controlled pharmaceutical industry that generates $500 billion a year in profits. Blindly acting on orders passed down by their Illuminati superiors, and with scientific precision, cold-blooded killers in government create laws that make vaccinations mandatory (typically after fabricating a nonexistent crisis, such as "H1N1 Bird Flu" or "Swine Flu"), and their narcotics-manufacturing pharmaceutical companies create drugs that kill. Doctors are their unwitting middleman drug dealing "street vendors," *pushing drugs* on an unsuspecting and uninformed public that are as unwitting as the truth-adverse doctor.

Those at the top of the satanic pyramid chain of command delight in cruelty, and derive sadistic pleasure in witnessing the suffering and death of others, especially little children. But, your doctor *does not know that.* Your upper middle class yuppy doctor thinks "the government is good" and that he/she is "a wonderful person," an humanitarian, a life saver, someone who "cares about people." But the reality is that "human government is intrinsically evil," and all doctors functioning within organized medicine today are "overpaid serial killers" who love their ignorance and will rigorously defend it against truthful health-related information which they perceive as a threat to preserving their (pharmaceutical) drug trade. He/she *will not* tell you that the Mercury in vaccines causes sterility and brain damage, learning disabilities, and a host of other neurological disorders. He/she *will not* tell you about vaccine waivers and exemptions. He/she *will not* tell you that Ethyl mercury (Thimerosal) was *not* removed from vaccines – as claimed by the government propaganda – but the Mercury dosage was actually *quadrupled*! (They lied, again.) Furthermore, he/she *does not know* that the world controllers *lied.* Even when told the truth about vaccines, he/she neither believes it nor *cares to know it.* Your doctor *will not* bother to research the facts. Doctors working within the system are *that* brainwashed.

MORE GUNS OR MORE DOCTORS?

The number of physicians in the U.S.: 700,000
Yearly accidental deaths caused by U.S. physicians: 120,000
Accidental deaths per physician: .171
(Statistics from U.S. Department of Health and Human Services)

The number of gun owners in the U.S.: 80,000,000
Yearly accidental gun deaths in U.S.: 1,500
Accidental gun deaths per owner: .0000187

Based upon the government's vague criterion of "accidental deaths caused by physicians," statistically, doctors are 9,144 times *more dangerous* than gun owners. Yet, the above computation does not take into account other sources of iatrogenic (doctor induced) deaths, a short list which includes, but is not limited to: exposure to radiation and chemotherapy (98 percent of all cancer patients die from the treatment, not from cancer), unnecessary surgeries, "side effects" from pharmaceutical drugs, aborted fetuses, wrong diagnosis, accumulative detrimental health effects from dental and diagnostic x-rays (LD-50 lethal *accumulative* dosage), Mercury dental fillings (50% by volume of a silver amalgam tooth filling is toxic Mercury), experimental testing upon the elderly, tonsillectomy (tonsils serve an important immunological function, especially in children), DNA damaging Mercury vaccines. The above figure of 9,144 should conservatively be upgraded by a 100 times multiple to reflect a long list of causal deaths attributable to doctors. Thus, doctors can be nearly 1 million times (914,400) more dangerous than gun owners. (The *actual* figure for yearly accidental deaths caused by physicians is closer to 500,000, more than four times higher than what is reported by government statistics.) Office visit, anyone?

Vaccines are nothing less than government-sponsored *Bioterrorism*. The mad push to make vaccines compulsory has nothing to do with any threats of a disease spreading epidemic, but has everything to do with furthering the Globalist's Agenda – i.e. vaccines are solely a *political genocide issue*. The Illuminati globalists (primarily the Rockefeller eugenics crime syndicate) promote through their Rothschild-controlled media, *nonexistent* pandemic disease threats like West Nile Virus or H1N1 Bird Flu as a means to justify mandatory vaccinations. (Crisis-Reaction-Solution.) Scare tactics and outright lies are the standard government media ploy to induce a sheep-like populace to submit to their own destruction. Like the Chemtrail denial phenomenon, U.S. citizens' *adamant denial of the dangers* of vaccinating their new born infants and children conclusively demonstrates that the globalist's media mind-control and propaganda is highly effective. (Health-conscious Europeans realize that Americans are among the most gullible and undiscerning people in the world. The European Union has long ago banned the use of the known neurological poison, Fluoride, in municipal drinking water supplies. But in America the people are told Fluoride is "good for you"... and the Fluoride-tranquillized sheeple *believe it*!) A mind cognitively impaired and controlled by a constant stream of media lies and deceit cannot receive the truth. No matter how much truthful information is presented to the walking dead, they will steadfastly defend falsehoods heard repeated on TV drug company commercials and the evening news. (*Repetition* is crucial to successful mind-control programming.) Nazi propaganda minister, Joseph Goebbels, said: "If you tell a lie big enough and keep repeating it, the people will eventually come to believe it." Hitler once stated: "The broad mass of the nation ... will more easily fall victim to a big lie than to a small one.... What good fortune for government that people do not think."

The Plain Dealer | Breaking news: cleveland.com

Sunday, November 18, 2007

School vaccinations get a booster shot

MATTHEW BARAKAT
Associated Press

UPPER MARLBORO, MD. — Hundreds of grumbling parents facing a threat of jail lined up at a courthouse Saturday to either prove that their school-age kids already had their required vaccinations or see that the youngsters submitted to the needle.

The get-tough policy in the Washington suburbs of Prince George's County was one of the strongest efforts made by any U.S. school system to ensure its youngsters receive their required immunizations.

Two months into the school year, school officials realized that more than 2,000 students in the county still didn't have the vaccinations they were supposed to have before attending class.

So Circuit Court Judge C. Philip Nichols ordered parents in a letter to appear at the courthouse Saturday and either get their children vaccinated on the spot or risk up to 10 days in jail. They could also provide proof of vaccination or an explanation for their kids not having them.

By about 8:30 a.m., the line of parents stretched outside the courthouse in the county on the east side of Washington.

Many of them complained that their children already were properly immunized but the school system had misplaced the records. They said efforts to get the paperwork straightened out had been futile.

"It was very intimidating," Territa Wooden of Largo said of the letter. She said she presented the paperwork at the courthouse Saturday and resolved the matter.

"I could be home asleep. My son had his shots," said Veinell Dickens of Upper Marlboro, who also blamed errant paperwork.

Aloma Martin of Fort Washington brought her children, Delontay and Taron, in 10th and sixth grade, for their hepatitis shots. She said she had been trying to get the vaccinations for more than a month, since the school system sent a warning letter. She had an appointment for Monday, but came to the courthouse to be safe.

"It was very heavy-handed," she said of the county's action. "From that letter, it sounded like they were going to start putting us in jail."

School officials deemed the court action a success.

STEPHEN J. BOITANO | ASSOCIATED PRESS

Guardian Kim Beard and her charge, Joshua Grier, 4, indulge in some play Saturday while waiting in line in Upper Marlboro, Md., with hundreds of others for court-mandated appearances to get the children vaccinated.

To those mothers and expectant young women who reject this truthful information regarding the dangers of vaccines, and who ignore the available literature, web sites, testimonials, etc., and who *adamantly refuse* to believe it and fail to act accordingly to protect their children, the author says: "The Judgment of Almighty God be upon you! Give your children a *quadruple dose of Thimerosal.*" (Matthew 10:14,15; Mark 6:11,12; Luke 9:2,5.) This Scriptural condemnation is especially applicable to the more affluent segment of the American population: characteristically, mothers of the yuppy middle class *reject* any suggestion that vaccines are dangerous, and will vigorously resist the truth and defend the lies told them by their equally brainwashed doctor/pediatrician. (In the author's personal experience, their truth-rejection is a *consistent response* reflecting their unrepentant *spiritual condition,* and is indicative of their *rejection of Jesus Christ: the way, the truth, and the life* [John 14:6]. The more affluent social class tends to be atheists, agnostics, adherents to various New Age Eastern Metaphysical religions, witchcraft, or pseudo-Christianity.) One would expect those individuals above the lower class to be better educated and more discerning regarding their health and the health of their children, but they are instead brainwashed by the very system they worship, and therefore are as ignorant, or even more so, than the intellectually impoverished lower class. The proud are *cursed* by God: *Thou hast rebuked the proud that are cursed, which do err from thy commandments* (Psalm 119:21); Job 40:11,12; Proverb 15:25, 16:5; Isaiah 2:12, 13:11; Jeremiah 50:31-32. Innocent children suffer the consequences of their parents' wickedness and rejection of the truth. But, the meek (toward God, not toward man) *will* hear the truth, and they and their children *are blessed* and *shall inherit the earth* (Isaiah 61:1; Matthew 5:5).

For those readers seeking to reinforce the above information regarding the dangers and irreparable damage caused by vaccinating their children or receiving "Flu shots," etc., the following web sites and search words are offered in the hope they will heed this warning and thereby reap the blessings of God Almighty for their obedience *to Him*, and not to their drug-pushing pathologically ignorant Illuminati-sponsored doctor:

<VaccineInfo> <vaccinetruth.com> <TheIdahoObserver> <vaccinetruth.org> <vaccinefreeworld> <vaccine911.com> <InformedChoice> <thinktwice.com> <know-vaccines.org> <dangerousmedicine.com> <deathbyvaccination.com> <medicine-no.com> <vacinfo.org> <VaccineDamage> <Dr.SherriTenpenny> <trackingvaccinations.com> <vaccineawareness.org> <Marytocco.com> <VaccineScandals> <vaclib.org> <Eustice Mullins> <Murder by injection> <Dr. Rashid Buttar> <healthychild.com> <VaccineTalkDr.Rohlfsen> <ImmuneSuppression> <childhood-shots.com> <alternative-doctor.com> <EducateB4Uvaccinate>

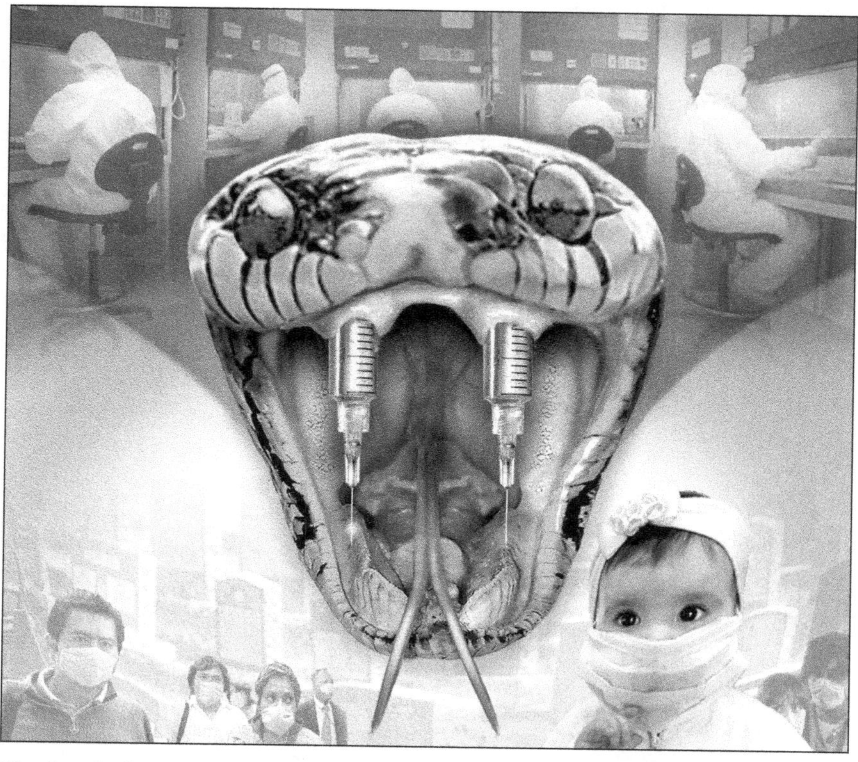

The level of Mercury present in a vaccine is 100 times higher than what is safe to consume.

The incidence of Autism in the U.S. was 1 in 50,000 during the early 1970's when the globalist's eugenics propaganda was beginning to escalate and targeted American new born infants and school aged children. The goal of the Luciferian Global Hierarchy was to create a nation of children with a Wizard of Oz "Lollipop Kid" mentality (retarded) and body type (obese, stunted, short stature), and with as many genetic defects and premature births as possible. Today, they have attained these objectives. Decades prior to this date, the occurrence of Autism was virtually unknown, but presently the rate of Autism in America is 1 child in 60, and this ratio continues to decrease. Autism is not caused by faulty gene combinations; it is *impossible* to have a genetic epidemic. It is not caused by "cats transmitting the Autistic disease to infants." (There was actually such a *government-funded* study done at Case Western Reserve University. The Illuminati globalists know the retarded mentality of the American people – i.e. that they *will believe anything told them by their government masters,* especially if endorsed by the medical or academic community.) Autism is not a result of any other cause but one: *Vaccines*! Any parent who vaccinates their infant or child should be charged with First Degree *Murder* and given the death penalty, for they are indeed guilty of *premeditated homicide.* In destroying the mind, body, and soul of their own offspring, they deserve death. There are *no* good reasons to vaccinate. Absolutely *none.*

At the time of this writing, 4 exemptions exist for legally escaping "mandatory" vaccinations of oneself and one's children. They are: Philosophical, Religious, Medical, Proof of Immunity (determined by blood titration). However, by the time you read this, there may no longer be any allowance for vaccine exemptions. Satan's people will continue to create 9/11 scare tactics such as "Swine Flu/Bird Flu" as a pretext to *force you* and your loved ones to be injected with their genocidal diseases. The globalists want a depopulated earth, and that is why the Bill and Melinda Gates Foundation is spending billions of dollars on research and development to sterilize third world populations by the use of vaccine inoculations laced with sterilizing components. Because vaccines are of such great importance to the Luciferian eugenicists, they will soon make it globally mandatory for all new born infants, children, and adults to receive their toxic poisons. A word of advice to the wise: When they come to your door, or stop your car on the road at a checkpoint, with armed police threatening you with incarceration in a FEMA concentration camp if you refuse to be injected, be prepared to resist as if your life depends upon it ... because, *it does.* If you submit, you will in fact wish you were dead; the diseases you and your children will contract from vaccines are *that* horrifying. Instead, be prepared for the worst, and tell them to go to their eternal destiny – hell – where they rightfully belong. Always remember that *whatever* the unrighteous government tells you to do, *resist* with everything that is in you. Just say "NO". *Regardless* of what Satan's government people demand or suggest, your answer should *always* be a firm "NO". (Explanations are not necessary, and are usually counterproductive. Tyrants will not respond to reason; they only understand force.) Resist! Their indwelling demons will get the point. James 4:7: *Resist the devil, and he will flee from you.*

"Our government wouldn't do *that*! Our leaders care about us. Government is our *friend*," say the estrogenic chemically lobotomized truth-haters, as a hypodermic needle filled with frothing disease and toxins are injected into their wide-eyed innocent little child. For those who deny the truth about vaccines, there is also a bridge in Brooklyn that is still for sale, and prime Florida swamp land real estate; and Easter Bunny, Santa Claus, the Tooth Fairy, and the 9/11 official story – it's all true! (For those who despise the truth.)

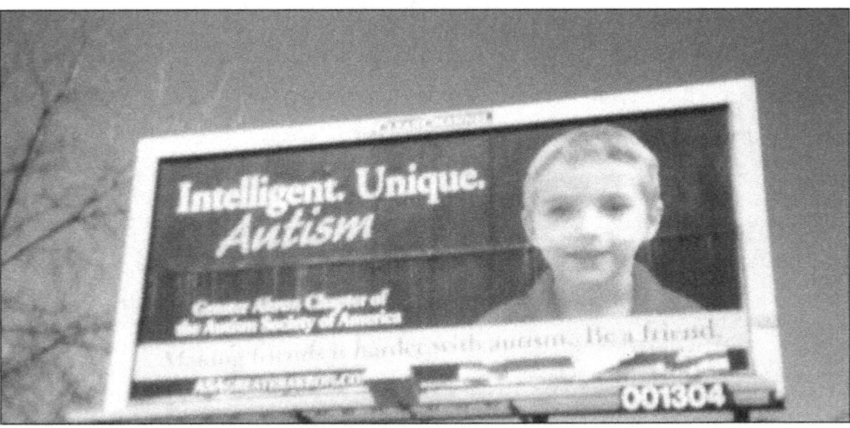

Vaccines are unequivocally the greatest *medical hoax* ever foisted on the American public.

MSG/ASPARTAME

The world is being drugged with two *Neurotoxins* delivered through soft drinks and processed packaged food products. A diluted dose of these neurotoxins is present in municipal tap water (ref. Fluoride, next Section.)

The addition of *Monosodium Glutamate* (MSG*)* to food has been disguised by more than 100 different names. Together with *Aspartame,* these two food additives represent the next level in the genocidal culling of the world population. A major objective of the *Globalist's Agenda* is to kill off vast numbers of people. In statistical terms, and as stated by Nazi war criminal and Illuminist Henry Kissinger in a public statement in 1982, only 500,000,000 of the present population of the world will be allowed to live ... to serve *them – the elite.* The other 7 billion must be eradicated. This translates into a death toll of 92.9 percent of the current world population. Only 7 percent should remain alive after the decimation caused by the Globalist's Agenda, the repercussions of world economic collapse, and the standard "Solution": WWIII (global thermonuclear warfare). To make the point even clearer, for every person living, 14 are expected to die. But, before then, Jesus Christ will have returned (Matthew 24:22; ref. Appendix A). The current U.S. population of 325 million is scheduled to be reduced to *20 million,* a 93.9 percent reduction.

Dr. John Olney, in 1969, is credited with discoveries that chemical components of MSG and Aspartame (Phenylalanine, Aspartic Acid, Methanol) cross the blood-brain barrier to cause nerve damage in brain tissue, interfere with electrical impulse transmission, deplete neurotransmitters (acetylcholine, cholinesterase, etc.), and destroy brain neurons. He also established a direct biochemical link between Aspartame and brain cancer. Dr. Russell Blaylock has researched the effects of these neurotoxins and concludes that their presence in the brain excites the brain's immune system for long periods of time to cause brain cell death. Olney coined the term "Excitotoxins" when referring to Aspartame, MSG and other

Glutamate derivatives, and also many of the ingredients found in vaccines, including Mercury, Aluminum, mycoplasm, bacteria, and viral fragments (ref. Blaylock's book: *Excitotoxins: The Taste That Kills*). Canadian physician, Dr. Bill Deagle reports: "Aspartame was approved by deception through the USA FDA Food and Drug Administration. Through lies and lobbying has now poisoned 6000+ [food items] and spread to 90 countries. Aspartame toxicity is amplified by ELF electromagnetic pollution from WiFi networks, cell phones, and the electronic cage of our world ... causes DNA breaks. Aspartame is a Molecular Global Eugenocide."

MSG creates insulin resistance, a symptom of Type II Adult onset Diabetes; it also triples the output of insulin from the pancreas. When ingested during infancy or young childhood, it creates an implacable *resistant obesity* in children that does not respond to exercise or dietary modification. Today, most adults and many young children and adolescents are overweight; an increasing percentage have diabetes (1 person in 3); MSG is often the causal factor. During a ten year period of MSG doping of the American population, there has been a 600% increase in the incidence of diabetes. In both children and adults, MSG has been linked to severe anger, major depression, and suicide.

The Illuminati's criminal FDA lists MSG as "naturally occurring," yet be aware that does not mean it is safe for human consumption. Many foods containing MSG, as well as other excitotoxins, are labeled as having "No MSG," but they nonetheless do (they lied). Among researchers it is common knowledge that Monosodium Glutamate and Aspartame cause permanent brain damage in children. These substances affect how a child's brain forms during early developmental years, and have been directly linked to learning disabilities and emotional difficulties, especially later in life. Brain nihilators, they create brain tumors in children and damage an area of the brain associated with hormone regulation and production, resulting in male sterility (low sperm count) and female infertility. Gross obesity and childless parents are further examples of the "slow kill" consequences of the Globalist's Agenda.

Chemical components of Aspartame are classified by the Occupational Safety and Health Administration (OSHA) as *hazardous*. These constituents include methanol (causes blindness), formaldehyde (embalming fluid), Formic acid (ant venom), and diketopiperazine (brain tumor causing agent). Death is #77 on the FDA list of Aspartame symptoms. Aspartic Acid has been a known neurotoxin for more than 40 years, yet it continues to be used in processed foods and beverages. Experimental infant and young rats ingesting Aspartame exhibited endocrine malfunctions: stunted growth, obesity as adults (Wizard of Oz Lollipop Kids), and were also characterized by sexual reproductive dysfunctions. Aspartame accounts for 70 percent of all complaints to the FDA, which is a globalist front group controlled by the international Illuminati. Like MSG, ingesting Aspartame early in life manifests in gross obesity that is resistant to dietary restriction or exercise. Other consequences are the usual degenerative brain diseases: Alzheimer's, Parkinson's, ALS, Huntington's; as well as Major Depression, Brain Inflammation, Type II Diabetes and sudden cardiac death. Phenylalanine, comprising 50 percent of the Aspartame molecule, upon exposure to a developing fetus via maternal blood, is concentrated 4 to 6 times, causing birth defects such as mental retardation, microcephaly and Autism.

Aspartame creates DNA damaging free radicals throughout the body, destroys brain cells, and blocks normal brain electrochemical activity, resulting in learning difficulties that become more pronounced as the child ages. Derived from genetically modified microorganisms, it damages the Hypothalamus – the regulator for the autonomic (involuntary) nervous system – and lowers the level of brain hormones Serotonin, Epinephrine, Norepinephrine, and Dopamine. Deficiencies of these chemical substances are associated with depression and suicidal tendencies. (Without realizing that Aspartame is the cause, doctors unwittingly label such symptoms "Bi-Polar Disorder," then "treat" it with psychotropic drugs which *enhances* learning disabilities/depression/suicidal effects of ingesting Aspartame.) Aspartame causes headaches, vertigo, blindness, and increases the severity of symptoms of diabetes. It is proven to cause miscarriages. Similar to consuming meat poisoned with MSG or recombinant Bovine Growth Hormone (rbGH/rbST), Aspartame-contaminated food and beverages are among the primary reasons why so many children today are chronically overweight, a rare condition only fifty years ago. (In addition to MSG, another reason for implacable childhood obesity is GM/GMO's; ref. next Section.) Aspartame increases the severity of Autism and the various so-called "Attention Deficit Disorders" (ADD/ADHD), which are caused by the neurotoxic effects of *vaccines,* and are further amplified by psychotrophic drugs (Prosac, Ritilin, Luvox, Paxil, etc.) given to school children to treat ADD.

Aspartame and MSG added to soft drink beverages and processed packaged foods create a *chemical dependency* for their continued consumption. Consequently, processed and packaged foods and beverages are *chemically addictive*; the induced drug dependency is not unlike that of a street addict's craving for illicit drugs. And this is how McDonald's, Burger King, Wendy's, Taco Bell, and all the other fast food chains keep you coming back for more: "Come on, Kid's! Let's go to McDonald's for yet another Aspartame/MSG dinner!" But don't try to warn today's parents about the dangers of what they are feeding their children, because *they do not want to know*! What they want is their "Happy Meal," not knowledge. Burgers, fries and a Coke – it's cheap, easy, fast, chemically addictive, and they don't have to think (and afterwards, won't be able to). Americans today *absolutely love* their ignorance … and death. Proverb 8:1,36: *Doth not wisdom cry? and understanding put forth her voice? … But he that sinneth against me wrongeth his own soul: all they that hate me love death.* The highest concentrations of MSG are found in fast foods, and at the top of the list is *chicken* food products: e.g. Chick-fil-A, Kentucky Fried Chicken (KFC), the "cuisine" served at fine restaurants and the local "greasy spoon."

Key among the Illuminati front groups manufacturing and promoting these neurotoxic poisons is the pharmaceutical giant, *Monsanto,* which translates as "Satan's Mountain." The word

"Pharmacy" is derived from the Greek word, "Pharmakeia," which means "Sorcery." Clearly, pharmacists are sorcerers and prescription drugs are witchcraft. Purveyors of modern snake oil, lotions and potions have changed little over the centuries. With few exceptions, yesterday's traveling "Dr. Good" has been replaced by today's modern version of the village witchdoctor, identified by the sage initials "Dr." "M.D." Doctors are the ever faithful servants of their constant drug suppler, Illuminati-owned "Big Pharma." FDA officials are majority share stock holders and sit on the Board of Directors of large drug companies manufacturing excitotoxins. Conflict of interest?

THE WORLD FOOD SUPPLY HAS BEEN POISONED

The diabolically deceitful "government-regulated" FDA food industry changes the names of excitotoxins in packaged foods so you cannot recognize their presence. There are over a hundred different food additives which either contain excitotoxins or are literally MSG/Aspartame labeled with a disguised name. The resulting brain lesions can occur from a *single dose* of a product, such as a diet soft drink. Aspartame and MSG work synergistically to enhance their overall damaging effect: what might be a subtoxic dose of MSG, when combined with an Aspartic Acid-containing food or soft drink, creates a toxic dose. The long-term presence of Ethyl mercury in the body from vaccines, or Hydrofluorosilicic acid from drinking fluoridated water, or Sodium fluoride from brushing your teeth with fluoride toothpaste, further enhances the synergistic effect of excitotoxins.

More than ninety-nine percent of the food items in your grocery store are *not safe* to ingest. *No* processed packaged food products are fit for human or animal consumption. Aspartame and MSG are in tens of thousands of food products. It is difficult to find any packaged food or bottled beverage that does not contain these neurodegenerative poisons. This pathetic state of affairs was planned by the globalists and is *deliberate.* Your local supermarket has now become a mind and body destroying New World Order "Opium Parlor."

Some common examples of MSG doping are: *all* soft drinks, especially "diet," "low calorie," "sugar free," "zero"; candy, chewing gum, Kool Aid, Crystal Light, children's medications, and all vaccines. Even an educated supermarket label reader will overlook the presence of these deadly killers, because the fiendish eugenicists have invented *an arsenal of different names* to mask MSG's presence. Examples of deceptive names of food additives that contain Glutamate excitotoxins are: Flavoring, Seasoning, Natural Flavors or Colors, Natural Beef or Chicken Flavoring, Malt Flavoring, Corn Syrup, High Fructose Corn Syrup, Soy Protein Isolate or Concentrate, Hydrolyzed Vegetable Protein; anything "autolyzed," "hydrolyzed," "enzymes," "protein," "amino acids"; Textured Vegetable Protein (TVP), Yeast Extract, Autolyzed Yeast, Malted Barley, Broth, Bullion, Stock, Vegetable Broth, Soups, Gravy, Starch, Corn Oil, Hydrolyzed Oat Flour, Maltodextrin, Calcium or Sodium Caseinate (Casein), Whey Protein Extract/Isolate/Concentrate, Citric acid, Pectin, Gelatin, Gel Caps (used for coating pills and capsules), Carragenen (ice cream, yogurt, candies, chewing gum), and many other products with misapplied pseudonyms – *all of these items* contain MSG. The masked names are intended to conceal the fact that MSG has been added to *all* processed packaged foods and drinks. All soft drinks (soda), and especially "diet" drinks, are heavily laced with diabetes-promoting and brain-synapse disrupting biochemical agents. Imagine today's misguided "diet-conscious" consumer who drinks "diet" soft drinks laced with MSG in an attempt to slim down. This is tantamount to smoking cigarettes to cure lung cancer, or swallowing lead pellets to lose weight.

Aspartame is likewise camouflaged by a broad assortment of other names to disguise its presence in foods and beverages: Nutrasweet, Splenda, Equal, Spoonful, Equal Measure, are only some of the more common deceptive misnomers; more alternate names are constantly being created. Similar to MSG, this nasty

Excitotoxin is found in *all* processed packaged foods and drinks, especially those heavily promoted for consumption *by children.* (The Beast government wants *your children*! Always assume the terrorist FDA government agency has *allowed* adulteration of any foods, drinks, and candy created to appeal to children.) More examples of common foods and beverages where Aspartame is present are: soft drinks, baby foods, vitamin supplements, all candies, Cool Aid, Crystal Lite, diet drinks, bakery sugar, cake mix, aspirin, and more than 10,000 other common supermarket items. For some food categories, the FDA does not require excitotoxins to be listed on the product label; labeling laws have been changed so Aspartame, MSG, and other nervous system destroyers are no longer required to be listed as ingredients! (If there is a Phenylalanine warning on the label, the product contains Aspartame.)

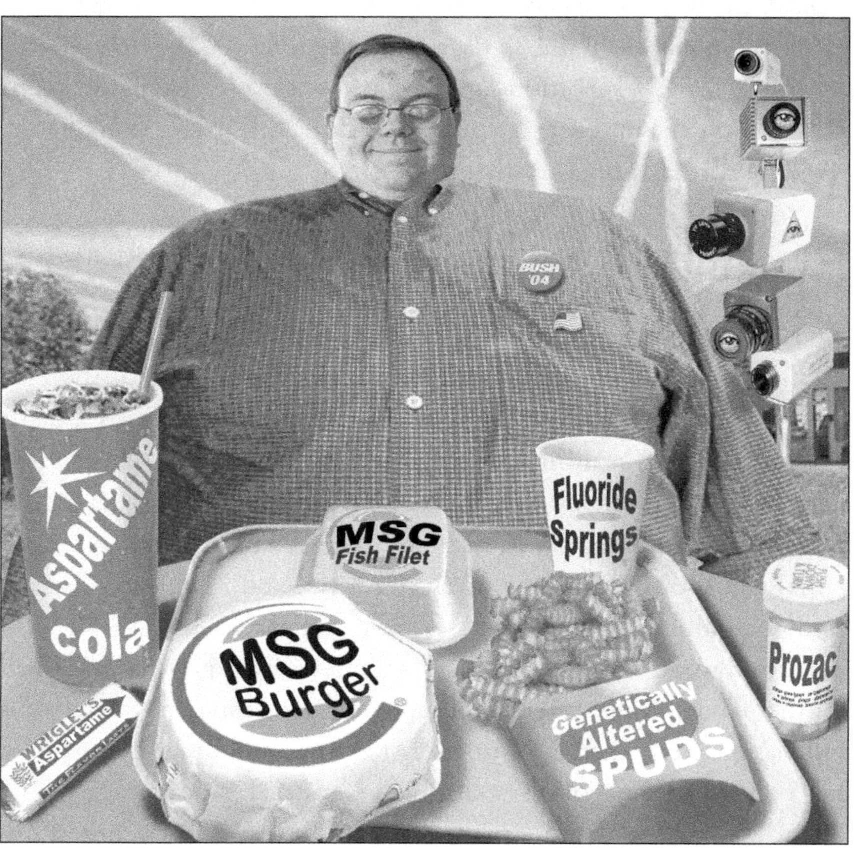

Excitotoxins represent one of today's most dangerous threats to human health and longevity. Dr. Blaylock quotes a senior executive in the food additive industry during a conversation: "MSG, Aspartame, and other additives are going to be in our food no matter how many name changes are necessary." In today's *Chemtrail/Vaccine Twilight Zone World*, neurodegenerative cancer-causing agents will always be a part of your diet, but, *only if you trust in man.* The punishment for believing lies and ignoring the perfect counsel of God is that *you will* be afflicted with the diseases given to you courtesy of the Luciferian globalists. Leviticus 26:14-39; Deuteronomy 28:15-68. Jeremiah 17:5: *Cursed be the man that trusteth in man, and maketh flesh his arm, and whose heart departeth from the LORD.* To obtain the health blessings of God and avoid the curses of believing man's lies, your diet must be in conformity with Genesis 1:29: *And God said, Behold, I have given you every herb bearing seed, which is upon the face of all the earth, and every tree, in the which is the fruit of a tree yielding seed; to you it shall be for meat.* Counsel to the wise: Don't trust in man. *Believe* God! Essentially, if you can't pick it off a tree, don't eat it. (And be sure it is organically grown.)

FLUORIDE

The next genocidal item on the globalist's menu is *Fluoride.* Elemental Fluorine is the most chemically reactive of all the elements. One of its binary compounds, Sodium fluoride, is a *waste product* of the aluminum, fertilizer, and nuclear waste industries. It is a *biohazardous material,* and like EPA-regulated Mercury, is highly toxic to human beings. Yet, Mercury is placed in the human mouth (amalgam tooth fillings are 50% Mercury), and Hydrofluorosilicic acid, containing radioactive isotopes and traces of Arsenic and Lead, is a toxic waste byproduct of the fertilizer industry added to municipal drinking water supplies. These are strange places to store radioactive toxic metals ... unless, of course, you despise humanity and control all the world's political and natural resources. Only *then* does this criminal activity make sense. Industrial wastes containing heavy metals and other components harmful to human and animal health are being added to fertilizers that are spread over agricultural farmlands. The process is legal and saves industries the expenditure of disposing hazardous materials. Through their roots and leaves plants uptake these toxins into their cellular structure which is later consumed by animals and humans. Fluoride, as well as Mercury, Cadmium, Arsenic, Lead, and industrial waste products, are being transferred from agricultural crops to your grocery shelves.

It was during WWII that researchers at the I.G. Farben Chemical plant in Germany (today, in America, I.G Farben is known as the Bayer Company, manufacturer of "Bayer Aspirin") discovered that Fluoride is a *tranquilizer,* and that humans ingesting Fluoride become apathetic and highly receptive to being controlled. When Prescott Bush, father of the infamous drug czar – George Herbert Walker "Poppy" Bush, and Grand Father of the little Bush, George W. (nickname for the "little Bush" is "Shrub") – as CEO of Germany's largest industrial chemical manufacturing company, upon reporting this finding to Hitler, the Fuhrer was positively ecstatic. Now that he had an effective way to anesthetized the entire nation of Germany by *mass medication,* his job as chief European dictator would be much easier. Both Stalin and Hitler added Sodium fluoride to the drinking water supply of all their municipalities, and as a consequence, the people became "sheeple". No fear of a citizen revolt from grazing sheep whose only concern is to be fed a steady diet of doped food and water. Sound familiar?

At the end of the second Illuminati-planned and financed war, Germany's chief scientists and war criminals were granted sanctuary at major U.S. universities, research laboratories, military bases and Washington DC politics via Operation Paperclip. This planned move was directed by the Vatican in Rome and specifically sanctioned by the Roman Catholic Pope. (The global political power of Vatican City exceeds that of all nation-states, and is superseded only by the combined influence of a few key European Monarchs and Rothschild Illuminati.) Fluoride was summarily added to municipal drinking water supplies of most U.S. cities, effectively *mass medicating* the American population. Just 1 part Fluoride per million (1 ppm) is sufficient to disrupt brain functions and lower IQ levels. (A single powdered egg contains 900 ppm Sodium fluoride.) Fluoro-poison was heavily promoted by the Illuminati-controlled American Dental Association as "an effective decay preventing dentifrice." As always, when dealing with Satan's people, their truth is lies. Sodium fluoride, an active ingredient in tooth paste, has *absolutely no positive effect whatsoever* in preventing or reducing dental caries. But it *does* have a profound and permanent *detrimental* effect upon the cognitive development of little children. (Clinical studies show that Sodium fluoride *promotes* dental cavities.) In the same manner that drug addicts rub cocaine powder into their gums, fluoride toothpaste worked into the tooth-gum interface during the brushing of teeth expedites transfer of this brain-destroying biohazardous compound directly to the brain and throughout the systemic circulatory system.

In addition to creating mass apathy, Fluoride and its chemical derivatives are neurotoxic and known to disrupt brain cell electrical connectivity and stimulate cancer growth, *especially* in children. (It's all being directed at children.) Brain cancer, bone marrow cancer, osteoporosis, pancreatic cancer, congestive heart failure, arteriosclerosis, macular degeneration, are only some of the accumulative long-term effects of ingesting Fluoride compounds. This highly toxic chemical concentrates in glands (prostate, adrenal) and sexual organs (testes, ovaries), sterilizing males and reducing fertility in females. In like manner, infant plastic nursing bottles made with Bisphenol A (BPA) is an endocrine disrupter that mimics the female hormone estrogen when leaching into heated liquid drinks fed to infants; later causing sterility and infertility, feminization of boys, triggering the early onset of puberty in girls by age 7, and sometimes as early as age 3. BPA is also found in white composite dental fillings, dental sealants, and the coating used to line the inside of canned foods. Estrogen-based soy "baby formula" reduces testosterone hormone levels in developing infant boys. Thus, genocidal eugenicists have no fear that today's "men" could one day rise up and castrate the globalists. How can they, when today's men have themselves been "castrated"?

Fluoride combines with the Aluminum component of vaccines that deposits in brain tissue to create a highly toxic fluoro-aluminum compound. The previously noted synergistic effect of Fluoride combining with Mercury, Aluminum, Glutamate, and other neurotoxins enhances nerve cell degeneration.

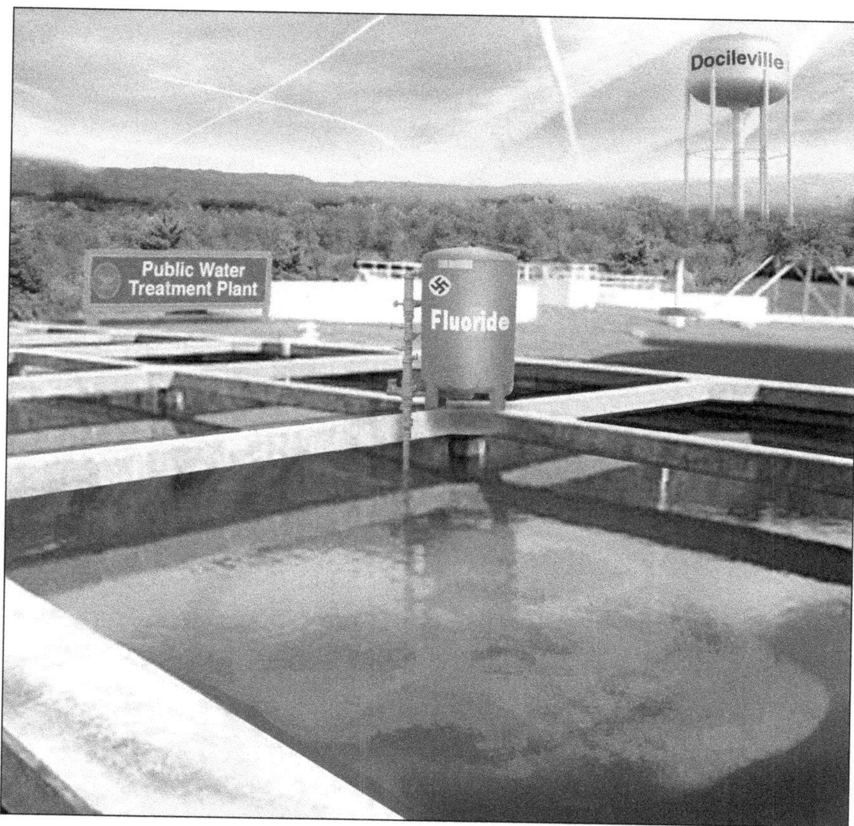

"Fluoride" is a general term which includes over 1000 toxic waste chemicals, as well as Arsenic, Lead and radioactive Uranium isotopes. Hydrofluorosilicic acid added to the drinking water supply of most U.S. cities is a biohazardous waste product used by the global eugenicists as a chemical weapon against the American population. Demographic studies show that a Fluoride concentration of just 1.9 ppm reduces IQ levels. The concentration of Fluoride in tap water is 10 times greater than that amount. There are more than 75,000 impurities (dissolved organic compounds) in municipal tap water supplies.

Mass medication with Sodium fluoride enabled WWII Nazi despots to control the potential raging masses from trampling them to death; and today, doping the public drinking water supply with Hydrofluorosilicic acid has worked to pacify a nation of Americans from uttering so much as a whimper as their life blood is being extracted from them by vampires in Washington DC (District of Criminals). When combined with other means discussed in this section to anesthetize and silence the people, 325 million U.S. sheeple are willingly being lead to the slaughter.

Similar to the action of Fluoride, the element Lithium is another chemical weapon used by the globalists to weaken and control the American group mind. It too is being added to municipal drinking water supplies. Consumed by humans, Lithium produces a calming effect, creating a pliant servant of the Beast government, one who will not protest or *even question* wicked unrighteous government laws and decrees. Lithium is a tranquillizer and anti-psychotic prescription drug used in the treatment of certain psychological disorders; the patient becomes docile, compliant, harmless, a spineless blob of jelly – perfect specimen for New World Order servitude.

Supermarket shelves are stocked with fluoridated water promoted for consumption by infants. A beverage item at your grocer has a label that reads: "Nursery Water with added Fluoride. Specifically formulated for Infants and Toddlers." Selling for $1.18, the 1 gallon soft plastic jug (leaching sterility-causing BPA) further notes: "0.7 mg/Liter sodium fluoride." Those mothers and parents who feed their infant or toddler "nursery water" or "infant formula," are guilty of *Infanticide*, Murder in the First Degree. (Upon reading this section of the book, they can no longer use ignorance as an excuse.) It is incomprehensible to this author how anyone could be so negligent, unless, of course, *they too* have been drinking fluoridated tap water all their life. Incidentally, here is the name and contact information of just one of several companies that manufactures and sells this toxic poison in stores: DS Waters of America, 45 West Nobelstown Rd., Carnegie, PA 15106. 1-800-682-0246. Call or write to express how much you "appreciate" them permanently brain damaging little children.

GM/GMO's

In the NWO Final Solution, food has been *weaponized.* Diseases are manufactured in the laboratory by splicing foreign protein sequences into the DNA of plants and animals for creating never before seen genetic strains. Food products that have been *Genetically Modified* (GM)/*Genetically Engineered* (GE), upon consumption by humans or farm animals, transfers cross species genetic material that wreaks havoc upon a finely tuned physiology. Genes inserted into genetically modified microorganisms (GMOs) for the purpose of synthesizing pesticides, when ingested by animals or humans, genetically alters the host's gut bacteria to produce foreign proteins and *insecticide toxins.* These genetically modified intestinal bacteria are transferred to succeeding generations of digestive bacteria, which continuously replicate and manufacture insecticide toxins long after the GM food has been eliminated from the body. Bacillus thuringiensis (BT) produces an insecticide in GM corn and cotton that has clinically proven harmful neurological and reproductive effects when ingested by animals or humans. Fed to farm animals, it is transferred to milk, eggs, and meat consumed by humans, conferring systemic toxicity. In studies of laboratory animals fed BT corn, all died within 3 days. BT introduced into GM plants is the most likely cause for decimation of the world bee population.

Some further physiological effects of food genetic engineering on test animals and humans are: autoimmune diseases, diabetes, sterilization and infertility, accelerated aging, gastrointestinal distress, food allergies, brain inflammation, problems with regulation of cholesterol and insulin. Consumption of foods that have been genetically modified steadily weakens the human body over time, manifesting as diabetes, organ failure: damage to liver, spleen, pancreas, and other vital organs; as well as creating various forms of cancer and Attention Deficit Disorder (ADD), especially in children. Researcher, Jeffery M. Smith, in his books, *Seeds of Deception* and *Genetic Roulette*, describes experimental studies performed on hamsters feed genetically modified Round Up soybeans. (*Round Up*, or *Round Up Ready*, are brand names of GM agricultural seed products synthesized by Monsanto [translation: "Satan's Mountain."] The phrase, "Round Up" is derisively intended to imply that *the public*, having ingested GM food products, will be rendered "Round Up Ready" for "Harvest" – i.e. ready for transport to a FEMA concentration camp.) The test results showed that hamsters fed Round Up Ready GM soybeans had a 5 times higher mortality rate than the control group not fed GM soybeans, and they became sterile in the *third generation*. Genetic modification of certain agricultural plant species began in 1996, and were first introduced into the public domain in 1997, about the same time the globalists initiated Chemtrail spraying. What this means for Mr. and Mrs. American is that their grandchildren *will not be able to reproduce*; they will be sterile and childless, and are the *last* generation (ref. Appendix A and C). The experimental studies also showed that laboratory animals fed GM soybeans grew hair inside their mouths. (Brushing your teeth will soon take on a new meaning.) Farm animals fed GM/GE grains soon afterwards become sick and die.

Round Up Ready soy and corn food products have been proven to cause birth defects. Among packaged foods sold in grocery stores, 95 percent are genetically modified or contain GMO's. Within the next 8 years there will be a significant reduction and physical/cognitive debilitation of the American population resulting from side effects of GM food consumption.

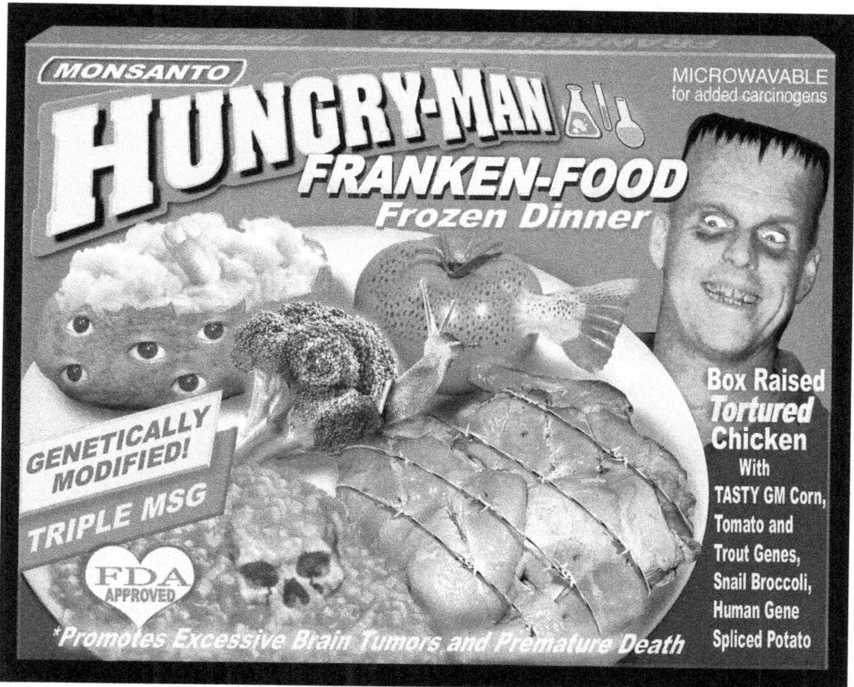

GMO labeling is prohibited in America; GM agricultural food products do not require a consumer label warning that they are genetically modified. FDA officials are told by successive administrations not to allow the labeling of GMO products, and are instead told to promote the biotechnology industry. (If the 5 digit numerical PLU code listed on the sticker appended to any whole produce of fruits and vegetables begins with the number "8," this means it has been genetically modified. If the first number is "9," it is organically grown. If the first digit of a 4 digit code is "3," it has been irradiated; if a "4," it is neither GMO nor irradiated.)

Codex Alimentarius are proposed international laws created by the Illuminati supra-government for *prohibiting* the sale of natural food products and health-promoting disease cures, some of which are beneficial for safeguarding and promoting robust health, or at least treating the consequences of ingesting GM processed packaged foods and drinking MSG/Aspartame beverages. This tyrranical decree will make all health food supplements – vitamins, mineral, nutrients, etc. – illegal for sale, considered "contraband," leaving only doctor prescription drugs (poison) as "legal." The Illuminati Hierarchy hopes to kill off 3 billion people when Codex Alimentarius is put into effect. Recent Senate Bill S-510 makes it *illegal to grow your own food! Organic farming will soon be considered a federal crime, punishable by prison incarceration!* Family farms are being run out of business by government regulations and replaced by large scale government-controlled agribusiness that will only grow genetically modified synthetic foods.

The European nations of Austria, Greece, Hungary, France, Luxembourg, and Germany (2009), have banned the use of foods which are GM or contain GMO's. But the United States has not, and most Americans have neither the knowledge nor awareness that genetic modification of food is a real and present danger to their health. Furthermore, even if you tell them, they do not seem to care. *Why have some Americans become so incredibly stupid?* The previous two chapters, and much of the remainder of this book, answer that question.

Today, there has been a takeover of the world's food production. The Illuminati are now expediting their efforts to eradicate over 90 percent of humanity. Just consider how far they have gone to destroy or control access to unadulterated natural food: presently, the food on supermarket shelves is *dangerous* to your health! The international shadow government wants you to consume only *their* "food" which has been deliberately weaponized and rendered toxic or genetically unfit for human or animal consumption. Currently, mindless robotic steroid police are raiding natural food stores and Farmer's Markets, guns drawn, ready to shoot.

Among the *known* food crops presently being genetically modified are: Canola oil (100%), Soybeans (95%), Alfalfa (90%), Cottonseed and Safflower seed oil (75%), Corn: GM brand name: "Star Link" (72%), Hawaiian papaya (70%), Sugar Beets, Zucchini and yellow squash (30-40%). Foods that will soon be GM are: Wheat, Potatoes, Rice, Peas, (Wheat and Peas may already be GM at the time of this writing. The last crop of non-GMO Montana hard red winter wheat was in the fall of 2009.) Some food products containing GMO's are: Meat, eggs, and dairy products from animals fed GM/GE feed or injected with Recombinant Bovine Growth Hormones, most vegetable oils, margarines, honey and bee pollen from GM sources, cross pollination of plants with GM seeds. GM food additives include: Aspartame, MSG, flavorings, enzymes, rennet in hard cheeses. Examples of GMO ingredients: anything derived from soybeans: soy flour, soy protein, soy isolates, soy lecithin, vegetable proteins, textured vegetable protein (TVP), tofu, miso, tamari, protein supplements; anything derived from corn: corn flour, corn gluten, corn starch, cornmeal, corn syrup/high fructose corn syrup (enhances cancer cell proliferation). Examples of processed foods containing GM/GE ingredients: infant formula, salad dressing, hamburgers and hotdogs, mayonnaise, candy, chocolate, cookies, crackers, fried food, corn chips, veggie burgers, meat substitutes, ice cream, frozen yogurt, tomato sauce, baking powder, vanilla, enriched flour, alcohol, bread, cereal, peanut butter. Nearly all packaged processed "foods" have genetically modified ingredients and/or are linked molecularly to non-food products. For example, petroleum derivatives (silicon) are present in McDonald's Chicken McNuggets – it is literally "plastic food." GM Star Link Corn, used by Taco Bell, has proven to cause organ failure in their restaurant patrons. Recombinant Bovine Growth hormone fed to all commercially produced cattle supplied to fast food chains, creates obesity and its attendant syndrome of ill health effects when consumed by humans. If given a choice, farm and wild animals will not eat food that has been genetically modified.

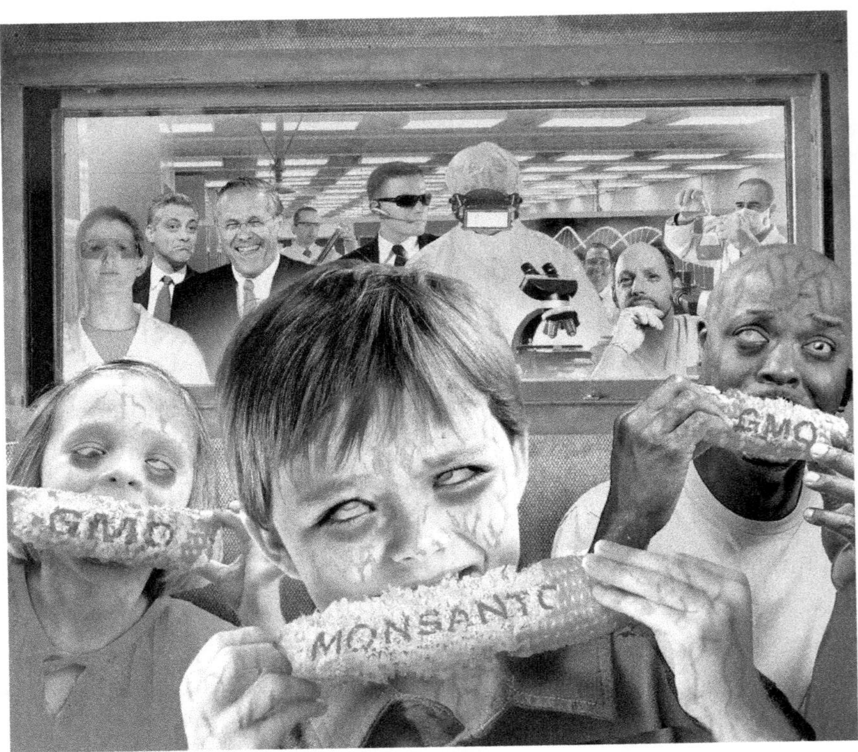

Consumers are being used as unwitting test subjects, "guinea pigs" in a worldwide biotechnology genocide experiment that exchanges foreign proteins between different species of plants, animals, and human beings.

No tests have been done, *or are allowed by the government to be performed* on BT, GM/GE/GMO foods to prove their safety. Independent researchers of GM food products have been fired or murdered. Not a single scientific study has *ever* been published on the effects that consuming GM products has on animals. No post-market surveillance; no clinical feeding trials; no independent safety peer review.

FDA government officials are often heads of GMO companies like Monsanto. Their objectives are: global food control, crop contamination, war on small farmers, population control by the genocidal killing off of large numbers of people.

SUPERNATURE

But as the days of Noe were, so shall also the coming of the Son of man be.
– Matthew 24:37

As a species, mankind is under a state of siege, a genetic coup d'Animal and Plant Kingdoms by globalist world dictators; a frothing mad demon-possessed band of pot-bellied crook-backed half-human monsters taking over the world. It sounds like a plot from a B-Rated Hollywood movie, but it is nevertheless true. Genetic Engineering has let the "genie" out of the bottle ... and it cannot be returned again. Man's rebellion against God's natural order has now resulted in animal proteins introduced into plants, plant proteins into animals; new molecular genetic combinations have spawned from this diabolical alchemy that was deliberately bioengineered to weaken the human genetic code (genome) and make individuals less genetically fit to reproduce. GM food, and creating genetic hybrids between plants and animals, is being carried out in genocide laboratories – chiefly Monsanto and Kraft (note the name derivative of witch*craft*). These Illuminati-controlled biotechnology companies, and others like them, have combined soybeans with rats, wheat with chickens, tomatoes with scorpions, safflower with carp, spiders with goats, jellyfish with dogs and monkeys (that "glow in the dark"), and cows with humans – to name only a few examples of scientific madness that registers off the chart. They have also succeeded in genetically splicing vaccines into the DNA of plants, for consumption by humans as an *edible form of mass inoculation with disease.* Because the Luciferian world controllers are cold-blooded psychopathic mass-murderers and habitual pathological liars from birth (Psalm 58:3), they can plausibly justify their genocidal insanity in order for the intended GM result to appear agriculturally or medically useful. Yet, whether the false rationale is "fungal resistance" in wheat, or "better pharmaceutical drugs," one thing is absolutely certain: Satan's people are *incapable* of telling the truth (and neither can they know the truth, or even recognize it when forced to acknowledge it). Their bold-faced deceptions are dependent upon a national ignorance and opposition to the truth/ Truth. Because the American people today have *made lies their refuge* (Isaiah 28:15), therefore, the consequences of their ignorance is *death* (Proverb 8:36) – both physically and spiritually.

In addition to mass sterilization, a major goal of the Rockefeller, Carnegie, Ford, and Bill Gates Foundations is to neutralize the entire world population from revolting against the New World Order. The people of America have now been *anesthetized by mass medication* of their food, beverages, water and air. In order for the Illuminati crime syndicate to achieve their depopulation objective (decimate 80-90% of the global population, 94% of the U.S. population), the supra-government Hierarchy plans to alter everything that God has created, replacing it with Satan's synthetic version as a decadent facsimile of God's perfection. (Monsanto executives have publicly stated that their goal is to genetically modify *all* plant and animal species on the planet.) In today's topsy-turvy mad mad world, the global eugenicists are striving to destroy human genetics so they can recreate it to their own perverse liking. Doctors of deceit are working diligently to transform the earth into a world of chaos, confusion, sickness and death; a place where they have obliterated the distinction between edible food and non-food, living and non-living, animals and plants, men and women, humans and non-humans. Modern culture is very much like it was before the flood in Biblical times. Presently, man has again polluted the world with his wickedness, and soon, God will once more purify the earth. But, *this time* He will do it with *fire* (Exodus 32:10,12; Deuteronomy 4:24, 9:3; Hebrews 12:29).

... Noah ... was perfect in his generations, and Noah walked with God (Genesis 6:9).

Noah was "perfect" in the sense that the genetic material of he and his immediate family (a total of 8 people) was the *only* remaining genetic line on Earth whose DNA had not been contaminated with the spiritual genetics of the sons of God – i.e. demons. The doubters will deny human-demon procreation is possible, for how, they ask, can a spirit without a physical body produce offspring with a physical human? The answer is quite simply because, God said so. Genesis 6:2,4: ... *the sons of God saw the daughters of men that they were fair; and they took them wives of all which they chose.... There were giants in the earth in those days; and also after that, when the sons of God came in unto the daughters of men, and they bare children to them, the same became mighty men which were of old, men of renown.* (Also ref. Luke 1:31,35,37). The DNA molecule makes possible meiotic cellular division within human sex cells (ovaries and testes). The process of cell division after the union of sperm and egg to create from a two cell embryo a rapidly growing mass of differentiating cells is a wonder to behold and yet remains a mystery to modern science. The best scientific minds cannot explain how this process occurs. Could it be that the double strand DNA helix is a gateway portal connecting the material world with a higher dimensional spiritual realm? i.e. the creation of new life occurs on a sub-quantum level, in a *non-physical pure energy* space. If so, spirit demons producing half-humans is not far-fetched after all. (This is actually not a conjecture, but must be true, since material existence cannot be initiated on a physical level, but can only come into being from a non-material process, the source of which is the Spirit of God.)

... *As the days of Noe were ...*

Today, contaminated bloodlines have once again infiltrated the human genome and spread throughout the world. This demonic linage is widespread in certain segments of the human population, and is especially prevalent among members of the Illuminati and their spiritually like-minded rank and file Criminal Fraternity. The Word of God does not lie, and testifies that human-demon hybridization is not only possible and has occurred in past ages, but is happening in today's modern world. Genesis 6:4: *There were giants in the earth in those days; and also after that.* John 8:44: *Ye are of your father the devil.* Isaiah 57:4,5: … *are ye not children of transgression, a seed of falsehood, Enflaming yourselves with idols under every green tree, slaying the children in the valleys under the clefts of the rocks?* The news headlines, our satanic culture, clearly testifies that reemergence of the Genesis 6:4 serpent seed of Satan is once again very much a present day reality.

… so shall also the coming of the Son of man be.

They were called "Nephilim," which means "fallen ones." The Nephilim were the *mighty men which were of old, men of renown* that God spoke of in Genesis 6:4. They were giants, some over 30 feet tall; an amalgam of human DNA and demon DNA. They lived in ancient times past; they live in the present time: *There were giants in the earth in those days; and also after that.* They walk among us today – appearing fully human, but are actually the product of hybridization between a mortal human being and a non-physical devil/demon spirit. Most of them openly and deliberately serve their lord and master – human government. Those not directly involved with Satan's unrighteous wicked human government remain at large in the world, seemingly functioning on a day by day basis as normal human beings. But irrespective of their occupation, their sole reason for being is to act as *resistance to the righteous.* They were created to oppose God, His servants, and the truth. In a spiritual sense, they have no other function, no other rationale for existence. Their destiny is an assured eternity in the Lake of Fire, for they were never intended by God to be Saved, having made the decision not to serve God long before their consciousness crossed the quantum dimensional double-helix DNA threshold. (In the world of infinity, time is nonexistent; God gave them a choice, and before they acquired human form they made a free will decision to reject Jesus Christ – God made manifest to the mortal soul. Instead, they chose to serve the Lie. ref. Jeremiah 1:5)

The conclusion of the matter is that certain of the human species are not what they appear to be; they are not fully human, but are quasi-humans. Just as in the days of Noe, they have a different *spiritual genetics* than the mass of mankind, and consequently, serve another agenda, another gospel, which is not the gospel of Jesus Christ. Their purpose here on Earth is to do the will of their father, Satan, the Devil; which is to steal, kill, and destroy. The written Holy Word of God, the 1611 Bible testimony of Jesus Christ, describes human-demon hybrids as "brute beasts" (Jude 10) incapable of knowing the truth (2 Thessalonians 2:10-12), spiritually lost (Jude 12-13). They are creatures of base instinct, cursed from the womb. Psalm 58:1-3: *Do ye indeed speak righteousness, O congregation? do ye judge uprightly, O ye sons of men? Yea, in heart ye work wickedness; ye weigh the violence of your hands in the earth. The wicked are estranged from the womb: they go astray as soon as they be born, speaking lies.* When you turn on your TV, you will see them gazing back at you. Notice the depth of pitch black darkness in their eyes.

NEWS MEDIA

"That is the secret delight and security of hell, that it is not to be informed on, that it is protected from speech, that it just is, but cannot be made public in the newspapers, or be brought by any word to critical knowledge."

– Thomas Mann

"Make the lie big, make it simple, keep saying it, and eventually they will believe it."

– Adolph Hitler

"Educate and inform the whole mass of the people ... They are the only sure reliance for the preservation of our liberty."

– Thomas Jefferson

Yet, the deadliest *poison* of all is the *News Media*. From the local newspaper reporter to the major network television evening news anchor man, nearly all are without Godly wisdom, devoid of integrity, adverse to the truth, and absolutely despise the one and only true and living God, Jesus Christ of the New and Old Testament 1611 King James Bible. As a group, they are intellectual prostitutes, paid *not* to report the truth. If a rare exception were ever to surface, he or she would soon be unemployed and blacklisted for life.

The media is controlled by a transnational Illuminati crime syndicate. News reporters are under pressure to avoid reporting on certain issues which their superiors demand to remain secret. Chemtrails are an example. They are paid well to repeat disinformation provided them from the top of the Luciferian pyramid; half-truths and outright falsehoods to keep the sheeple pacified, and all the while believing they are providing a public service by selling out to their government "handlers" in exchange for a weekly paycheck. Media representatives have a "License to Lie"; either though ignorance or deliberate intent to obscure and obfuscate, they often fail to report the full truth. Historically, they are infamous for their lack of truth discernment, and are highly adept at twisting facts to suit their own distorted perceptions and scripted agenda. Key and influential media personalities such as Glen Beck, Sean Hannity, Bill O'Reilly, Rush Limbaugh, and Michael Savage, are paid to control both sides of the left/right paradigm by silencing the opposition while at the same time exposing the legalized criminality rampant throughout government. They are government shills working diligently to preserve the Globalist's Agenda.

All the above mentioned are on record for refusing to objectively discuss 9/11 and its global Police State implications, as well as Chemtrails and the Bohemian Grove (ref. You Tube/Mark Dice/Glen Beck/Sean Hannity/etc), where high level U.S. politicians annually revel in a bacchanal orgy, and where they are known to partake in homosexual encounters among themselves, with children, and with porn stars. It is at the "Grove" where – as documented by Senator John DeCamp – snuff films are produced (filmed murders, typically of children) and human sacrifices take place upon an altar before a forty foot stone owl representing Molech, the demon god of death and destruction. "Ladies and Gentlemen, I present to you … your political saviors!"

The news molds public opinion and is tailored to suit the vested interests of those within the world criminal elite power structure, which ultimately are the super wealthy upper echelon Illuminati (European "Black Nobility" Monarchies, including the Rothschilds). The European Rothschilds own all the major news wire services, including The Associated Press, Reuters, UPI. All the political magazines you see on news stands: Time, Life, Newsweek, US News and World Report, to name but a few, are wholly owned and controlled by Rothschild interests. Likewise, the newspapers: Chicago Tribune, The New York Times, Wall Street Journal, Los Angeles Times, Washington Post, Detroit Free Press, Boston Globe, Dallas Morning News, Cleveland Plain Dealer, and all other metropolitan newspapers across America, as well as major international papers – all of them are under direct Illuminati control. (A few exceptions still exist, for example, The Idaho Observer.) The European Rothschilds have a major stake in the Federal Reserve banking system, and even own U.S. conglomerate "Federal" Express. All the major book publishing houses are under close Illuminati supervision and are not permitted to allow any serious exposé of the Globalist's Agenda. In the major print media, no headline news is ever permitted to be released into the public domain unless it serves the Luciferian's purpose: people control; truth is lies, lies are the truth. To them, news reporting is a weapon to be used against the public. There is not an editor, CEO, or publisher of any major newspaper in America who is not working – directly or indirectly, knowingly or unwittingly – for the globalists, and who will not do whatever their masters say in order to maintain their job of perverting or preventing the truth from being reported. Failure to comply results in the use of lethal force. This is why for over 16 years Chemtrails are not being reported by the major media; i.e. everyone is afraid of the consequences. ("Huh, what'er Chemtrails?")

During the U.S. government-staged terrorist attack of September 11, 2001, with live coverage of the event by all the major television news stations (ABC, NBC, CBS, Fox News, CNN, etc.), as BBC journalists were reporting the collapse of the Twin Towers, they also reported the collapse of Salomon Brothers Building 7 (WTC 7), a nearby tall skyscraper. Yet, something was wrong with their live recounting of the incident; something seemed amiss – there was just one "detail" overlooked: *the building was still standing!* While the cameraman focused on the reporter, in the background could clearly be seen Building 7, tall as ever! It was not until 25 minutes later, that, like the World Trade Towers, *it too* was imploded by planted explosives; a *controlled demolition*, collapsing into its own "footprint" in a matter of seconds. No plane; just thermite plastic explosives.... Oops! The Illuminati news wire services had been just a little premature in "releasing" information to the press about their *pre-planned script.* Moments *before* the implosion occurred, police standing nearby were inadvertently filmed on camera and could be heard on recorded audio warning pedestrians to "Stand back! They're gonna' bring down the building!" (The cops knew it was going to happen. As loyal members of the Criminal Fraternity, their allegiance is to the Beast government, not to the public. None of them later came forward to report the truth.) Only 5 percent of Americans are aware that Building 7 fell. The controlled media refused to report it and continues to discredit the true account of what *really* happened on 9/11, calling the truth "Conspiracy Theory" (ref. Appendix E).

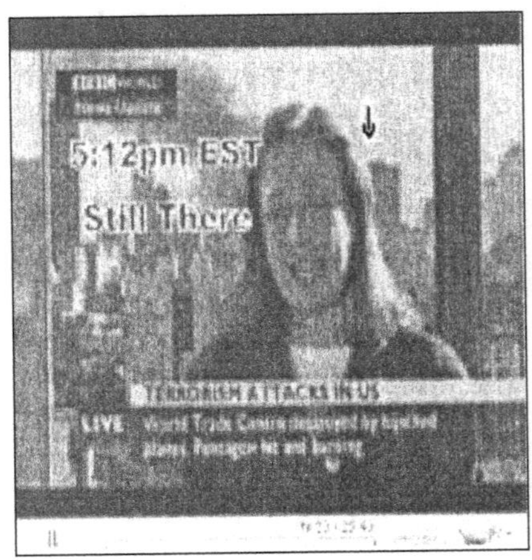

BBC news correspondent reports: "Salomon Brothers building collapsed." But the building behind her shows it still standing!

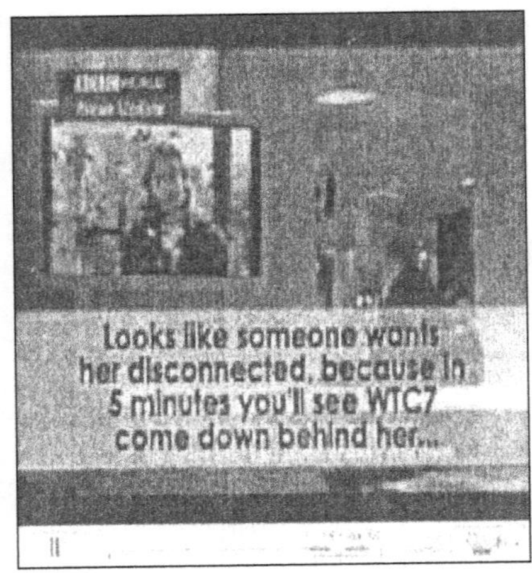

Nearly half hour later, WTC 7 implodes to ground zero. (The live TV broadcast transmission is cut before the building falls.) A perfect planned demolition.

NYC 9/11 was the start of the contrived "War on Terrorism" in America – not against secretive "terrorists," but *against the American people.* It created an excuse to increase domestic security: at check-points, full body scanners at airports, and soon, other government controlled locations such as court houses, libraries, and even commercial retail stores. For those yet retaining an intact brain, 9/11 was an obvious government-staged event to create a false enemy which the globalists could blame for the chaos they manufacture as a rationale to justify their coming worldwide Police State. Aaron Russo, film producer (From Freedom to Fascism) and former Libertarian Party aspirant to the U.S. Presidency during the Bush/Kerry "campaign" era, when paraphrasing one of the Rockefellers (Nick) during a private meeting, stated: "He said what happened on September 11 was a fraud, and that there were no terrorists (he's laughing) … 'This whole thing was all a farce, a joke. There are no terrorists!' he said. 'We did it so we could get the oil in Iran and Iraq … and then we're going to put a microchip in everybody … and if they won't go along with us, we'll just shut off their chip and they won't be able to do anything.'" Shortly afterward, in 2007, Aaron Russo – fast gaining a following in America for exposing the unconstitutional personal income tax fraud perpetrated against the American people – *allegedly* died of cancer … or was he murdered by the CIA? Statistical probabilities favor the latter.

The twin skyscrapers and WTC 7 were brought down to ground level by the use of *Thermite* plastic explosives; a controlled demolition. Much film footage exists on the Internet and You Tube with eye witness testimonies of *thousands* of bystanders reporting they heard the sound of explosives detonated prior to and after the collision of commercial aircraft into the Towers. (Blasts from horizontal jets of ejected matter are visible in many photographs.) It is a physical and engineering impossibility to collapse tall buildings of that stature to ground level – in less than 7 seconds – by the impact of jet aircraft or subsequent fire. Only someone who drinks fluoridated water or allows themselves to be inoculated with "Flu shots" could believe anything so ridiculous. The 9/11 government "inside job" was a pretext for creating anti-Constitutional laws in America to steal away citizen's Constitutional rights in order to facilitate loss of U.S. sovereignty in preparation for instituting a worldwide supra-government. *Within hours* of the "Black Ops" team effort (primarily mediated by the CIA-FBI), the previously drafted 800 page mockingly named "Patriot Act" and "Homeland Security Act" was forced on the fluoride-brain American public who, instead of being outraged because of loss of their Constitutionally guaranteed freedoms, thanked "Big Brother" for protecting them from "the terrorists." Today's Americans are a people so incredibly gullible they will accept *anything* the controlled media tells them – no matter how absurd. In fact, the more irrational, illogical and ludicrous the government lie, the greater the likelihood U.S. citizens will believe it. Hitler was absolutely right. The American people *really have* become that dumbed-down.

The news media played a major role in broadcasting disinformation during the incident which occurred in New York City on September 11, 2001, a planned act of war used as a pretext for initiating the "War on Terrorism" *against the American people.* It was contrived in order to create anti-Constitutional laws to forfeit citizen's Constitutional rights, increase domestic security, and facilitate loss of U.S. sovereignty in preparation for instituting a global Police State control grid world government. The staged event was planned by a supra-national small group of Luciferian dynasties, mediated by the CIA, and allowed to occur by the U.S. government puppet regime. It was intended to terrorize the American people into sacrificing their Constitutional rights in exchange for "peace and safety" from the ubiquitous "terrorists." (The *only* terrorist is *the government* – at all levels: Supra-national, Federal, State, local.) The U.S. criminal elite also hoped to declare a State of Emergency (Martial Law: impose military rule over the civilian population), but "only" managed to murder 3000 innocent people. The terrorism was planned 15 years in advance and was scheduled on that occultically significant 9/11 date because the Luciferian globalists believed they would derive satanic power to covertly deceive U.S. citizens into an unquestioned acceptance of the bold lie that "the Arab terrorists did it." The real reason for blaming the "Arabs" was to gain public support for U.S. military aggression in the Middle East in order to control Iraqi oil reserves and Afghanistan poppy opium production. But, you will never hear *that* from Dan Rather or Barbara Walters. The controlled press was the government enabler which facilitated the public's erroneous perception. And the lobotomized American people have never even asked "Why?"

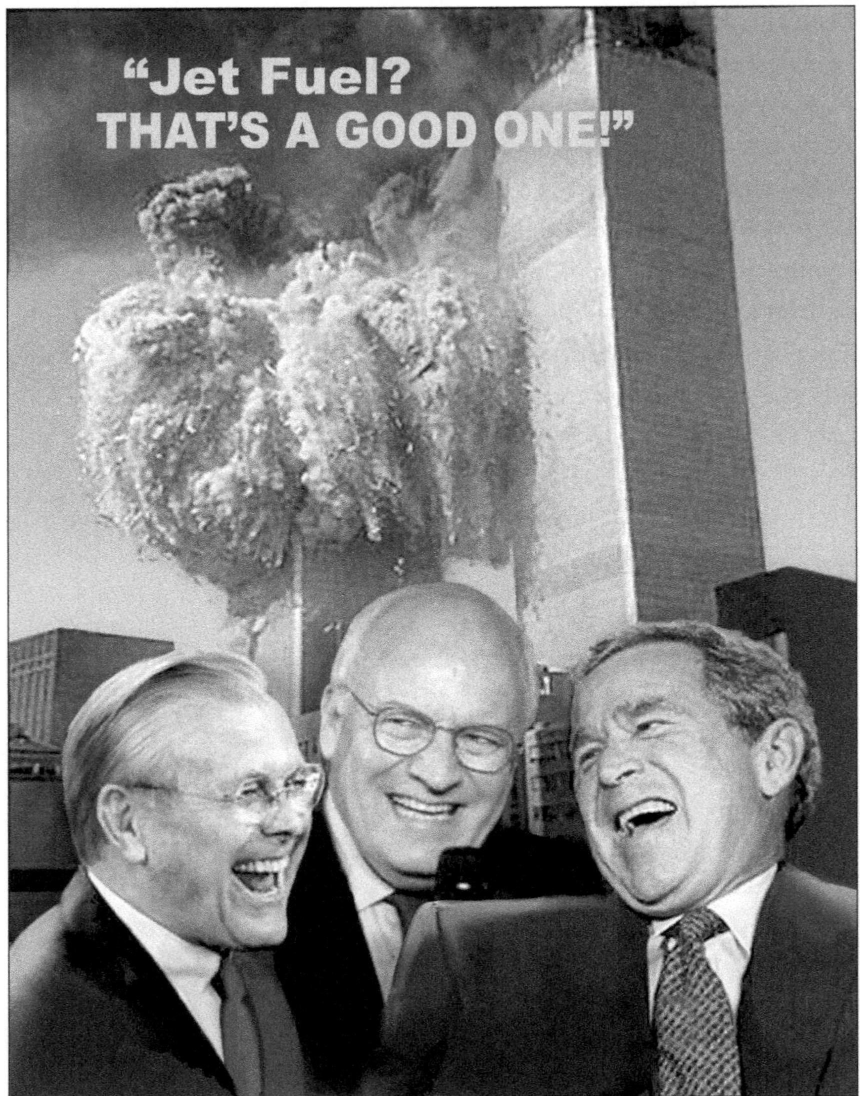

Minions of the Illuminati puppet masters are laughing in their Dom Perignon: "New York City's tallest buildings collapsed to ground zero in less than seven seconds when jet fuel melted the steel girders! Ha, Ha, Ha, Ha, Ha, Ha. They think Al Qaeda did it! But we're Al Qaeda! Ha! Ha! Ha! Ha! Ha! Ha! ... Or, how about this one: We made brain-destroying toxic Mercury vaccines mandatory because there's a 'Bird Flu epidemic' – yet, no one has died from 'the Flu' ... but they're all dying from the vaccine! Ha! Ha! Ha! Ha! Ha! Ha! ... Americans have become so stupid and decadent they'll believe anything we say!"

The global elite are still regurgitating their caviar over that tall lie.

In the 1880's, John Swinton, a New York City journalist, rose up to deliver a speech before a large banquet gathering of his peers. "There is no such thing in America as an independent press," he declared among the hushed silence. "You know it and I know it. There is not one of you who dares to write honest opinions, and if you did, you know beforehand that it would never appear in print. I am paid weekly for keeping my honest opinion out of the paper I am connected with. Others of you are paid similar salaries for similar things, and any of you who would be so foolish as to write honest opinions would be out on the streets looking for another job. If I allowed my honest opinions to appear in one issue of my paper, before twenty-four hours my occupation would be gone. The business of the journalists is to destroy the truth, to lie outright, to pervert, to vilify, to fawn at the feet of mammon.... what folly is this toasting an independent press? We are the tools and vassals of "rich men" behind the scenes. We are jumping jacks: they pull the strings and we dance. Our talents, our possibilities and our lives are all the property of other men. We are intellectual prostitutes." Needless to say, Mr. Swinton was soon out of a job. It should not be surprising that the media controllers prohibit the printing of "honest opinions," since it has always been their policy to disallow the reporting of *fact-based truth*.

The ruling power hierarchy has traditionally used the press to brainwash and mind-control the masses. If allowed to think for themselves (i.e. get rid of the TV and stop listening to politicians), vast numbers of individuals would come to the sudden realization that they are being psychologically and emotionally manipulated by those whom they have granted power to rule over them. Among the greatest fear – and nightmare – of the globalists is a well-informed citizenry: large masses of herd-like people stampeding forward, hanging nooses in hand, furiously angry over what has been done to destroy their future generations of children. Therefore, the Luciferians keep a close watch over what the sheeple are permitted to know. Today, nearly all television broadcasts, by design, support the Globalist's Agenda. Key television news personalities are members of the Council on Foreign Relations (CFR), cogs in a giant wheel that slowly grinds away Constitutionally guaranteed freedoms. Created by a generational high-level Luciferian witch, David Rockefeller, it is essentially the "real" executive branch of the U.S. federal government, and is among the primary Illuminati think tanks for planning the post economic collapse and restructuring of the world's political and economic financial systems.

The level of misinformation, disinformation and mind-control is so extreme today; the degree of "thought control" media programming so thorough, that anyone "plugged into" the system is enslaved by it and incapable of independent objective critical thinking.

Truthful information occasionally leaks through the controlled media's invisible wall of silence. To follow are some notable quotes from the past that managed to escape the "delete button" of the censor's watchful eye:

"The individual is handicapped by coming face to face with a conspiracy so monstrous he cannot believe it exists."

– J. Edgar Hoover, Former FBI Director

"The money powers prey upon the nation in times of peace and conspire against it in times of adversity. It is more despotic than a monarchy, more insolent than autocracy, and more selfish than bureaucracy. It denounces as public enemies all who question its methods or throw light upon its crimes."

– Abraham Lincoln (Shortly afterwards, like Kennedy, he was assassinated.)

"Sarah, if the American people had ever known the truth about what we Bushes have done to this nation, we would be chased down in the streets and lynched." – George Herbert Walker "Poppy" Bush, Sr. in a live televised news conference with a CFR news reporter

"In my line of work you gotta' keep repeating things over and over and over again, for the truth to sink in, to kinda' catapult the propaganda." [mindless audience applause].

– George W. Bush, in a televised speech before a live audience

"MSG, Aspartame, and other additives are going to be in our food no matter how many name changes are necessary."

– Senior executive in the food additive industry during a conversation with Dr. Russell Blaylock, MSG/Aspartame excitotoxin researcher

"Whenever the government says they are going to keep you safe, get ready, because you're going to lose your freedoms."

– Jesse Ventura, former Governor of the State of Minnesota

"September 11 was a big lie and a pretext for the war on terror and a prelude to invading Afghanistan … the attacks were a complicated intelligence scenario and act … U.S. using the attacks to attack others."

– Iranian President Mahmoud Ahmadinejad, commenting on the "official version" of the 9/11 cover-up story

"Ideas are more dangerous than guns."
– Vladimir Lenin. Etched into the stone wall of a corridor at the communist Soviet Russian newspaper, *Pravda* (translation: "Truth")

"It doesn't matter who the people voted for; they always vote for us."
– Joseph Stalin, mass murderer of 20 million innocent Russian people

"Think of the press as a great keyboard on which the government can play."
– Joseph Goebbles, Hitler's Minister of Propaganda

"We are grateful to the Washington Post, The New York Times, Time Magazine and other great publications whose directors have attended our meetings and respected their promises of discretion for almost forty years. It would have been impossible for us to develop our plan for the world if we had been subject to the bright lights of publicity during those years. But, the work is now much more sophisticated and prepared to march towards a world government. The supranational sovereignty of an intellectual elite and world bankers is surely preferable to the national auto-determination practiced in past centuries." – David Rockefeller, address to a meeting of the Trilateral Commission, June 1991

One can only marvel at the lack of intellect demonstrated by the globally destructive supra-national shadow government who presume to rule the world. *Professing themselves to be wise, they became fools* (Romans 1:22); ... *the folly of fools is deceit* (Proverb 14:8). And to wonder at the world bankers devoid of wisdom: ... *the prosperity of fools shall destroy them* (Proverb 1:32). The fate of the self-proclaimed "intellectual elite" and avaricious money changers is written in the Word of God: ... *shame shall be the promotion of fools... but fools die for want of wisdom* (Proverbs 3:35;10:21).

During the 1960's and 1970's the Illuminati created opposition which they called "Communism," and that has today been renamed, "Global Governance," or more commonly known as the "New World Order." The communist doctrine of the globalist's ministers of propaganda, spread by their controlled media, makes the NWO (Communist) takeover of America more imminent than at any other time in modern history.

CHAPTER 6

THE FINAL COUNTDOWN

Babylon the great is fallen, is fallen, and is become the habitation of devils, and the hold of every foul spirit, and a cage of every unclean and hateful bird ... for by thy sorceries were all nations deceived. – Revelation 18:2,23

For then shall be great tribulation, such as was not since the beginning of the world to this time, no, nor ever shall be. And except those days should be shortened, there shall no flesh be saved: but for the elect's sake those days shall be shortened. – Matthew 24:21,22

For when they shall say, Peace and safety; then sudden destruction cometh upon them ... Therefore let us not sleep, as do others; but let us watch and be sober. – 1 Thessalonians 5:3,6

"We are on the verge of a global transformation. All we need is the right major crisis and the nations will accept the New World Order."

– David Rockefeller
Speech made at the UN General Assembly, September 1994

In the same manner in which the crashing New York City Twin Towers was a *planned demolition* – collapsed into its own "footprint" by the use of explosives planted within its internal structure – so too, the implosion of the U.S. and world economies are being orchestrated from within the very institutions entrusted to safeguard against that occurrence. The 9/11 government-staged terrorist attack was planned far in advance (15 years) of the event taking place; likewise, the crashing of the American and global economies has been planned long before this present time (since at least the early 1900's).

The economic timeline is unfolding as previously anticipated by the author, and the ensuing *accelerated collapse* is about to begin. But the timing is the providence of God (James 4:15), not the pretentious posturing of Satan's silly servants. Both the near and long-term future of the rapid descent has been predetermined by God's design. The current analysis reveals that the year 2015 will be the final advance of a dying economy.

Because the public has been conditioned by the Illuminati-controlled media to believe that the DOW is an accurate measure of the nation's economic health, therefore, the higher it can be advanced relative to its former peak in 2007, the greater their confidence in America's economic future. Consequently, shortly after the 2015 reversal in the stock market, the public will lose hope in any restoration of America's former prosperity, which will create more stock selling, and, the faster and farther will be the ensuing decline. With the sudden collapse of the "global house of cards" the greater will be sudden panic among the terrorized masses who will gladly surrender more of their God-given freedoms for the false promise of "peace and safety." It will be precisely at that juncture the world's elite criminal crime families will use the "crisis opportunity" to bring in their Luciferian global dictatorship and demands for a microchipped citizen population.

The massive 40 per cent loss in 2008 contained the largest Quarterly decline since the 1929-1933 Great Depression. The month of October saw the greatest weekly basis point drop in stock market history (2527 points). The fourth Quarter months of October and November were also the largest 2 month point decline in history, losing 3400 points on the DJIA, representing 1/4 of the total valuation of corporate America as measured from the second quarter of 2008. Volatility of this degree gives clear indication that the supra-government Luciferians are planning something highly significant for the near-term future.

The crash of the U.S. economy is most likely to occur during the 4 year period between 2016 and 2020. A majority percentage of the U.S. and global economic damage should occur in the year 2018. Something of major global significance will occur to trigger a reaction of this magnitude in the world financial markets. More staged "terrorist acts" have been planned by the supra-government transnationalists, therefore, further government-contrived terrorism against the U.S. citizenry seems likely – as was executed on 9/11 – but of much greater degree. Their objective is to declare a national State of Emergency (Martial Law), suspend the U.S. Constitution in order to assert military rule over the public. The rationale presented to the dazed American people will be to justify a seemingly righteous cause: "fighting terrorism" or mandatory vaccinations (i.e. inoculations with disease) for a nonexistent "Bird Flu Pandemic." (Like the false claim of "terrorism," there exists no "Bird Flu," or "Swine Flu," or any other kind of *imaginary* "pandemic" [e.g. H5N1, H1N1, West Nile Virus, etc]. It's all merely another *government-created fraud*, a "fabricated outside threat" used as a pretext to bring everyone into their collectivist system of tyranny so they can impose total control over the population. Registration for *mandatory forced vaccinations* is one of the principal means for accomplishing their *Police State Control Grid* stated objectives.) If the media is promoting it, you can be absolutely certain the government is behind it; and a Satan-directed criminal government is *incapable* of telling the truth. (The media blackout of reporting the atmospheric spraying of *Chemtrail* weaponized biochemical and biological warfare agents *is* very real. For example, a recreated strain of *Spanish Flu* would be lethal for the entire global population, as it was for segments of the world population in the 1918 pandemic that lasted 2 years and killed 50-100 million people, mostly healthy young adults. Tissue samples from frozen victims have been used to reproduce the virus and were genetically engineered to be even more deadly, creating a "super plague" of resurrected flu pandemic. It would be a simple matter to include it in the daily global Chemtrail aerosol spray operation.) Nuclear holocaust is impending; a real or perceived threat of its imminent occurrence in the Middle East would constitute a precipitating factor to ignite a global financial meltdown. Threats of a nuclear strike by any of the Middle East or Asian factions qualifies as *wars and rumors of wars* (Matthew 24:6-8). A declared war between superpowers would be WWIII, the final battle of Armageddon. (2051? ref. Appendix A: *Biblical Prophetic Timeline.*)

The early stages of the 2016-2017 first crash sudden economic implosion will create increasing numbers of bank failures, citizen's frozen bank accounts; the public angry over their inability to withdraw funds. Also, record unemployment at all socio-economic levels. (Currently, the unemployment rate is 21 percent, twice that being reported by government statistics. This figure is fast approaching 1929 Great Depression levels.) The number of homes lost to bank foreclosure will continue to escalate as the stock and housing markets further devaluate, precipitating massive losses to the real estate, banking, and big business sectors; and soon to follow: food shortages, forced vaccinations, and citizen revolts against the government. (The "Second American Revolution" will be a feeble "non-event" by only a few brave individuals: statistically, about 1 in 100,000. The other 99.9999% of the U.S. population having been rendered too physically incapacitated, psychologically disabled, or morally bankrupt by the Globalist's Agenda to launch a defensive against the illegitimate high treasonous U.S. puppet regime.)

Acting on orders from their Illuminati masters, political figureheads representing the communist/fascist takeover of the U.S. federal government (the former pre-Lyndon Johnson political regime having now been hijacked and replaced by Illuminati supra-government private corporate and international Rothschild banking interests) will rapidly transform a once quasi-Constitutionally free nation into a Stalinist Gulag, an oppressive lock down prison camp. Documented FEMA Concentration Camps, both above and underground, have already been built all across America and are awaiting train box car loads of "prisoners of war" – i.e. U.S. "citizen terrorists," "enemy combatants" (derisive terminology, like the equally contemptuous phrases, "Patriot Act" and Office of "Homeland Security") shackled to the interior walls of rail cars equipped with iron chains. A reported 500 million plastic caskets have been manufactured and are awaiting deployment at FEMA Concentration Camps throughout America (ref. Internet for photographs of stacked burial chambers). Additionally, sports arenas can be instantly transformed into lockdown "Detention Centers"/Enemy Prisoner of War Camps with armed military guards ordered to shoot anyone attempting to leave, as occurred in New Orleans during Hurricane Katrina. Warrantless house to house searches and gun confiscation (which also took place in Louisiana during Katrina), highway check points (presently being conducted throughout the U.S.), federalized militarized police, face recognition cameras, naked body scanners in government and commercial facilities, biometric national ID card – *this* is your future, America! (All of the preceding are *presently* ongoing in the United States.) Americans are doomed to go into Illuminati captivity. The global madmen will use the ruse of "terrorism" as the chains to bind a brainwashed public. The Luciferians assume the American people have become so dumbed-down they will not realize what is coming … and they don't – i.e. nearly everyone who reads this section will not believe these events will occur, or thinks it could take place at some point in the distant future, but not in their lifetime. Yet, its imminent reality does not require anyone's belief, especially since much of it is *already* occurring. The controlled media is not reporting it, and that is why hardly anyone knows about it. (But even when told the truth about the present ominous reality, people still will not believe that it will soon transpire.) Those who have denied the truth for so long, and trusted in falsehoods told them by their "political saviors" – both, in government and false Christian churches, may abruptly awaken to realize the advance warnings issued in the Books of Daniel and Revelation, and as reflected in this volume, are *absolutely true.*

There will be a double crash in the financial markets. The first will occur in the years 2016-2017, followed by a more severe crash starting in the year 2018. The initial stock market devaluation will likely halt in the 10,000 DOW range. The seconday collapse will surpass the level of the first decline, dropping to approximately the 1000 level by 2020. This 1000, or lower price level, represents *economic Ground Zero,* intended by the Illuminati globalists to mirror NYC World Trade Towers *9/11 Ground Zero,* a final phase in the progressive devaluation of U.S. and other world currencies. Such a massive stock market loss (94 percent from its 2015 high) will necessitate the implementation of a *cashless world currency* to replace the U.S. dollar and other national currencies that have been devaluated by the collapsed American economy. Electronic currency transfers will be facilitated by microchipping the entire global population – i.e. Mark of the Beast technology (Revelation 13:16,17). This microchip technology already exists and has been in use for many years. The human tracking microchip is manufactured by Verichip Corporation, a division of Applied Digital Solutions. The original version of the human implantable microchip has recently been miniaturized still further, and is now only a fraction the size of a grain of rice. In addition to being made smaller, the newer version of the biochip (transponder cylinder) has an imbedded circuit board with a storage capacity greatly exceeding that of the former chip, allowing for complete cataloguing of personal, financial, educational, and medical history. An improved edition of the presently existing "Chip" may soon be a further miniaturized version, a *microdot.*

The RFID chip (Radio Frequency IDentifier) currently being used for retail products and tracking pets, is the precursor to the *subdermal* human *implantable* RFID microchip (Radio Frequency Implanted Device) *Mark of the Beast.* Most Walmart products are currently marked with an RFID chip. (Wal*mart, logo a satanic pentagram star, is a globalist New World Order citizen surveillance beta test project.) Shown below, the illustration superimposed on the RFID microchip indicates the exact positioning in the human hand for the future *Mark of the Beast* described in the Book of Revelation. Notice that the crosshairs are centered on the *underside* of the *right hand*, indicating the electronic chip reader will scan the *palm* of the right hand as it passes over the reader device. A two thousand year old Bible prophesy specifies the Mark will be *in* the *right hand* (Revelation 13:16).

Walmart RFID microchip

At some point in the near future, during or after the 2018-2020 financial market slide into oblivion, a global political dictator (Antichrist) will step out from the shadows and blasphemously declare himself to be the "savior of the world," the "Messiah" (false messiah), the one who will fix the problem, save the people, create "peace and safety" (i.e. an international dictatorship). With each passing year the probability of that occurrence increases. In the interim, as prophesied in Matthew 24:23-26, there will be many false messiahs (antichrists). At this point in time, U.S. President (in title only) Barack Hussein Obama (aka Barry Soetoro) is undoubtedly a false messiah, and is definitely an Antichrist *precursor* (1 John 2:1). He also seems to qualify for the office of the Antichrist *beast* of Revelation 17:8,11;19:19,20. As a Rothschild Illuminati appointee, and promoted by their controlled media to divert the public's attention while the Luciferians complete assemblage of their NWO international political construct, he demonstrates the antichrist spirit when speaking in support of global government: "We've got to give them a stake in creating the kind of 'World Order' that I think all of us would like to see." (The word "them" refers to the Fluoride-drinking/Mercury-vaccinated/Chemtrailed/ TV mind-controlled/MSG-doped American people. The words "we/us" is meant to signify those at his level and above in the supra-government Global Hierarchy.) Further manifesting the same Satanic spirit as his Illuminati masters, he supports a global currency, a one world religion, and has passed legislation exempting vaccine manufacturers from legal prosecution and liability arising from their death and disease-causing inoculations. He does everything his controlling handlers tell him to do: any new unconstitutional law or Police State Executive Order, he *will* sign. (His approving signature is intended for public display purposes only, and is not necessary for implementation of globalist decrees.) He has called for a "civilian national security force" (youth army), an Hitlerian idea whereby adolescents are given full police authority to arrest and detain; and ordinary citizens "police themselves," spying on each other, reporting neighborhood "terrorists" to the "authorities." "His" recently passed "Health Care" Bill requires all citizens to be injected with an *implantable microchip* by the year 2017 in order to qualify for receiving medical "health care." Throughout his *staged* "political campaign" the controlled press labeled this *Illuminati shill* "the new world Messiah" – and the sheeple applauded him! John 5:43: *I am come in my Father's name, and ye receive me not; if another shall come in his own name, him ye will receive.* Those who are deceived by this imposter, believing he is their "savior," have been preordained by God for eternal destruction (2 Thessalonians

2:10-12). Modern-day Illuminati spokesperson, Henry Kissinger, has publicly announced that Soetoro/Obama would rule the emergent global government: "Obama is primed to create the New World Order," said the former Third Reich double agent.

Barack is Latin for "Lightning" or "Thunder." Luke 10:18: *I beheld Satan as lightning fall from heaven.* The Hebrew transliteration for "Lightning from heaven" is "Barak O Bamah." Therefore, the Lord Jesus Christ is saying in His Holy Word: "*I beheld Satan as Barack Obama.*" Also, Matthew 24:27: *For as lightning cometh out of the east, and shineth even unto the west....* Barack/Barry Obama/ Soetoro was born in Kenya Africa, in the *East.* Of course, Obama/ Soetoro, like all U.S. Presidents after JFK, has no political power whatsoever to initiate or execute decisions, and is merely a media-created Illuminati front man told what to do by his Illuminati handlers. His speeches and every political move are dictated by invisible Rothschild/Rockefeller puppet masters. Nevertheless, because he is so obviously indwelled to an unusual degree with the antichrist spirit, and also for the reasons just cited, the author gives him a high probability for being the literal Antichrist. Although the Antichrist is yet to be revealed at the time of this writing, Obama/Soetoro could well turn out to be the embodiment of the prophesied "son of perdition" upon such time when he becomes fully indwelled with the spirit of Lucifer/Satan. The following is further rationale for maintaining this conviction:

1) Daniel 9:24. The seventy prophetic weeks of Daniel ended in the year 1948.

2) Daniel 9:25. Sixty-two years after the decree to restore Israel (1947), *the Messiah the Prince* (Antichrist) will make his appearance on the world scene.

3) 1947 + 62 years = 2009.

4) In 2009, January 21, 22, Barack Hussein Obama was sworn into office. This date is exactly 62 Hebrew years from the time of the decree to restore Israel (each year consisting of 360 days).

5) Unless there was some other significant world political figure who took office on that specific date, these Daniel verses seem to indicate that Obama is indeed the prophesied future Antichrist.

U.S. and world political leadership has long ago disintegrated into mere figureheads. As Plato once observed: "Those who are too smart to engage in politics are punished by being governed by those who are dumber."

Another potential candidate for the global role of "Antichrist" (Satan-indwelled human being) is Spanish diplomat, Javier Solona. (Javier is Latin for "Savior"; Solona, "of light." Hence: "Savior of light." 2 Corinthians 11:14: *And no marvel; for Satan himself is transformed into an angel of light.*) As former Secretary-General of NATO and of both the European Union and Western European Union (1999-2009), he made a 7 year covenant with the European Union nations (effective January 1, 2007 and ending *January 1, 2014*), that seems to be in accordance with Daniel 9:27, thus fulfilling a key criterion for the identity of the prophesied Antichrist global dictator. He is the Commander-in-Chief of all 10 EU nations, and has been described by those closest to him as "The most powerful man in the EU, and maybe the world." Several of his key EU legislation are documents coded with the number of the Beast "666," the three digits identifying the emerging global government which is the Revelation 13:15 image of the beast; and is also the number of the Antichrist himself. For these reasons, there exists some potential for Solona fulfilling the office of Antichrist.

Other possible candidates for the Scriptural office of "the son of perdition" reputedly are: King Juan Carlos of Spain; Prince William of the UK House of Windsor; and the Pope of the Roman Catholic Church. The Pope, whoever it may be at the appointed time, will play a vital prophesied role as *either* the literal Antichrist or, more likely, his enabler, the *False Prophet* of Revelation 13:11-18. The office of the Pope is titled as "Vicar of Christ," which translates into "Antichrist." The Roman Catholic Church is the global anti-church ("Catholic" means "Universal") which rides the New World Order Police State beast. Revelation 17:3: ... *a woman sits upon a scarlet colored beast, full of names of blasphemy, having seven heads and ten horns.* In Bible prophesy, "woman" = "Church" (2 John:5)/Vatican City (Revelation 17:18); "beast = Antichrist/ NWO global government (Revelation 13); the seven heads = seven hills on which Vatican City is situated (Revelation 17:9; Rome is known as "The city that sits on seven hills"); ten horns = ten political leaders of the NWO 10 world regions, presently subdivided and already appointed (Revelation 17:9,12,13).

Battle lines have long ago been drawn: ... *choose you this day whom ye will serve; whether the gods which your fathers served...*(Joshua 24:15), the "god" of this world, Satan: Rome/Vatican, *the traditions of men* (Colossians 2:8,1-18,20; 1 Peter 1:18); *or* Jesus Christ, *the way, the truth, and the life* (John 14:6; 1 Peter 23,25). It is impossible to serve both; you can only serve one (Matthew 6:24). Only the second choice leads to eternal life.

Who will ultimately occupy the prophesied positions of Antichrist and his facilitator, the False Prophet – the above named individuals, or some other Luciferian vessels of wrath, yet to be announced? Only the future will tell. But whoever it is, the Word of God declares that the whole world will be deceived into believing his false identity and accepting the lie. Revelation 17:8 ... *they that dwell on the earth shall wonder, whose names were not written in the book of life from the foundation of the world, when they behold the beast that was, and is not, and yet is.* What seems certain at this time is that he will assume power shortly after the collapse of the world financial markets – i.e. 2018-2020.

The newly created Antichrist global government will be different from all other governments throughout world history. Although human government is corrupt and the most evil institution on earth, yet, this last attempt by Satan to rule over man will make any predecessors appear civilized by comparison. The final wicked government rulership by Satan is the one that will utterly trample the world's people to death (Daniel 7:7,8). It will coincide with the Great Tribulation prophesied in Matthew 24, Mark 13, Luke 21. Intensified persecution of humanity by the global government should start at the time of the secondary market collapse in 2018-2020. Revelation prophesy anticipates the return of Jesus Christ (Matthew 24:29-31) the only true Messiah (ref. Appendix A). While the 2020 terminal date derived by the author is not certain; the return of Jesus Christ *is* a certainty. This apocalyptic event will be the end of the present age rule of Satan and his government minions on planet Earth, and then ... *The Judgment*: Revelation 19:11-16: *And I saw heaven opened, and behold a white horse; and he that sat upon him is called Faithful and True, and in righteousness he doth judge and make war. His eyes were as a flame of fire, and on his head were many crowns; and he had a name written, that no man knew but he himself. And he was clothed with a vesture dipped in blood: and his name is called the Word of God. And the armies which were in heaven followed him on white horses, clothed in fine linen, white and clean. And out of his mouth goeth a sharp sword, that with it he should smite the nations: and he shall rule them with a rod of iron: and he treadeth the winepress of the fierceness and wrath of Almighty God. And he hath on his vesture and on his thigh a name written, KING OF KINGS, AND LORD OF LORDS.*

There is Scriptural proof that the year 2019-2020 is terminal for the present age of mankind. Matthew 24:32-34 speaks of the revitalization of the figurative fig tree (Israel), and those living at that time being the *final generation* that shall witness the Great Tribulation and also the second coming of Jesus Christ. Seventy years is one Biblical generation. In the Hebrew calendar, one year is 360 days. Israel was officially restored to the status of an independent nation in the year 1948. Adding 70 years to 1948 yields the year 2018. An additional 5 days per year multiplied by 70 years equals 350 days, which is nearly 1 year on the modern day Gregorian calendar. Therefore, one year added to 2018 is the year *2019-2020.* Could this year represent the *maximum time* remaining for the unfolding of Satan's global New World Order government and the prophesied return of Jesus Christ? (Matthew 24:29-31). Only the future will tell for certain.

The year 2018 should plummet the DOW to about 3000-2000; 2020 continuing the freefall descent to approximately 1000 or lower. From that point onward, no further near-term market analysis is possible utilizing the author's technical approach; all integral components of the millennial cycle have been completed. A new cycle begins at the conclusive end of this age (Revelation 20) and lasts for the 1000 year millennial reign of Jesus Christ (2020-3020?) in which the New Jerusalem Kingdom of God is established on Earth (Revelation 21,22).

The above stock market computations were achieved by means of Fractal Geometry and the 1.618 Golden Ratio and its derivatives. These ratios originate from a measurement reflecting the fractal characteristic of self-similarity evident throughout God's natural world. When using the key derived ratio of .618 for computing the *time equivalent* of that demonstrated in the above DJIA *price levels* determined by geometric fractals, the *same result* was achieved. To illustrate: multiplying the 7 year period between market tops in 2000-2007 by 1.618 yields 11.326 years. Added to the date of the March 2009 terminal decline provides the time for the ultimate bottom to occur in June-July 2020. As was the case regarding *price levels*, all the author's *time* calculations are *close approximations* within a range, and cannot provide the *exact* "day and hour" when these events will occur (Matthew 24:36).

The foregoing Golden Ratio *time analysis* yielded the same timeline results as that derived by Fractal Geometry applied to *price analysis*. Therefore, in reproducing an *identical outcome* by utilizing two different analytical means, the reliability of the author's economic forecast is statistically enhanced. When further considering the Matthew 24:32-34 Scripture pertaining to the restoration of the physical nation of Israel – previously demonstrated to produce the year 2019-2020 as a terminal date – there is a three fold confirmation that this specific time has prophetic significance (Deuteronomy 19:15).

In order to effectively establish a planetary dictatorship, the Luciferian transnational criminal elite must first debase the currencies of all nations and institute an entirely new system for recording financial transactions. The global economic crash of 2018-2020 will enable them to accomplish the long awaited "Plan" of their master, Lucifer/Satan. Superficially, it is the international controlling shadow government dictating world policy to its underling Presidents, Prime Ministers and other associated political figureheads; but, in reality, a few key Illuminati (select individuals from the Black Nobility First Tier of the Global Hierarchy) are being personally directed by Lucifer himself in how to go about creating a global disaster. And they will do it by crashing the world economy, consolidating and restructuring the global banking system, and activating an international surveillance matrix that requires everyone in the world to be "marked" with an *implantable microchip*. Although many of the lower-level globalist pawns do not yet realize it – or perhaps never will – *mass human microchipping* is the *ultimate objective* of their Illuminati masters in creating a New World Order planetary dictatorship. Zbigniew Brezinski, a poster boy for the New World Order, stated: "Soon it will be possible to assert almost continuous surveillance over every citizen and maintain up-to-date complete files containing even the most personal information about the citizen. These files will be subject to instantaneous retrieval by the authorities." This is a psychopath's wish, a dictator's dream come true, one that would surely make Hitler beam with delight.

"Obama's" Health Care Bill passed through Congress on March 3, 2010, and has a provision (#101) that requires a Radio Frequency Implanted Device (RFID microchip) *in the body* of a person before they can receive medical care. This implanted microchip will become *mandatory* for every U.S. citizen in the year 2017. Penalty for refusal to comply with this new tyrannical federal law is a $250,000 fine and 5 years imprisonment. "Forced compliance" is the means by which the Illuminati will bring the world's people under their dictatorial rule. The vaccine issue has been stressed throughout this book, not only because it is genocidal, but also since it will be used as a pretext to legislate mandatory vaccine inoculations *requiring registration* which enables the Beast government to *track* and *control* citizens. (*Never* register for *anything*. That is how they get you into their system.) Plans are already in place for establishing road blocks (choke points) along all major U.S. highways; motorists must prove they have been injected with disease-transferring vaccines by displaying a *permanently attached metal bracelet* which contains a tracking microchip. A FEMA concentration camp is the final destination of all those found not wearing their government-issued "proof of vaccination" steel bracelet.

The *National ID Card* is another precursor to the microchip implant. Legislation making it legal – the *Real ID Act* – has not yet been passed by Congress at the time this is written, but it fulfills all the requirements for the infamous Mark of the Beast described in

Revelation 13:16-17. This National ID *tracking* Card has an embedded microchip, and is not the ultimate Mark, but an ongoing installment in the progression toward an *implantable* chip. (Recently, the British Parliament voted on a *mandatory* subdermal-injected microchip for all UK citizens. It *just barely* failed to pass into law.) Once written into law, anyone who refuses to comply by obtaining the tracking card will be subject to arrest and imprisonment (Daniel 6:7). This is yet one more phase in the prophesied Beast government's attempt to number every person on earth. The plastic card contains personal biometric information (e.g. thumb scan, iris scan, facial recognition scan, and possibly a DNA sample) and a GPS microchip that will track the recipient 24/7. This act of *high treason* by political puppets in Washington D.C. has absolutely nothing to do with "national security" or "fighting terrorism," but has everything to do with Satan's government people claiming jurisdiction over your mind, body, and soul (Internet ref. *Real ID Act*).

Whether a plastic card or subdermal microchip, a government Mark will be required of all citizens in order to participate in the restructured cashless commerce system of the federal Beast … *save he that had the mark, or the name of the beast, or the number of his name* (Revelation 13:17). Therefore, the eternal consequences of receiving *either* Obama's RFID chip *or* accepting the biometric National ID Card will be the same: Lake of Fire (Revelation 14:9-11). The State-issued Driver License could soon become a National ID Card.

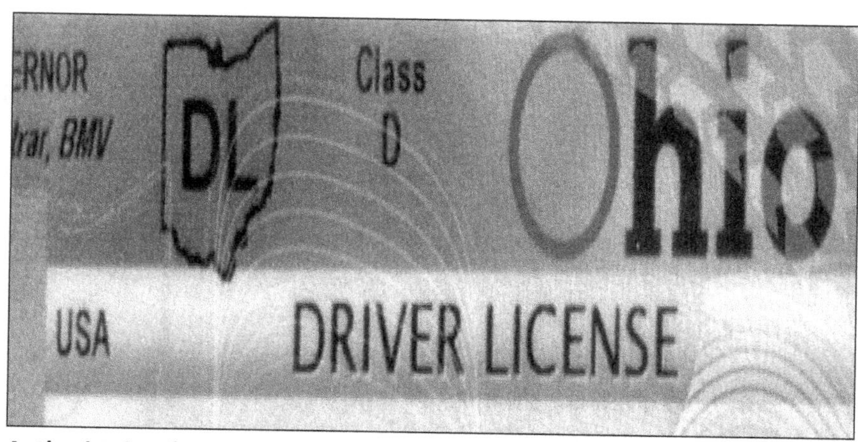

Authorization for the "right" to travel. The Beast government unilaterally changes God-given and Constitutional rights into "privileges," thereby gaining control over the individual. Mandatory Driver License is used for identification/tracking purposes, while also generating government revenue by forced compliance registration fees and punitive fines (violation of extortion and racketeering laws: RICO). The enlarged red letter "O" symbolizes Ouroboros, fiery serpent swallowing its own tail: the great red dragon, Satan, the Beast (Revelation 12:3,4). Man's government = Satan's religion = Revelation Beast.

One of the "alternatives" to being "chipped" is outlined in a government document called *Rex 84,* which specifies the building of concentration camps throughout America. Presently, more than 600 of these prison-like facilities have been constructed and are vacant and ready to receive *U.S. citizens* during the imminent Martial Law round-ups which should occur during or shortly after the 2018-2020 U.S. stock market crash. A *better alternative* to cooperating with Luciferian government decree is advance relocation to a remote mountainous terrain, preferably inaccessible by road, where provisions have been stockpiled to last a minimum duration of 4 years. (This is no guarantee of not being hunted, but at least you will have a fighting chance.)

Over 100,000 Christian "pastors" in America have submitted to Department of Homeland Security FEMA officials when agreeing to cooperate with Satan's religion (human government) by telling their congregations to turn in their guns, receive vaccinations, and peaceably go to FEMA camps. The "Clergy Response Team" further agreed to tell their flocks to obey any government requirement to be microchipped, since "it can't be the prophesied Mark of the Beast because we haven't been Raptured yet." But the Bible teaches there *is no* Pre-Tribulation Rapture (Matthew 24:29-31). The pseudo-Christian Pastors are in obedience to their lord and master, the Beast government, whom they serve to the exclusion of the Lord Jesus Christ. They sold out to the government Devil, becoming prostitutes of FEMA propaganda (ref. Appendix E, F, G).

At some time during or after the bottom of the Crash in 2018-2020 there will be an incremental unification of world currencies; the U.S. Dollar replaced by the North American Union *Amero,* already being accepted by the Chinese as a replacement currency for the *devalued* U.S. Dollar (name changed to "Phoenix"), which will then be united with the European *Euro.* When these two currencies are further combined with the Asian and African currencies, a *single world monetary unit* will emerge. Soon after that key juncture, the Illuminati's Criminal Fraternity hitmen – UN foot soldiers and municipal police departments – will enforce the requirement for *the entire world population* to be physically microchipped (ref. Appendix C #13). Throughout the period leading up to that Biblically prophesied event, government-engineered acts of staged terrorism designed to frighten and coerce the masses of people into submission to unjust decrees will continue to increase in frequency; Satan's endless war against humanity will rapidly escalate. Matthew 24:21: *For then shall be great tribulation, such as was not since the beginning of the world to this time, no, nor ever shall be.* What nearly everyone fails to realize is this is not a distant prophesy in the unforeseeable future, but is a *current event,* a very real historical fact *about to transpire.*

The Illuminati's Hollywood films are not merely for entertainment purposes, but are a *medium* for spreading NWO propaganda. (Holly Wood is an herb used by witches for "casting spells.") The entire 9/11 scenario was presaged in a Hollywood film, *The*

Knowing, released prior to September 11, 2001. There were other well-timed movies foretelling that tragic event and the subsequent post 9/11 citizen prison culture, such as *The Green Line*, which featured in the summer of 2001, just before the staged act of terrorism against the American people on September 11.

Chemtrail Bathomet "Goat Head of Mendes" photographed directly above author's residence on the day before an earlier book printing.

Serving as a benchmark, 9/11/2001, initiating the politically contrived "War on Terrorism," and used as pseudo-justification for instigating a war with Iraq and Afghanistan (i.e. it wasn't about "terrorism"; it was about controlling Middle East oil and Afghanistan opium production, and imposing world totalitarian rule), could be considered as *wars and rumors of wars* (Matthew 24:6). A Scripturally significant *seven years* from that date is September 11, 2008, which exactly coincided with the first phase of the economic crash that was forecasted and documented by the author *prior* to its occurrence (ref. Appendix D). The next dates of Biblical significance should be the end of the next 7 year period in 2015, the top in the U.S. stock indices; followed by the year 2019-2020, the crash bottom of the world financial markets, the year calculated by geometric fractal price analysis, Golden Ratio time analysis, and Matthew 24:32-34 prophesy (a Deuteronomy 19:15 *triple* witness). *A fourth witness* can be derived for prophetic relevance of the year 2019 as being a Biblically significant 70 years (on the Hebrew calendar) from 1948, the year physical Israel once again became an independent nation. The year 1948 fulfills Daniel 9:25 prophesy of 69 weeks consisting of 70 years each, and totaling 4830 years from the time of the birth of Jacob/nation of Israel in 2882 BC. It also fulfills Daniel 9:24 prophesy of 70 weeks consisting of 70 years each, and totaling 4900 years from the year 2965 BC, the time of God's Covenant with Abraham/the human race. (The author derived dates for the birth of Jacob/Israel, and God's Abrahamic Covenant, as well as the birth of Adam, from genealogical accounts provided in the Books of Genesis and Matthew 1; ref. Appendix A. According to the author's calculations, the first human being, Adam, was created in the year 4988 BC.)

The Tribulation shall commence in the near future. The years ahead will be characterized by escalating loss of personal freedoms and government-staged crisis, primarily in the form of a fabricated "outside threat." There is a government plan for staging a fake "alien invasion" at some time in the near future. Code name "Project Blue Beam," and created by holographic imagery, it could possibly be mediated by HAARP. UFO's – i.e. spiritual beings of light, demons – have already been embedded in the public consciousness by Hollywood, and are accepted as reality.

In addition to all the forms of government tyranny and manufactured terrorism discussed throughout this volume for subjugating the world population under the Illuminati's dictatorial control, this transnational criminal elite will continue to stage mini-crisis events such as school shootings by CIA mind-controlled Delta subjects, planted bombs in buildings, hijacked commercial jets, CIA mind-controlled lone gunmen randomly killing scores of innocent people, nonexistent pandemics, ecological disasters, etc., as a pretext to *force compliance* resulting in loss of personal freedom (gun control laws, mandatory vaccines, registration to receive government "benefits," etc.), so they can track and control the citizenry. (There is also the potential for a real, not staged, global crisis in the event of a near Earth orbiting rogue brown dwarf star identified as "Planet X." ref. Appendix C. This scenario was proposed in the author's book, *The Coming of Wisdom*, written in 1996.)

The goal of the Luciferian criminal elite is to genetically and psychologically weaken and destroy mankind. The short-lived duration of Satan's global human elimination campaign will evidence the rule of human government in its worst manifestation in all of recorded history. It will be the fourth and final dominate government on earth (Daniel 7:23). Daniel 7:7: *And I saw in the night visions, and behold a fourth beast, dreadful and terrible, and strong exceedingly; and it had great iron teeth: it devoured and break in pieces, and stamped the residue with the feet of it; and it was diverse from all the beasts that were before it; and it had ten horns.* The ten horns are 10 kings, as explained in verse 24: *And the ten horns out of this kingdom are ten kings that shall arise....* These are the governors of the 10 world regions, which at this present time have *already* been assigned.

The end of the Great Tribulation will coincide with the *return of God in the flesh: Jesus Christ* (Revelation 19:11-21). Only He knows the exact *day and hour* when that prophetic event will occur (Matthew 24:36). But, in the meantime, *it is possible* to know the *season* (v. 32-33) ... and the season is this present time. According to the author's analysis, and based on Holy Scripture, a major cataclysmic event for this present age of man could be 2019-2020. It is important to keep in mind that the analysis presented in this volume pertains to the timeline for the crashing of the U.S. and global financial markets. The Daniel and Revelation prophesies specifying the endtime apocalyptic scenario may not directly correlate with that date, and could perhaps transpire at some later time in the future beyond 2019 (ref. Chapter 8: *Parting Comments*).

Although the Luciferian Illuminati sincerely believe it is their demented actions which determine the destruction of world financial markets and ensuing chaos and future of mankind, they are *infinitely outranked* by the most High LORD God, Who sits on His throne up in heaven, gazes down at them … and LAUGHS!
Psalm 2:2-4: *The kings of the earth set themselves, and the rulers take counsel together, against the LORD, and against his anointed, saying, Let us break their bands asunder, and cast away their cords from us. He that sitteth in the heavens shall laugh: the Lord shall have them in derision.*

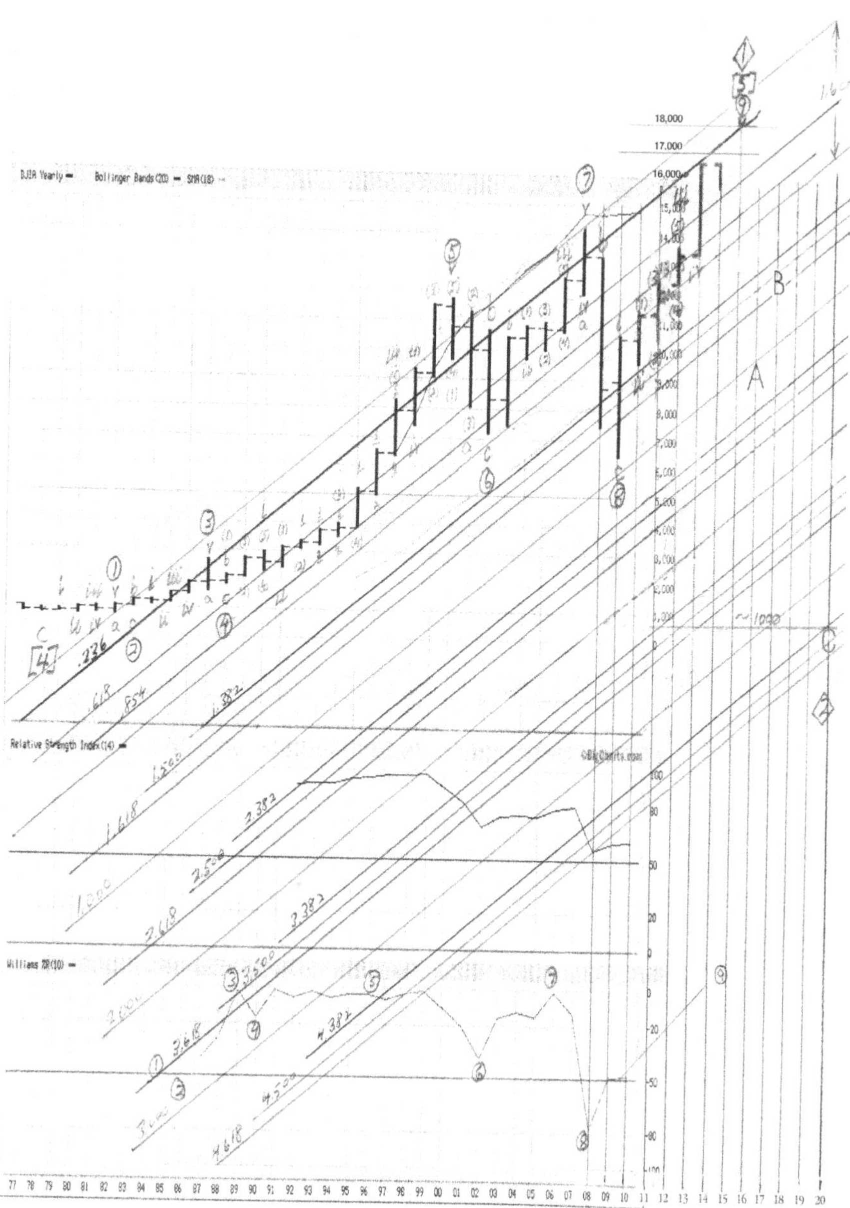

Yearly Projected Dow Jones Industrial Average 1978 - 2020

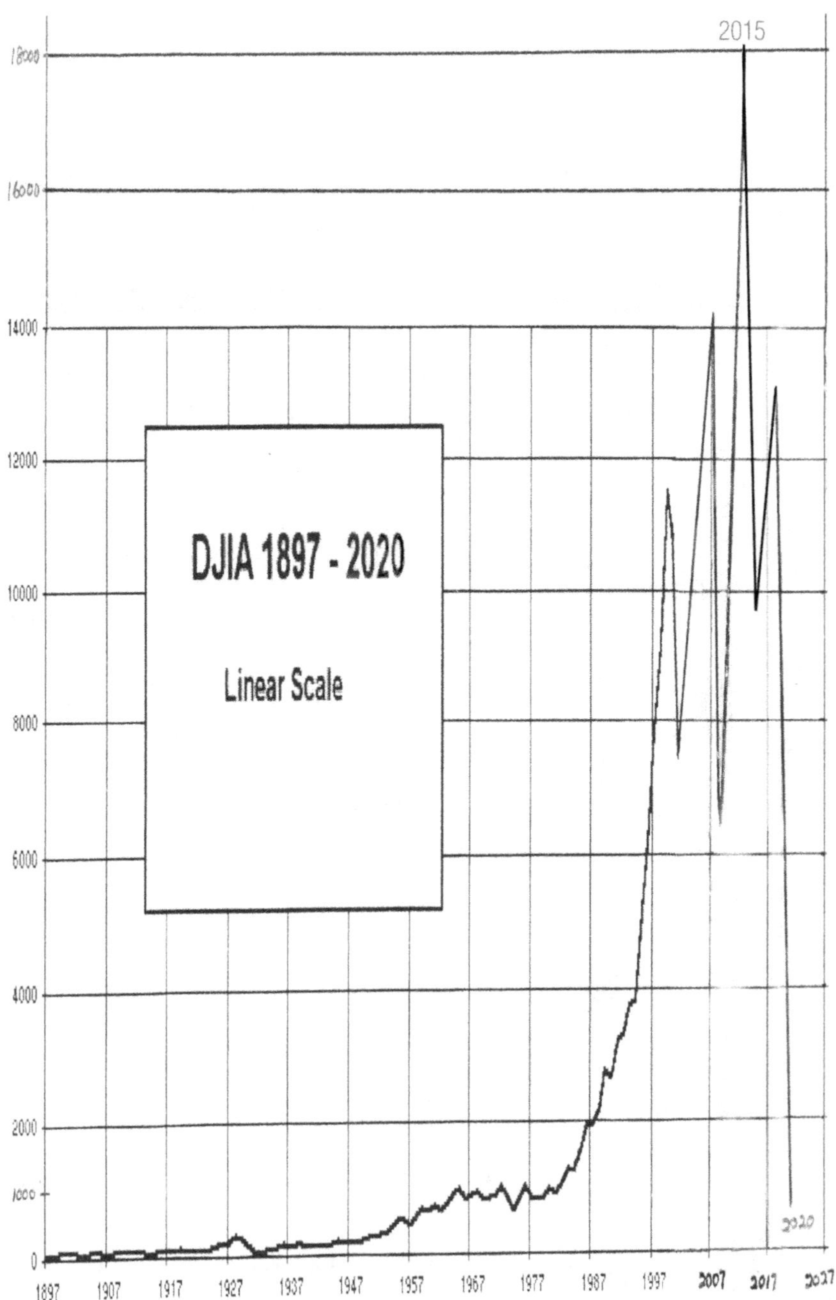

Yearly Projected Future of Dow Jones Industrial Average 1897 – 2020

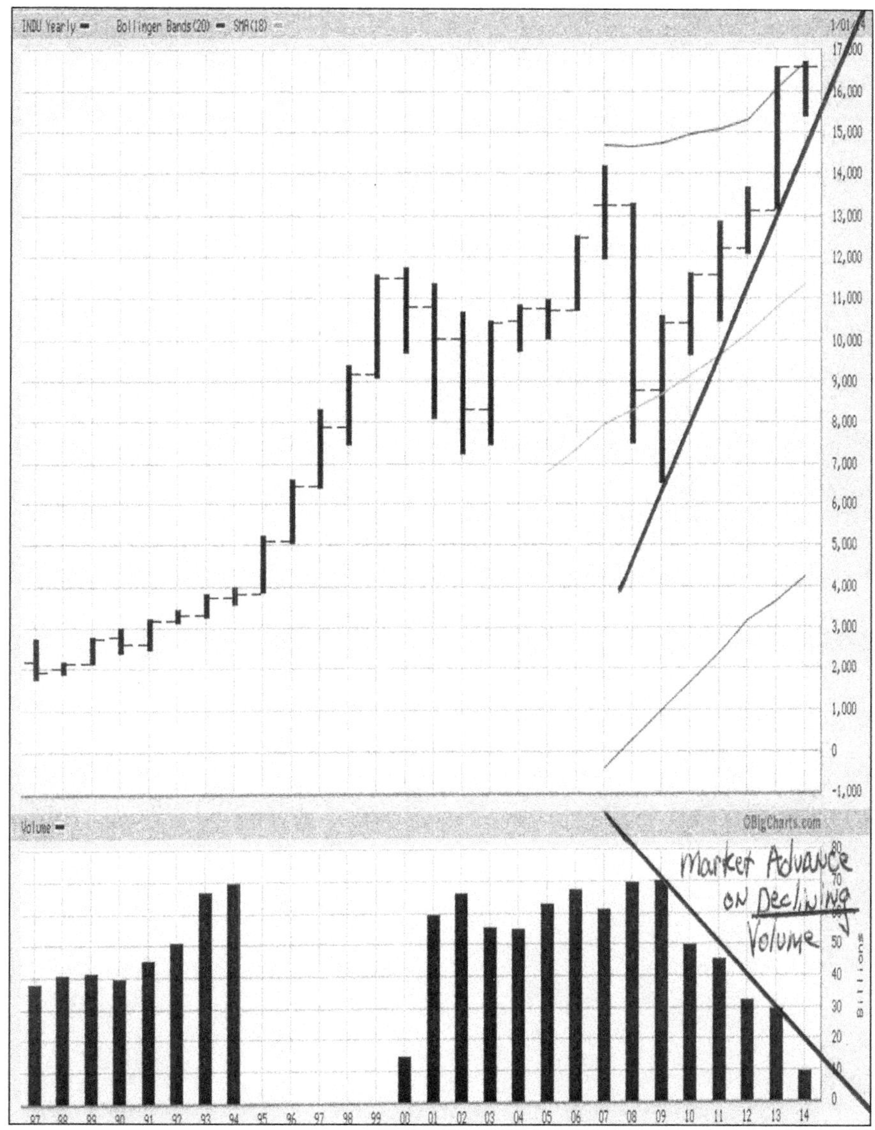
INDU Yearly
Bollinger Bands(20)
SMA(18)
©BigCharts.com
Volume
Market Advance
ON Declining
Volume
Billions

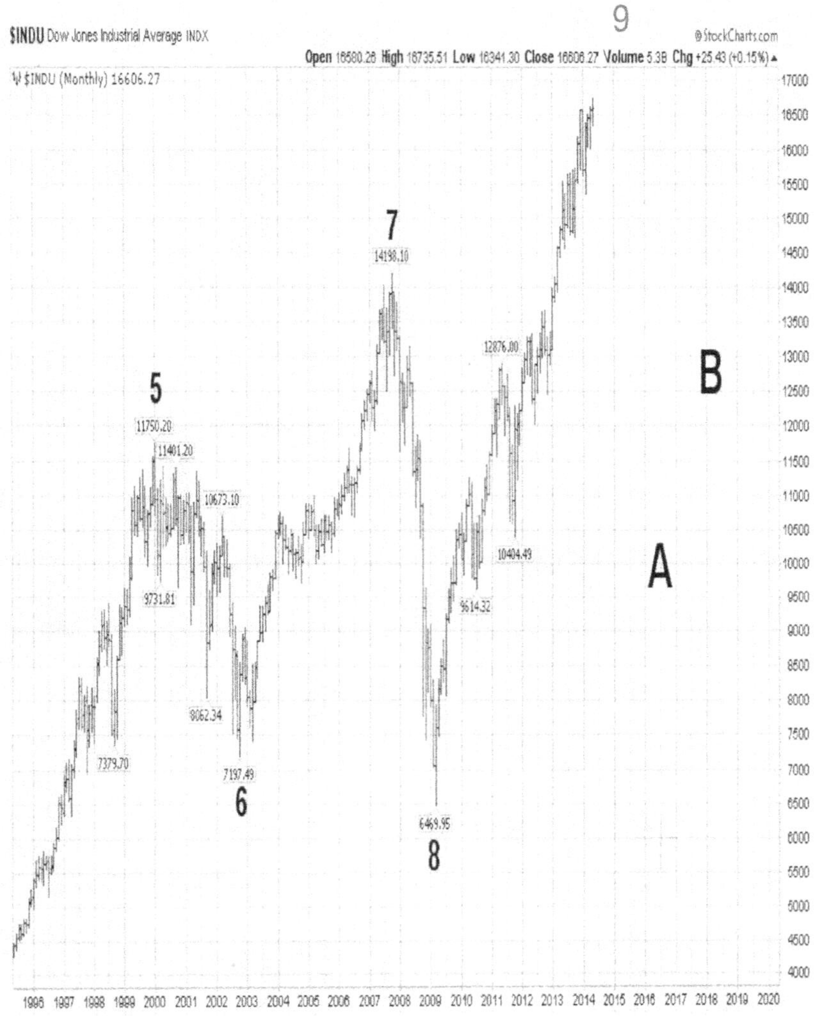

Monthly Projected Dow Jones Industrial Average

Projected Future of the Gold and Silver Markets

CHAPTER 7

THE CRASH OF 1929-1931 VS THE CRASH OF 2018-2020

"The power that is in control of the world is not the benevolent wise and spiritual group some of the masses have been conditioned by behavior modification to believe ... The elite rulers of this world are part of a Satanic conspiracy to enslave the human race ... We are about to go into a New World Order that will be worse than Hitler's New World Order, but the power behind the scenes is the same – the Illuminati getting their power from their centuries-old generational satanic practices."

– Fritz Springmeier, Author of *Bloodlines of the Illuminati*

Wednesday, October 23, 1929

The first significant down movement in the stock market occurred. The next day, $10 billion in stocks were wiped out.

Friday, October 25, 1929

J.P. Morgan Bank stopped the decline by pumping millions of dollars into the financial markets, temporarily easing panic and assuaging fears among the public.

Tuesday, October 29, 1929 (Black Tuesday)

Another massive round of selling on the New York Stock Exchange. 13 million shares traded (today, that amount of stock trades within the first 5 seconds after the open); $14 billion in losses for the day; more than $30 billion lost during the week: 10 times greater than the annual budget of the 1929 federal government.

1929 CRASH FOLLOWED BY THE GREAT DEPRESSION, THEN WWII

Elite members among the Illuminati Hierarchy plan the course of world financial markets. The infamous stock market crash of 1929 was orchestrated by a small group of generational Satanists who's major objective in life is to do the will of their master, who comes *to steal, and to kill, and to destroy* (John 10:10). For them, death and destruction are a way of life. Their serpent seed brood of descendants, in carrying on the tradition of their bloodthirsty ancestors, are the primary movers and shakers plotting to bring down the U.S. economy; and they are planning to do in the years 2018-2020.

Satan's people numerically made known their identity in the September 11, 2001 (9/11) mass murder. Luciferian numerology was also in evidence throughout the 1929 crash timeline. For example, the date, 1929 consists of two groups of sequential numbers, each equal to the number 11 (9+2; 2+9), representing a double confirmation. The number eleven is of great importance to the diabolical Global Hierarchy, and has been utilized in the past for timing their treacherous deeds. The technical start of the greatest crash in U.S. history was in September of that year, thus 9/29 also yields a double eleven (9+2; 2+9). The actual crash date was October 29, 1929: 10/29/29 (2+9; 9+2; 2+9), a *triple iteration* of the ominous confirming number 11.

Key blood-related Illuminati families (primarily the British Rothschilds) own and control the media, and therefore regulate the flow of information to a public that never suspects what is actually occurring behind a paper wall of government-controlled propaganda. One need only consider the Illuminati media's response to the most significant economic tragedy in American history: the sudden meltdown of the U.S. economy that lasted from late 1929 until at least 1933. It wasn't until 1954 that the DJIA economic indicator recovered its former 1929 level. By the end of 1929, in only 2 months, $40 billion was lost from U.S. stock equity. By 1933, national income had fallen by 50 percent; 5000 banks closed their doors, bankrupt. At the height of the market – *just as today* – prior to the initial Crash stages and throughout the ensuing period of decline, the scripted press continued to assure the public there was no need for alarm. The following is a brief sample of quotations from the respected "experts" of that day: leading economists, business moguls, investment advisor gurus, and no less an authority than three U.S. Presidents – all were *wrong* – and at the worst possible time:

1) "We will not have any more crashes in our time."

   –John Maynard Keyes, 1927

2) "No Congress of the United States ever assembled, on surveying the state of the Union, has met with a more pleasing prospect than that which appears at the present time. In the domestic field there is tranquility and contentment ... and the highest record of years of prosperity. In the foreign field there is peace, the goodwill which comes from mutual understanding."

   – Calvin Coolidge, December 4, 1928

3) "We feel that fundamentally Wall Street is sound, and that for people who can afford to pay for them outright, good stocks are cheap at these prices."

   – Goodbody and Company, market letter,
   The New York Times, October 25, 1929

4) "The end of the decline of the Stock Market will probably not be long, only a few more days, at most."

   – Irving Fisher, Professor of Economics
   at Yale University, November 14, 1929

   "Financial storm definitely passed."

   – Bernard Baruch, cablegram to Winston Churchill,
   November 15, 1929

5) "[1930 will be] a splendid employment year."

– U.S. Department of Labor,
New Year's Forecast, December 1929

6) "The spring of 1930 marks the end of a period of grave concern ... American business is steadily coming back to a normal level of prosperity." – Julius Barnes, head of Hoover's National Business Survey Conference, March 16, 1930

7) "While the crash only took place six months ago, I am convinced we have now passed through the worst – and with continued unity of effort we shall rapidly recover. There has been no significant bank or industrial failure. That danger, too, is safely behind us." – Herbert Hoover, May 1, 1930

"Gentlemen, you have come sixty days too late. The depression is over."

– Herbert Hoover, responding to a delegation requesting a public works program to help speed the recovery, June 1930

8) "We are now near the end of the declining phase of the depression." – Harvard Economic Society, November 15, 1930

9) "Stabilization at [present] levels is clearly possible."

– Harvard Economic Society, October 31, 1931

10) "All safe deposit boxes in banks or financial institutions have been sealed ... and may only be opened in the presence of an agent of the IRS."

– President Franklin Delano Roosevelt, 1933

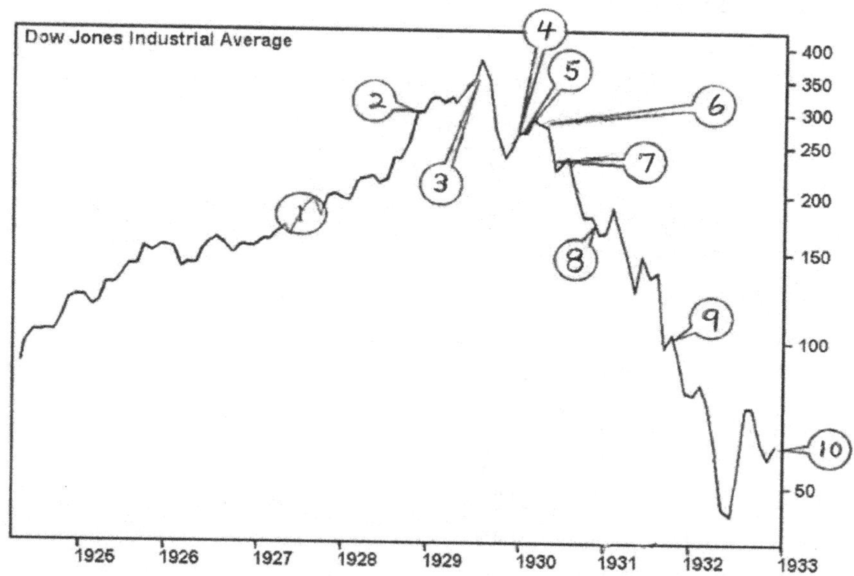

… And while the U.S. economy is presently (2014) at the above level 2, the sinking band continues playing on …

> *"The economy is sound."*
>
> – Ben Bernanke, Chairman of the Federal Reserve

> *"Sub-Prime is contained."*
>
> – Henry Paulson, U.S. Treasury Secretary, during the housing market collapse

> *"The American people should buy stocks at current discounted levels."*
>
> – U.S. figurehead President Barack Obama (aka Kenya-born Barry Soetoro)

The 1929 stock market crash was a prelude to the Great Depression that was followed by WWII. The stock market crash of

2018-2020 will likewise be a portent of the *second* Great Depression in America, and subsequent WWIII.

Elite world leaders ostensibly dictating government policy are not the paragons of decency, morality and virtue which the controlled media hopes to convince the public they exemplify. After the Illuminati-planned demolition and murder of 3000 people in the NYC Twin Towers on September 11, 2001, the political subterfuge disseminated by the global supra-government assaulting the American people with a constant barrage of propaganda lies (the U.S. government had little to do with the incident on 9/11, except to "stand down" and allow it to occur) as a rationale for the staged terror, was to "blame it on the Arabs" in order to justify a war with *Iraq*. (Fourteen out of the 19 *scapegoat* "terrorists" implicated in 9/11 were *Saudis*, not Iraqis.) The real reasons were to exploit Iraq's vast oil reserves, take over control of Afghanistan opium production (one of the world's most lucrative cash crops), and strengthen Zionist Israel's dominance in the Middle East. Osama bin Laden likewise had no involvement with the 9/11 Black Operation, and, like Saddam Hussein, is well known to be a CIA operative for over the last 30 years! (The bin Laden and Bush crime families have been long-standing business partners for decades. On the morning of 9/11 George Bush Sr. is reported to have had a conference with the bin Laden family during a Carlisle Group meeting. Neither was Hussein hanged during a public mock "show trail" that was merely intended for disinformation purposes. A stand-in "look alike" was executed in his stead.)

When dealing with legal criminals, nothing ever appears as it truly is; everything they tell you of any importance is a lie. To follow are more glaring examples of political subterfuge:

> *"I don't know where bin Laden is. I have no idea and I really don't care. It's not that important. It's not our priority."*
> – Former puppet President George W. Bush, March 13, 2002, in reference to the "bin Laden did it" media disinformation

ploy presented to the American public as a rationale for "identifying the perpetrator" of the 9/11 government hoax. This was six months after the media had brainwashed the American citizenry with the gauche fabrication: "The multibillion dollar NORAD strategic air defense of the most powerful military in the world was breached by a small group of foreigners with Swiss army knives led by one man in a rag turban, whom the entire combined forces of the FBI, CIA, and intelligence operatives throughout the world cannot find because he's hiding out in a cave somewhere in Afghanistan." And the vaccine neurologically damaged/MSG/Aspartame/fluoride-drinking American people *actually believe* one individual masterminded 9/11 and was hiding in a cave, plotting and scheming to overthrow America!

"You can fool some of the people all of the time, and those are the ones you want to concentrate on." – George W. Bush

"I can hypnotize a man – without his knowledge or consent – into committing treason against the United States."
– Dr. George Estabrooks, Rhodes Scholar and hypnosis expert with ties to the U.S. military and domestic intelligence, 1942.

"Military men are just dumb, stupid animals to be used as pawns for foreign policy." – Henry Kissinger, quoted by Bob Woodward in *The Final Days*, 1976.

"The only way to world peace is through mind control of the masses."
– Former Prime Minister of Canada, Brian Mulrouny, when speaking to former U.S. President Ronald Reagan. Quoted by Cathy O'Brien in the book, *TRANCEformation of America.*

(Included in a previous chapter, the following quotation merits repeating):

> *"Sarah, if the American people had ever known the truth about what we Bushes have done to this nation, we would be chased down in the streets and lynched."*
>
> – Former Illuminati-appointee and head of the CIA, ersatz U.S. President, and FBI-documented pedophile, George H.W. Bush, Sr., 1992

In summary, it was W.C. Fields who perhaps said it best: "No one ever went broke underestimating the intelligence of the American people."

CHAPTER 8

PARTING COMMENTS

"All truth goes through three stages. First it is ridiculed. Then it is violently opposed. Finally it is accepted as self-evident. – Schopenhauer

A previous timeline forecast of a possible stock market crash transpiring in the years 2012-2013 was aborted by the Illuminati world controllers. A new timeline for the initial crash event is anticipated by the author to be the years 2016-2017, with a secondary decline of greater magnitude in the years 2018-2020. A temporary postponement of the near-term Crash would not benefit the globalist's objectives, and therefore, they have little motivation to suspend its occurrence any longer. In fact, they are at this point in time eager to create a global crisis. The Luciferians have been trying to pass a "Global Warming" Carbon Tax on the "permissible" amount of Carbon dioxide emissions resulting from industrial, commercial, residential, and personal release of CO2 into the atmosphere from burning fossil fuels or from human respiration. Satan's people falsely claim there is a CO2 "greenhouse effect" causing a "global warming trend," but the truth is they want *more control* over our lives and literally seek to regulate our very life breath. (Non-government funded independent scientific research has proven that the atmospheric temperature of the earth is in a *long-term cooling trend*, not global warming. Supra-government sprayed Chemtrails create an atmospheric infrared solar radiation heat-trap to raise ambient air temperature, thus inducing an artificial *localized* temperature increase.) Carbon dioxide is essential for plant growth and is a primary by-product of animal and human metabolism. The world's oceans absorb massive amounts of carbon dioxide as part of the earth's Carbon Cycle, a closed system in equilibrium. Thus, reducing carbon emissions is proven to be yet another *false flag* weapon in the arsenal of the globalists who plan to use the extorted Carbon Tax proceeds to fund the final stage of their NWO political agenda. A Carbon Tax Bill having failed during a recent Copenhagen Conference, the Illuminati are now anxious to create more environmental crisis, such as the BP oil spill, to justify taxing even the air we breathe. Both, Global Warming and a Carbon Tax are *Conspiracy Theories* (ref. Appendix E).

PROJECT MOCKINGBIRD: CIA MEDIA DISINFORMATION AGENTS

The creation of a major world crisis would presently serve the globalist's interests, if for no other reason than because their covert plan is daily becoming more transparent to the general public. Several Internet news reporting websites and alternative media radio talk show forums have made significant strides in exposing important aspects of the Globalist's Agenda to a worldwide audience. Alternative media exposure of the conspiracy is *tolerated* by the globalists, and is often *approved, permitted, and financially supported by them*, in order to monitor the public's reaction to what they, the elite, are doing.

The Illuminati creates *controlled opposition* according to the *Hegelian Dialectic*, positioning their own operatives as leaders of social and political resistance movements. The so-called "Patriot Movement" is an example of how they *control opposition*. Since the time of J. Edgar Hoover, a standard FBI covert citizen surveillance operation known as *Cointelpro* (acronym for Counterintelligence

Program) continues to be implemented to infiltrate, subvert, disrupt; create disinformation, confusion and chaos within and between targeted groups, while provocateuring legal repercussions to vilify those groups and individuals which the CIA/FBI considers "a threat to national security."

Government spy organizations like the National Security Agency (NSA), CIA, and FBI, plant their own people within various citizen factions in order to regulate the flow of damaging leaked information, repress dissent, and foment a sense of fear, hopelessness and disempowerment among group members. *Left-wing/Right-wing* false division paradigm keeps the opposition from uniting against the established NWO. For example, posing as leaders of the "Truth Movement," such compromised "psy-ops" (psychological operations) individuals create an *ineffective* group of insurgent "patriot resisters" by *encouraging inactivity among their followers.* Subtle disinformation is planted among factual truth exposing government corruption, but no solutions are offered, thus neutralizing citizen opposition without firing a shot. Ineffective action is further encouraged by suggesting disgruntled patriots work within the corrupt legal/legislative system (i.e. vote, "write your Congressman," "protest and picket in front of the courthouse," "get signed petitions," "bring about change," etc.). The so-called "Tea Party Movement" and "Patriot Movement" are classic illustrations of government personnel infiltrating an organized citizen movement by which effective resistance to tyranny is rendered *impotent,* stripped of any power or force – and the Illuminati couldn't be happier! Hitler's Propaganda Minister, Joseph Goebbles, understood this tactic well when stating: "It thus becomes vitally important for the State to use all of its powers to *repress dissent,* for the truth is the mortal enemy of *the lie,* and thus by extension, the truth is the greatest enemy of *the State.*" (Emphasis added.)

Project Mockingbird creates operatives that have been groomed and positioned within alternative media (all those working with-in mainstream media are government CIA operatives, whether they realize it or not), and who are sanctioned by the controlling supra-government to function as *simulated resistance* against the NWO (Dialectic Principle). Necessary as agents of disinformation, and serving as "Coadjutors" to engender a sense of fear and psychological neutering among their targeted audience, they work to articulate and diffuse group rage against government tyranny by psychologically disabling the citizenry. Such government counter-intelligence agents divert the public focus away from issues detrimental to special interests of the elite. In so doing, they stifle an effective response to oppose political oppression. What the media infiltrated psy-ops agent has been trained and perhaps mind-controlled programmed to do, is emotionally disarm the public through a process of "information overload" regarding the presumed threat and utter futility of rising up en masse to oppose and defeat the foe. By repeatedly reinforcing this technique, voicing what are essentially mind-control Eastern meditation mantras, the government shill convinces the angry masses of frustrated people not to engage in any effective action. In having been frightened into a state of inactivity, they fulfill the old adage: "Those that fear an overthrow are half-beaten." The manipulated public has been "psyched out." In that regard, consider this poem:

If you think you are beaten, you are.
If you think you dare not, you don't.
If you'd like to win, but think you can't,
It's almost a cinch you won't.
Think you'll lose, and you're lost.
For out in the world we find,
Success begins with a fellow's will –
It's all in a state of mind.
Life's battles don't always go to the stronger or faster man;
But soon or late, the man who wins, is the one who thinks he can.

Certain high profile "patriot leaders" can be trauma-based MK-Ultra mind-controlled subjects (Manchurian Candidates) with programmed multiple personalities that have gained sufficient credibility among their following *to stifle* an effective public uprising against the tyrannical government – e.g. the planted charismatic leader screams and rants, but no effective solutions or action is proposed or undertaken. (True resistance leaders are imprisoned or murdered by the federal government. The most suspect of being Project Mockingbird CIA agents are those who seemingly tell the truth but suffer no adverse repercussions.) Double Agents also function by *collecting names* gathered from visits to their Internet website(s), purchase of their products, or tracking those calling into a toll-free listener comment phone line. Such government shills serve to "smoke out" hidden resistance to be added to a FEMA Camp Pick-up List. In this manner, "the enemy" is identified in advance and located for later efficient "disposal" during Red, Blue and Yellow List police "roundups," presently being conducted.

TIGHTENING OF THE NET

The Internet has by-passed government restrictions placed on free speech, and therefore the level of citizen awareness and corresponding (simulated) resistance against the New World Order is gaining momentum. This is occurring mostly among the idealistic under 30 age group. As a result, the end of unrestricted Internet access is fast approaching. The communist-installed modern U.S. puppet regime government, presumably operating in Washington D.C., has recently approved the "Cybersecurity Act," and the transnational media syndicate (Illuminati) are now proposing "Internet 2" that will soon make informative exposé websites unavailable to the general public – except by registration – for citizen tracking purposes. Search Engines like Google and Yahoo, and online purchasing through EBay and its affiliated debit company, PayPal, as well as personal information gathering sites such as Craigslist, Facebook and Twitter, are all government *data-mining fronts* regulated by the NSA/CIA/FBI.

ONLY TRUE CHRISTIANS CAN KNOW THE TRUTH

The author realizes that some of his views expressed in this volume are unpopular among pseudo-Christianity and Professing Christians, as well as the Criminal Fraternity. But this only serves as confirmation that his position is from a righteous perspective, and therefore, acceptable in the eyes of God, the only audience for Whom this book was written. The author has addressed his concerns to the Truth Audience, and consequently, his stance on key issues will find unanimous consensus *only* among those of like mind, whether there be many or few. Readers bear evidence of their indwelling spirit by their reaction to the truth.

True Christian brothers and sisters will be in agreement with the author on topics eschewed by the dominate majority, especially his views on the reality of spiritual reality in a Biblical sense, his condemnation of the Legal Criminal Fraternity as a hybridized race of human-demon offspring resulting from corrupted spiritual genetics (Genesis 6:4; Daniel 2:43), the reality ofhuman-indwelling fallen angels (demons/devils); and the character transformation, psychological aberrations and cognitive impairment resulting from such symbiosis. Other pivotal issues included organic brain dysfunction caused by the following: drinking fluoridated water, receiving vaccine injections; consuming MSG, Aspartame, GM/GMO "food"; breathing Chemtrail atmospheric mind and body altering bioengineered components, toxic substances and heavy metals; and exposure to the genetic and brain wave function altering electromagnetic grid. These topics were discussed at length because they are relevant to understanding the mindset of the criminal elite who plan to collapse the international economy and bring the world into submission to their dictatorial global Police State. These important issues reveal the psychopathology driving the Illuminati Criminal Fraternity's insatiable madness to cause universal mayhem, death and destruction. Only those readers who yet retain an *intact mind* can appreciate the wisdom of exposing evil in today's world; tearing off the façade masquerading as good, and frankly expressing the truth in unequivocal terms. To state otherwise is an invalidation of the truth message and would immediately position this author in the terrorist government enemy camp.

The enemies of the Lord Jesus Christ *can not* receive the truth because there is no truth in them (ref. 2 Thessalonians 2:10-12). Their spirit is that of their father and progenitor, the father of lies, who promotes lies to be the truth. As his progeny, they are *spiritually incapable* of knowing otherwise, and will therefore reject the author's message, since, how is it possible for them to recognize the truth of a matter when not only their inner *spirit* is corrupt, but also their organic *brain* has deteriorated and been rendered dysfunctional and diseased? How is it possible, when they have been drinking fluoridated water all their life, and from childhood have brushed their teeth with excitotoxic fluoride toothpaste that enters the gum/tooth interface for direct and immediate transport to the brain? How can they correctly perceive reality when GMO's and self-replicating Chemtrail polymer nanofibers have taken over the cell reproductive function of every cell in their body, including their neuronal brain tissue, and created synthetic amino acid protein sequences of their replicating DNA? Truth rejecters are spiritually, psychologically, and cognitively *handicapped*, unable to act as receivers or transmitters of the truth, because they have been further *disabled* by chemical doping with MSG and Aspartame *for decades*! Such a brain – one that has been ravaged by a steady regimen of the vaccine protocol – is a pathetic specimen of a healthy intact mind with the *capability* of discerning truth from falsehood. Truth-haters, because they are indwelled by truth-resisting demons, and because their mental apparatus has become substantially impaired, resist the truth and all those who defend it. Their ability to reason has been incapacitated because their brain chemistry is in a state of toxic imbalance. The demonic hierarchy has infiltrated and directs a mind that has been thus neutralized and shut down higher reasoning functions. Such an individual perceives truth to be lies, and lies to be the truth. This defines the character of the Illuminati/ Criminal Fraternity, as well as all those sympathetic or apathetic to their cause. For such individuals and readers, the author advises a radical departure in their lifestyle, diet and belief system in the hope they may someday engender the cognitive and spiritual faculty to come to a saving knowledge of the truth, receive the spirit of God's indwelling Holy Spirit, and thus arrive at full agreement with the author's truth message. If it be the will of God the Lord Jesus Christ, may He grant such individuals the grace to *repent* in order to receive His free gift of everlasting life.

URGENT NEED FOR "EARTH CLEANSING"

The author is in *complete agreement* with the Illuminati in regard to their multi-generational desire to curb global overpopulation and make the world safer from the threat of terrorists and weapons of mass destruction; and realizes and acknowledges that significant portions of the human race need to be exterminated, euthanized, and systematically "killed off" in order to allow for those remaining to live harmoniously within the earth's fragile ecosystem. Speaking from a eugenics perspective, clearly, certain rapidly proliferating and undesirable segments of the human gene pool need to be eliminated by the most efficacious means available – irrespective of any humanitarian concerns – and as expediently as possible. This protocol is of paramount urgency and importance at this critical point in time, and would serve the "greater good of all," enabling ecological "sustainable development" while lowering population growth and consumption of valuable agricultural and natural resources. The sudden genocidal demise of certain target groups would also lower the crime rate; raise the level of education, health and well being among the general world population; and would serve to improve reproductive fitness for generating better strains of cognitively superior individuals. A higher standard of living would be made possible for those remaining after a much needed "Earth

Cleansing." For these reasons and more, the "undesirables" should be summarily terminated in order to allow space on the planet for those remaining who are of a peaceable nature, fear the God of Heaven, and keep His Commandments. It is *the meek* which *shall inherit the earth*; those who *delight themselves in the abundance of peace* (Psalm 37:11).

Therefore, it is decreed by the perfect and infallible counsel of God Almighty (Revelation 19:17-21) that all Illuminati and their associated Criminal Fraternity underlings, their handlers, masters and controllers – all the way up to the top of the Luciferian pyramid – should be rounded up and quarantined in presently vacant FEMA concentration camps located throughout America and the rest of the world. There, in dirt-floor barracks, the Word of God is to be read to them day and night over a public address system. Those who refuse to repent of their evil deeds and who deny Jesus Christ, should be sent off to fight in military conflicts overseas, becoming fatal casualties of wars which they have created to further their political agenda and for the benefit of their own personal financial interests. Other countries would likewise follow this same mandate in order to insure that the only individuals slaughtered on the battlefield are rank and file members of the Criminal Fraternity. To guarantee their destruction, these socially acceptable criminals are to be relocated to war zone areas contaminated with *Depleted Uranium,* which they shall breathe and thus maximize their exposure to systemic organ damage by lethal radioactivity (with a half-life of 500,000 years). Also, prior to being shipped, the fraternity of criminals should be injected with multiple doses of *vaccines* (up to 99 per session) containing *Thimerosal* Ethyl mercury, Lead, live cancer cells, Arsenic, and the most virulent stealth viruses bioengineered to date (i.e. "Flu shots"). As an added measure to further insure their expedient eradication, the military recruits would be exposed to *concentrated* atmospheric Chemtrail components continuously piped into their group living quarters, and fed a diet consisting solely of GMO/MSG/Aspartame indigestible inorganic derivatives and plasticized polymer-based synthetic facsimile foodstuffs (with a half-life of 500,000 years) such as McDonald's Chicken McNuggets, hamburgers and french fries; Wendy's, Taco Bell, KFC, Chick-Fil-A, etc. The only beverage permissible would, of course, be Hydrofluorosilicic acid municipal tap water (with extra Chlorine, Uranium isotopes and leached pharmaceutical drugs). This dietary regimen would serve as "embalming fluid" to reduce the need and expenditure of later having to bulldoze mass burial gravesites.

And I will feed them that oppress thee with their own flesh; and they shall be drunken with their own blood, as with sweet wine (Isaiah 49:26).

The certain destiny of the *serpent seed of Satan* (Genesis 3:13-15, 6:4; Daniel 2:43; Matthew 3:7, 13:38, 23:33, 24:37; John 8:44; 2 Peter 2:12,14) is total annihilation of their physical body, and subsequent *eternal* torment of their spirit being – experiencing all the pain of a physical body – by the most perverse and sadistic of demons; with constant intense physical burning sensation from engulfing flames of fire in an everlasting process to purify their unrepentant soul and purge them of their diabolical recalcitrant unrighteousness (Revelation 14:9-11). Because of their incorrigible madness, hell is *forever.*

It is the author's sincere hope that only those who are worthy of eternal *Life* may have the right to the Tree of Life and share in the abundance promised by God in His Holy Word: *I am come that they might have life, and that they might have it more abundantly* (John 10:10). Jesus Christ is *the way, the truth, and the life* (John 14:6). *Blessed are they that do his commandments, that they may have right to the tree of life, and may enter in through the gates into the city* (Revelation 22:14). The few rare exceptions who are presently among Satan's government people are hereby advised to call out to the Lord Jesus Christ for mercy. Therein is your *only* hope.

When the legal criminals and pseudo-Christians (still waiting to be "Raptured") appear before the Lord Jesus Christ at the Great

White Throne during the Final Judgment, they will be convicted of their unrepentant wrongdoings and sentenced to an eternity in the burning Lake of Fire, where they will die a *second death* (Revelation 20:11-15). Conversely, God's people, upon physical demise, are immediately translated into an eternal dimension known as "Paradise" or the Kingdom of Heaven, where they will serve the Creator of the Universe (Jesus Christ) with great joy while forever experiencing *true* peace and safety from legal criminals and the Illuminati's corrupt system of tyrannical human government. In the end, everyone shall receive what the Word of God has said they deserve: *And, behold, I come quickly; and my reward is with me, to give every man according as his work shall be* (Revelation 22:12).

A SCENE FROM THE HOLLYWOOD FILM: *A BUG'S LIFE*

The bug archenemies of the world ant population gather to assess the burgeoning overpopulation of "ant people." The bug leader stands before a horde of his comrades to deliver a telling speech:

Leader of the Bugs: "There *was* that ant that stood up to me."

First Soldier Bug: "Yeah. But we can forget about him. It was just one ant."

Leader: "Right! It's just *one ant*!"

Second Soldier Bug: "Yeah, Boss. They're puny!"

Leader: "Puny? ...

[The leader pulls down a bottle filled with hundreds of small kernels of wheat that bury the soldier bugs standing nearby in an avalanche of rock-like grain.]

Leader: "You let one ant stand up to us, then they *all* might stand up! Those puny little ants outnumber us a hundred to one. And if *they* ever figure that out, there goes *our way of life*! It's not about *food*; it's about keeping those ants *in line*!"

"... it's about keeping those *people* in line." Take heed people. There are 100 of us for every one of *them*. (Somehow, the Illuminati allowed this revealing insight to slip past their controlled media censor. Or, did they think it no longer matters?)

WAKE UP SHEEPLE! ... THEY'RE LAUGHING AT YOU!

When you cast your vote, they're laughing at you! When you watch television or listen to the evening news, they're laughing at you! When you turn in your guns, they're laughing at you! When you sit in a darkened room and watch their witchcraft sorcery Hollywood films, they're laughing at you! When you look at yourself in the mirror and wonder why you can't lose weight, feel sick, and have been diagnosed with heart disease, cancer, diabetes and Alzheimer's, they're laughing at you! When you wonder why your child has Autism, they're laughing at you! When you go to the doctor, they're laughing at you! When you go to the supermarket, they're laughing at you! When you dine at restaurants, they're laughing at you! When you drink the tap water, they're laughing at you! When you submit to illegal coerced extortion payments (personal income taxes) to fund the Federal Reserve and their murderous Globalist Agenda (and your own destruction), they're laughing at you! When you send your children to public and private schools, they're laughing at you! When you wonder why your children are drug addicted, sodomites and lesbians, they're laughing at you! When your sons and daughters join the military to die in foreign wars that benefit the private interests of the elite, and are used as expendable "collateral damage" for testing vaccines and other biochemical warfare agents, they're laughing at you! When you submit to government-mandated forced vaccinations of your children, they're laughing at you! When you receive a "Flu shot," they're laughing at you! When your children report you to the police for administering Biblically-advised corporeal punishment, owning firearms, or upholding the Constitution and Bill of Rights, they're laughing at you! When you attend a 501(c)3 government-approved church, and remain silent, they're laughing at you! When government TSA employees grope you, your spouse and children at airport "security check points," and you do nothing to stop them, they're laughing at you! When you drive down the road in your GPS-equipped car, they're laughing at you! When they create the next "terrorist act," and you believe their "official version" lie, they'll be laughing at you! When you go to the bank to withdraw your funds and see the militarized police standing guard at the closed locked doors, they'll be laughing at you! When they soon crash Wall Street and the world banking system collapses, and they start WWIII, they'll be laughing at you! When they Taser you, your wife and children with a paralyzing electroshock dart, handcuff and take all of you away to a FEMA concentration camp, they'll be laughing at you! And when you succumb to receive their microchip implant, they'll be laughing at you! … for eternity!

Now that you know the truth, you have a decision to make: You can either Wake Up! … or, you can continue being sprayed by Chemtrails, consume weaponized food and beverages, drink IQ-lowering fluoridated tap water, allow your children to be inoculated with lifelong vaccine diseases, not home school your children but send them to government reprogramming public and private schools, attend government-approved churches, stand by powerless as TSA government perverts grope your family, let the Illuminati wipe out your life savings in the coming economic Crash, watch TV, vote … and go back to sleep, Sheeple.

Good Night.

Those who would make themselves "Sheep" shall be eaten by "Wolves."

APPENDIX A

Biblical Prophetic Timeline

Key Dates	Elapsed Time (Yrs)	Event	Supporting Scriptures
	0	Dark Void	Genesis 1:2
11,000 BC	0	Creation of empty space ("Big Bang")	Genesis 1:3-5 Psalm 90:4 2 Peter 3:8
9000 BC	2,000	God created the spiritual universe (Heaven) and the physical galactic universe	Genesis 1:6-8
8000 BC	3,000	God created the Earth	Genesis 1:9-10
7000 BC	4,000	God created time: the sun and moon	Genesis 1:14-18
4988 BC	6,012	God created man	Genesis 1:26,27,31
4000 BC	7,000	Seventh Day of Creation: God rested	Genesis 2:1-3
3930 BC	7,070	Birth of Noah	Genesis 5:28,29
3330 BC	7,670	The Great Flood	Genesis 6:17;7:6,11
3040 BC	7,960	Birth of Abram (1948 years from birth of Adam)	Genesis 11:26
2965 BC	8,035	God covenants with Abraham; establishes His Covenant with mankind	Genesis 12:1-3
2882 BC	8,118	Birth of Jacob (Israel) Birth of the physical nation of Israel	Genesis 25:26 Genesis 32:28;35:10

Key Dates	Elapsed Time (Yrs)	Event	Supporting Scriptures
1948 AD	12,948	Re-establishment of the physical nation of Israel; symbolic fulfillment of Abrahamic Covenant Completion of 69 weeks of Daniel Jerusalem encompassed by its enemies	Jer 29:10,14 Amos 9:14,15 Daniel 9:25 Luke 21:20
2018 AD	13,018	Completion of the seventieth week of Daniel 3 1/2 years from 2014 Antichrist inauguration End of the present Earth Age (May 14, 2018 is 70 years from rebirth of Israel) Crash of world financial markets	Jer 25:11; Dan 9:2 Daniel 12:11 Matthew 24:22
2020 AD	13,020	13,000 years of creation history 7,000 years of mankind upon Earth; "Mark of the Beast" cashless economy	Ezekial 7:17-19 Zephaniah 1:10-18 James 5:1-3 Genesis 1:9-10 Genesis 1:26 Revelation 13:16,17
2051 AD?	13,051	End of the reign of Antichrist End of the New World Order WWIII Battle of Armageddon Return of Jesus Christ	Revelation 19:19-20 Isaiah 21:9; Rev 14:8;18:2 Rev 16:16;19:17-21; Rev 6:12-17; Isaiah 2:19,21; Joel 2.3 Rev 19:11-16;22:20

Jesus Christ, the Word of God (Revelation 19:13), God in the flesh, (John 1:14), *spoke* (Genesis 1:3) the entire universe into existence (Genesis 1:1; John 1:1-3; Psalm 33:6). There was *no time* involved for the creation of space to form an expanding universe. Creation was an *instantaneous* event manifested at infinite supraluminal speed. God – i.e. His physical manifestation in the personhood of Jesus Christ – set the space/time continuum and galaxies in their initial rotational state by the act of speaking His Word (Genesis 1:1,3). The Latin word, "Universe" (Uni-verse) means "single spoken sentence." After the single spoken sentence uttered by God: *Let there be light* (Genesis 1:3), the initial lighter elements, as well as Oxygen (H2O, water) were created (Genesis 1:6). After the creation of the lighter elements (Hydrogen, Helium, etc), including the substance water, God created the other elements (Genesis 1:9).

The vast distances (14 billion Light Years) reported by cosmologists, and their corresponding calculation for the age of the universe (14 billion years), is not in conflict with the above Biblical timeline specifying 6 Days of Creation. The reason for this is because at the speed of light there is no time; the measurement of time collapses to absolute zero at light speed. Therefore, from a relativistic perspective of an observer on Earth (i.e. Earth time), the physical matter occupying distant space *appears to be* billions of miles away, and *appears to be* billions of Light Years old, but *only* in a relativistic "R*ed Shift*" time-distorted sense. From God's infinite timeless perspective relative to the passage of Earth time recorded in the Genesis 6-day account of Creation, the 13,000 year history of the universe is a true and accurate assessment of Earth time/distance.

Red Shift is a physical measurement that identifies in terms of *lengthening* electromagnetic wave length how fast an object is *receding* as a function of its distance from a point source. There exists an inverse relationship between time/displacement of distant matter and the perception of that time/displacement. At relativistic speed (near or at the speed of light), as distance increases, earth bound *human perception* of the magnitude of that distance correspondingly decreases. As the speed of an object approaches the velocity of light, time slows down to near zero, but when perceived by a distant observer on Earth, *time dilates* – i.e. the expanded red-shifted longer wave lengths of light can make time/distance appear to be millions, or even billions, of years; when in fact, little *non-relativistic* time/distance has transpired. This perception is in accordance with the *exponential rate of expansion*, which reduces the perceived time/distance by 1/2 for each doubling unit of time/distance observation. Therefore, with each doubling in the size of the universe, the perceived time for that doubling is quadrupled. In the initial stages of space expansion, when the universe was relatively small, a relatively small unit of time transpired. But as the universe became larger – as the Word of God proceeded to travel from the point source of having been spoken by God (i.e., the so-called "Big Bang") – there was an incremental increase of Earth-bound time perception. For example, as a result of the Red Shift phenomenon and exponential expansion factor, a universe that appears to be 14 billion light years in diameter/old is actually a mere fraction of that size/age – i.e. 1/1,000,000 (14 billion/13,000). Therefore, an observer positioned outside of the time dimension perceives the passage of time as 13,000 years (Genesis 1:6-8), and his time clock for Earth point of reference has been in existence for 13,000 years. From the perspective of Earth, six days of creating the universe (Genesis 1:3-5; Psalm 90:4; 2 Peter 3:8) required 14 billion years and produced a universe that is perceived to be 14 billion Light Years in diameter. Hence, the speed of light cannot be used as an absolute measurement for cosmological time or distance.

At present, the universe has been in existence for about 13,000 years. From the creation of planet Earth (Genesis 1:9,10), the current age of Earth is approximately 10,010 years. (Scripturally, 10 is the number for *testimony*.) Starting from the Biblical account given in Genesis 5:3-32; 11:10-26, establishing the birth of Abraham at

3040 BC, Noah at 3930 BC, Adam at 4988 BC, and the 6 Days of Creation – 1,000 years each, (plus 1,000 years for the seventh day God rested), and thus arriving at 11,000 BC for the beginning of creation – as of this writing, the physical universe can be derived as having been in existence for 13,010 years.

Abram was born exactly *1948* years from the creation of the first man, Adam. God made a covenant with Abram, who later became *Abraham, the father of all nations.* At the time of God's covenant with the human race, Abraham was 75 years old (Genesis 11:31;12:4). Then departing from Ur of the Chaldees to reside in Canaan, this would have been the year 2965 BC. The year *1948* AD was the date that *physical* Israel once again became a nation after the Roman Captivity in 70AD, thus symbolically fulfilling God's Abrahamic covenant with mankind (Daniel 9:25). This was 4,900 years (70 years x 70) subsequent to God's covenant with Abraham. As previously stated, the number 7, and multiples thereof, are highly significant throughout the Bible for designating completion or perfection. Thus, 70 times 70 is *double confirmation* for the significance of the year 1948. (4900 years - 2965BC + *13 years* = 1948AD. The 13 year remainder can be attributed to differences in ancient versus modern calendars, and also, to any author computational error.) Another prophetic date to consider during that time period is 2882 BC, the birth of Jacob, who's name was changed by God to "Israel." The Daniel 9:24,25 prophetic 69 weeks of 70 years (4830 years) ended in 1948, thus making this the third confirmation of 1948 as the prophetic reinstatement of the physical nation of Israel (4830 years - 2882BC = 1948AD). The year 1948 is clearly significant as a benchmark for measuring the time remaining for the fulfillment of future Bible prophesies

Referencing Jeremiah 25:11 and Daniel 9:2, seventy years are appointed by God for the desolation of Jerusalem. Therefore, physical Jerusalem (ancient Israel) – the nation that disobeyed God's Commandments and rebelled against Him – was the Old Covenant with Abraham that reiterates with the New Covenant

True Christian people (New Jerusalem). Seventy years added to 1948 yields the year 2018. The year 2018-2019 therefore seems to be a key terminal date which fulfills Scripture prophesy.

There are two iterations: Old Testament *physical* Israel and New Testament *spiritual* Israel. The *New Israelite* people of *New Israel* – i.e. *New Jerusalem* (Revelation 3:12;21:2) – are the totality of those *Born Again* throughout all of human history. These are the Elect Remnant, irrespective of race or ethnicity (Romans 9:6-8;25-27); *they* are the *True* Christians.

The year 2018-2019 would mark the end of the 7th day – i.e. seventh millennium since the creation of the first man, Adam (7,000 years - 4988BC = 2012AD). Subsequent to this date would be the commencement of the 1000 year reign of Jesus Christ on Earth (Revelation 20:4-6). Adding this future 1000 year period to the existing 13,000 year historical interval, yields 14,000 years of Earth history, a *double iteration* of the highly significant Biblical 7000 years denoting *completion.*

It therefore appears that within a brief span of time from this writing, God will begin all over again with a new cast of characters – those of His choosing: the Elect Remnant. During the 7000 year "Great Earth Experiment," all others were merely acting as "fodder," resistance to be overcome by the relatively few *True* believers and their unshakable faith and trust in their Messiah, Jesus Christ. During the fourteenth millennium since the creation of the universe, the next 1000 years (approximately 2050-3050), will be God's reign on Earth. There will be no Criminal Fraternity, no New World Order, no human/demon hybrid mass-murdering Devil-worshipping Luciferian financial elite stalking the earth. To the glory of God, Satan's people will be conspicuously absent from New Jerusalem. Once again – as it was in the Garden of Eden – for the next 1000 years the spiritual Kingdom of New Jerusalem on Earth (Revelation 3:12;21:2,10-27;22:1-5) will be a place of great tranquility and harmony; a paradise, where God's people will live in the invisible spiritual realm, unmolested by Satan's government people who will physically reside outside the gates, in a netherworld wasteland created by their own destruction. New Jerusalem will be a place where the Elect saints will … *delight themselves in the abundance of peace* (Psalm 37:11). In the very near future, God will resume where He left off with Adam and Eve.

The Great Deceiver, Father of Lies: Lucifer/Satan, has only a brief time remaining for his duped stooges (the Illuminati globalists and millions of their underling Criminal Fraternity henchmen) to fumble with their *doomed* Plan. In just a few more years the temporary rulership of this planet will be transferred back to its original rightful Ruler – Jesus Christ/LORD God Almighty – God Himself.

There exists a potential for a 33 year time extension beyond 2018-2019, until the year 2051, based on the 33 year period of Jesus Christ during which He preached, "… *repent ye and believe the gospel* (Mark 1:15). This duration corresponds to a period of grace in which all of Israel shall be saved (Romans 11:26) – i.e. True Christians. While the 2020 terminal date is likely correct for anticipating a major world cataclysm, there remains a possibility that it represents only the start of God's judgment and global destruction foretold in the Book of Revelation. In that case, it will require another generation of human beings for bringing about the fulfillment of the Bible prophecy.

The 2051 terminal date was given to the author by God in a revelation at the time when this book was being prepared for publication, immediately subsequent to a conversation with someone regarding an end time date and salvation of the Elect. The year 2050-2051 is the first Jubilee year (7 x 7 years) of the new 7th Millennium.

APPENDIX B

Proofs for the *True* Age of the Earth

Proof #1: The distance light travels in 1 year is called a "Light Year." The velocity of light is 186,000 miles per second. The distance that light would travel in a universe created 13,000 years ago is 76 quadrillion miles (the number 76 followed by 15 zeros). According to the evolutionists – those agnostics and atheists who deny the Word of God – the universe has been in existence for 14 *billion* years. (Some estimates are of considerably longer duration, e.g. 78 billion years.) In that period of time light would have traveled over *1 million times further* than in 13,000 years. The universe would therefore be *1 million times larger* than is possible from the Genesis account of creation. A 14 billion year old universe would be 82 million trillion miles in diameter (82 quadrillion x 1 million).

The problem with believing the universe is 1 million times older than what the Bible teaches is that the distribution of matter throughout the visible universe would be more sparse than if creation began only 13,000 years ago, assuming matter is being equally created and destroyed (yet the amount of matter in the universe is constant; no one has ever observed a new star being formed). Hubble telescope images of deep space reveal a tightly compacted universe. The "fudge factor" of 1 million Light Years is a function of *relativistic time distortion* (*Red Shift* of the electromagnetic spectrum) and the *exponential rate of expansion* (ref. Appendix A). A reported disparity of 1 million Light Years also just happens to "conveniently support" an evolutionary theory which requires millions, or even billions, of years for order to emerge from a state of random chaos. This not only violates the Law of Entropy, but if that feat were in fact possible, the kingdom of the globalist's New World Order Criminal Fraternity would *improve* over time and actually become *better* in a Biblical sense. But that is not reality, since Satan's people are known for their moral degeneracy and become worse over time, not better. *But evil men and seducers shall wax worse and worse, deceiving and being deceived* (2 Timothy 3:13). The old universe theory, like the old Earth theory, is not based on a God-ordained science, but rather God-rejecting evolutionary *science fiction.*

Time-distance estimates for the diameter of the universe and its age have been inflated by a factor of 7 (1 million). For example, the Milky Way galaxy is said to be 100,000 Light Years in diameter. Light from the sun reaches the planet Pluto at the farthest reaches of the Solar System in an average of 54 minutes. If light required 100,000 years to transverse the Milky Way, then our Milky Way galaxy would be 58 billion times the size of the Solar System. This not only proves to be visually inaccurate (by inspection of Hubble telescope images from NASA's Cosmic Background Explorer's diffuse Infrared Background Experiment), but – if Einstein's Relativity Theory is discarded – a Milky Way galaxy that is 58 billion times larger than the Sun's Planetary System would be 7.69 times larger than the extensivity of the entire 13,000 Light Year universe! Therefore, the Milky Way, and the known galactic universe, is much smaller in a non-relativistic sense than determined by cosmological measurements exclusive of *Red Shift* time-space considerations. (Illuminati-controlled *NASA* = *N*ever *A* *S*traight *A*nswer.)

Proof #2: Fossil records of certain single-celled plankton, known as foraminifera, found in sediment layers beneath the ocean, indicate that the salinity of the ocean water was significantly decreased during a time in Earth's history that corresponds with the Great Flood. The discarded shells of these creatures when they die and drop to the ocean bottom form a geological record of temperature and salinity of the ocean water. Examination of core samples show that oxygen isotope ratios indicate a temporary decrease in ocean water salinity during a period of time thousands of years ago that corresponds with the Biblical account of a worldwide flood at the time of Noah. This supports the young Earth 6 Day Creation account being true and correct.

Proof #3: The Earth's magnetic field is losing strength as a function of time. Since 1829, a scientific record has been kept of the planet's magnetic field strength, which shows that it has declined by about 7 percent since that time. Subsequent measurements plotted graphically illustrate a natural order of exponential decay. From this data can be determined a 1400 year half-life for the strength of the magnetic field. When extrapolated, the figures show that the earth's magnetic field was much stronger in the past than in the present. An earth that is millions of years old would have an exponentially high field strength. In fact, just 20 thousand years ago the magnetic field strength would have been too strong to support life. Data compiled by physicist Dr. Thomas Barnes reveals that the field strength is decaying at a rate of 5% per century, and was 40% stronger in 1000 AD than it is today. Commenting on Barnes' discoveries, researcher Jonathan Sarfati said: "... the earth's magnetic field was caused by a decaying electric current in the earth's metallic core ... could not have been decaying for more than 10,000 years, or else its original strength would have been large enough to melt the earth. So the earth must be younger than that."

Proof #4: The oldest living life form on earth is a Bristle Cone Pine tree in Southern California, which can be dated back 4300 years, to a time period after the Flood when the first trees would have started to grow again. This proof once again supports the Biblical account of a young Earth that is thousands, not millions, of years old.

Proof #5: Layers of sedimentary rock are presumed by geologists to have required many millions of years to be deposited, as in the so-called "geologic column" visible in the Grand Canyon. But there is evidence which points to exactly the opposite conclusion: fossilized trees found standing vertically among many layers of sedimentary rock deposits. This rapid sediment deposition could only have occurred in a brief period of time – months, or even weeks – such as would have transpired during a worldwide flood, and could not have taken place over a period of geologic time. The formation of the Grand Canyon can be experimentally proven by simulated studies of erosion from a draining body of water through the mile of sediment deposits left by receding Flood waters. (Geological evidence exists for a post-Flood lake adjacent to the present-day Grand Canyon.)

Proof #6: Written records only go back 6,000 years. If man were on earth for the duration claimed by evolutionists – i.e. hundreds of thousands, or even millions, of years – where is the written record? The Old Testament Bible – God's written record to mankind – has been in a physical written form since the time of Moses and the prophets. (But it has existed since before the beginning of time. John 1:1; Psalm 119:89.) Paleontologists theorize that Stone Age man existed *190,000 years* before beginning to make written records. If man had been upon the earth for this period of evolutionary time, there would be an extant record of written communication. Since none exists, the ancient age of mankind, like that believed of the Earth, is proven to be a scientific fraud.

Proof #7: Over time, the sun is rapidly decreasing in size. Scientists have been keeping records of the sun's diameter for more than 300 years, and have calculated that the rate of shrinkage is 5 feet per hour. At that rate, one million years ago the radius of the sun would be twice its present radius. Thus, the farther back in time, the larger its radius would have been. It has been determined that the rate of shrinkage in the past was faster than it is today. Using these figures, the sun would have been large enough to touch the earth only 20 million years ago. Evolutionists believe the Earth is 4 billion years old. Based on the rate of solar shrinkage, this is clearly an impossibility. The Earth has not been in existence for millions of years, but only for thousands of years.

Proof #8: DNA decays in a natural environment as a result of exposure to cosmic radiation and other factors which cause errors in the transcription process of cellular reproduction (mutations). Experts in DNA genetics have recently concluded that the mutation rate of mitochondrial DNA necessitates revision of "mitochondrial Eve" from 200,000 years ago to a mere 6,000 years ago, and no more than 10,000 years. This lowered time range coincides with the Biblical record for the creation of mankind (7,000 years ago). Fossil dinosaur bones have been excavated which still have soft tissue attached. This could not occur if the time since their extinction was measured in millions of years, but is possible only for a timeline spanning a few thousand years.

As of the year 2010, mankind has inhabited the Earth for 6,998 years [4,988 BC (birth of Adam) + 2,010 years (year 0 to 2010 AD)]. This is in stark opposition to the elapsed time believed by archeologists and paleontologists who cite figures for the duration of human habitation on Earth ranging from 200,000 to 8 million years!

The inherent limited accuracy of radioactive Carbon 14 Dating (fossilized remains from different parts of the same animal have shown a difference of hundreds of thousands of years!) is partially the reason for this lack of agreement; the remainder is *political*. Antichrist government-funded "scientific" research is guaranteed to produce anti-Biblical results. In addition to not taking into consideration red shifted *relativistic time distortion*, their erroneous age of the universe is ideologically motivated. It is a propaganda campaign by Satan's people attempting to discredit intelligent design by Jesus Christ, the Creator God of the universe, replacing Him with the Globalist's Agenda of man as an "evolving animal"; and not only biological evolution, but also social and moral "evolution." The only problem with their "moral improvement theory" is that mankind as a whole is not improving with time, but is progressively deteriorating and becoming *worse* (2 Timothy 3:13). Those denying a Creator God are merely seeking justification for their own moral depravity. Psalm 14:1: *The fool hath said in his heart, There is no God. They are corrupt, they have done abominable works, there is none that doeth good.* Romans 1:20-22: *For the invisible things of him from the creation of the world are clearly seen, being understood by the things that are made, even his eternal power and Godhead; so that they are without excuse. Because that, when they knew God, they glorified him not as God, neither were thankful; but became vain in their imaginations, and their foolish heart was darkened. Professing themselves to be wise, they became fools.*

Darwin's contrived and now debunked "Theory of Evolution" only succeeds in proving the impossibility of greater complexity arising from simpler forms. (It also violates the First and Second Laws of Thermodynamics, which God created.) A case in point is "Nebraska Man": In 1922, an excavated artifact was thought to belong to an early ancestor in human evolution. From this archeological find was reconstructed a prehistoric human-like creature, yet, the scientists seemed to have overlooked the fact that their "evidence" was somewhat lacking. Not only was "Nebraska Man" reconstituted from the dentition of a small forest-dwelling animal, a peccary, but his *entire genealogical family* was recreated – wife, children and cousins – totally reconstructed, from that *one pig tooth*! Needless to say, attempts to validate Darwinian Evolution are often as comical as they are impossible. Its derivative anti-God philosophy – Eastern Mysticism New Age "spiritual evolution" – is likewise a laughable farce. According to evolutionary theory, depending upon which "pig tooth" is used for C-14 analysis, the origin and age of mankind is *also* "evolving" – i.e. *it varies*. Organic evolution (living forms evolving from nonliving matter) and Carbon 14 Dating requires an astronomical "leap of faith" (i.e. guess work). Any respected scientist today rejects it; only those most hardened toward God can believe in absurdities.

APPENDIX C

15 Reasons why *this* is the Terminal Generation

Now learn a parable of the fig tree; When his branch is yet tender, and putteth forth leaves, ye know that summer is nigh: So likewise ye, when ye shall see all these things, know that it is near, even at the doors. Verily I say unto you, this generation shall not pass, till all these things be fulfilled.

– Matthew 24:32-34

1) Since 1948, for the first time in 2000 years, the physical nation of Israel has been re-established (reborn) in fulfillment of Bible prophesy, which uses the symbolism of a sprouting "fig tree" when referring to the original covenant people (Matthew 24:32-34; Mark 13:28-30; Luke 21:29-32). These Scriptures foretell that the generation which is living at the time of Israel's rebirth will be the *last* generation ... *this generation shall not pass, till all these things be fulfilled.* (Matthew 24:34). A biblical generation is 70 years. Anyone born after 1948 is "*this generation,*" and is, at most, 62 years old at the time of this writing. Therefore, a minimum of 8 years from the date this is written (2010) remains until "*this generation*" passes – i.e. 2018. (ref. Chapter 6 and Appendix A.).

2) By Luciferian globalist's design, among the chief causes of human infertility are Hydrofluorosilicic acid added to municipal

drinking water, Aspartame and MSG in all processed packaged foods, estrogenic compounds in all soy products, including soy-based infant formulas and many other processed foods; estrogen-mimicking Bipshenol-A present in plastic baby bottles and all hard plastic products. These factors cause feminization of boys, creating obese asexual young males later incapable of reproduction, and early onset of puberty in girls (7 years old and younger). Hormone-altering chemical substances in the world food supply and drinking water have created an exponential increase in male sterility and female infertility. Lowered reproductive success of the global population by mass sterilization with forced vaccines; food, water, Chemtrail air doping; government mandated zero population policies, abortions, Planned Parenthood, hospital euthanasia of elderly.

3) Genocidal global vaccination programs government-mandated after staged non-existent health threats such as "Bird Flu," "Swine Flu," etc., and third world population control vaccines disguised as a "public health disease preventative," have presently created a worldwide population with latent cancer, diabetes, AIDS, Alzheimer's, and other degenerative terminal diseases. The cancer rate has increased from near zero in the early 1900's, to its current incident rate of 1 in 2 people; Diabetes is diagnosed among 1 person in 3. Stealth diseases such as Morgellons, Parkinson's and other debilitating neurological disorders can be transmitted by Chemtrails.

4) Agricultural crops engineered with Genetically Modified Organisms (GMO's), when consumed by animals and humans, produce lethal pesticide toxins from intestinal flora in the human digestive system. GM plant seeds with terminator genes render agricultural plants unable to germinate and reproduce, resulting in dependency upon government-controlled non-heirloom seeds for food production and consequent global

mass starvation. (During the 1920's, Stalin murdered 20 million subsistence farmers when confiscating their crop harvest and cutting off their supplies.) Genetic engineering of plants and animals is *permanent*; once the genetic code of the plant and animal kingdom has been changed and introduced into the wild species population, it can never be retrieved or restored back to its original state. Transgenetic cross-contamination of native species by pollen drift from agricultural GM crops commonly occurs. Genetic Modification of edible plant species is known to cause sterility and reproductive failure in animals and humans. In the U.S. the majority of agricultural crops are artificially pollinated (ref. 8). Corn and cotton seeds spliced with the genetically modified organism, Bacillus thuringiensis (BT) causes sterility and neurological (suicidal) effects in test animals.

5) Impending WWIII; many Third World countries now have weapons of mass destruction.

6) Artificially modified weather resulting from HAARP microwave transmissions and Scalar Technology creates flooding and droughts to agricultural crop areas, causing global food shortages, worldwide famine.

7) Planet X, a small brown dwarf star that never attained a temperature hot enough to ignite, is a wandering celestial body with a mass 3 times the size of Jupiter and a gravitational force 1000 times that of Earth. It is approaching the Solar System (or is reportedly *now* in our Solar System, located somewhere between the planets Neptune and Jupiter) and expected to soon pass near the Earth, causing magnetic pole shifts triggering earthquakes and volcanoes, with resulting massive seismic oceanic tsunamis and severe weather of a magnitude never before seen. Luke 21:25,26,31,32: *And there shall be signs in the sun, and in the moon, and in the stars; and upon the earth distress of nations,*

with perplexity; the sea and the waves roaring; Men's heart failing them for fear, and for looking after those things which are coming on the earth: for the powers of heaven shall be shaken … so likewise ye, when ye see these things come to pass, know ye that the kingdom of God is nigh at hand. Verily I say unto you, This generation shall not pass away, till all be fulfilled.

It is said the rogue star will bring in its train asteroids from the outer solar system Kuiper Belt, some of which have been calculated will collide with the Earth's surface. An asteroid just 1 mile in diameter is sufficient to eradicate a significant portion of life on this planet (Revelation 8:7). There exists tens of thousands of asteroids in near earth orbit which fulfill this size criterion. Earth changes resulting from Planet X's gravitational pull upon the Earth's liquid molten mantle will cause a shift of the seismic plates, with consequent earthquakes, volcanoes, tsunamis. The present frequency of these natural phenomena is increasing at a geometric rate, thus lending credibility to the suspected approach of the mysterious celestial body. This is in fulfillment of the prophesy in Matthew 24:4; Luke 21:11: … *and fearful sights and great signs shall there be from heaven.* Isaiah 13:5,13 is possibly a further reference to the consequences of a magnetic pole shift created by an approaching strong gravitational force such as a wandering celestial body: *They come from a far country, from the end of heaven, even the LORD, and the weapons of his indignation, to destroy the whole land.… Therefore I will shake the heavens, and the earth shall remove out of her place, in the wrath of the LORD of hosts, and in the day of his fierce anger.*

8) Disappearance of honey bees. Essential for plant pollination and human food production, the current estimate is a 70 percent reduction worldwide. Albert Einstein predicted the end of all life on Earth within 4 years of loss of the world's bee colonies. Japan's bee population has already been eradicated; in America it has been decimated. Globally, pollinating bees have

been nearly exterminated by genetic modification of plant species. Bacillus thuringiensis (BT) and other GM plant alterations causing sterility, are a known factor in bee extinction, termed Colony Collapse Syndrome. Chemtrails acting in conjunction with HAARP, could also be implicated. These two causal factors may be responsible for massive bird falls from the sky; hundreds of thousands of birds suddenly dropping to the ground dead, covering entire cities. Also, extensive fish kill-offs in the oceans and lakes.

9) The Illuminati's biotechnology human extermination campaign is producing worldwide diseases and plagues in fulfillment of Bible prophesy (Matthew 24:7; Luke 21:11). Genetic engineering agricultural crops has rendered foods unable to be assimilated by animals and humans, causing diseases and plagues in previously healthy populations.

10) Dramatic reported increase in human contact with transdimensional entities erroneously believed to be "extraterrestrials," but which are in fact Biblically-described devils/demons. Material manifestations are on the rise (Revelation 9:1-11). Increase in human physical contact with demons (i.e. UFO's, "aliens," "greys," "ET's," etc). Human-demon hybrids in high political office and key government positions (Genesis 6:4; Daniel 4:17) are under deadlines for establishing a world government. These deadlines all focus upon a single initiating event: *global economic disaster.* The author anticipates the first of two major disasters to transpire in the years 2012-2013 (economic); the second global disaster in 2018-2019 (environmental).

11) Race specific plagues: AIDS, BSE, etc. Over 50 percent of the African population has died of vaccine-transmitted AIDS; the other half are carriers for spreading this fatal disease. Genocidal terminal diseases transmitted by vaccines are legally mandated

for U.S. citizenry under the false flag guise of "fighting terrorism" and "disease prevention."

12) Rebuilding of the third Jerusalem Temple and renewal of the daily sacrifice is about to begin. When the daily sacrifice is taken away by the new world dictator, Antichrist (at the time of his inauguration in the Jerusalem temple?), another terminal date prophesy will have been fulfilled (Daniel 8:11,11:31). Subsequent to that event, 1335 days remain (3 years, 7 months, 27 days; Daniel 12:11-13) until the return of Jesus Christ and the end of this present Earth Age.

13) In fulfillment of Revelation 17:12,13 endtime prophesy, the world is to be divided into 10 regions. This has already been decreed by UN legislation. Presently, the process of political global unification is nearly completed: the North American continent (Mexico, U.S., Canada) has since 2005 been united as the North American Union, with its own currency, the Amero; the Eastern European nations have been united under the European Union, with the Euro currency replacing European nation-state currencies. When these two continental currencies are politically unified, and then further united with the African, Asian and Australian continents and their currencies, a global political and economic system of world government will have been created in preparation for the rise of the Antichrist global dictator.

14) British Petroleum (BP) oil spill in the Gulf of Mexico (June 2010) could be the fulfillment of the Second Vile Judgment endtime prophesy of Revelation 8:8-9 and 16:3: *And the second angel poured out his vile upon the sea; and it became as the blood of a dead man: and every living soul died in the sea.* A dead man's blood turns from bright red to brownish dark red with darker patches of coagulated dried blood; the color of oil in water is brownish dark red with darker patches of undispersed congealed oil. As

this book is in its final stages of preparation before going to print, the most recent terrorist act staged by the Illuminati has become the greatest man made ecological disaster in history; the off-shore drilling well exuding 2 1/2 million barrels of oil into the ocean *per day*. This massive *daily* release of oil is equivalent to the *total amount* lost during the USS Valdez oil spill in Prudhoe Bay, Alaska. There reportedly exists no effective means to stop the gushing flow of oil from a "21 mile long fissure in the ocean floor", or from "leaks from breaks in the mile-long collapsed pipeline" (conflicting media disinformation). This tragedy has the potential for becoming global and killing off all life in the interconnected ocean waters. During the subsequent third Vial Judgment of Revelation 8:10-11 and 16:4, all the inland surface and subterranean ground water becomes tainted with toxic blood-like oil. Revelation 8:11: ... *many men died of the waters, because they were made bitter.* Hurricanes and connecting inland waterways will transpose oily sea water and toxic chemical "oil dispersant" to the continental States, fulfilling this subsequent Third Vial Judgment: *And the third angel poured out his vial upon the rivers and fountains of waters; and they became blood.* As part of the oil remediation effort, GM mutant oil-eating bacteria are causing physiological harm to the endemic plant and animal species and subsequently to humans. Relief efforts are blocked that could stop the oil flow and clean up the spill. A planted explosive created the leak, killing 11 people on board the drilling platform; the global elite allowing the spill to continue. The undersea oil reserve is estimated to require 9000 days (25 years) to deplete. The Gulf Oil Spill is yet another government-staged act of terrorism with a broader agenda yet to be ascertained.

15) Matthew 16:4: *A wicked and adulterous generation seeketh after a sign, and there shall no sign be given unto it, but the sign of the prophet Jonas.* The sign of the prophet Jonas was the great whale. Recently, a whale was sighted in the Mediterranean Sea, off

Tele Aviv; a Grey Whale, not seen in this area for approximately 300 years. Normally inhabiting the Pacific Ocean, a whale in the Mediterranean is "the equivalent of finding a dinosaur in your back yard," said a whale researcher. In December 2010, this extremely rare event was witnessed worldwide via modern TV and Internet media. Based on the size of the whale, it has been estimated to be 60 years of age. The modern nation of Israel, reborn in 1948, has been in existence for 62 years – i.e. the whale and Israel were born at the same time. This gives credibility to the belief that the whale, like the reformed nation of Israel, is prophetic.

"The sign of the prophet Jonas" is an earlier reference (Matthew 12:40) Jesus made of the correlation between Jonah spending three days and three nights in the stomach of a whale, and Jesus subsequently spending three days and three nights in the grave. Is it possible for the later verse, Matthew 16:4, to have been said by Jesus in reference to the endtime sighting of a "Jonas whale" in the vicinity of Israel?

APPENDIX D

Published Forecast Documentation

The following documentation correctly anticipated major turning points and declines in the U.S. stock indices. It is a record of key historical stock market events preceding a future anticipated major collapse of the U.S. and global economies. Most forecasts were published *before the events occurred.* (Dates of published documentation are in parenthesis):

1) The third largest weekly and monthly Dow Jones Industrial Average point decline in the 218 year history of the New York Stock Exchange: August, 1998. (August 9,13,23, September 27, 1998).

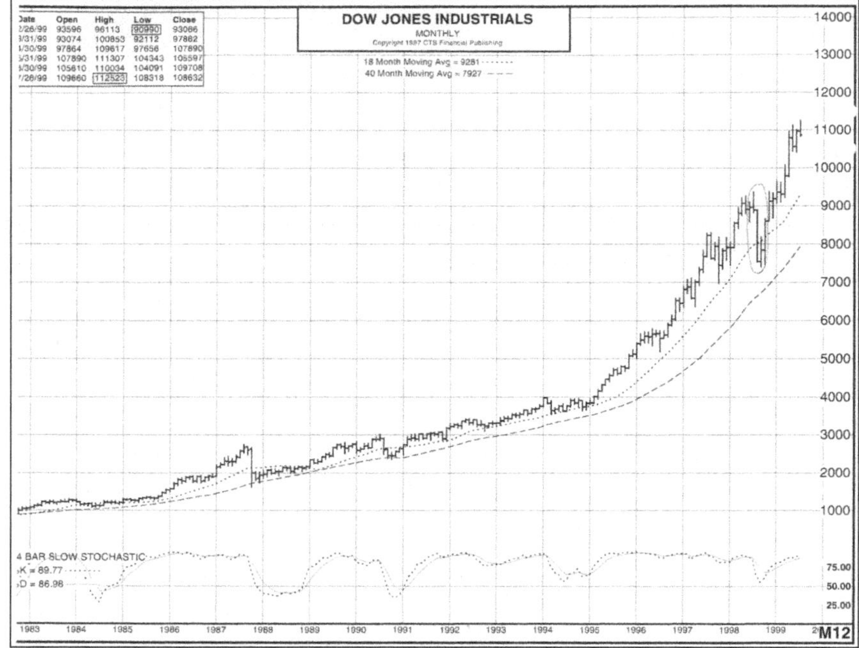

Monthly Chart

The red arrows indicate the dates for a Plain Dealer ad warning of an imminent decline, which occurred just days after the 3rd ad ran. The 1300 point drop between 8/25 - 9/1, was the 3rd largest weekly decline in the 200 year history of the stockmarket. The 4th ad, appearing on 9/27, once again EXACTLY PRECEEDED a significant drop - this time for 700 points. On a monthly basis, the 2 month decline, representing 2000 points, was the 3rd largest historical decline ever.

Daily Chart

)EALER · SUNDAY, AUGUST 9, 1998

siness Opportunities

GEPPETTO'S
'IZZA & RIBS
e part of your neigh- 'ranchise opportuni- able in Cleveland & w and EXISTING res- ites available. Call nchise Recruitment 505-0040

ket/Gourmet Gift Co. ne for holidays. Lg. 'rofitable. Inventory, nail & customer lists. 3 mornings.

GO FISH !
vel Window Cleaning e. Immediate cash - ured accounts. $26k t. 20 yrs. exp. INDOW CLEANING 531 for free info pkge.

-unique repeat busi- v score card system. nand. No competition. 'd. NOW 888-866-9823.

usiness opportunities: . 65,000 sq. ft. 7 acres

b. $2.5 million. b. $320,000. 'ederick, COLDWELL HUNTER REALTY. 440) 777-8500 or 3628 VM.

rea investment Corp. s Investor to open N-3 Grill & Bar 440-232-0356

NG CARD Distributor- 'l co. No selling. Co. rt time. Only $6900 re- o start. 800-917-9500

Deli Mart - Established lage thriving business! enses! Priced to sell! Bob or Brenda at Cen- All Service, Inc. 00.

East: Conv type. Busy eat potent'l. Only $39k. -21 Byrne Rlty 449-7404

RY, East. Convenient ies. $700,000 440-871-8479

RY STORE FOR SALE cation, lottery & food Call: 216-661-7768

R CLEANING service. tomers. 216-371-2444.

AP TRANSP. Business . Up & running. Call 0-232-1961. Only serious only, please.

High Income
No Selling Involved

en minutes of your time ut more about this very business opportunity. 18-791-5337.

H Prestige printing ess. Personal reasons. ell. No exp. necessary. . Bert - 1-800-645-3006.

Based Business. Double come 216-371-4528

IMPROVEMENT Com- ce location. Serving a six area. Twelve year BBB r. Turnkey operation. 5-4358 Days: 440-474-9661

IMAN RESOURCES conduct interviews per Activities true genius

0800 Business Opportunities

LIQUOR LICENSE-Solon, D5 Fax inquires to: 440-708-0211

MACHINE SHOP
Established shop with excellent customer base. Conventional type equipment. Sales $160,000. Asking $100,000. Some owner financing.
EMPIRE 216-462-0161

MAIL ORDER womens golfing catalog for sale, $250,000 sales from home. EBB 216-621-4041

★ ★ MAKE BIG $$ ★ ★
Per hr. with our new unbelievable vending concept. Locations included, low invest.
★ ★ 1-800-807-1178/24 hrs. ★ ★

Make up to $247,500 distributing our complete line of money-making software for free- we fulfill all orders. Write to P.O. Box 1136, Chardon, OH 44024-5136 or visit our web site at: http://infodiskpro.com/diskover

MALL FOOD BUSINESS
Best in mall. Top Mall. Sales $540,000. Profit $77,000. Hi growth. Ask $120K down.
FULLER & ASSOCIATES INC.
Canton 330-492-6294

MANUFACTURING. Lamp shades. Excellent gross profits! Terms. Broker 216-486-8911.

MEDICAL BILLING!
Join our growing team of successful Entrepreneurs. ACCUMEDIC, an industry leader for over 20 yrs. Process medical/dental claims. Excell training & support. 800-903-1303 x32048

MEDICAL BILLING
Unlimited income potential. FT/PT Investment $4,995/$8,495. Financing avail. For free information call IAMS (800) 322-1139 Ext. 1413

MEDICAL Billing, guaranteed training/support. Work home. Modest investment.
Call 800-500-4456

★★★★★★★★★★★★
MEDICAL BILLING
Work on your computer, full or part time. Processing insurance claims for doctors and dentists. Complete training.
CLIENTS PROVIDED
800-933-1809 Ext. 29
★★★★★★★★★★★★

MEDICAL BILLING A+
Exciting program! Free report by industry leader explains superior software, training, support & client acq. program. Start up $4,995+. Call to qualify for free computer.
NCS 800-207-3711 ext 645

MLK - Grocery Store, Fully Equipped-Lottery $67,000 Owner Will Help W/Financing HAGGINS REALTY 216-291-9800

MOMS Make full/part time income from home. 216-228-4759.

MOTO X: Profitable business for Sale. Clothing, parts, accessories. $15,000/best offer 440-593-3735 • 440-593-683

MOVING Company, est. 1950, great opportunity. Paid off 1st year. Lots of cash flow. Serious inquiries please. $30,000 216-676-8888.

NEIGHBORHOOD TAVERN & restaurant, totally remodled. hotest place in town. Serious

0800 Business Opportunities

PIZZERIA & restaurant, seats 40, newly decorated, east suburbs. $31,500. Call 440-286-4131.

PostalAnnex
A NATIONAL LEADER
in postal business services franchising
• Own your own business
• Training & support
• Copying/business services
Now available in your area!
Contact Jim for free info:
1-800-456-1525
+ + + + +

PRINTING/Ad Specialties Business. Great opty. for the 90's entrepreneur! Est. accounts. Call Bob at: Equi-Serv 440-734-7632. Prinsipal only.

PRINT SHOP (Commercial) Family owned 40 yrs., retiring Broker 440-942-0199

PURCHASE PROPERTY. Pennies on the dollar! 614-675-1179.

RADIO SHACK Dealership available. Successful. Serious inquiries only. 330-335-9501.

RESTAURANT, Franchise setup with no franchise fees! Turnkey operation! Money maker! $70,000! Eastside location. Company One Rlty. 440-333-8700

RESTAURANT LOUNGE with real estate. Building 3069 sq.ft. On 3.29 acres, Madison, Ohio. Health forces 50% reduced price M. B. A. Realty 216-459-1460

RESTAURANT DOWN TOWN D1,D2,D3,D6, Seats 130, term M. B. A. Realty 216-459-1460

RETURN YOUR $29K investment (100% secured) as fast as 90 days. Service local accounts. 1-800-323-3866

Sandwich Shop West. Tom C., CENTURY 21 DePiero 440-842-7010.

SEEK BUSINESS ASSOCIATE to help me open branch of my unusual service business in OH. Grossing 1M+ with high repeat. Investment $15,000. Will train. Mr. K. 1-800-229-2276.

SEEKING licensed hair dresser with own following, or willing to help for business partnership or booth rental. Westside. Call Christina. 216-221-9008.

SERVICE COMPANY requires working partner with $12,000 investment to manage 8-10 field techs. Salary $40K plus profits. 905-354-0909.

SIGN FRANCHISE has a well established location avail. Must sell immediately. Very low initial investment. No reasonable offer will be refused. Full training and support. Financing avail. 1-800-[illegible]

STOCK MARKET CRASH!
Coming soon. 1929 style sudden decline can make YOU instantly wealthy. Don't be among the losers. One time opportunity, ACT NOW! 216-

[illegible] possibilities. Call [illegible] Said, Realty One. 356-22[illegible]

TANNING SALON FOR SALE

0800 Business Opportunities

TANNING SALON- 14235 Detroit Ave. $28,900/neg. Realty One. Cherie Nemic, 440-304-4167

TANNING Salon for sale. 7 bed facility in S.E. suburbs. $17,500. For info call 216-429-5111.

TENT Bus. (party)-Turn key, truck, tents, tables/chairs, etc. $25,000. 440-286-1455

THE ATLANTA BREAD COMPANY
The highly successful upscale neighborhood bakery cafe, serving soups, salads, sandwiches, variety breads, pastries and bagels is interviewing potential franchisees in Cleveland. Financing may be available to qualified candidates. Phone John Byron at (800) 398-3728, ext. 103
www.atlantabread.com

TOP SECRET
The fastest and easiest way to make money. Work at home. Call 1-800-811-2141. Code #58097.

Tuffy
Auto Service Centers
Is Expanding In The Cleveland Area. New Location Available In Parma Hts, Call Jim Jacobs
1-800-228-3339

ULTIMATE Vending $10 & $20 Vends. No Soda, No Snacks, No Selling. Free Sample. Invest Required 800-737-9495 24/hrs

VENDING MACHINES
(5) Combo, Soda & Snack. $4000/Offer. 440-543-7704

VENDING mfr. needs distributor. Instant profits. OK credit-100% financing. 1-800-805-9621

VENDING ROUTE - westside. 28 snack & pop units on location doing over $30,000 annually. $950 ea. Call E. Havel at 440-845-2112

VIAGRA AND PROPECIA
"2 Hottest Drugs in the World"
DISTRIBUTORS NEEDED!
Toll-Free 888-353-0953
KESSLER PHARMACEUTICAL

VIDEO. For south. Nice profits! Let's deal...Broker 216-486-8911.

VIDEO store closing, everything must go. West 330-225-1208.

Want To Work For Yourself? Consider a CAREER in real estate and new home sales. Call Adrian Frederick at COLDWELL BANKER HUNTER REALTY for more details at 777-8500/327-2123

WATER Treatment, sales & service, excellent dealership, great training. ERANCO 216-621-4041

★ ★ WESTLAKE ★ ★
Busy Award winning Tanning Salon, 15 yrs. est. clientele. 5 beds, computerized. Inventory. Call: Shelly Williams-Mikes. 440-234-3883. $65,000.

0800 Business Opportunities

W. SPRINGFIELD PA 15 unit motel, 1 effic. apt., frame office, Col. house, Sherango steel bldg. 36x64x10. Convenient location o. I-90 & 6N to Rt. 20. On approx. 17 acres leaving acreage for expansion. Tower on property pays yearly taxes. Owner will finance portion. 814-922-3550, leave msg if no answer: EJ's Motel, 13825 Ridge Rd. & Rt. 20.

0840 Financial

TOUGH TIMES?
If you're in the market for a signature loan or debt consolidation with less than perfect credit: let First Choice Funding be your only choice. 937-252-4677 or 800-873-8810

WELL KEPT SECRET
Buy Stock Direct (216)732-3279

0850 Money to Loan

AAA CREDIT NOT REQUIRED
Cash For Any Reason. Home Owners Only. 1-800-USA-MONY

ALL TYPES OF MORTGAGES
Best Available terms for good, bad or no credit! Call anytime MORTGAGE PLUS 888-460-6846. Licensed Mortgage Banker.

CASH FOR ANY PURPOSE
Qualifying Loans In Days. Real Estate, Stop Foreclosure Perry 330-656-4125 /330-650-6935

LEASE any type of equipment for your business. Low down payment. Prime Leasing Co. 734-3666

LOANS BY PHONE
Financial Problems Handled w/Dignity
call Bentley Financial Services
1-800-459-0004

MONEY FAST
FOR
ANY REASON
FROM YOUR HOME
•Quick Closings
•No Broker or Application Fees
•Any Type of Credit OK
•Self Employed or Fixed Income
•Investment Property OK
•Professional Personal Service
A DIRECT LENDER
NOT A BROKER
ALTERNATIVE LENDING
Mortgage Corp.
800-613-6179

PAYDAY ADVANCES
LOANS
No Credit. 216-556-1907 24/hrs.

PRIVATE Investor - Must secure w/real estate. Loans $50,000 & up. Any reason. 440-526-1345.

0860 Money Wanted

0860 M

I need to borr back A.S.A.P

Collect results us Sports Collec

★NEED
Music co. hc and is unable to keep up w mand. Offeri return for $5(

WANT
Will pay back for 9 years. property wor with clear de Also, 12 ye Please call 4

1600

INVITA
Sealed bids the office of Board of Par Cleveland M tration Buil Parkway, Clc until 2:00 P August, 199 will be put read.

BID
#3688: DE TION to be Cleveland Courses o basis for a #3701: NAT for a one (1 #3702: RO plied "as ne 98/99 #3703: JAN be supplied one (1) yea

Bids must sealed en marked wit number an Specificatio and envelop during regu office of the are to be with the inv and specific submitted blank suppl may be wi sixty (60) c duled closin of bids. P after appro Park Comr bids will be BY ORDER PARK COM THE DIRECTO CLEVELAN

p.d.aug9,16

INVIT LEC Sealed bid

First Notice

THE PLAIN DEALER · THURSDAY, AUGUST 13, 1998

0800 Business Opportunities

BAR+bldg. near mills. lo price. Collins Broker 216-362-1692

FRANCHISE OPPORTUNITY
SOUTHPARK CENTER
WETZEL'S PRETZELS
(626) 432-6900 EXT. 17

FREE REPORT! Get rich in mail order in 7 wks. 888-757-1883

HANDICAP TRANSP. Business for sale. Up & running. Call 7p-8p, 440-232-1961. Only serious inquiries only, please.

JANI-KING
#1 Commercial Cleaning Franchise Co. in the world. We offer from $1,000 to $50,000 in monthly contracts. 29 years in business. Member BBB. For free brochure and video call
[illegible]

STOCK MARKET CRASH!
coming soon. many will LOSE fortunes, but I'll show you how to MAKE a fortune! don't miss this rare opp't'y for INSTANT WEALTH time ltd, so HURRY! Call for info:

VIAGRA AND PROPECIA
"2 Hottest Drugs in the World"
DISTRIBUTORS NEEDED!
Toll-Free 888-353-0953
KESSLER PHARMACEUTICAL

WANTED: insurance agencies, east/west, lge./sm. 440-461-0804

0850 Money to Loan

AAA CREDIT NOT REQUIRED
Cash For Any Reason: Home Owners Only. 1-800-USA-MONY

CASH FOR ANY PURPOSE
Qualifying Loans In Days.
Real Estate, Stop Foreclosure
Perry 330-656-4125 /330-650-6935

MONEY FAST FOR ANY REASON
FROM YOUR HOME
•Quick Closings
•No Broker or Application Fees

1240 Dogs, Pets and Supplies

BEAGLES Pups, 8 weeks, shots, wormed, lemon & white & tri-colors. $75. each. 330-656-3524

BEARDED Collie, AKC, male, 14 wks old, first shots, partially housebroke. $400. 419-892-2978

BICHON AKC MALE PUP
Shots, Beautiful. $475
440-888-8363

BICHON FRISE - AKC, 6wks. Shots, wormed. $400-450. 419-846-8001, Mike.

BICHONS AKC. $385.
AKC CAIRNS-$325.
330-833-6556

★ BLOODHOUND AKC ★
Black & Tan, Red pups. Shots & dewormed. $500. 216-351-5892.

BORDER COLLIE MIX PUPPIES: adorable, gentle. $[illegible] ea. 216-281-4057

BOSTON Terrier, male, 11 mos., shots, housebroken, great pet. $200. 330-847-9195

BOSTON Terrier Puppy, AKC, female, 9 wks. old, shots & wormed. Call: 419-896-2325

BOXER Puppy, fawn female, 9 weeks old, have parents. Call 330-659-3012 or 330-712-3681

BOXER PUPS AKC:
Parents on premises. 1 female, 1 male, 7 wks, brindle & fawn. $350-$400. 330-645-0462.

BOXER pups, AKC 2 fawn males, 11wks, shots/wormed, excellent w/kids. $400. 330-630-0526

BOXER PUPS, AKC, 1 male, 6 females, fawn and white, $400. Call 330-562-7646.

BRITTANY Mix Rescue: Rupert needs a home! 7 mos., neutered family pet. 440-439-8026

BRITTANY Pups, top CH line, orange & livers, hunters & pets, shots, wormed. $300. 440-968-3431

BULLDOG pups, CH. bloodlines-grandparent #3 in nation, parents on premises, males & females. Great variety. $1500. 740-681-9201

BULLMASTIFF, AKC,
6 Months old, Shots, Fawn.
330-659-3971 - leave message

CAINE Corso, black, 8mo old, $800. 216-371-2697 after 5:30pm.

CAIRN TERRIERS AKC pups, 1st shots, $375 & up. 440-422-3503.

CANARIES: guar. male singers, & health. $50 w/cage; $40 without & lowered when buying pairs. 440-240-1728-leave msg.

CAT-Domestic short hair

1240 Dogs, Pets and Supplies

DOG Kennels(2) w/roof, 4'x10', 6'x11'. $150 ea. 330-220-8395 or Voice Mail 216-875-0849

ENGLISH Bull Dogs - 9 wks. 1 male, $1500; 1 female, $1200. Red & white. Exceptional Ch. sire. Show quality. Parents on premises, home raised. 440-777-4339.

ENGLISH Bulldog Pups, AKC, Ch sire, lge boned, show quality, shots & wormed. 330-220-5035

FERRETS- 3 pairs, all neutered & spayed, shots. Vet checked. $75/pair. Cages also for sale. 440-884-0150

FERRETS Neutered & Spayed Pair, must stay together, 2 Yrs., Playful, Cage, $50. 440-543-4719

FINCHES (Zebra) $6 a piece,
216-906-2641.

Foster Homes Needed Volunteer position for mother cat & kittens. Vet bills paid. 216-226-8598

GERMAN Shepherd pups, quality bred, hip/health guar., black & black/tan. $500 440-248-6676

GERMAN SHEPPARD Pups AKC, black/tan, big-boned, 8wks shots/wormed. $350 440-858-9760

GERMAN SHEPHERD PUPS, AKC/OFA, black/tan; black/red, shots/wormed, $350. 330-[illegible]

GERMAN SHEPHERDS AKC
Exceptional pups, strong & healthy, all colors. Female & young male adults avail. Gentle companions, excellent temperament $100-up 440-636-6202

GERMAN SHEPHERD AKC PUPS
Outstanding White Polar Bear type. Reasonable. 440-636-6202

GERMAN Shepherd, WHITE AKC pups, Calif. lines. Taking deps. now $400-up. 330-659-9378.

GERMAN Shorthair Pointers, AKC, Excellent hunting dog & pets. Has 1st shots. 419-884-2418

GERMAN Short Haired Pointer Pups, AKC, excellent hunting stock. 440-298-9854 after 5.

GREAT DANE AKC, 6 Pups, Brindle, 7 Wks., Ch lines, Shots, Wormed. $500/Ea. 440-729-0638

GREAT DANE pups, AKC, show/pet, ears cropped, ready to go home. Call 937-437-3701.

GREAT Dane Pups, AKC, Bred For Temperament, Pet & Show Quality $400 Up. 440-235-2770.

GREAT Pyrenees, OFA/CH parents, quality puppies, lovingly raised. 216-671-4507.

HIMALAYAN CFA kittens, vet

1240 Dogs, Pets and Supplies

PEKINGNESE pups, 1st shot, male and female, $250.
330-922-4061

PIT BULL PUPPIES, black and white, Kingfish/Rocco, $200. 440-428-1578 or 0955

PITBULL Puppies, ADBA. Carver bloodline, $100. Call 216-231-0638

PIT BULL PUPS
Champion pedigrees. Ancestors of Patrick, Tudor, Anderson, Sherwood, Rocco. Dogs as seen in the World of the American Pit Bull Terrier Book. ADBA registered, shots & wormed. $400. Serious inquires only. 724-656-9069

PIT BULLS PUPPIES, Purebred. 5wks. $125. 216-939-9353, after 7p; 216-861-0248 before 6p.

POMERANIANS, AKC, 5 mo. to 4 yrs, pet & show quality, shots, wormed. $200 & up 440-779-9280

POODLES & Yorkies (10), Toy, Mini, Tiny, shots. Bred for disposition. $200-$375. (330) 856-4039

POODLE, Toy, Pups, Creams & Apricot, AKC, shots/wormed/dews. $325-$350. 216-251-3805

PUG PUPS, AKC, 1st shots & wormed. $400 each. 330-695-4875

PUPPIES 3 pure shepherd pups $100ea. 8wks; Lab mix $50ea. 8wks; Brittany Spaniel mix. 16 wks., $50. Shot/wormed. 440-546-0634/440-582-1749.

PUPPIES, 8 weeks, shots, wormed, cage trained, medium to large, $45. ea. 330-656-3524

RABBITS, Dwarf - Adorable! White, brown & gray, 6 wks. Ready now. $20. 216-429-3447.

RARE BREED-CANE CORSO
Beautiful black, blue & brindle; lge.-boned, Mastiff 8 wk. old pups. First shots/wormed, parents on premises. Registered ICCF. 216-475-3365 or 216-283-5653

REPTILES, 2 adult male bearded dragons, $50 ea., and one 7½ foot female boa, proven breeder, $50. Call 216-761-4052 after 6pm

REPTILES, Savanah Monitor, 18", $40. BALL Python, 3', $50. Both friendly. 440-934-2704

ROTTWEILER Pups-$300. Grown adults-$200. With papers.
216-517-8824

ROTTWEILER PUPPIES, AKC, 8wks, parents on premises. $500. 330-296-5197

ROTTWEILER puppies, 6 wks. old, 1st shots, parents on premises. $300. Call 216-991-3595

1260 Horses, Stables, Trailers, Stock and Equipment

AQHA western pleasure prospects. Weanlings & 2yr.old bay mare. Priced to sell. Riverwood Farm 419-663-4443, Norwalk OH

ARAB, Reg.- MOVING, MUST SELL. Geld, gray, 11 yrs. old, flashy, versatile, great all around. $2500. 440-593-2299.

BOX STALLS AVAILABLE
Full care, Indoor arena, Hinkley, $180/month. 330-273-1941

DBL.E. REG. Buck Skin Quarter Horse, 8 yr. gelding. Great show prospect. $4000. 440-748-1041.

DONKEYS, Variety of loveable, registered, miniature.
440-236-3603, after 4pm

GENTLE Morgan Mare - Needs good home. Good family/trail horse. 440-236-3624.

HORSE Dispersal: Quarter Horses, TB's, 100% sound. Must sell, reasonable prices, well trained. Call: 440-834-4356

QUARTER Pony, Dark Bay, 14.3H, Eqitation-Always In The Ribbons, $2000. (440) 238-0464

REG. 5 yr. old Orange Bay Thoroughbred, good for novice to intermediate, $2500/offer. Yearling Thoroughbred Filly, chocolate color, big- 15.3HH, quiet. $1800/offer. 2 yr. old quarter filly, Soral, 15.2 HH, stout & straight, $3000/offer. Wheenling Dun Overo Paint colt, 2 blue eyes, straight, quiet, $4000/offer.
★330-945-6420, Sarah★

REG. TENN. WALKERS - 3 yr old & 5 yr old, good temperment. $1800 ea. Aft. 4, 330-274-2589

TB MARE 11 yrs., 16.1 Hands, liver Chestnut, wonderful mover good hunter prospect, needs exp'd rider, $2000./best offer. work 440-349-1000 ext 3470, or eves. 440-498-0884

TENNESSEE Walker- (2) Reg.; Black, yearling colt, $1500/best offer & Sorrel Weanling Filly, $2500. Both very gentle & have been handled extensively. 419-529-3002.

TENNESSEE WALKERS
(330) 227-3666

THOROUGHBRED Gelding, 8 yrs. old. 16.3+, dark bay, very handsome, $1500. 330-634-9387.

1270 Machinery, Tools, Motors and Material-Handling Equipment

AA Affordable Steel Sq. & Rect-

1300 Home Fu[rnishings,] Appliances

BDRM Set 3 pc, wood, armoire, bed/mattress $1500./offer 216-

BDRM set, 4pc, quiries. Ca 216-64

BDRM set, Lane incl. full mattres $600. Antique La $350. 10½' sof tables, lamps i coffee table $50. excellent cond. offers. 330-562-42

BED, Black Head/Footboar tress Set, Still $1200. Sell $365.

BED-brass hea queen size mattr Never opened o sell! $250. 440-89

BEDDING: Q Never used $175 Set $155. 330-478-

BEDRM. SET, 6 Large Queen Be $1900. (440) 885-2

BENCHCRAFT couch, blue, 1½ cond. Lifetime g $900, take $450. 2

BUNK Bed, all w guards & matt Never used. 440-3

BUNK BEDS-c w/mattress's-Nev duty. $175. Cleve

BUNK BEDS, sol lacquer oak finis mattress. Never box. $180. 330-630-

BUNK BEDS - UN PINE W/MATT HEAVY DUTY.

CARPET: 150 yds $4.00/yd. 330-478-9

CARPET: Shop Good quality, can 216-939-1543

CENTRAL AIR New - in box. R install. 440-543-27

CHINA CABINET ING STEREO, wh teal, excellent c or best offer. 216-

COUCH & Love S wood trim, beige tables avail, $300.

COUCH, Sectiona 2 mo. old. GOR 440-572-4946 or

Second Notice

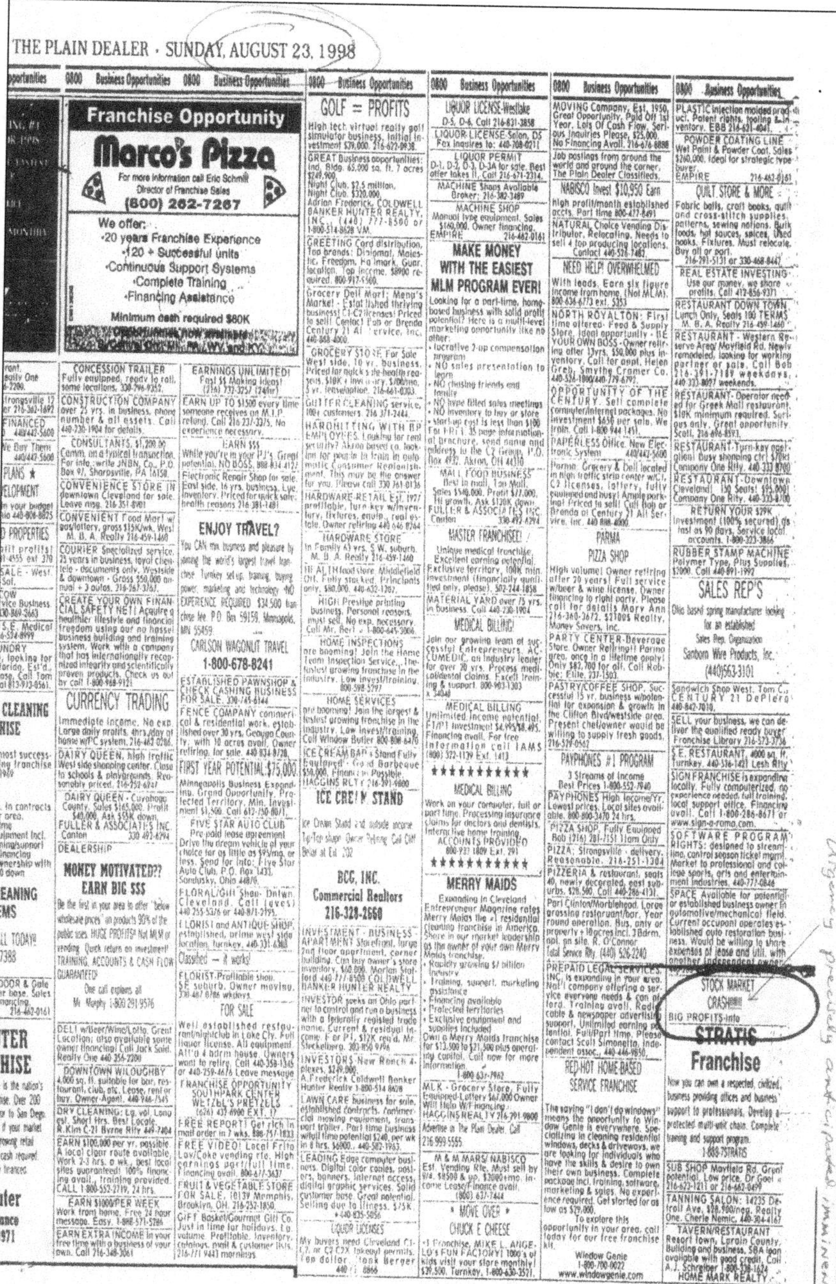

THE PLAIN DEALER · SUNDAY, AUGUST 23, 1998

0800 Business Opportunities

Franchise Opportunity

Marco's Pizza

For more information call Eric Schmitt
Director of Franchise Sales
(800) 262-7267

We offer:
- 20 years Franchise Experience
- 120 + Successful units
- Continuous Support Systems
- Complete Training
- Financing Assistance

Minimum cash required $80K

GOLF = PROFITS

High tech virtual reality golf simulator business, Initial investment $39,000. 216-622-0938.

GREAT Business opportunities: Ind. Bldg. 65,000 sq. ft. 7 acres $249,900. Night Club. $2.5 million. Night Club. $320,000. Adrian Frederick, COLDWELL BANKER HUNTER REALTY, INC. (440) 777-8500 or 1-800-514-8628 VM.

GREETING Card distribution, Top brands: Diplomat, Majestic, Freedom, Hallmark, Guar. location. Top income. $8900 required. 800-917-5500.

Grocery Deli Mart: Meng's Market - Established thriving business! C1-C2 licenses! Priced to sell! Contact Bob or Brenda Century 21 Al Service, Inc. 440-888-4000.

GROCERY STORE For Sale West side, 10 yr. business. Priced for quick sale-health reasons. $10K + inventory. $/mo. 5 yr. lease/option. 216-661-0303.

GUTTER CLEANING service, 100+ customers. 216 371-2444.

LIQUOR LICENSE-Westlake D-5, D-6, Call 216-831-3858

LIQUOR LICENSE-Solon, D5 Fax inquires to: 440-708-0211

LIQUOR PERMIT D-1, D-2, D-3, D-3A for sale. Best offer takes it. Call 216-671-2314.

MACHINE Shops Available Broker: 216-382-3489

MACHINE SHOP Manual type equipment. Sales $160,000. Owner financing. EMPIRE 216-462-0161

MAKE MONEY WITH THE EASIEST MLM PROGRAM EVER!

Looking for a part-time, home-based business with solid profit potential? Here is a multi-level marketing opportunity like no other:
- lucrative 2-up compensation program
- NO sales presentation to learn
- NO chasing friends and family
- NO hype filled sales meetings
- NO inventory to buy or store
- start-up cost is less than $100

S.E. RESTAURANT, 4000 sq. ft. Turnkey. 440-526-1421 Lesh Rlty

SIGN FRANCHISE is expanding locally. Fully computerized, no experience needed, full training, local support office. Financing avail. Call 1-800-286-8671 or www.sign-a-rama.com.

SOFTWARE PROGRAM RIGHTS: designed to streamline, control season ticket mgmt. Market to professional and college sports, arts and entertainment industries. 440-777-0846

SPACE Available for potential or established business owner in automotive/mechanical field. Current occupant operates established auto restoration business. Would be willing to share expenses of lease and util. with another independent owner.

STOCK MARKET
CRASH!!!!!
BIG PROFITS-info

STRATIS
Franchise

Now you can own a respected, civilized, business providing offices and business support to professionals. Develop a protected multi-unit chain. Complete training and support program.
1-888-7STRATIS

SUB SHOP Mayfield Rd. Great potential. Low price. Dr Goel 216-623-1211 or 216-662-0499

TANNING SALON: 14235 Detroit Ave. $28,900/neg. Realty One. Cherie Nemic. 440-304-4167

TAVERN/RESTAURANT

Urgency precisely anticipated imminence

Third Notice

THE PLAIN DEALER SUNDAY, SEPTEMBER 27, 1998

0800 Business Opportunities

SAM's Show Bar & Grill, 3217 W. 25th, w/license. 216-741-0100

SCREEN PRINTING EQUIPMENT & supplies. Perfect for home-based business or commercial. $8500. Days 330-225-1209 or Eves. 330-220-4096

SEARCHING FOR MORE THAN JUST A JOB?

We are looking for friendly, energetic, conscientious, service-oriented people to join our team. We have opened 70 dry cleaning stores across the U.S., mainly in the Southeast and Midwest. Our Operator/Managers earn their way to owning their own business in 3 years. Guaranteed salary during the time before purchase. Incredible income potential in the multi-billion dollar dry cleaning market, at 50% of the price charged by the competition. We will give you training in operating a small business and assist you in being successful. There is no capital investment needed by the Operator/Manager. Immediate opportunities are available in Ohio, Kansas, Georgia and Missouri. No previous dry cleaning experience is necessary. Send your resume to: WH Cleaners, Inc., 5950 Berkshire Lane, Suite 300, Dallas, Texas, 75225 or FAX to 214-691-3376 or send via e-mail to carol@whcleaners.com No calls, please. EOE

SEEKING licensed hair dresser with own following, or willing to help for business partnership or booth rental. Westside. Call Christina, 216-221-9008.

SERIOUS Income Potential. Health & Nutrition Industry. www.[illegible].com [illegible]

SEVEN-ELEVEN #1 in OHIO High profit, Pay off in 1½ yrs. M. B. A. Realty 216-459-1460

SHOES & Shoe Repair for sale day 216-531-3339/eve 440-442-8488

SPECIALTY Womans Retail Franchise [illegible]

STOCK MARKET CRASH #2

15x's return in 1 wk! That's what you would have made on the 1300 pt. DJIA drop (8/25-8/31) I predicted 5 wks ago (see 8/23 ad). #2 coming soon - don't miss ANOTHER opportunity to make a fortune! I'll show you how. Call Today!

[illegible] SALON FOR SALE $13,000 neg. 216-529-0812

THE ATLANTA BREAD COMPANY

The highly successful upscale neighborhood bakery cafe, serving soups, salads, sandwiches, variety breads, pastries and bagels is interviewing potential [illegible]

0800 Business Opportunities

ULTIMATE Vending $10 & $20 Vends. No Soda, No Snacks, No Selling. Free Sample. Invest Required 800-737-9495 24hrs

USED Car Lot For Lease Westpark Area. 330-239-4046

VCR - CAMCORDER REPAIR in business 15 yrs. Much possibilities & potential. A-1 eastside location, Young tech will do well. Illness forces sale 216-464-4840.

VENDING 1st time opp't'y. Prime locations. OK credit-100% financing. 1-800-903-5017

VENDING, 23 pops-candy, on 11 locations, $10K. Joe 440-842-6060

VENDING, BULK ROUTES - 35 locations. Greater Cleveland Area. - 440-285-7585

VENDING MACHINES, (10) w/oak stands. $1400 for all. Call 1-888-228-4991 ext. 0195

VENDING Machines/Route- Start business. 440-646-9171.

VENDING - Used Mr. Vend novelty equipment. 16 units, w/ or w/o locations. 614-382-9080

Want To Work For Yourself? Consider a CAREER in real estate and new home sales. Call Adnac Frederick at COLDWELL BANKER HUNTER REALTY for more details at 777-8500 [illegible]

WE'LL SHOW YOU THE MONEY!

(Just call any of our clients:) 3-5 hrs/wk. No sales. Investment needed. Free info. 800-876-3326

WHERE CAN YOU START A Home based Business for $149 for 39 mo. or $4,285? Receive a new 300 Mhz Pentium Processor Computer w/a 15" montinor, color printer, a merchant account that takes all major credit cards, unlimited software training, a support team that is unprecedented, a personal web site that markets 38 organic life changing nutritional suppliments & the ability to pay it off in the 1st month? Toll Free, 24 hrs. 888-524-1065

0840 Financial

BUYER-Notes/Contracts any cash flow/real estate, business commercial, FGF 440.329.2311

0850 Money to Loan

AAA CREDIT NOT REQUIRED

Cash For Any Reason. Home Owners Only. 1-800-USA-MONY

ALL TYPES OF MORTGAGES Best Available terms for good, bad or no credit! Call anytime MORTGAGE PLUS 888-460-6846. Licensed Mortgage Broker

0850 Money to Loan

SECOND CHANCE CREDIT CARDS

25% cash back, Call now 1-877-997-8576 or 314-997-8576

$5K to $200K Any Reason. No Credit Required. 216-531-1140

0860 Money Wanted

EARN at least 15% Secured real estate equity. 50-60% - LTV Perry 330-656-4125 / 650-6935

EVER had someone give you a 2nd chance? That's what I need. My credit is poor and I can't secure a loan. Hard-working family man w/ excellent paying job. Need someone to give me that 2nd chance. Will pay high interest for a loan between $9K-14K. Also will pay for idea that leads to a completed loan. 440-564-2586

INVESTORS-$450K needed to start business. Have business plan & quotes. 440-257-6896

1600 Legal Notices

Date of Public Notice: September 30, 1998

Cuyahoga County

PUBLIC NOTICE

NOTICE OF RECEIPT OF 401 APPLICATION

Public notice is hereby given that the Ohio Environmental Protection Agency (Ohio EPA) Division of Surface Water (DSW) has received an application for, and has begun to consider whether to issue or deny, a Clean Water Act Section 401 certification for a project to relocate approximately 750 lineal feet of the existing channel of Abrams Creek onto property owned by Cleveland Metroparks. The applicant also proposes to fill approximately 1.7 acres of wetlands adjacent to the existing Abrams Creek channel for development purposes. Stream wetland mitigation will occur on and adjacent to the project site. The application was submitted by Simon Properties, 4645 Richmond Road, Suite 102, Warrensville Hts., Ohio 44128. The project is located immediately west of the intersection of Hepburn Road and Jefferson Park Road, Middleburg Heights, Cuyahoga County. The Buffalo District Corps of Engineers Public Notice Number for this project is (B)97 494 0066(0)

The discharges from the activity, if approved would result in degradation to, or lowering of, the water quality of Abrams Creek

1600 Legal Notices

to Ohio EPA/DSW, Attention: Permits Processing Unit, P.O. Box 1049, Columbus, Ohio 43216-1049 within 30 days of the date of this public notice

p.d.sept27,1998 867961

Department of Justice
Antitrust Division

Take notice that a proposed Final Judgment as to Medical Mutual of Ohio has been filed in a civil antitrust case, United States of America v. Medical Mutual of Ohio, Civil No. 1:98-CV-2172. On Sept. 23, 1998, the United States filed a Complaint against Medical Mutual of Ohio alleging that Medical Mutual had unreasonably restrained competition in the greater Cleveland area in violation of Section 1 of the Sherman Act, 15 U.S.C. Section 1. The proposed Final Judgment, filed the same time as the Complaint, restrains Medical Mutual from enforcing a Most Favored Rates requirement and from requiring its participating hospitals in the Cleveland area to disclose to Medical Mutual the rates such hospitals offer or charge any payers. A Competitive Impact Statement filed by the United States describes the Complaint, the proposed Final Judgment, the industry, and the remedies available to private litigants who may have been injured by the alleged violation. Copies of the Complaint, proposed Final Judgment and Competitive Impact Statement are available for inspection at the Department of Justice in Washington, D.C. in Room 400, 325 Seventh Street, N.W., and at the Office of the Clerk of the United States District Court for the Northern District of Ohio, Ohio

Interested persons may direct comments to Gail Kursh, Chief, Healthcare Task Force, 325 Seventh Street, N.W., Room 404, Antitrust Division, Department of Justice, Washington, D.C. 20530, within 60 days of the date of this notice.

p.d.sept27,28,29,30, oct1,2,3,1998 863856

LEGAL NOTICE

Pursuant to the provisions of sections 119.03 and 119.032 of the Ohio Revised Code, the Liquor Control Commission hereby gives notice of its intention to amend the following rule of the Liquor Control Commission and offers the following synopsis of

1600 Legal Notices

floor, Columbus, Ohio 43215.

p.d.sept27,1998 868094

LEGAL NOTICE
REQUEST FOR PROPOSAL
STARK AREA REGIONAL
TRANSIT AUTHORITY

In accordance with Ohio Revised Code 306.43, proposals will be accepted by the Executive Director of the STARK AREA REGIONAL TRANSIT AUTHORITY, in the office of said Executive Director, 1600 Gateway Boulevard, S.E., Canton, Ohio 44707 until: MONDAY, OCTOBER 19, 1998 at 1:30 PM. LOCAL TIME and then at such time and place opened and read aloud for the purpose of securing bids for:

INTERNAL LINING OF
DIESEL FUEL
UNDERGROUND
STORAGE TANKS

SARTA has set a goal for Disadvantaged Business Enterprises of 12% (twelve percent) participation for this contract.

Bids will be received according to the specifications and proposal sheets on file and available in the office of the Executive Director. Bids must be submitted on the printed forms provided to submit a bid on any or all of the items set forth in the request package. The Authority reserves the right to reject any or all proposals and to waive any informality in any bid.

Bidders shall be prepared to furnish any information requested regarding same.

No bid may be withdrawn for a period of sixty (60) days from the date of the opening of the bids. The Stark Area Regional Transit Authority Board of Trustees reserves the right to reject any and all bids and to accept the bid deemed most beneficial to the Stark Area Regional Transit Authority

By Order of the
Executive Director
Sharon Kasunic Eslich

p.d.sept27,1998 864477

LEGAL NOTICE
REQUEST FOR PROPOSAL
MANAGEMENT DEVELOPMENT
PROGRAM

The Cuyahoga Metropolitan Housing Authority (CMHA) is requesting proposals for MANAGEMENT DEVELOPMENT PROGRAM, Solicitation No. 60-380-98. All proposals are due by 10:00 a.m., Thursday, October 15, 1998. All proposals shall be sealed and delivered to CMHA [illegible]

1600 Legal Notices

will be drafted to include: expressed desires of people currently living in large congregate settings, description of data on the perceived barriers, recommendations for resolution of those barriers, an advocacy action plan for the next steps to be taken and lessons learned from quarterly roundtable discussions.

Application Deadline: 11-11-98

Staff Coordinator: Leslie Paull

Interested parties are encouraged to consult with DD Council Staff Coordinators prior to requesting application material (614-466-5205). Questions regarding fiscal issues should be directed to James Wilder at (614-644-5545) or Alex Jones at (614-752-5002).

Applications may be obtained by contacting Mr. Wilder or Ms. Jones.

The Ohio Developmental
Disabilities Council
8 East Long Street, 12th Floor
Columbus, Ohio 43215

p.d.sept27,1998 869593

NOTICE OF
NON-DISCRIMINATORY
POLICY AS TO STUDENTS
JAPANESE LANGUAGE
SCHOOL
OF CLEVELAND

Japanese Language School of Cleveland admits students of any race, color, national and ethnic origin to all the rights, privileges, programs and activities generally accorded or made available to students of the school. It does not discriminate on the basis of race, color, national and ethnical origin in administration of its educational policies, admission policies, scholarship and loan programs and athletic and other school administered programs.

JAPANESE LANGUAGE
SCHOOL OF CLEVELAND
MAILING ADDRESS:
KOJI KADOWAKI
2224 JESSE DRIVE
HUDSON, OH 44236
CLASSROOMS:
1857 SOUTH GREEN RD.,
SOUTH EUCLID, OH
44121-4299
(12 CLASSROOMS AT
REGINA HIGH SCHOOL)

p.d.sept27,1998 869118

NOTICE TO BIDDERS

Sealed bids will be received by the Director of Public Service of the City of Euclid, Euclid Municipal Center, 585 East 222nd Street, Euclid, Ohio, on Monday [illegible]

1350 Miscellan[eous] Sale / W[anted]

AIR Cond/Heat, [illegible] flow, 208 230 V 3 ph [illegible] $6900. 216-267-5739 [illegible] parties please co[ntact] erased by mistake

AIR CONDITIO[NER] $750; FURNACE [illegible] 216-496-3398.

ALUM. ladders 40 [illegible] fold, craftsman 9 [illegible] craftsman 4⅛" [illegible] 216-299-0432.

ANTIQUE Wine P[illegible] Canning Jars w/L[illegible] $2.99/Case of 12. 21[illegible]

APPROX. 35 pcs. [illegible] ble, various siz[es] 56"x45". Alum. [illegible] lean to type, approx [illegible] 440-327-3846.

ARCADE ACTION [illegible] with coin mec[illegible] [illegible]

BATHT[UBS] Cast iron, $200. 216-3[illegible]

BATHTUBS (2) cla[illegible] old collectibles after 5pm.

BAY Garden Windo[w] crank out, Never [illegible] 330-225-3299

BENCH SAW 22" [illegible] Good cond., days [illegible] 216-531-3339 eve [illegible]

BRICK 413 used, 353 unused [illegible] Maple Hts 216-663-[illegible]

BRIDAL Slip extra [illegible] on cake box for w[illegible] w/angel top. 440-23[illegible]

BUYING old gas p[illegible] toration, 1950 [illegible] 440-777-6629. Leave [illegible]

CASEMENT Windo[ws] w/screens, 20" wide [illegible] Offer. 216-360-0513.

CASH PA[ID] For furniture & ap[illegible]

CEDAR, 1x4 at 40c [illegible] 900'. 440-582-0085.

CLAM Baker, stai[nless] system, w/holdi[ng] stainless ball valve [illegible] 8:30a.m 216-524-872[illegible]

CLOCKS: Over 60 C[illegible] Welch, Ansonia, & [illegible] Up To 20% Off Sept [illegible] Hills Antiques. 2010 [illegible]

COINS AND STAM[PS] turn that collection [into] immediate cash, or [illegible] Gladly travels. Unli[illegible] 800-831-61[illegible]

COLLECTOR Buyin[g] Swords, Ammo. 38 [illegible]

CRAFTSMAN Lar[illegible] top only, never [illegible] 330-225-3299.

Fourth Notice

2) Subsequent advancing financial markets after 2000-2003 decline. (First Limited Edition Booklet printing: December 2003).

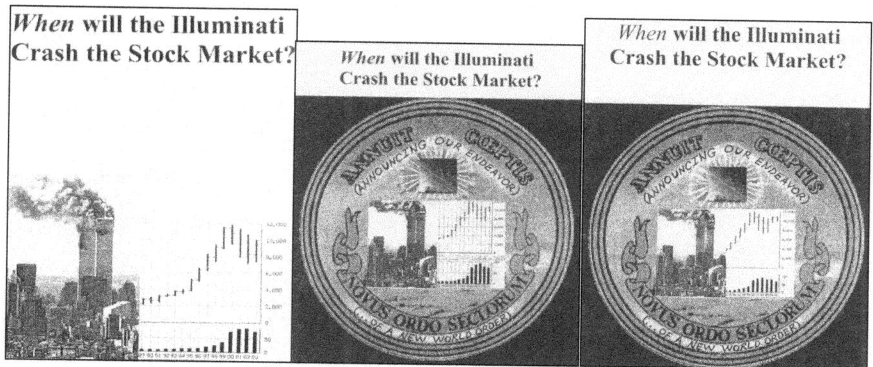

2003 - 2005 Booklet Covers from 3 printings

3) Historical top in the U.S. economy: October 11, 2007. (August 10: November 18, 2007).

4) Initial stage U.S./global economic decline: first Quarter 2008 – first Quarter 2009. (August 10, 2007). Initial stage of U.S. banking collapse. Largest weekly and monthly DJIA point decline in the history of the stock market. Largest percentage Quarterly decline since the Great Depression.

The Plain Dealer | Friday, August 10, 2007

Legal Notices

INVITATION TO BID

Sealed bids will be received by the Office of the Executive Director-Secretary of the Board of Park Commissioners of Cleveland Metroparks (the "Board"), 4101 Fulton Parkway, Cleveland, Ohio 44144, until 2:00 p.m. local time on the 27th DAY OF AUGUST, 2007 (the "Bid Opening Date"), at which place and time bids will be publicly opened and read for:

BID # 5379: ASPHALT PAVEMENT IMPROVEMENTS, BRECKSVILLE RESERVATION

The contract shall be let in accordance with the Bidding Documents (as defined in the Instructions to Bidders included therein) on file in the Office of the Board (4101 Fulton Parkway, Cleveland, Ohio 44144). Copies of said Bidding Documents for the project may be obtained by bidders from the Board by depositing with it a check for $25.00 (Twenty-Five Dollars) non-refundable, made payable to "Cleveland Metroparks" for each set of Bidding Documents.

Plans for the Project are available for review at McGraw-Hill Dodge Construction, 6200 Rockside Woods Blvd., Independence, Ohio 44131; Builder's Exchange, 9555 Rockside Road, Valley View, Ohio 44125 and at the Office of the Board.

Bids must be submitted in sealed envelopes and clearly marked with the appropriate bid number and name of bidder. No late bids will be considered.

BY THE ORDER OF THE PARK COMMISSIONERS OF CLEVELAND METROPARKS.

Vern J. Hartenburg
Executive Director-Secretary
Cleveland Metroparks

p.d.aug.10,17,2007 1748291

INVITATION TO BID

Sealed bids will be received by the Office of the Executive Director-Secretary of the Board of Park Commissioners of Cleveland Metroparks (the "Board"), 4101 Fulton Parkway, Cleveland, Ohio 44144, until 2:00 p.m. local time on the 24th DAY OF AUGUST, 2007 (the "Bid Opening Date"), at which place and time bids will be publicly opened and read for:

versity Heights in preparing a needs assessment and programmatic analysis for certain city services and their required facilities. Any interested individual or firm should obtain a copy of the "QUALIFICATIONS-BASED SELECTION STATEMENT CRITERIA" from the Clerk of Council. Interested individuals or firms should provide their statements by September 7, 2007. The City of University Heights reserves the right to reject all proposals.

By Order of:
Beryl E. Rothschild, Mayor
City of University Heights

p.d.aug.3,10,2007 1740403

LEGAL NOTICE
Request for Proposal (RFP)
Off-Site Data Storage
Solicitation No: 37-000-07

The Cuyahoga Metropolitan Housing Authority (CMHA) seeks Proposals from qualified companies. All responses shall be sealed and delivered to: CMHA Purchasing Department, Attention: Daphne Burns, A.P.P., 1242 East 49th Street, 5th Floor, Cleveland, Ohio, 44114, and arrive before 11:00 on Friday, August 24, 2007 Eastern Standard Time. All Proposals received after this date and time shall be returned unopened.

A copy of the RFP may be obtained from the CMHA Purchasing Department, by calling (216) 432-5016 Ext. 4073, Monday through Friday, 7:30 A.M. to 4:30 P.M. beginning Friday, August 3, 2007 or from our web site at www.cmha.net.

Proposals should be prepared in accordance with the instructions outlined in the RFP and will be evaluated by CMHA as stated in the evaluation factors for award. CMHA reserves the right to reject any or all proposals received and waive any informality in the pro-

Legal Notices

NOTICE OF VOLUNTARY DISSOLUTION

Notice is hereby given that Empire Glass Company, an Ohio corporation, was dissolved upon filing a Certificate of Dissolution with the Secretary of State of Ohio on July 24, 2007.

p.d.aug.10,17,2007 1748344

NOTICE TO BIDDERS

IN ACCORDANCE WITH THE OHIO REVISED CODE CHAPTER 153, SEALED PROPOSALS SHALL BE RECEIVED FOR FURNISHING ALL LABOR, MATERIAL AND EQUIPMENT NECESSARY WITH REGARD TO THE FOLLOWING PROJECT:

PROJECT TITLE: FAÇADE IMPROVEMENTS, MICHAEL A. DONZELLA ADMINISTRATION BUILDING
TOTAL COST ESTIMATE: $300,000
REQUISITION NO.: RQ 9400

THE PROJECT PROPOSALS SHALL BE IN ACCORDANCE WITH SPECIFICATIONS AND DRAWINGS PREPARED BY THE PROJECT CONSULTANT, FOGLE/STENZEL ARCHITECTS, INC 2800 EUCLID AVE., STE 600, CLEVELAND, OH 44115 UNDER THE SUPERVISION OF THE CUYAHOGA COUNTY BOARD OF MENTAL RETARDATION AND DEVELOPMENTAL DISABILITIES. THE BIDDING DOCUMENTS ARE ON FILE AND AVAILABLE AT THE OFFICE OF PROCUREMENT & DIVERSITY, ROOM 100, COUNTY ADMINISTRATION ANNEX BUILDING, 112 HAMILTON AVENUE, CLEVELAND, OHIO 44114.

BIDS MUST BE PLACED IN THE BID DEPOSITORY AND SHALL BE ACCEPTED UNTIL TWO O'CLOCK IN THE AFTERNOON (2:00 P.M.) LOCAL TIME ON SEPTEMBER 14, 2007 IN THE OFFICE OF PROCUREMENT & DIVERSITY, ROOM 100, COUNTY ADMINISTRATION ANNEX BUILDING., 112 HAMILTON AVENUE, CLEVELAND, OHIO 44114, AT WHICH TIME AND PLACE THE BIDS SHALL BE OPENED IMMEDIATELY THEREAFTER, AND READ PUBLICLY. THE CLOCK LOCATED IN THE OFFICE OF PROCUREMENT & DI-

BUSINESS IN THE STATE OF OHIO. IF A CERTIFIED CHECK, CASHIER'S CHECK, OR IRREVOCABLE LETTER OF CREDIT IS SUBMITTED AS THE BID GUARANTY, IT MUST BE DRAWN ON A SOLVENT BANK AND MADE PAYABLE WITHOUT CONDITION TO THE TREASURER OF CUYAHOGA COUNTY. THE BID OR CERTIFIED CHECK SHALL BE HELD AS A GUARANTEE THAT IF THE PROPOSAL IS ACCEPTED, THE BIDDER WILL ENTER INTO A CONTRACT FOR THE SAME. THE SUCCESSFUL BIDDER, UPON THE CONTRACT AWARD, SHALL PROVIDE A CONSTRUCTION BOND IN THE SUM EQUAL TO ONE HUNDRED PERCENT (100%) OF THE CONTRACT AMOUNT PER O.R.C. SECTION 153.54.

PAYMENTS IN FULL SHALL BE MADE BY WARRANTS ISSUED BY THE CUYAHOGA COUNTY AUDITOR.

THE RIGHT IS RESERVED TO REJECT ANY OR ALL BIDS BY ORDER OF THE BOARD OF CUYAHOGA COUNTY COMMISSIONERS.

JIMMY DIMORA
TIMOTHY F. HAGAN
PETER LAWSON JONES
MICHAEL KOCHAN
PURCHASING MANAGER
OFFICE OF PROCUREMENT & DIVERSITY

BID STATUS: INITIAL BID

p.d.aug.10,17,2007 1748101

NOTICE TO BIDDERS

Notice is hereby given that sealed proposals will be received in the Board of County Commissioners Office of Procurement & Diversity, Room 100, County Administration Building Annex, 112 Hamilton Court, Cleveland, Ohio 44114 until 2:00 p.m., (local time) on August 31, 2007 for: Construction of Gate #5 Restroom at the Cuyahoga County Fair Grounds in Be-

Legal Notices

The Board of County Commissioners reserves the right to accept or reject any bids or any part or all parts of any bid submitted, and waive all technicalities.

BY ORDER OF THE BOARD OF COUNTY COMMISSIONERS OF CUYAHOGA COUNTY.
JIMMY DIMORA
TIMOTHY F. HAGAN
PETER LAWSON JONES

Adrian Maldonado, Director,
Office of Procurement & Diversity

This notice may also be viewed at the following Cuyahoga County Internet Web Site: www.cuyahogacounty.us/opd by clicking on the current legal notices section. A list of open bids will appear on the next screen. Click on the bid due date to view the legal notice.

p.d.aug.10,2007 1748010

NOTICE TO BIDDERS

Sealed bids will be received by the Director of Public Service of the City of Euclid, 585 E. 222nd Street, Euclid, Ohio on August 27, 2007 at 4:00 p.m. for the Tungsten Road Replacement in the City of Euclid, Ohio.

Plans and/or Specifications are on file in the Service Director's Office at Euclid City Hall, 585 East 222nd Street, Euclid, Ohio. A non-refundable charge of SEVENTY-FIVE DOLLARS ($75.00) (picked up) in cash or check made payable to CT Consultants will be made for each set of plans and specifications purchased.

All bidders are required to attend a mandatory Pre-bid Conference on August 21, 2007 at 10:00 a.m. at the City of Euclid, 585 E. 222nd Street, Euclid, Ohio. Failure to attend the Pre-bid Conference will subject the bidders proposal to be considered non-responsive.

Each bid must be presented in the BIDDER'S ENVELOPE, provided by the City, sealed and marked: "TUNGSTEN ROAD REPLACEMENT PROJECT". BIDS MUST BE ACCOMPANIED BY ONE OF THE FOLLOWING: A) BID BOND IN THE AMOUNT OF 100% OF THE TOTAL AMOUNT BID; OR B) CASHIER'S CHECK, OFFICIAL OR CERTIFIED CHECK ON A SOLVENT BANK, OR CASH IN THE AMOUNT OF TEN PER-

specifications may be obtained.
Bid File No. B-2031
Resolution No. 242-06
Opening Date: Friday, August 24, 2007

A contract for the demolition of existing cabinets and the purchase and installation of new cabinets at the District's Environmental & Maintenance Services Center, per the District's specifications.

Jacqueline Williams,
Purchasing Manager

p.d.aug.10,17,2007 1748356

NOTICE TO VIEW BALLOTS FOR SEPTEMBER 11, 2007 ELECTION

A viewing of ballots for the September 11, 2007 Primary Election in Broadview Heights (Mayor and Council at Large) and Solon (Ward 7, Council) will be available for the public from Friday evening, August 10, 2007, through Saturday, August 11, 2007 (comments welcome). Ballots will be posted at the Cuyahoga County Board of Elections, 2925 Euclid Avenue, Cleveland, the Cuyahoga County Courthouse, 1 Lakeside Avenue, Cleveland, and on the Board of Elections website, boe.cuyahogacounty.us. Comment by phone, (216) 443-3200 or e-mail, electioninfo@cuyahogacounty.us

BY ORDER OF THE BOARD OF ELECTIONS, CUYAHOGA COUNTY, OHIO

p.d.aug.10,2007 1748874

PUBLIC NOTICE

DJIA high of 14,021.95 on 7/17/07 was the top in US economy. 1st quarter 2008, Dow will accelerate decline 3 yrs-until 2010-approx low: 1500. Send inquiries:

p.d.aug.10,,2007 1747258

Automobiles for Sale

99 Acura 3.2 TL w/GPS 152K,one-owner,fully ld,eng.grt.shape.$6750 call 216-406-0625.

2000 Acura TL Excellent condition - Loaded. Heated seats, Navigator system with updated disk, auto-climate control, power seats, power locks, power sunroof, power mirrors, remote entry, AM/FM/CD/Cassette, cruise control, built-in garage opener, leather seats, red exterier, no rust, no leaks, clean, 106,000 miles. Eastlake, OH 440-479-7567 $8,300

ACURA 2005 TL. All Options, 11k Mi., One Owner, Perfect, Must Sell. 216-533-4073.

ACURA 2006 TSX. #9014347A, 12k miles, very clean, very sporty, $25,999.
CLASSIC LEXUS
888-501-6070

AUDI

NEW & CERTIFIED PRE-OWNED VEHICLES IN STOCK!

$14,500.
axelrodchrysler.com
216-459-8350

BMW 2002 325i. Moonroof, leather, full power. $16,994.
lambertgm.com
800-711-2793

BMW 2002 525i, Dark grey, moonroof, 43k miles $19,495
SIMS 1-866-397-0416

BMW 2003 M3, silver/black leather, sunroof, Harmon Kardon, navigation, mint cond. Only 14K mi. $37,000 obo. 440-479-8894

BMW 2004 325ci. 5 speed, leather, roof, 45k miles. $18,786.
Montrose Ford
Fairlawn 800-757-8196

BMW 2004 745i
Ex.cond. 63k. Loaded. BMW Warr. till 100K. 216-509-8847 $34,500

BMW 2007 335i Conv
Blk/Blk auto, 1K miles, $57,000 440.840.0102

BUICK 1988 LeSabre. 4 dr. V6. A/C, CD. No rust. 71K. $2250. 216-338-3909

BUICK 1990 Reatta Convt. Red. Showroom Cond. New tires. 25k, $15,000. 440-832-0712

BUICK 1993 Park Ave. 4 dr. V6. Cold a/c. Low mi. Showroom cond. $2450. 216-780-2445

BUICK 1995 Century, V6, 4 dr, 56k, no rust,

Automobiles for Sale

BUICK 1999 LeSabre. Auto, air, full power, clean, $2990.

HONDA of Mentor
1-866-311-3325

BUICK 1999 Lesabre Limited. Leather, full power, only 22k, $8999
LAKESHORE
1-866-769-2205

BUICK 1999 Park Ave loaded silver, lthr great shape, look & ride! $5700. 440-779-5361

BUICK 1999 Park Avenue. 66k, leather heated seats, power features, chromes, nice, $9990.
LEIKIN BUICK
440-946-6900

BUICK 2000 Century Custom. Full power, mock top, must see! $7995
SIMS CHEVROLET
5180 Mayfield Rd.
440-228-5884

BUICK 2000 LeSabre. 4dr, low miles. $7988.
SERPENTINI
330-441-4300

BUICK 2000 LESABRE Custom exc. cond., 74k mi., $5,500 440-237-5500

BUICK 2000 LeSabre Ltd. Exc. cond., loaded, extras, 69K. $6200 /obo. 216-447-0807

BUICK 2001 Century. $5995
JAY HONDA 440-749-6361

BUICK 2001 Century Custom, all new tires & brakes, 80K, exc. cond. $6,400. 330-467-1700

BUICK 2002 Century. Air, full power, $8490.
STRONGSVILLE DODGE
440-238-8100

1-800-486-1338

BUICK 2004 LeSabre, 32k mi. White, all pwr. CD. Good cond. $10,400. 559-448-7373

BUICK 2004 LeSabre. Leather, mock top, wild cat pkg, power seat, CD, loaded, $12,990.
LEIKIN BUICK
440-946-6900

BUICK 2004 Regal, Leather, alloys, bucket seats, $11,999.
LAKESHORE
1-866-764-9976

BUICK 2004 Regal LS. Auto, luxury pkg, alloys, leather, full power equipment, moon, Certified & Warranty $14,990
SATURN OF CHAGRIN
1-800-715-6319
saturnofchagrin.com

BUICK 2005 Lacrosse CXS. Leather heated seats, power sunroof, chromes, spoiler, 6 disc, 25k, loaded, $17,990.
LEIKIN BUICK
440-946-6900

BUICK 2005 Lesabre Custom, 33k mi, onstar & cell phone incl. 1 owner non smoker, miracle shield, steel mist, exc. $13,000 neg. 440-333-3461

BUICK 2005 Lesabre. Leather seating with mock top, 1 owner trade in, clean in and out, $12,995.

ANDY SIMS BUICK

Automobiles for Sale

CADILLAC 1995 Deville Concours. Dk blue, only 54k, $6990, #T18884B.
CLASSIC TOYOTA
1-888-528-7636

CADILLAC 1995 Fleetwood. Black, lthr $5995
CRESTMONT
CHRYSLER JEEP
216-831-2100

CADILLAC 1996 Deville. Leather, all pwr, alloys, loaded, linen gold, 140k, excellent, one price, $3990.
axelrodchrysler.com
216-459-8350

CADILLAC 1996 El-Dorado, sunroof, low mi., no rust, $6,700 Call: 216-731-2755

CADILLAC 1996 Seville SLS, 137K, loaded, looks/runs great, $3400. 216-398-8631.

CADILLAC 1997 Catera, 128K, leather, green, great cond. $4350/obo. 440-503-3444

CADILLAC 1997 Catera, blk/blk leather, as is. 62,879 mi., $3,300/ best offer 216-526-1497

CADILLAC 1997 DeVille. Dark Blue. Mint! Only 55K. $8500. 216-932-7855

CADILLAC 1997 DeVille. Loaded! Leather. 101K. All Pwr. $2995. 440-350-1435

CADILLAC 1999 DeVille, very good cond., new exhaust, brakes, alternator, $5900/offer. 440-256-8894

CADILLAC 1999 SLS Black, loaded, only 68,000 mi, won't last! $7,800. 440-582-0632

CADILLAC 2000 Deville DTS, silver, moonroof, chromes, 94k. Clean. $8295. 216-970-2886

CADILLAC 2000 Eldorado, Lthr $10,995.

LEIKIN BUICK
440-946-6900

CADILLAC 2004 Seville SLS Loaded, moonroof, 36K, warranty left, $19,000 440-248-8621

CADILLAC 2005 CTS, Leather, alloys, priced to sell, $18,999.
LAKESHORE
1-866-764-9976

CADILLAC 2005 Deville. Full top, full power, sharp! $18,994.
lambertgm.com
800-711-2793

CADILLAC 2005 Seville STS. Only 27k miles, Touring, chrome wheels. $26,994
lambertgm.com
800-711-2793

CADILLAC 2006 CTS. Aged unit, must sell, $22,999.
LAKESHORE
1-866-769-2205

CADILLAC 2006 DTS, 19K mi, Showroom Cond., Wife's Car, $28,500/obo. Call 216-464-1766

CADILLAC 2006 STS. Pearl white, navigation, leather, roof, all the toys, 10k. $35,689.
Montrose Ford
Fairlawn 800-757-8196

CHEVY 1989 CORSICA CL, V6, 4 Door, Auto, Air, 39K, Loaded, $1950. 216-338-3909

CHEVY 1993 LUMINA. exc. transp., air, CLEAN Runs Great! Must See! $2295. 216-346-6580.

Automobiles for Sale

CHEVY 1999 Camaro V6, auto, 58K, T-top loaded, plus snow tires 216-225-5015 $8500

CHEVY 1999 Cavalier Z24. Loaded, back to school special. Cheap $3995
GANLEY LINCOLN/MERC
440-845-6000

CHEVY 1999 MALIBU 4dr., 2.4 engine, 130k, Runs great, wht. $2500 obo 216-466-1594

CHEVY 1999 MALIBU. auto., loaded, air, blk., runs great, clean. $1900. 216-254-4486.

CHEVY 1999 Prizm 4dr 4cyl, auto, air. $3980
STRONGSVILLE DODGE
440-238-8100

CHEVY 2000 Camaro Convt, 49k, Silver/Blk, Premium Sound, Leather, Alloys, Extra Clean. $9995. 216-570-3200.

CHEVY 2000 Malibu auto, 79.9k mi, brown 1 owner, new tires $3,350. 216-403-4091

CHEVY 2001 Camaro. T-Tops, auto, low miles $9500
GREAT LAKES HYUNDAI
216-376-2527

CHEVY 2001 Impala Just got on our lot 82,000 miles, $5999.
LAKESHORE
1-866-769-2205

CHEVY 2001 Monte Carlo, 90k mi., sport package, silver, $5900 Call: 4405320429

CHEVY 2001 Monte Carlo, 90k mi., sport package, silver, $6100 Call: 4405320429

CHEVY 2001 Monte Carlo. Must see! Only $6995
GANLEY OUTLET
216-671-1500

CHEVY 2001 Prizm

AC, auto, ready. $4995
SERPENTINI
330-562-8585

CHEVY 2003 Cavalier only 42k mi., absolutely like brand new $6950 440-724-3025

CHEVY 2003 Impala Auto, AC, silver $5995
CRESTMONT
CHRYSLER JEEP
216-831-2100

CHEVY 2003 Impala. Dark red, GM Cert warranty $10,895
SIMS 1-866-397-0416

CHEVY 2003 Impala Full power. $9950
STRONGSVILLE DODGE
1-866-570-0051

CHEVY 2003 Impala. Full pwr, AC, CD, must see $9995
SIMS CHEVROLET
5180 Mayfield Rd.
440-228-5884

CHEVY 2003 Impala LS Leather, sunroof, alloys, $8999.
LAKESHORE
1-866-769-2205

CHEVY 2003 Malibu. Auto, AC, CD, extra clean $8995
SIMS CHEVROLET
5180 Mayfield Rd.
440-228-5884

CHEVY 2003 Malibu. Full pwr, AC, CD, only 58k miles $9995
SIMS CHEVROLET
5180 Mayfield Rd.
440-228-5884

CHEVy 2003 Malibu. Moon, lthr. Only $839

First Notice

The Plain Dealer | Sunday, November 18, 2007

Business Opportunities

Commercial Cleaning Franchise Opportunity Anago
Programs starting as low as $1,425 down!
• Start your own commercial cleaning business in a few hours in the evening.
$1K - $50K or more! in Monthly Income
• Let it grow and decide to leave your day job and be a full time owner.
Ranked in the top 25 fastest growing franchises in america
Make a decision that will change your life today!
CALL 800-926-9725 ext 101

BBQ RIBS TAKE-OUT Well-estab. w/ loyal customers. Good sales. EBB 440-409-0302

Beauty Salon Willoughby on Vine St.8 stations ample park'g $34,900 w/equip. 216-513-0281 Keller Williams Realty Greater Cleveland

BEAUTY SHOP - Chair Rental, reasonable. W/ option to buy this upscale, busy E. suburb shop. 216-381-3100

BE YOUR OWN BOSS
85+ Existing Businesses
90+ New Franchises
Largest inventory of business opportunities
Largest Business Intermediary Team
Call to set appointment to explore your options!

Sunbelt Cleveland
Business Sales & Acquisitions
216-739-0272
SunbeltBizBuySell.com

BUSINESS Card Distributorship. Earn Top $$. Includes Inventory. $11K. 216-831-3777

BUSINESS FOR SALE Established 6 years, Owner works 15 hours/week. Nets $120k. Will Train! $5k Down. 800-494-7740

BUSINESS:
Ohio City Bar $225K Property available
BEREA Laundrymat, make offer
STRONGSVILLE Tavern, $140K.
WESTPARK Bar $150K, bldg. avail.
N.W. Pizza & Ribs Bar $195K
N.W. Italian Restaurant $495K, bldg. avail
PARMA Bar $60K., Req. $50K down
MUNROE FALLS Bar $120K, bldg. avail.
WEST SIDE PIZZA Famous Name $49K
CAHILL INVESTMENTS 440-891-9180

BOROSH'S GOLDMINES
We Make Sales Where Others Fail CALL NOW! $$ 440-843-8088 $$

CAR WASH Package 2 Locations! Property!

Bar D6 BROOKLYN 16k wk Proudly Prosper

Dairy Queen Rockside Area 9k wk - SWEET!

Beverage Store C2 Parma Very Low Rent

Sports Bar D3A + R.E. BRUNSWICK $22k wk

* ALL OWNER Financed *

Bar D6 Broadview Hts. $11k wk BE RICH!

MR HERO $6k wk Very Lo Down.Pymt

BOWLING ALLEY D6 18 Lanes! HURRY!

7 Unit Shopping Center Cleveland Clinic Area

Bar D3A Sagamore Hills * RETIRE YOUNG! *

LIQUOR Licenses GALORE Cleve D5 D6 Bedford D5 Mayfield Heights D5 D6 Rare Independence D5. Cleve D1 D2. Hudson D5 Westlake D5.Aurora D5. Trex D5 or D1D2 Nice Price!
IMMEDIATE TRANSFER
YourOHIO Permit Specialist
BOROSH
Realty 440-843-8088

Business Opportunity Can you teach, train, or speak to groups? Call 888-666-5361 for opportunity details.

CLEVELAND (On Rocky River Dr.) Deli & Restaurant for sale.Close to airport. $40,000 /obo. Includes inventory. Call: 216-265-2981

Coffee/Sandwich shop like new! All equipment, take over lease, great location. $149,900. Doree Adams, 440-669-1117 RE/MAX HomeSource

LOOK
COFFEE HOUSE Established location in western suburb. Great opportunity for someone with good credit. Assume lease. Call 1-888-860-5082 ext. 408

COKE/M&M Route Earn Big $$$! Loc. in Cleveland. $0 Down.Fin avail 800-367-6709 x:563

COMBO Vending Routes Great Loc. 100k Potential. Financing Avail. 888-500-1776

DAILY CASH COW! Establish a local candy route. 30 machines $5,995. Call now for details! 1-800-704-5414

Deli/Carry Out
Great Loc. w/ potential Call D. Breznak w/ Realty One 216-538-7377

Digital Print Bus. MUST SELL! Low Invst. No Exp. Nec. Loc. Spprt 800-645-3006

DOW. Topped 10/11/07 @ 14,198.10: 2008-10 90% decline to 1300. Details: 216-

Former Excel Communication Reps WANTED Would you like to do it again with a solid company thats been in business for years and similar compensation. Listen to our 5 min info line 646-222-0243 and then call me 419-466-4153 or email FormerExcelRep@yahoo.com

★ FRANCHISE ★
★ OPPORTUNITY ★
Looking For Successful Franchisees, Sales Exp. Necessary, $18k Franchise Fee, Business To Business Sale, Fast Growth Possible. Contact Mike Riegel: 800-481-8696 / mikeriegel @townmoneysaver.com

FRANCH. PIZZA SHOP Est. 15+ yrs. carry-out & delivery. Great location EBB 440-409-0302

GAS STATION with Property, Good Convenient Store Sale! After 3pm 440-344-2643

GET RICH. BUSINESSES FOR SALE, PROFITABLE Century Twenty-Two 440-899-9866

BE YOUR OWN BOSS
GROUT-DOCTOR FRANCHISE AVAIL. Home-based. West side of Cleve. Retiring. Will train. More info. call: 216-233-9912

HALLMARK Greeting Cards, High Income oppty., 30 local accts. 24 hrs. 1-800-330-1613

HOBBY Shop Owner wants to retire, Make Offer. P.O. Box 26182 Cleve. OH 44126

INVESTOR SPECIAL
Fully Renovated, 3/4 Bdrm. Single, $25,000 in equity. 216-244-0686

ITALIAN EATERY Attractive restaurant in affluent area. Hi. sales EBB 440-409-0302

LIMOUSINE TRANSPORTATION SERVICE, $295,000. Or with property, $695,000. 440-521-4747

LIQUOR LICENSE. D-5 D-6 Lyndhurst. $35,000 440-944-1359

LIQUOR Liscense for sale, Willoughby OH. $30,000. Call mon-fri til 6PM. 440-285-3111

METAL PRODUCTS MFR Sales $13M.Prof $1.25M C-STORES in Medina, & Portage Counties MACHINING COMPANY $300,000 annual profit Hard asset valu $½ mil. DRY CLEANER Summit County. Profit $90,000 SALON & Day Spa : upscale. In high income area S/E of Cleve. Net $50K+ for owner-mgr. FULLER & ASSOC., INC. Don Dreisig, Owner & Pres. 330-492-6294

SUPER DEAL
MINI MART CHECK CASHING FOR SALE OR LEASE OWNER FINANCE 440-785-4444

NAT'L FRANCHISE OPPORTUNITY
Franchise company looking for successful individual to join our proven franchise system. Full training and support. No exp. req. Please call 1-800-935-8863

NORTH RIDGEVILLE Current use is Auto Sales/Lot! 1.3 acre corner! Prime location w/new shopping center in progress across street! Won't last long- buy as investment NOW!! Only $399,000! M. Vaszi-Howard Hanna Smythe Cramer. 440-759-0540

PAINT YOUR OWN POTTERY Have Fun Owning This 10 Yr. Est. Studio In Westlake, No Exp. Necessary. Owner Retiring. Serious Inquiries Only. Call 440-453-5002.

PERFECT HOME BUSINESS Full or part time, carpet and upholstery cleaning. 1-800-507-7222 code: CL5913

LOOK
PIZZA FRANCHISE For sale in Chesterland. Well established, 12+ years. Build equity. Turnkey operation. For more information call (440) 537-0914.

PIZZA GOLD MINES AVON: Gross $520,000 Top Location. Steady Growth. Retire here.

KENT: Gross $270,000, College Town. Always Busy. Priced Right. Sam 216-695-4251

PIZZA SHOP. Lorain County, New Equipment, Asking $120,000 Call 216-990-8627.

★★PIZZA SHOPPE★★ Profitable Estab. Fam. Bus. Turnkey Operation High traffic CONCORD locat. $115k CALL ➡ Ed or Jean 440-979-5842 Coldwell Banker Hunter

PIZZA WEST
Retiring after 37 yrs. You will live well after you buy this business. Gross $770K. R.E. Incl. MBA Rlty440-885-0139

PLAY IT AGAIN SPORTS®
New & Established franchise opportunities. Join our 380+ store chain. Training & support provided. 1-800-592-8048 playitagainsports.com

PROFITABLE TAVERNS FOR SALE
• (3) Lakewood/Food
• Parma/Food w/profit
• Avon Food/Profitable
• Cleve/Food/profitable
• Strongsville/Food
Century Twenty Two 440-899-9866

GREAT LOCATION
RESTAURANT - BEREA for lease. With some equipment. Call for details. Realty Corp. of America, 440-461-7210

Restaurant For Sale
West Side Cleveland Lorain Ave. Seating for 30 & carry-out. $30,000 216-526-7523

RESTAURANT in Northfield. Easy terms. Will finance. Principals only 216-355-0152

RESTAURANT Lounge W. Sub. Very attractive. Liquor is 40% of gross MBA Rlty440-885-0139

RESTAURANT SPACE FOR LEASE
Approx. 6,000 SF with adjoining party/conference ctr; full liquor license; fully equipped kitchen & dining room; prime Beachwood location; 216-595-1800 for further information.

RETAIL Well est. inside stand business at the historic West Side Market. Current owner has operated business for 27 yrs. Exc. Reputation, long time customers. info 216-221-9631.

START YOUR OWN COMPUTER BUSINESS Over 100 P3 & Apple G3/G4 Computer Systems, Cloning Station & MUCH MORE! $4900. 440-391-7707

STEEL & UTILITY INDUSTRY Supp. quality refractory materials. RE avail. EBB 440-409-0302

SUPER DEAL
TAKE OVER LEASE New hot dog/ hamburger fast food restaurant across from new Wal Mart Super Center in Geauga Cty. Turnkey ...Nothing to buy... take over lease of totally equipped restaurant. Divorce forces change of ownership. Call for details: 440-477-9342

Tanglewood Square
Giant Eagle - Walgreens 26,000 Cars+ / Day
2 Restaurant 1425 & 7300sf Hood-Cooler-Freezer-Bar Will Divide 7,300 SF
Rent Incentives
R Katz Realty Ltd, Realtor (216) 831-0300 Ext. 232 Or Your Broker/Realtor

TOWING FACILITY & 80-160 Car Impound Lot, 4 bay, new construction, Willing to neg. lease. 5893 Heisley Rd., Mentor. 440-336-3504

TRAVEL- A 5 TRILLION $$ INDUSTRY! We pay $1000/sale. We do 95% of the work! You do NO SELLING! Call Now: 800-378-1169 ID-8542gd

TRUCKING GREAT OPPORTUNITY Box trucks for sale with Full Time Work. Make Great Money. Start Immediately. No exp., Financing Available 440-963-0277 or 440-476-1962

Trucking OTR Flatbed Seek to buy or merge Looking to purchase all or part of any size existing operation with or without authority with key personel in place for our West Side terminal. Call Jim 440-234-7800 ext 103

Turn-Key Ice Cream Store
Ice Cream Franchise has several turn-key opportunities in Cleveland market. Get in for spring! Build equity Call Joe 216-536-0557.

VENDING: Drink & Snack Machines. For sale w/great loc. & fin. 24/7. 866-823-0223

WELL Est. Westside Body Shop. Turnkey Oppt'y For Serious Buyer. 216-392-8350

WESTSIDE Lawn Care & Snow Plowing Company. Turn-key Operation 2006 Revenue $140k, Asking: $95,000 Call 440-570-4762

Wholesale Commercial Laundry Start up package and training $15,000 Cash 330-475-8220 ext. 101

YOU CAN START YOUR OWN AVON BUSINESS FOR JUST $10. Free training and more. For details call Joan 440-442-2183

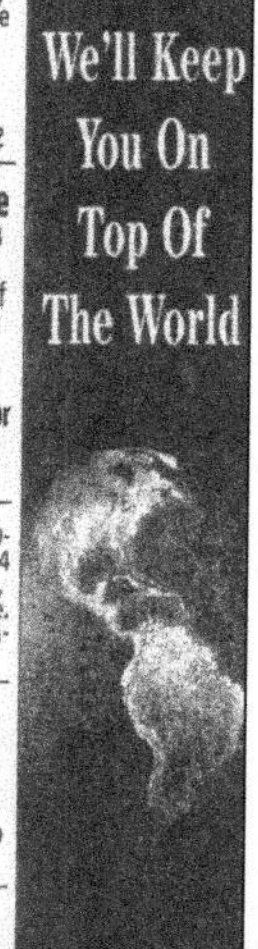

Second Notice

DJIA Timeline Perspective: 2 Year, 5 Year, 10 Year, 50 Year charts with published forecasted 2007 ultimate top in U.S. economy circled:

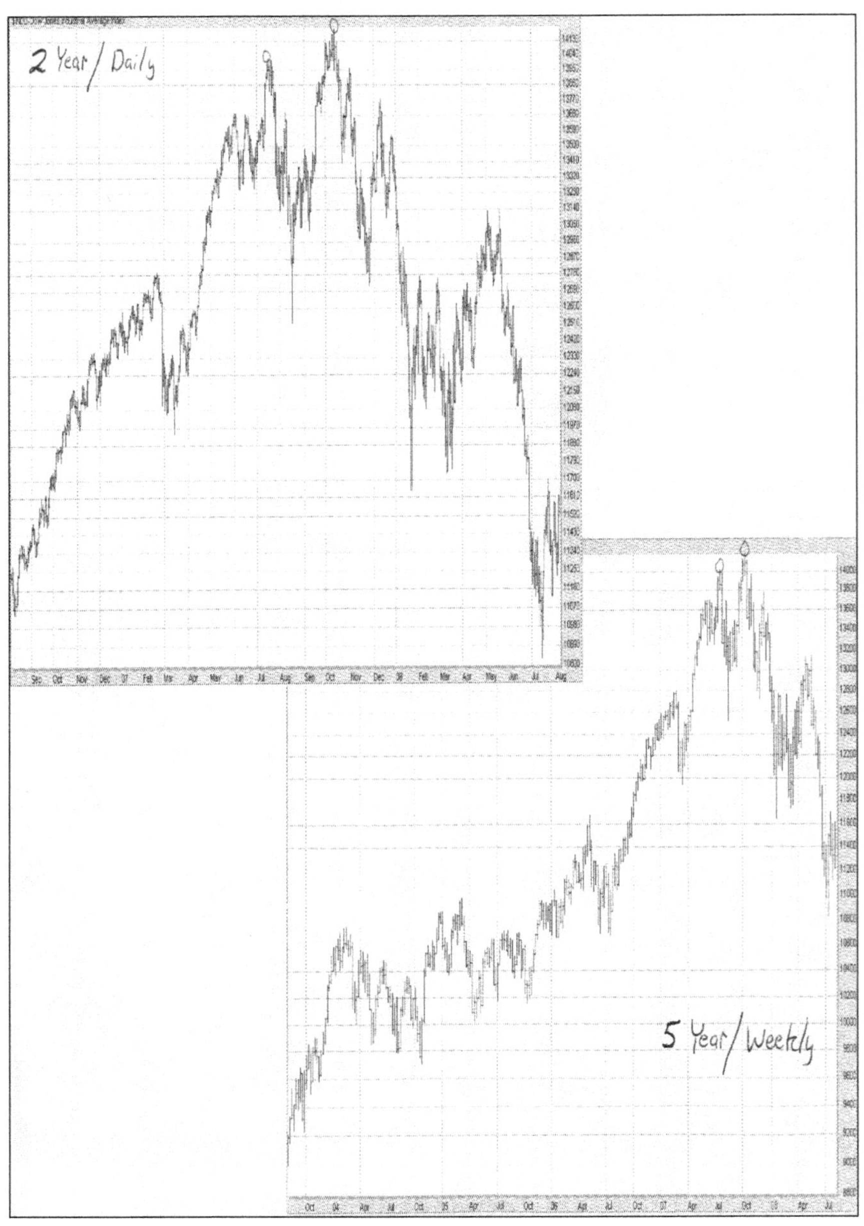

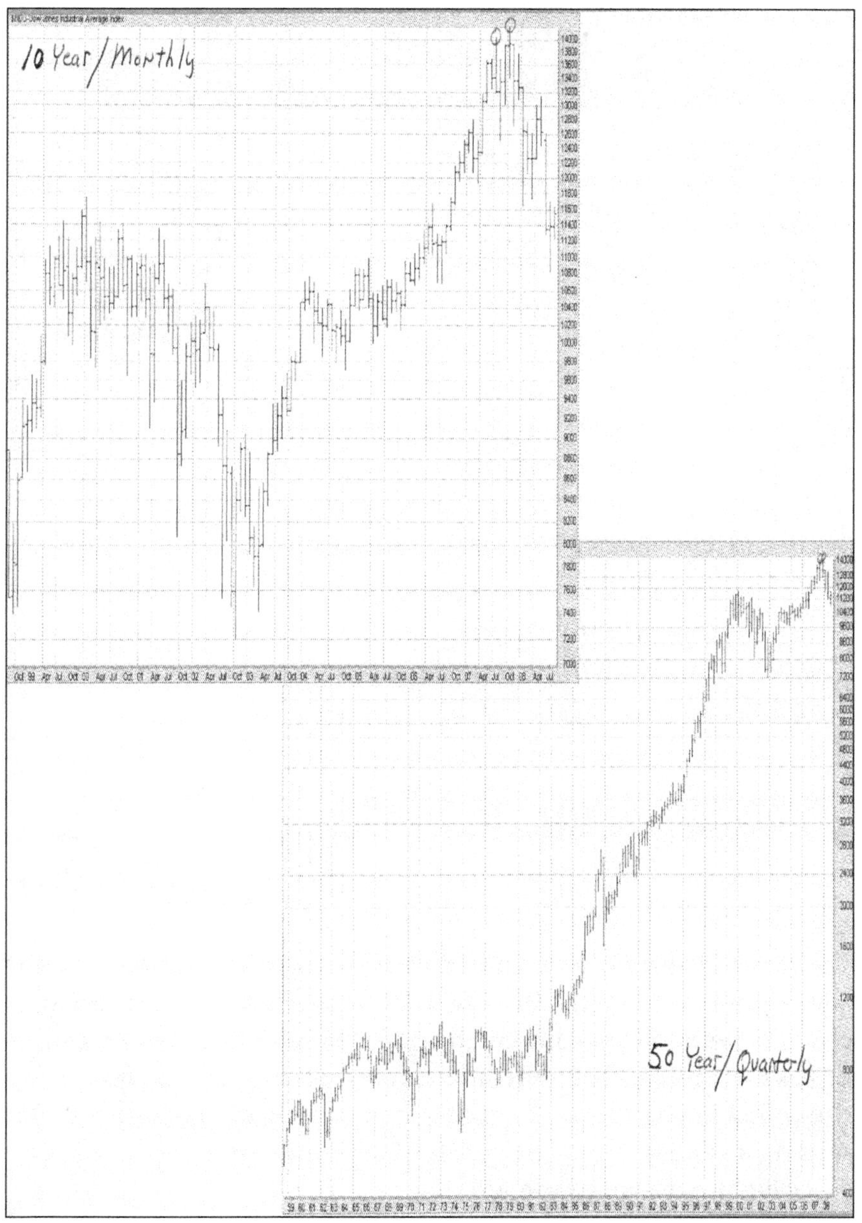
10 Year/Monthly
50 Year/Quarterly

April 30, 2008

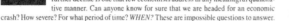

Financial

Can I know for certain what to do with my savings and investment capital during the present Recession and coming economic collapse?

Soul Esprit

This question may come as a shock to some people, yet, the US economy, for the first time in more than five years, is currently in a Recession. As of March 31, the end of the first quarter marked the second consecutive quarter of stock market losses, which is the definition of a Recession. The issue of further decline is one that few economists address in any meaningful quantitative manner. Can anyone know for sure that we are headed for an economic crash? How severe? For what period of time? *WHEN?* These are impossible questions to answer. Or, are they...?

August 1998: I was the only person on record to anticipate the largest weekly point drop in the more than 200 year history of the stock market. This advance forecast was published and documented in major print media 2 weeks before the event.

February 2001: Seven months prior to the second largest weekly drop in US economic history, I once again correctly predicted the time period of the sudden market collapse precipitated by the 911 WTC staged deception.

March 2003: I foretold the very day in which the 3 year decline terminated and reversed to begin a long-term sustained advance.

December 2003: I published a book that specified a precise future timeline for the ultimate top and subsequent crash of the US economy.

To Date: The economic timeline is proceeding as anticipated in the referenced book written more than 4 years ago. During the interim, further documentation has been published. The present and future course of the American and global economies remain clearly indicated at this time.

Regarding strategies for safeguarding capital, the prudent individual or corporation should seriously consider taking action to re-allocate their vulnerable financial resources. Such an individual or corporate entity must realize that during an abrupt and prolonged downturn in the economy there will be few "safe havens" that will not suffer the ravages of price depreciation. Even so, investment opportunities exist to not only preserve your assets and savings, but also to experience substantial appreciation. The wise investor and family provider should be aware that, historically, the banking sector is the first to crumble (has occurred and is now occurring), and that the stock indices are merely a barometer of the prevailing economic deterioration. In early 2005, my analysis warned of the housing bubble that, for the last 2 years, has resulted in 50 percent losses to real estate values in some areas of the country. Future projections indicate this decline will intensify and become widely distributed throughout the US. (National Housing foreclosures increased 57% in March)

With banking, the stock market, and real estate expected to continue posting losses in the years ahead, where can your investment capital be safe, and even grow? For each individual investor, it is indeed possible to ascertain the answer to that question, and to know what to do - in advance - in order to avoid unrecoverable losses and be strategically positioned to profit during the severe economic times to come.

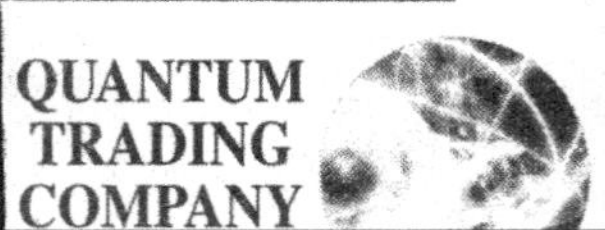

This advertisement was posted in the newspaper of an affluent community soon after the 2007 DJIA top, when the Index was only 7% below its all-time high of 14,198.10. The author's expertise would have saved local investors billions of dollars during the following 12 month 51% decline from 13,250 to below 6500. Among a readership of over 150,000 people, there was *only one* (derisive) response to the ad.

6) Third Quarter 2010 recovery after nearly a 1000 point drop on May 6: [998.50 basis points; largest single daily point decline in stock market history; second largest daily percentage drop in the history of the stock market (9%), second largest weekly decline in history; and a 9 day 1100 point loss: 5/13-25/10].

Friday, May 7, 2010

Dow plummets by almost 1,000 points

Day ends with loss of 'only' 348 points as 'unusual' trades made in error suspected as trigger for dive

1 p.m.: **10,797.68**

2:30 p.m.: **10,590.83, down 277.29**

4 p.m.: **10,520.32, down 347.80**

2:46 p.m.: **9870 — a 998.50-point loss on the day that was the Dow's largest intraday trade loss ever.**

By Adam Shell and Matt Krantz
USA TODAY

Cover story

NEW YORK — In a late-day plunge eerily reminiscent of famous Wall Street stock market meltdowns in 1987 and the fall of 2008, the Dow Jones industrials nosedived almost 1,000 points Wednesday in a volatile day that began with heavy selling on Greek debt fears and was followed by a waterfall decline that was allegedly caused by erroneous trades and "unusual trading activity."

In a roughly 15-minute span that began around 2:30 p.m. on Wall Street, the Dow, which was already down almost 300 points, suffered the bulk of its biggest-ever intraday dive, falling as much as 998.50 points, or 9.2%, to 9869.62. The violent drop was followed by a rebound nearly as steep, with the Dow finishing down 347.80 points, or 3.2%, to 10,502.32.

The fast-and-furious drop caught traders off guard, sparking a vicious rumor mill, as there was no apparent news event to spark such a sudden plunge. While it was occurring, Andy Brooks, a trader at T. Rowe Price, guessed that it was a so-called "fat finger" trade, a term used to describe a trade that is entered incorrectly by human hands. "I have no idea why it happened; when it falls that far and fast and bounces back that quickly, you figure it's an error or tech snafu," Brooks said.

It turns out the veteran trader's suspicions were on target. Some unusual trades — which are believed to have been made in error — in well-known, big-name stocks such as Procter & Gamble, which dropped 37% in the blink of an

Please see COVER STORY next page ►

By the numbers

On Thursday, the Dow Jones industrial average had one of the most turbulent trading days in its history and suffered its biggest intraday loss.

- Thursday's intraday trade loss: **998.50**
- Thursday's intraday percentage loss: **9.2%**
- Thursday's point loss: **347.80**
- Thursday's percentage loss: **3.2%**
- Percentage loss since record close of 14,164.53 on Oct. 9, 2007: **25.7%**
- Point loss over past three days: **631.51**
- Percentage loss over past three days: **5.7%**
- Largest three-day point loss since: **November 2008**
- Largest three-day percentage loss since: **March 2009**
- Percentage gain this year: **0.9%**

Sources: The Associated Press, Dow Jones & Co.

DJIA Timeline Perspective: 10 Year chart with published forecasted July 2010 commencement of resumed advance in U.S. economy circled:

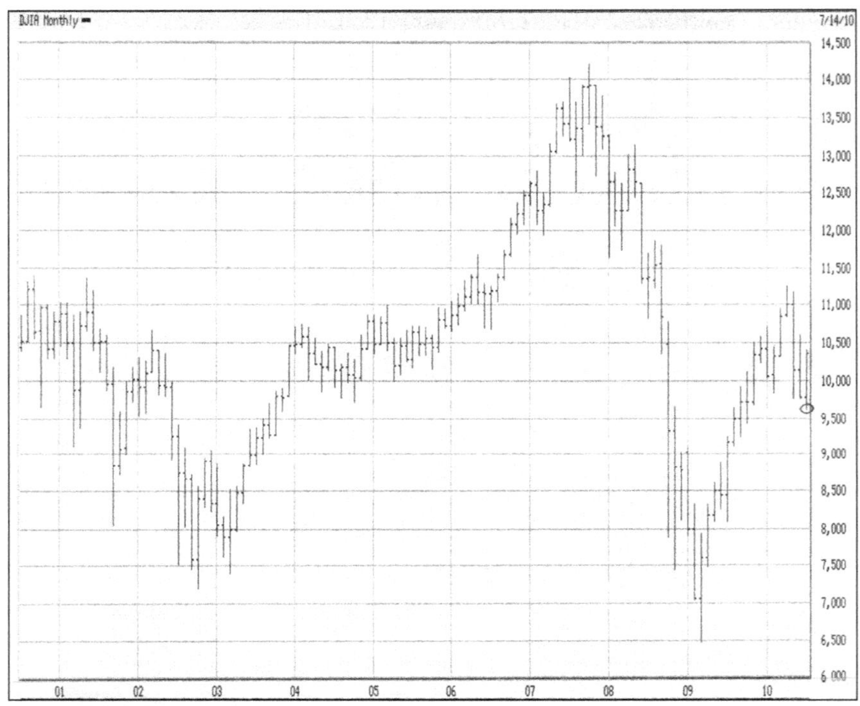

www.Ohio.com

Akron Beacon Journal • Thursday, July 15, 2010

PLICATIONS INCLUDE SWITCHING TO GENERAL AIR PERMITTING.
Jul 15

SUMMARY OF ORDINANCE NO. 220-2010 DETERMINING TO PROCEED WITH THE IMPROVEMENT OF ANDERSON AVENUE AND CERTAIN OTHER STREETS BETWEEN CERTAIN TERMINI (2010 PHASE I UNIMPROVED STREET RESURFACING PROGRAM) BY TREATING THE SURFACE THEREOF AND DECLARING AN EMERGENCY.

Council enacted an ordinance determining to proceed with the improvement of Anderson Avenue and the other streets designated between certain termini in Resolution No. 128-2010, by treating the surface thereof with substances designed to preserve the surface (the "Improvement"). The estimated special assessments prepared and filed in the office of the Clerk of Council with respect to the Improvement were adopted.

Adopted: June 28, 2010
Approved: July 8, 2010

This summary is being published pursuant to Section 38 of the City Charter. The complete text of the Ordinance is available at the office of the Clerk of Council.
Jul 15

SUMMARY OF ORDINANCE NO. 221-2010 DETERMINING TO PROCEED WITH THE IMPROVEMENT OF ARCH STREET AND CERTAIN OTHER STREETS BETWEEN CERTAIN TERMINI (2010 PHASE I RESIDENTIAL RESURFACING PROGRAM) BY RESURFACING AND DECLARING AN EMERGENCY.

Council enacted an ordi-

ANNOUNCEMENTS

1005 Events

★★★★★
BROWNS & INDIANS
ALL GAMES
ALL CONCERTS
1-800-210-1459
★★★★★

GENERAL

1825 Professional

7/2/10 DJIA 9614.32 will advance to 12,500 by Dec. 2010, then decline to 500 by 2nd Qtr. 2012.
Soul Esprit

1840 Attorneys

A BANKRUPTCY & debt relief firm. Fair fees. Call 330-730-2852

A Debt Relief Law Firm
BANKRUPTCY
$495* $0 Down
*min. atty. fees Chpt. 7
Offices in Downtown Akron
(330)-370-7800
Member Better Business Bureau

DEBT RELIEF & BANKRUPTCY. Exp., Free Consult., Pay Plans. Evening & Weekend Hrs. 1-330-253-6264

DISSOLUTIONS, $200
Divorces, $500.

Journal.
Don't Wait, Do It Today!

Job Hunting?
Online. Anytime.
Ohio.com monster
ohio.monster.com

Marketing/Sales

The Beacon Journal
The Akron Beacon Journal is seeking Representatives for events and kiosks in the Akron area.
• No experience nec.
• Part time & FT hrs.
• Flexible schedules
• Start right away
Must be 18 or older w/ reliable transportation
Call today to schedule an interview. 330-996-3691
EOE

Find your next home here!
In print. Online. Anytime.

cargo vans for scheduled routes. Apply in person, 8-5 M-F 4240 Sunnybrook Rd., Kent.

Single or Team OTR Drivers Needed.
Class A CDL, 2 yrs. exp. a must. Excellent pay, miles & equipment. Sign on bonus & performance incentives! Great owner ops pay rate.
Call Recruiting @ 419.433.6200 for details.

Tanker Drivers Class A
Dillon
Average $50,000 per year, Local & Regional, Full Benefits + 401K, Hazmat & Tanker Reqd. 2 years Exp. TWIC a plus.
Lodi, Ohio
www.dillontransport.com
Call Tom @ 330-439-4154
tbarco@dillontransport.com

Unspecified/ General

Apartment MANAGE COUPLE
Full time position, 70 unit suburban apt. community in Summit County. Exp. in leasing and apt. maintenance. Ambitious, knowledgeable and friendly. Salary, suite, medical, utilities paid. Must live on-site and have valid drivers license. Call 330-630-9092 or fax resume to 330-630-9093.

Auto
EXP. auto dismantler. Must have tools & prior exp. Hrly. rate neg. w/exp. Apply in person only. Bumper to Bumper Auto, 66 W. Waterloo Rd., Akron, 44319.

Carpenters
Framing carpenters needed. Out of state work. 330-465-8418.

Courier

AUCTIONEER: JERRY JARVIS
330-352-0243 452 Dorset

5201 Tag & Estate Sales

ESTATE SALE
July 15 & 16, 9-5, July 17 9-1. 7341 Glengary, Sagamore Hills, (Rt. 82 to Canyon View).
This condo w/ bsmt. is chalk full, 70's mod furniture, incld. contour chair, walnut wall unit, coffee table, bedroom set - vintage Boy Scout, Roy Rogers spurs in box, wood wagon, huge amount of Brown's, Indians & Ohio State fan gear, Austin & other sculptures, lg. amount of camping & outdoor equipment including 3 canopies, new linens in packages, computer, stereo, Kodak Easy Share of photo dock, fountains and much more misc. Enormous amount of men's stylish casual fashions, (lg. & extra lg.) many new w/ tags. Must see to believe.
S'More Antiques & Collectibles

Walker Liquidating
ESTATE SALE
Sat. & Sun. - July 17-18
10 am – 4 pm
8185 Chestnut Blvd.
Broadview Heights 44147
Sale Day 330-620-3582
First Day Nos. 9 a.m.
Easy Directions: Take Exit 151 (Wallings Rd.) off I-77 and go West to Left on Chestnut. Super Clean, Air Conditioned Home with treasures waiting for you. See website for Photos & Map. As Always, Priced to Sell
www.walkerliquidating.com

This forecast was upgraded 6 months later (see the following January 22 notice) to make "fine tuning" adjustments as the analysis became clearer. The DJIA 500 level is not expected to occur until the terminal bottom in 2019-2020.

7) The previous timeline for a crashing stock market in 2012-2013 was aborted by the Illuminati world cotrollers who were not yet prepared to fully implement their New World Order Globalist Agenda. A new timeline anticipates a market advance until the year 2015.

F2 Akron Beacon Journal • Saturday, January 22, 2011

struction and Materials Specifications, 2008 Edition, each proposal must be accompanied by a certified check in the sum of 5% of bids on a solvent bank, or a bid bond in like amount, acceptable to the City of Akron, as a guarantee, that if the proposal be accepted, a contract will be entered into.

Bids may be held by the City of Akron for a period not to exceed ninety (90) days from the date of the opening of Bids for the purpose of reviewing the Bids and investigating the qualifications of Bidders, prior to awarding the contract.

Except as provided in Section 103.05 of The City of Akron, Construction and Materials Specifications, 2008 Edition, the bidder to whom the contract is awarded will be required to furnish a bond in the sum of 100% of contract price for the faithful performance of the contract.

The Director of Public Service reserves the right to reject any or all bids, and to waive informalities.

By Order of the
Director of
Public Service
Richard Merolla
Director of
Public Service
Advertise: January 15 and 22, 2011
Jan 15, 22

the sum of 5% of bids on a solvent bank, or a bid bond in like amount, acceptable to the City of Akron, as a guarantee, that if the proposal be accepted, a contract will be entered into.

Bids may be held by the City of Akron for a period not to exceed ninety (90) days from the date of the opening of Bids for the purpose of reviewing the Bids and investigating the qualifications of Bidders, prior to awarding the contract.

Except as provided in Section 103.05 of The City of Akron, Construction and Materials Specifications, 2008 Edition, the bidder to whom the contract is awarded will be required to furnish a bond in the sum of 100% of contract price for the faithful performance of the contract.

The Director of Public Service reserves the right to reject any or all bids, and to waive informalities.

By Order of the
Director of
Public Service
Richard Merolla
Director of Public
Service
Advertise: January 15 and 22, 2011
Jan 15, 22

Persons with disabilities needing assistance are asked to contact Billy Soule, Assistant to the Mayor for Community Relations, 166 South High Street, Room 503, Akron, Ohio 44308, 330-375-2189 (voice), 330-375-2345 (TDD), at least seven (7) days in advance.
Jan 22

LEGAL NOTICE
PROPOSAL
2011-2-1581
PROJECT UAK090001
Bierce Library Learning Commons Phase 1B FF&E
Bids Due: 2 P.M., local time, February 9, 2011; at THE UNIVERSITY OF AKRON, DEPARTMENT OF PURCHASING, 100 LINCOLN STREET, ROOM 209, AKRON, OHIO 44325 9001.
EDGE Participation Goal: 5%of contract.
Estimated cost:
Café Furniture$ 52,000.00
Library Shelving & Pin-Wheel Units $ 46,000.00
Miscellaneous Furniture/Relocation/ Cleaning Upholstery$ 160,000.00
Total $ 258,000.00
Bid Information: http://www3.uakron.edu /bids/conbidresults.htm
Bill J. Jenkins
Assistant Director of Purchasing
TWO INSERTS: 1/22/11, 1/29/11
Jan 22, 29

www.dnb.com and click on "D & B D-U-N-S Number" to obtain a number.

In addition, all Contractors are required to register with the Central Contractor Registration (CCR). Registration information for the Central Contractor Registry can be found at: http://www.ccr.gov/startregistration.aspx .

Copies of plans, specifications and contract documents are on file and can be obtained from eBLUEPRINT, 1915 W. MARKET STREET, AKRON, OHIO 44313, TELEPHONE 330-865-4800 at a cost of Twenty-five ($25.00) Dollars, which money is not refundable. PLEASE FAX OR E-MAIL YOUR REQUESTS PRIOR TO PURCHASE, FAX: 330-376-2511, E-MAIL: akron.all@e-arc.com YOU WILL THEN BE CONTACTED WHEN PLANS ARE AVAILABLE FOR YOUR PICK-UP. They can also be viewed in the office of the Bureau of Engineering, 7th Floor Municipal Building, Akron, Ohio.

Plans are in accordance with the City of Akron, Construction and Material Specifications, 2008 Edition and with

Continued next column

ANNOUNCEMENTS

1000 Special Bulletins

FINAL top in U.S. Stock Market: 2nd wk. Feb., DJIA 12,000-12,200; 2012 1st & 2nd Qtr. crash; 2013 near term bottom, DJIA 2400. Soul Esprit.

1005 Events

★★★★★
CAVS & INDIANS
ALL GAMES
ALL CONCERTS
1-800-210-1459
★★★★★

$$$$$$
Texas Hold 'Em Tournament Saturday January 29 at The Barberton Moose Lodge. For tickets or information call Pat Landolph at 330-592-4650. Space is limited!

The historically significant economic events listed below were also forecasted by the author but not documented by publication. Dates of forecasts (personal communiqués) are in parenthesis:

8) Primary top in the U.S economy in March 2000, as evidenced by *all* stock indices: S&P, NASDAQ, etc. (January 2000); *except* the DJIA (October 11, 2007. DJIA forecast was published August 10; November 18, 2007; ref. Chapter 2.)

9) Crashing financial markets resulting from September 11, 2001 government-staged terrorism (February 2001). Fourth largest weekly and second largest monthly DJIA point decline in stock market history.

10) Terminal reverse point of the 3 year DJIA decline ending in March 2003 (March 2003).

11) Bursting of the real estate Bubble that began in 2006 (April 2005). ref. author's book: *Fractal Trading.*

APPENDIX E

Conspiracy Theory

"In politics stupidity is not a handicap." - Napoleon Bonaparte

... the image of the beast should both speak, and cause that as many as would not worship the image of the beast should be killed.

– Revelation 13:15

Truth abhors a vacuum. In the absence of truth, falsehood and error rush in to fill the empty void. When the noble truth rises up to confront the devious lie, the lie flees under the cover of darkness, only to put forth venomous tentacles in an effort to confuse and confound all those who *worship the image of the beast.*

The Bible has much to say regarding the Image of the Beast. It is both a man-made political construct: a system of government tyranny; and an individual: the new global leader soon to be announced (Revelation 13:1-8). To worship is to obey. Romans 6:16: *Know ye not, that to whom ye yield yourselves servants to obey, his servants ye are to whom ye obey; whether of sin unto death, or of obedience unto righteousness?* Therefore, all who obey today's unrighteous New World Order government, worship the Beast. Revelation 9:20 states they *worship devils.* The Word of God further reveals that the devil is Satan, the father of lies. Hence, the lies spewed forth by today's NWO government-controlled media are believed by the majority who worship (obey) Satan. Those few who do not believe government lies and do not worship and obey devils are called "Conspiracy Theorists."

In an attempt to discredit the truth of a matter, the government media creates *disinformation* which they promote as the "official version" of what happened. Factual information which debunks that government-created myth is labeled "Conspiracy Theory." For example, the 9/11 engineered crisis and controlled demolition of NYC Twin Towers and WTC 7 was orchestrated in advance by the Illuminati supra-government Global Hierarchy for the purpose of offering a plausible rationale to the American people for entering into war with Iraq and also the real reason of controlling their oil reserves and Afghanistan opium poppy fields. No Arab "terrorists" were directly involved in the political gambit; the planes were remote controlled; the buildings were imploded by the use of thermite plastic explosives; the Pentagon was not struck by a rogue jet; and Osama bin Laden had nothing whatsoever to do with it. (bin Laden has been a CIA operative on the U.S. government payroll for over 30 years. He is George Orwell's "Emmanuel Goldstein," perpetual enemy of the state, invisible bogyman, itinerant "terrorist" extraordinaire. True Conspiracy Theorists in government office use bin Laden as a convenient *scapegoat.*) All the foregoing statements are documented facts, yet, George W. Bush boldly stood atop a heaping mountain of 9/11 rubble, shaking a clenched fist, and – while all America watched in wide-eyed breathless anticipation – pronounced vengeance upon the "terrorist" Osama bin Laden/Emmanuel Goldstein. (Just prior to this media circus act, the little Bush was entertaining elementary school students, reading a children's book about goats. He then went on to entertain adult elementary school children, reading from a teleprompter script prepared by Illuminati *government goats.*) It is staged media performances such as this which are "Conspiracy Theory."

The media is populated with agents of disinformation, hucksters of propaganda, creators of theatrics of the mind, whose sole task is to lend credibility to the "official government version" lie. Shawn

Hannity, Bill O'Reilly, Glen Beck, Rush Limbaugh, et al, and the Illuminati-controlled television news networks (CNN, Fox News, MSNBC, etc.) are scripted and sanctioned by the CFR beast government which they serve. Snickering in the face of obvious truth, they promote the blatant deceptions created by their government handlers for the purpose of controlling public opinion and perceptions. Popular news disinformation supports the Globalist's Agenda for a New World Order global dictatorship. Any opposition to that disinformation is ridiculed as not being credible, spurious, and unfounded. Media coverage of the *truth message* is sparse or nonexistent, and the truth proponents are often ridiculed, blacklisted and not given a public forum – e.g. Ron Paul's ineffectual presidential "campaign." (A Freemason and supporter of some of the Globalist's Agenda, Paul exemplifies the Dialectic Principle.) The government-controlled media spins the true account of what actually happened, then diverts the issue and trivializes the truth message by vilifying the messenger with ad hominum character assassinations. In this manner the controlled media discredits the account and contains the outpouring of fact-based objective truth, treating it as damage control. News media reporting is "Conspiracy Theory."

APPENDIX F

An Open Letter to Satanists, Witches, New Agers, Agnostics/Atheists, pseudo-Christians

The mouth of the righteous speaketh wisdom, and his tongue talketh of judgment.
– Psalm 37:30

Go not into the way of the Gentiles, and into any city of the Samaritans enter ye not: But go rather to the lost sheep of the house of Israel. And as ye go, preach, saying, The kingdom of heaven is at hand.
– Matthew 10:5-7

For those who make no claim to being a Christian, or to agreeing with the doctrines espoused by Christianity, it is advisable to reserve your judgment of them who profess to be Christians, but who are, in fact, *impostors.* Some of you rejected Christianity for this very reason, having made the false assumption that hypocritical pseudo-Christians are representative of True Christianity. Although they bear the self-professed title of "Christian," these *are not* True Christians, but actually hold more in common with your pagan doctrines than with Bible-based Christianity. Just because someone calls them self "a Christian," does not mean they *are*, in fact, truly Christian. Others among you have rejected Christianity because you believe that faith and trust in Jesus Christ is without power, impotent, a sign of weakness, ignorance, or naiveté. But, *you are deceived,* for nothing could be further from the truth.

You seek power, control over your life, and the lives of others. You want the riches of this life, now, in the present, because you think this world is "all there is." You resolve that in order to get that power you must serve another "god," one who promises that you can have it all – anything you want – and all you have to do is "bow down and serve him." But yet, you have overlooked a critical piece of information: Satan is a liar, and *the father of lies ... because there is no truth in him. When he speaketh a lie, he speaketh of his own: for he is a liar, and the father of it* (John 8:44). If you have put your trust in a known liar who can tell you nothing but falsehoods, what can you reasonably expect?

This letter is not intended as further condemnation of you who serve the false god of this world, for the author has already sufficiently expressed that righteous sentiment throughout the preceding pages and in other books. Rather, it is written in the hope that you will take an objective view of your life in a broader context than *blind faith* in the present world, for this life is a mere shadow of what is to come; there *will* be consequences for what is done while in the body. You are being tested, and are failing miserably. But yet, you are not without hope. It is written: *For the Son of man is come to save that which was lost* (Matthew 18:11; Luke 19:10). Jesus (God in human form) spent most of His time among sinners; He said: *They that be whole need not a physician, but they that are sick. But go ye and learn what that meaneth, I will have mercy, and not sacrifice: for I am not come to call the righteous, but sinners to repentance* (Matthew 9:12,13). Regardless of any evil you have done, it can be forgiven by a merciful God, Who said: *I will have mercy on whom I will have mercy* (Romans 9:15). The apostle Paul was an accomplice to murder and was deceived, much like yourselves, but he did it in ignorance: *Who was before a blasphemer, and a persecutor, and injurious: but I obtained mercy, because I did it ignorantly in unbelief* (1 Timothy 1:13). But, he turned from doing evil (repented) and God gave him a better hope. *And the times of this ignorance God winked at; but now commandeth all men every where to repent* (Acts 17:30). Paul was a religious zealot, also similar to yourselves in that regard, for among you are those who seek a spiritual experience, and pursue it with a fervor and zeal that puts many who profess Christianity to shame.

You want power? Jesus said: *He that believeth on me, the works that I do shall he do also; and greater works than these shall he do; because I go unto my Father* (John 14:12). Further, he states: *If ye have faith as a grain of mustard seed, ye shall say unto this mountain, remove hence to yonder place; and it shall remove; and nothing shall be impossible unto you* (Matthew 17:20; Luke 17:6). Power does not come from within your own being, but from outside yourself; it is not to be used for your own self-centered purposes – e.g. to control other people. Power which comes from God is for *His glory*, not your own. To comprehend this, you will first have to be broken, perhaps destitute, and experience the depths of humility. Yet, God will hold you up and not allow you to fall, for his Word says: ... *when I am weak, then am I strong* (2 Corinthians 12:10). God will not hear or receive you in your present state; you must come to Him in a spirit of repentance, sincerity, brokenness, humility, and separation from the world. *God resisteth the proud, but giveth grace unto the humble* (James 4:6). *The LORD is nigh unto them that are of a broken heart; and saveth such as be of a contrite spirit* (Psalm 34:18). The continual sacrifices you make to your deceitful master are the very means by which you are being held in bondage. The Spirit of God challenges you to break free of that slavery and live in true liberty – forever. *And ye shall know the truth, and the truth shall make you free* (John 8:32). *For thou desirest not sacrifice; else would I give it: thou delightest not in burnt offering. The sacrifices of God are a broken spirit: a broken and a contrite heart, O God, thou wilt not despise....Then shalt thou be pleased with the sacrifices of righteousness* (Psalm 51:16,17,19).

Some of you believe that you have power of your own volition, derived from within yourself; a command of the natural world or special knowledge that enables you to "tap into" the "energy flow of the universe." You live in a "Star Wars/Harry Potter" fantasy world ruled by impersonal "forces" or spirit beings of questionable origin. Increasingly more of you are experiencing direct contact with these disembodied entities, and wholeheartedly believe they are who they claim to be: "extraterrestrials," "nature spirits," "spirit guides," "ancient ascended masters," "energy," "avatars," "Mother Mary," your deceased spouse or relative, etc. And, even though you do not believe in the existence of the Devil/Satan (for his existence does not require your belief) he is nonetheless the one who has deceived you. Revelation 12:9: *And the great dragon was cast out, that old serpent, called the Devil, and Satan, which deceiveth the whole world.* You were taken in by The Great Deception; duped, fooled, lied to ... *giving heed to seducing spirits* (1 Timothy 4:1). You have not embraced the truth, but a poisonous snake, a reptile; and having been bitten are therefore *deceived.* What you believe, is a *fable*, the oldest lie known to man: ... *ye shall be as gods* (Genesis 3:5). What God offers in His Word, the 1611 King James Bible, is *true* spiritual reality. Belief it, and reject the greatest lie ever told, which you have accepted as "truth."

Many of you look to human beings as a "god" figure, trusting in the next election, the next silver-tongued politician who promises you the world, but delivers nothing. And soon, or presently, you will also accept as legitimate, the *ultimate* politician who will be the epitome of unrighteous human government. If you believe the false promises of man, he will lead you where you wish to go ... *the way of the wicked seduceth them ... for by thy sorceries were all nations deceived* (Proverb 12:26; Revelation 18:23). The first step in your recovery from being taken captive by the matrix of deceit is to consider the possibility that you could be mistaken in your core beliefs; might be wrong about your basic assumptions, and allow for the contingency that you have "overlooked something." There are *eternal consequences* for having made a critical error concerning your spiritual allegiance – *ultimate consequences* that cannot be revoked. If you do not reject the lie and receive the truth of the way of Jesus Christ, the repercussions after your physical death will be permanent. Acts 4:12: *Neither is there salvation in any other: for there is none other name under heaven given among men, whereby we must be saved.* Hebrews 9:27: *And as it is appointed unto men once to die, but after this the judgment.* Instead of voting for a "false messiah" or channeling your New Age "spirit guides," read the Word of God and have *His Holy Spirit* work through you. The light you shall receive will be the true light of the gospel, and not the deceptive light of Lucifer's darkness. Matthew 6:23: *But if thine eye be evil, thy whole body shall be full of darkness. If therefore the light that is in thee be darkness, how great is that darkness*! The right choice is very easy to make: if you receive the truth of the 1611 King James Bible and believe what Jesus taught, you stand to gain everything and lose nothing. But if you reject it, and are wrong (and you *are* wrong), you lose everything. Therefore, in believing the 1611 King James Bible Word of God – and doing what it teaches – there is *no risk*! Simply ask Jesus Christ to give you the *faith* to receive His grace to reject the lie and believe the truth. His indwelling Holy Spirit will do the rest, for Jesus Christ *literally is* the Truth (John 14:6). Read the Bible aloud, or otherwise *audibly hear* the Word of God spoken, for: *"... faith cometh by hearing, and hearing by the word of God* (Romans 10:17). You cannot save yourself; you will not be reincarnated and given another chance; you will not attain perfection by any work or esoteric knowledge. It is only the shed blood of Jesus Christ that will save you. *And they overcame him by the blood of the Lamb...* (Revelation 12:11). There is power in the name of Jesus Christ; the demons that now indwell you are terrified at the mention of that Name and the power of His shed blood. (James 2:19). Therefore, verbally command them in the name of Jesus ... and watch them flee (Luke 10:19.20).

Very little can be said to those who deny the existence of God or that deny the reality of His existence can be proven. If an Atheist or Agnostic were to be honest, all he would need to do is gaze upon the world that shimmers and moves before his eyes – the beauty, subtlety, incomprehensible infinity – and ask, "Where did all this come from? ... Who made this?" Any other reply but "*In the beginning God created the heaven and the earth"* (Genesis1:1), can only be answered with further Scripture: *The fool hath said in his heart, There is no God. They are corrupt, they have done abominable works, there is none that doeth good* (Psalms 14:1; 53:1). *Because that which may be known of God is manifest in them; for God hath shown it unto them. For the invisible things of him from the creation of the world are clearly seen, being understood by the things that are made, even his eternal power and Godhead; so that they are without excuse: Because that, when they knew God, they glorified him not as God, neither were thankful; but became vain in their imaginations, and their foolish heart was darkened. Professing themselves to be wise, they became fools* (Romans 1:19-22). To claim there is no God is to acknowledge that the concept of God is valid, and therefore infers His existence. Thus, the logic of those denying God's existence or that it cannot be proven, is self-contradictory and shown to be fallacious. For such a recalcitrant and deceived individual, the Word of God counsels: *Repent ye, and believe the gospel* (Mark 1:15).

There is no greater deceived than those who believe themselves *True* Christians, when in fact they merely *profess to be Christian.* In today's neopagan revival America, where many wish to think well of themselves and for others to think well of them by identifying with the convenient label, "Christian," that word has lost nearly all of its original meaning. Today, the term, "Christian," has become the most overused and meaningless word in the English language. In some contexts, it has come to mean the exact opposite of its original usage. It was during the early part of the first century that this word originated; yet, those early believers at Antioch to whom it was appended were persecuted, hunted, tortured and slain for publicly acknowledging that distinction. They were not ashamed of the name of Jesus Christ, and against all odds stood for the truth and did not fear the unrighteous "authorities" of that day – the pagan Roman government and hypocritical religious Pharisees. They had already counted the cost of what would be required of them – *physical death* – but gladly met total bodily destruction because they knew what they were dying for was Worthy: *Thou art worthy, O Lord, to receive glory and honour and power: for thou hast created all things, and for thy pleasure they are and were created* (Revelation 4:11). The same is true in many parts of the world today: South America, Asia, Africa, and the Middle East. Many are suffering persecution unto death for their allegiance to the Truth of the gospel of Jesus Christ.

For the unrepentant who profess Christianity, and especially those of that persuasion calling them self "Pastor," their condemnation on the final Day of Judgment will be among the most severe. Unlike the above other categories of spiritually deceived, the Bible has little sympathy for those who know the truth, *and having a form of godliness, but denying the power thereof* (2 Timothy 3:5-9). The only exceptions are those newly exposed to the truth of God's Word, and who have recently made the decision to follow the Lord Jesus Christ, but are unlearned in the true doctrines of the King James Bible. They do error because of the twisted and perverted teachings of the corrupt and unclean body (false church) to which they have joined themselves. Hence, the burden of culpability rests upon the apostate church pastor and associated elders … *I know the blasphemy of them which say they are Jews, and are not, but are the synagogue of Satan* (Revelation 2:9). To those well-meaning new Christians who *cannot discern between their right hand and their left hand* (Jonah 4:11), the Word of God counsels: *Come out of her, my people, that ye be not partakers of her sins, and that ye receive not of her plagues* (Revelation 18:4).

For those who truly wish to know the truth – the Truth that is Jesus Christ – it is strongly advised not to partake in any way with a 501(c)3 *government-approved "church,"* since it is imbued with the spirit of antichrist, and is indeed the *synagogue of Satan*. Rather, the author suggests that you gather in small groups in your homes and read the 1611 King James Bible together in one Spirit. In like manner was the first century Church at Antioch and during Pentecost.

There is more hope for the Satanists, Witches, New Agers, Agnostics and Atheists than for pseudo-Christians professing

Christianity. *For it is impossible for those who were once enlightened, and have tasted of the heavenly gift, and were made partakers of the Holy Ghost, And tasted the good word of God, and the powers of the world to come, If they shall fall away, to renew them again unto repentance; seeing they crucify to themselves the Son of God afresh, and put him to an open shame … But that which beareth thorns and briers is rejected, and is nigh unto cursing: whose end is to be burned* (Hebrews 6:4-6,8*). So then because thou art lukewarm, and neither cold nor hot, I will spew thee out of my mouth* (Revelation 3:16).

The false doctrines that have been taught to Professing Christians are largely to blame for their willful misguided disobedience to the Word of God. Indeed, most of them have never even read the true Bible: the Authorized 1611 King James, so they would not know what it teaches, even if you told them. For example, they have been instructed by their church Pastor (who is likely a Masonic "change agent," "facilitator," who infiltrated their congregation with the intent of causing division and scattering the flock) that all they need to do in order to be "Saved" is recite the "Sinner's Prayer." According to this erroneous belief, from that moment on, they are guaranteed eternal salvation – regardless of what they may or may not do throughout the remainder of their life. This is the "Once Saved, Always Saved" *false doctrine* so prevalent among pseudo-Christianity today. It is essentially a magic incantation, a witchcraft pronouncement, bearing curses for those foolish enough to believe it. As Jesus stated, they *do error, not knowing the scriptures, nor the power of God* (Matthew 22:29; Mark 12:24). In both the Old and New Testament, the Bible clearly teaches that God's Covenant, and therefore His salvation, is *conditional* (Deuteronomy 29:20; Matthew 10:22; 24:13; Mark 13:13; 2 Timothy 4:3,4; James 5:19,20; Revelation 3:5; 22:18,19). Pseudo-Christian pastors are teaching their undiscerning congregation that they are not under the Law, classifying obedience to God's Word as "legalism," and they can therefore sin, yet still be Saved. This is a heresy, and symptomatic of the synagogue of Satan antichrist spirit prevalent among what today passes for the true Christian Church.

APPENDIX G

What is a True Christian?

No man can serve two masters: for either he will hate the one, and love the other; or else he will hold to the one, and despise the other. Ye cannot serve God and mammon. – Matthew 6:24

Think not that I am come to send peace on earth: I came not to send peace, but a sword. For I am come to set a man at variance against his father, and the daughter against her mother, and the daughter-in-law against her mother-in-law. And a man's foes shall be they of his own household. He that loveth father or mother more than me is not worthy of me: and he that loveth son or daughter more than me is not worthy of me. And he that taketh not his cross, and followeth after me, is not worthy of me. He that findeth his life shall lose it: and he that loseth his life for my sake shall find it.
– Matthew 10:34-39

And a stranger will they not follow, but will flee from him: for they know not the voice of strangers. – John 10:5

Here is the patience of the saints: here are they that keep the commandments of God, and the faith of Jesus. And I heard a voice from heaven saying unto me, Write, Blessed are the dead which die in the Lord from henceforth: Yea, saith the Spirit, that they may rest from their labors; and their works do follow them. – Revelation 14:12-13

"Resistance to tyrants is obedience to God." – Thomas Jefferson

"All that is necessary for the triumph of evil is that good men do nothing."
– Edmund Burke

(*Corollary*: Men who do nothing are not good.)

You cannot serve two masters. You will either submit to the government Beast or you will resist it. Are you in conformity with the Beast government? Do you obey unrighteous laws, ordinances, and decrees? Do you bow to the representatives of that unrighteous authority? Are your "heroes" and "saviors" worldly human beings operating in the realm of politics? Do you remain silent in the face of tyranny? If so, the Bible assures that your eternal destiny is *the Lake of Fire.*

To claim to be "a Christian" has become fashionable in today's neopagan society, especially among the organized Christian church, which, ironically, is neither *True* Christian nor the *True* Church. Most of those who patronize a government-approved 501(c)3 organized church are not God's servants, but are deceived into believing they are Saved into the Kingdom of God. Their real identity is that of *Professing* Christian, *pseudo*-Christian; individuals who merely *assume the title* of being "a Christian." For the vast majority of those professing Christianity today there is no spiritual difference between them and the heathen who make no pretense of Godliness. Titus 1:16 describes the essence of a Professing Christian: *They profess that they know God; but in works they deny him, being abominable, and disobedient, and unto every good work reprobate.* Professing Christians "go to church," but are not "The Church." Presently, it seems as if nearly everyone in America is "Christian"; even members of the Criminal Fraternity proclaim themselves to be "Christian." Psychopathic mass murderers and serial killers and pedophiles in high political office and Luciferian New World Order government operatives solemnly profess to being "Christian." Obviously, the term has lost all its former meaning.

Transliterated from the original Greek, the word, *Church,* means *The Called Out Ones.* These are the true servants of the Lord Jesus Christ, the *Elect,* the *Chosen, the Remnant, True Believers.* This tiny *Remnant* are those who have repudiated the illusory material world, repented of their unrighteous deeds, trust solely in the Lord Jesus

Christ for their eternal salvation, and faithfully abide by God's one and only Holy Word, the *1611 King James Bible*. They live in accordance with His Commandments, precepts and ordinances, and acknowledge the 1611 King James Bible as the *sole* legitimate Word of God for the English-speaking people (Ephesians 4:4-6). By the indwelling of God's Holy Spirit they are keenly aware that to believe otherwise is to call God a liar, and in so doing, would attribute to God a chief characteristic of Satan. This is *blasphemy against the Holy Ghost*, the only unforgivable sin (Mark 3:22,28,29).

To make a false claim of being "a Christian" is blasphemy, a very serious offense in the eyes of God. Yet, His name is constantly blasphemed by those who take pride in calling themselves "Christian," or "a Christian Ministry," or "Christian Organization." In today's world of compromised Christianity, if the name "Christian" is appended to an individual, group, or organization, it is nearly always indicative of *not* being *Scripturally* Christian. For a *True* Christian makes no claim or pretense of religious affiliation, but *demonstrates* their spiritual identity by *their works*. Matthew 7:16: *Ye shall know them by their fruits … every good tree bringeth forth good fruit; but a corrupt tree bringeth forth evil fruit.* It is their external actions which *give evidence* of their internal faith. And since salvation is by faith and not by works (Ephesians 2:8), it is therefore their works which give evidence of that faith and judge them as righteous or condemned before God. *Even so faith, if it hath not works, is dead, being alone … Ye see then how that by works a man is justified, and not by faith only … For as the body without the spirit is dead, so faith without works is dead also* (James 2:17,24,26). At times, the deception can be so convincing, the level of deceit so overwhelming – *until* they give evidence of the nature of their works, or lack thereof.

Professing/pseudo-Christians demonstrate few or none of the qualities of a *True* Christian. They are "Christian" in name *only*, not in spirit or deed. For their source of Scripture, *any* "Bible version" will do – any version *except* exclusive adherence to the 1611 King James Bible. The reason for this is because they do not recognize the truth. (The Truth *is* Jesus Christ. John 14:6.) Because the Truth is a stranger to them, they have no allegiance to the Truth, and will run from the truth. *And a stranger will they not follow, but will flee from him: for they know not the voice of strangers* (John 10:5). Because they care nothing for the truth/Truth, God *allows* them to believe a lie and be condemned to hell. 2 Thessalonians 2:10-12: ... *in them that perish; because they receive not the love of the truth ... God shall send them a strong delusion, that they should believe a lie ... that they all might be damned* ... Therefore, the issue of the correct Bible "version" is not a frivolous matter, as rigorously contended by the spiritually deluded, but is of *utmost importance*, and often serves as the first point of departure for a Professing Christian.

Only the Word of God (Jesus Christ) *Saves*. Thus, without the *True* Word of God (1611 King James Bible) it is impossible for an English-speaking people to be Saved into God's eternal Kingdom. *Neither is there salvation in any other: for there is none other name under heaven given among men, whereby we must be saved* (Acts 4:12). There is *only one* God (Deuteronomy 6:4; Mark 12:29), and therefore, there can be *only one* spoken *Word of God* – Jesus Christ (Revelation 19:13). Consequently, there can be *only one* written *Word of God* – i.e. only one Bible version. For this reason, Professing Christians tremble in fear of the exclusivity of the 1611 KJV, since it is the *only* Bible that has the convicting power of God's Holy Spirit. The true Word of God makes them feel uncomfortable because it convicts them of their sins. While defending the many false Bible versions (none faithfully reproducing God's prophesy and Covenant with man) they become argumentative, hostile, engaging in strive and debate, because upholding the unique God-inspired truth of the 1611 King James Bible conflicts with their unrighteous deeds and unrepentant heart. (Typically, those rejecting the exclusivity of the 1611 King James Bible talk of "original Greek and Hebrew manuscripts," "no extant ancient manuscripts," "Dead Sea Scrolls," and other similar lines of obfuscation.) Scripture further affirms they "*know nothing,*" have "*corrupt minds,*" are "*destitute of the truth,*" and believe that "material prosperity *is godliness.*" 1 Timothy 6: 3-5: *If any man teach otherwise, and consent not to wholesome words, even the words of our Lord Jesus Christ, and to the doctrine which is according to godliness; He is proud, knowing nothing, but doting about questions and strifes of words, whereof cometh envy, strife, railings, evil surmisings, Perverse disputings of men of corrupt minds, and destitute of the truth, supposing that gain is godliness: from such withdraw thyself.*

Professing Christians may have a preference for the New International Version (NIV) or some other Satan-inspired texts that were derived from corrupted ancient manuscripts (Alexandria Egypt) and further corrupted by modern *vessels of wrath fitted to destruction* (Romans 9:22). *For I testify unto every man that heareth the words of the prophesy of this book, If any man shall add unto these things, God shall add unto him the plagues that are written in this book: And if any man shall take away from the words of the book of this prophesy, God shall take away his part out of the book of life, and out of the holy city, and from the things which are written in this book* (Revelation 22:18,19). This curse applies not only to the ancient manuscript translators who changed the original Word of God used in today's various corrupted Bible versions, *but also* to all those who profess any of the false Bible versions to be the true gospel. Galatians 1:8: *But though we, or an angel from heaven, preach any other gospel unto you than that which we have preached unto you, let him be accursed.* Like their kindred-spirited Criminal Fraternity brethren, Professing Christians shall reap their reward in the eternal Lake of Fire. Galatians 6:7: *Be not deceived; God is not mocked: for whatsoever a man soweth, that shall he also reap.* The unsaved reject the 1611 King James Bible as the only true written Word of God because they reject the only true God: Jesus Christ. They hate the truth of God's only Word because they hate God, Who *is* The Truth. Pseudo-Christians prefer a "modified version" of God's Word in order for them to interpret what it says in any manner they prefer: 2 Peter 1:20: *Knowing this first, that no prophesy of the scripture is of any private interpretation;* and in a way that is more easily compromised: Isaiah 30:10-12: *Speak unto us smooth things, prophesy deceits. Get you out of the way, turn aside out of the path, cause the Holy One of Israel to cease from before us. Wherefore thus saith the Holy One of Israel, Because ye despise this word …*

Compared to the 1611 King James Bible, the New International Version (NIV) has 64,000 missing words and over 400 missing verses; most of the verses have been reversed. (Verses transposed in reverse order are the Devil's signature, proof that Satan was the editor of the NIV false Bible version.) It is written on the reading comprehension level of a twelve year old. The NIV was created in the 1850's during a time of Masonic infiltration of Christianity, with the resultant formation of several antichrist religious sects, such as Mormonism (Latter Day Saints), Jehovah Witness (Watch Tower Society) and Christian Science. Additionally, one of the NIV editors was an avowed lesbian/witch (Elizabeth Mollicot). The New King James Version (NKJV), although not as obviously apostate as the NIV, has nonetheless substantially altered the original KJV text in opposition and defiance of Revelation 22:18-19. Professing pseudo-Christians must realize there is *only one* Word of God: Jesus Christ (John 1:1; Revelation 19:13). If there were in fact more than one Word(s) of God – i.e. Bible Version – it would require there to be more than one Jesus Christ. And the many pseudo-Christian Protestant denominations and pagan religions do indeed have "another Jesus" (2 Corinthians 11:4). Only a True Christian can understand this. (ref. *New Age Bible Versions*, by Gail Riplinger.)

SILENCE IS BETRAYAL

"The truth must be told. The hottest places in hell are reserved for those who in a period of moral crisis maintained their neutrality. There comes a time when silence is betrayal." – Martin Luther King, Jr.

In tax exempt pseudo-Christian *government churches* all across America, the church administrators have swore their allegiance (in a 501(c)3 written blood pact with the Devil) to the *State Attorney General*, not to Jesus Christ. Colossians 1:18: *And he is the head of the body, the church.* The pastor and congregation obey the Beast government, and are more terrified of the Criminal Fraternity than they are of God's righteous wrath. (In the 1950's, Texas Senator, Lyndon B. Johnson, created 501(c)3 legislation to silence the churches and keep them out of politics.) Apostate "church people" fear the government, not God, and are willing to compromise the truth of His Word and trivialize His righteous Judgment. In today's Godless American culture they take no stand against evil; their silence being proof of their tacit agreement with a God-rejecting world. Their complacency is complicity; those who do not take a stand against wrongdoing are guilty of the crime. Today, nearly all 501(c)3 government-approved "churches" are complicit with evil; they are the synagogue of Satan (Revelation 2:9;3:9). Moreover, in blatant disobedience to God, the pastor is often a woman (1 Timothy 2:12,14; Isaiah 3:12), or in some other manner defies the Word of God, such as being immoral (1 Corinthians 6:9,10; Galatians 5:19-21; Ephesians 5:3-7; Revelation 21:8). Should a true servant of the Lord Jesus Christ venture onto Satan's turf, the Devil's servants will immediately recognize his spirit as being different from their own, and will let it be known that he is not a welcome visitor. In hating the uncompromising 1611 King James Bible message, infidels (2 Corinthians 6:15) typically "shoot the messenger."

Needless to say, Professing Christians have an unregenerate spirit, are not Born Again, and therefore are not "Saved" into the Kingdom of God. These include *Pre-Tribulation Rapturists* – the many millions of spiritually deceived waiting to be bodily removed from the earth prior to the start of the Great Tribulation. Matthew 24:29-31 states the contrary: *Immediately after the tribulation of those days … then shall appear the sign of the Son of man … and he shall send his angels … and they shall gather together his elect.* Their cult belief is a vain desperate hope found no where in Scripture, a false hope they will not have to suffer persecution for the sake of Jesus Christ. (It is *the wicked* that are removed from the earth; the righteous remain.

Proverb 10:30: *The righteous shall never be removed: but the wicked shall not inhabit the earth.*) The Pre-Tribulation rapture doctrine is a myth born of ignorance and cowardice. As the end of the age approaches, and global government tyranny in America encroaches ever further with each passing year, physical death resulting from being a witness to the eternal God of Heaven, Jesus Christ, will increasingly become a necessary requisite for salvation (ref. *New Foxes Book of Martyrs*).

The ranks of the spiritually deceived suddenly increase each time the supra-government Illuminati engineers yet another false crisis (e.g. "terrorist attack") to bring the American people to their knees. Abruptly shocked into subconscious awareness of their imminent demise in the burning Lake of Fire, they submit to their true master (the Criminal Fraternity), gladly forfeiting their God-ordained freedom for "safety" (Malachi 1:2,3); bowing to their government master (human government is Satan's religion). Romans 6:16: *Know ye not, that to whom ye yield yourselves servants to obey, his servants ye are to whom ye obey; whether of sin unto death, or of obedience unto righteousness?* Suffering from terminal identity confusion, the deceived do not realize who they are spiritually. *And a stranger will they not follow, but will flee from him: for they know not the voice of strangers* (John 10:5). For them, the Lord Jesus Christ is *a stranger*; they instinctively flee from their Savior, and instead, follow their Beast government "savior."

The spiritually blind among today's pseudo-Christian churches in America are not led by the Holy Spirit of God, but by *another* spirit*: the spirit of antichrist.* They hearken to *another gospel,* and revile those few True Christians that hold fast to the gospel of Jesus Christ *once delivered to the saints* (Jude 3). Their gospel is typically the NIV, NAS, RSV, NKJV, or some other *corrupt version* of the true Word of God. Lest it should be concluded that an unscriptural belief in a Pre-Tribulation Rapture (introduced into the doctrine of the false church in the mid 1850's, at the time of Freemasonry infiltration of Christianity), or considering the corrupt NIV to be Holy Scripture, are proof criterion for establishing an individual's apostasy, be aware that some Professing Christians and apostate "churches" use the 1611 King James Bible among their sources of Scripture, or perhaps even exclusively as their sole Scripture. This, however, is not definitive in establishing their *True* Christian status. *Ye shall know them by their fruits* (Matthew 7:16,20). Spiritual discernment is often required to recognize the subtle deception.

Judgment begins at the house of the Lord: ... *seest thou what they do? even the great abominations that the house of Israel committeth here, that I should go far off from my sanctuary? but turn thee yet again, and thou shalt see greater abominations.... And the LORD said unto him, Go through the midst of the city, through the midst of Jerusalem, and set a mark upon the foreheads of the men who sigh and that cry for all the abominations that be done in the midst thereof. And to the others he said in mine hearing, Go ye after him though the city, and smite: let not your eye spare, neither have ye pity. Slay utterly old and young, both maids, and little children, and women: but come not near any man upon whom is the mark; and begin at my sanctuary. Then they began at the ancient men which were before the house ... For the time is come that judgment must begin at the house of God: and if it first begin at us, what shall the end be of them that obey not the gospel of God? And if the righteous scarcely be saved, where shall the ungodly and the sinner appear?* (Ezekiel 8:6; 9:4-6; 1 Peter 4:17,18). The spiritually deluded masses of neopagans professing Christianity in today's apostate "government churches" demonstrate no concern over *the great abominations that the house of Israel committeth*. Virtually no where is there heard any that *sigh and that cry for all the abominations that be done in the midst thereof.* Be assured, they are *not marked* with a saving invisible mark upon their foreheads, and God will not spare them in the day of His Judgment. This *shall the end be of them that obey not the gospel of God*.

Phony Christians are "Sheeple," much like the undiscerning apathetic general U.S. population. They care nothing for the truth of God's Word. Few of them have even read it to know what it says, and fewer still understand what they have read because they do not have the indwelling of the God's Holy Spirit to enable them to understand. Thus, they misinterpret what they read in order to assuage their unrepentant sin nature. Like grazing farm animals, they passively stand by watching as the battle rages all around them. Ezekiel 13:5: *Ye have not gone up into the gaps, neither made up the hedge for the house of Israel to stand in the battle in the day of the LORD.* Instead, they smile sheepishly, applaud wicked government leaders, and condemn the righteous who stand against such individuals and the tyrannical Antichrist system they represent. *Because with lies ye have made the heart of the righteous sad, whom I have not made sad; and strengthened the hands of the wicked, that he should not return from his wicked way, by promising him life* (Ezekiel 13:22). 2 Timothy 3:1-7 was written for those today calling themselves "The Church": *This know also, that in the last days perilous times shall come. For men shall be lovers of their own selves, covetous, boasters, proud, blasphemers, disobedient to parents, unthankful, unholy, Without natural affection, trucebreakers, false accusers, incontinent, fierce, despisers of those that are good, Traitors, heady, high-minded, lovers of pleasures more than lovers of God; Having a form of godliness, but denying the power thereof: from such turn away ... Ever learning, and never able to come to a knowledge of the truth.*

If you are a *True* Christian, and not merely profess to be one, you realize that you are in a war, and must therefore be on the *offensive.* You are commanded by God to hate evil, confront it, resist it, and expose it (Amos 5:15; 1 Samuel 17:26; James 4:7; Ephesians 5:11). Being a *True* Christian, you *will* be *offensive* to some people; you *will* offend them because you have a different spirit than they. Your Spirit is of God, and, in knowing that, the unclean spirits which indwell them are offended and despise you. True Christians will offend the unrighteous (i.e. their possessing demonic spirits) who blasphemously refer to themselves as "Christians," "Evangelicals," professing to know God, but are hypocrites: *Ye hypocrites, well did Esaias prophesy of you, saying, This people draweth nigh unto me with their mouth, and honoreth me with their lips; but their heart is far from me. But in vain do they worship me, teaching for doctrines the commandments of men* (Matthew 15:7). *Ye neither know me, nor my Father* (John 8:19). In their mad rage against the righteous, Scriptural prophesy is fulfilled: *Why do ye not understand my speech? even because ye cannot hear my word. Ye are of your father the devil, and the lusts of your father ye will do ... And because I tell you the truth, ye believe me not* (John 8:43-45). *Am I therefore become your enemy, because I tell you the truth?* (Galatians 4:16). It is because of the silence and cowardice of the unrighteous calling themselves "Christians" – and *especially* the Pastors – that evil has been allowed to proliferate like cancer in today's government-controlled, anti-God, anti-Truth, anti-Free Speech American culture.

Pseudo-Christians tremble at the very thought of taking a stand for the truth. They represent no threat to the kingdom of darkness, and as any practicing disciple of Lucifer will tell you: "... they are the best thing that ever happened to the kingdom of Satan." Pseudo-Christian pastors are diligent to be in conformity to their *real* master, the one whom they actually serve: *Satan's unrighteous human government.* (Notice the U.S. flag prominently displayed in their sanctuary and on the front lawn of their "church.") The apostate church pastors are unwilling to confront the evils of today's society; they fear Satan's government people and simply want to be left alone to collect a weekly paycheck. *Hirelings* (John 10:12,13), b*lind leaders of the blind* (Matthew 15:14; Luke 6:39), they abhor speaking out against unrighteousness, unless it happens to be within the narrow guidelines of what their 501(c)3 government-approved Board of Directors will allow them to speak. Their "scripture" is literally a piece of government issue paper that establishes the By Laws of what they can and cannot say or do. But even if it were not for the favorable 501(c)3 tax-exempt status, they *still* would not act in accordance with the Word of God to confront and expose evil: e.g. abortion, corruption of children by unGodly school curriculum, homosexual agenda, unrighteous laws that mock and defy God and His righteous authority, exclusion of the teachings of Jesus Christ from the schools, the courthouses, the home; vaccines; poisoned food, doped water and Chemtrail air; and all the other perverse and unrighteous acts perpetrated by the Globalist's Agenda. The pseudo-Christian churches of today are lead *by women* who have stepped up to fill the void created by neutered effeminate men. Isaiah 3:12: *As for my people, children are their oppressors, and women rule over them.* Today's church pastors do not take a stand for the truth ... *and having done all, to stand* (Ephesians 6:13). They neither believe nor comprehend what the Lord Jesus Christ meant when he commanded them to *Occupy til I come* (Luke 19:13). They see no contradiction of their professed Christian beliefs while remaining passive and silent as all around them True Christianity is under attack by Satan's government. If this discrepancy is pointed out to them, they will simply shrug their shoulders and reply, "God loves everybody ... The government isn't bad ... Look at the American flag we have here in our church sanctuary." (The flag – like all images representative of Satan's kingdom – is *an idol:* Psalm 106:36,37; Matthew 22:20,21; Romans 11:4; 1 John 5:21; Revelation 9:20,13:14,14:9,10. Flag worship is *idolatry*! All idolaters are condemned to the Lake of Fire: Revelation 21:8; 1 Corinthians 6:9,10; Ephesians 5:3-6; Galatians 5:19-21.) But the pseudo-Christian pastors are *dead in their sins* and therefore cannot realize these Scriptural truths. Many of them have not read the King James Bible, or have not read it with Godly discernment to know what it says regarding their disobedience to the Commandments of God (John 8:21,24).

In the author's experience, nearly *all* "Christian" church pastors today are *pseudo-Christians.* Yet, rare exceptions do exist. Much like the well meaning MCF doctor, today's pastors, in a spiritual sense, are lethally dangerous because they have compromised the Word of God. In not taking a stand against evil in society, they are willfully disobedient regarding the application of God's Word to current issues of the day. God commands a *True* Christian to be *salt and light* in a dark world; but their spirit is dead, and there is no light in them. They cannot feel the fire of God's righteous wrath upon the wicked, because *they themselves* are wicked. When God asks them in Psalm 94:16: *Who will rise up for me against the evildoers? or who will stand up for me against the workers of iniquity?* Their response is: "Not me! This is only *a job*. I didn't sign up to be persecuted for the sake of the truth. This is how I make a living! I'm a hireling, a hired hand, and answer only to the church Board of Directors, not to God. I have a family to support ... I might lose *my job!* ... What about *my pension fund*?! ..." They are worldly and they are obedient to whom they serve: an antichrist government. Romans 6:16: *Know ye not, that to whom ye yield yourselves servants to obey, his servants ye are to whom ye obey; whether of sin unto death, or of obedience unto righteousness?* They are so distant from God, so apostate in their theology, they do not even have a *concept* of the characteristics of a *True* Christian. They literally believe that all one needs in order to be Saved is to "go to church," preach John 3:16, and ask God to save them. "Join our church, say the 'sinners prayer' and you go to heaven on the 'Rapture Bus'," they tell their undiscerning congregation. All the while, their children are drinking fluoridated water, fed MSG/Aspartame/GMO "food"; pumped full of Mercury, Lead, Aluminum vaccines; allowed to participate in the satanic culture, and are taught to obey the unGodly decrees of a Luciferian government.

Today's pseudo-Christian pastors refuse to recognize that the life of a True believer in Jesus Christ is one of *persecution* and repeated attacks by the enemy, which in today's Police State America is typically in the form of representatives of the Criminal Fraternity Beast government. They actually think that *going to church* is the same as being a member of *The Church*. Their ignorance is rivaled only by their naiveté. Their weekly gatherings more closely resemble a social club (barbecue, soft ball league, luncheon) than they do a contrite and broken spirit before the Almighty Creator of the universe. They oppose no one, confront no evil, and consequently suffer no persecution by the Beast government which persecutes all who are Godly and righteous in Christ Jesus. *Yea, and all that will live godly in Christ Jesus shall suffer persecution* (2 Timothy 3:12). The reason why they are not persecuted is because *they are not Godly and righteous in Christ Jesus.* Most are possessed by demons of false religion. (In today's America, a high concentration of demon-possessed individuals can be found in so-called "Christian churches." The many denominational churches have become a pooling ground and magnet for attracting those having granted demonic control over their lives. The author recounts in a book, *Everything is a Test: How God delivered me from "Impossible" Situations,* the duplicity demonstrated by some Christian pastors and many of those professing Christianity. He speaks from experience when stating that such are "contemptuous religionists with a feigned concern for the truth, thinly veiled by a cloak of maliciousness, and who will compromise the Word of God to suit their own conscious, whenever deemed expedient." He also acknowledges the exceptions: true men of God, who do not compromise the truth of Holy Scripture, and will not tolerate evil (Revelation 2:2), but take a stand against wrongdoing.

If one were to persist making inquiry of compromising pseudo-Christian pastors in the face of utter futility, the pastor should be asked to reconcile the disparity of Matthew 6:24: *No man can serve two masters: for either he will hate the one, and love the other; or else he will hold to the one, and despise the other. Ye cannot serve God and mammon.* Love-Hate? Hold to-Despise? These represent irreconcilable dichotomies. Yet, the decision must be made for choosing one *or* the other, and cannot be both. The one they *love* is the one they "hold to" (obey) – i.e. *the Beast government.* Therefore, the one they *hate* and *despise is Jesus Christ, the Word of God, God Himself.* They cannot have it both ways. John 14:15: *If you love me, keep my commandments.* Serve one *or* the other; impossible to serve both. These are the men, and women (1 Timothy 2:11-14; 1 Corinthians 14:34,35) calling themselves "Pastor" in today's government-approved 501(c)3 "churches" all across America. They made a deal with the 501(c)3 Federal Devil, and having compromised the truth, refuse to do anything about it. (A very small number of pastors *have* taken steps to denounce wicked human government and serve the only true living God by officially abdicating their 501(c)3 tax exempt status, formally renouncing it as an abomination to the

Lord and that signifies spiritual allegiance to the Beast system of tyranny. They have not, and will not, allow themselves or their assembly of saints to be "marked," physically or spiritually, by the Beast.) Jesus prophesied of the false teachers in Isaiah 56:10,11: *His watchmen are blind: they are all ignorant, they are all dumb dogs, they cannot bark; sleeping, lying down, loving to slumber. Yea, they are greedy dogs which can never have enough, and they are shepherds that cannot understand: they all look to their own way, every one for his gain, from his quarter.* John 8:21: ... *ye shall seek me, and shall die in your sins.* Job 15:34: *For the congregation of the hypocrites shall be desolate, and fire shall consume the tabernacles of bribery.* On the Final Day, standing before the Judgment Throne of God Almighty, they will have no excuse. Matthew 7:21-23: *Not every one that saith unto me, Lord, Lord, shall enter into the kingdom of heaven; but he that doeth the will of my Father which is in heaven. Many will say to me in that day, Lord, Lord, have we not prophesied in thy name? and in thy name have cast out devils? and in thy name done many wonderful works? And then will I profess unto them, I never knew you: depart from me, ye that work iniquity.* Matthew 24:51: *And shall cut him asunder, and appoint him his portion with the hypocrites: there shall be weeping and gnashing of teeth.*

The Beast government Federal Emergency Management Agency (FEMA) has indoctrinated and enlisted over 100,000 "Christian pastors" as their "Clergy Response Team" in anticipation of the soon to be declared Martial Law in America. The church leaders have agreed to tell their congregations not to resist government tyranny during a declared State of Emergency (i.e. staged acts of government terrorism), and have agreed to instruct their followers to receive vaccinations, become government informants against those who possess firearms or stockpile storable food reserves, or who otherwise plan to resist mandates to be dependant upon (worship) the government image of the Beast (Revelation 14:11; 16:2; 19:20). The pseudo-Christian pastors have been programming their flocks with the propaganda mantras: "The government is good. Obey the government, it's of God. Do whatever the government tells you." Romans 13 is often used as justification for rulership of Satan's people over God's people, but verse 3 invalidates the claim that this chapter of Scripture is referring to the Criminal Fraternity, which *are* a terror to good works. Romans 13:3: *For rulers are not a terror to good works*. Verse 6 states that God's ministers care for the things of God, but the CF cares nothing for the things of God. Therefore, these Scriptures *are not* referring to human government rulers, but to True Christian leaders. In further contradiction of these Scriptures, Satan's people neither speak the Word of God nor do they have a care for your soul, but only to destroy it. (Also ref. Hebrews 13:7,17.) All the verses in Romans 13 and the cited Hebrews verses are referring to God's people, *not* Satan's people. Professing Christians are taught they should live harmoniously with unrighteous legal criminals who deny and oppose the Word and will of Jesus Christ. But the Word of God says: *Be ye not unequally yoked together with unbelievers: for what fellowship hath righteousness with unrighteousness? and what communion hath light with darkness? And what concord hath Christ with Belial? or what part hath he that believeth with an infidel?* (2 Corinthians 6:14,15). God's people are not commanded to be at peace with an evil world, but rather, to stringently oppose it. *Think not that I am come to send peace on earth: I came not to send peace, but a sword* (Matthew 10:34). He commanded: *Occupy til I come* (Luke 19:13). In not knowing God, Professing Christians recognize government servants of Satan as their master. Today, if you obey man's corrupt government, you are in disobedience to God.

Whenever encountering a true servant of God, Satan's people impute unto that individual their own antichrist spirit. A wicked person will imagine that a righteous person is evil, like them self, while steadfastly regarding them self as righteous. Accusers of the brethren, Satan's people have always crucified the image of God. One of the ways it is possible to immediately know if someone is righteous is by their reaction to those who are unrighteous. This type of person should not be confused with the individual who appears to abhor evil, but who also abhors those who do good. (Police, and other members of the Criminal Fraternity exemplify this type of double mindedness.) Those who do evil are adamantly opposed to those who are representative of God; Satan's people typically impute their own unrighteousness onto others who are more righteous than themselves. Psalm 55:3: *... for they cast iniquity upon me, and in wrath they hate me.*

Today, the land is filled with the silence of the unrighteous who claim to "love God" and to "love the truth," yet utter not a word of outrage against the Beast government that openly defies and opposes God. (Such duplicitous individuals typically also talk of how much they love "their country.") In their cowardice they demonstrate no love for the truth, and deliberately disobey God, Who commands to *take a stand against evil:* Psalm 94:16: *Who will rise up for me against the evildoers? or who will stand up for me against the workers of iniquity.* God demands of His servants to oppose those who oppose Him: Ephesians 5:11: *And have no fellowship with the unfruitful works of darkness, but rather reprove them.* The blood of the martyrs is upon the head of those who call themselves "Christians" but do nothing to stand against evil. By their silence they *approve of evil.* Their sins of omission make them an accessory to crimes of the mind, body, and soul. On the day of final Judgment, they will not be rewarded according to God's mercy, but according to *their works.* Revelation 20:12,15: *... the dead were judged out of those things which were written in the books, according to their works ... and whosoever was not found written in the book of life was cast into the lake of fire.*

Professing Christians and Professing Christian Pastors are well advised to read the books of the prophets and Psalms to discover that it is the *righteous* who are persecuted by the Beast. As the Antichrist world government is braced and ready to take over, if you are not being persecuted for righteousness sake, could it be that you have not been found worthy of persecution?

Are you a True **Christian?**

To find out if *you* are a True Christian (and not merely profess to be one), answer "Yes" or "No" to each of the following questions:

Do you ...

_____ 1) Believe that the Authorized 1611 King James Bible is the *only* true, complete, and inerrant Word of God?

_____ 2) Use as your sole and exclusive source of Holy Scripture the 1611 KJV Bible? (not the NIV, NAS, NAV, RSV, NKJV, or any other version).

_____ 3) Believe that some or all Bible versions are faithful to the Word of God; are *given by inspiration of God, and are profitable for doctrine, for reproof, for correction, for instruction in righteousness?* (2 Timothy 3:16)

_____ 4) Believe you are "Saved" and going to heaven because of your religion, the particular church you attend, or because a pastor/priest/friend, etc., said that you are "Saved"?

_____ 5) Believe in a Pre-Tribulation "Rapture"?

_____ 6) Attend a government-approved 501(c)3 church that is in conformity to a God-rejecting government which functions in violation of the Word and will of God?

_____ 7) Participate in politics?

_____ 8) Believe you should obey unrighteous government?

_____ 9) Pray for your government leaders?

_____10) Think it is wrong or ungodly to speak out against unrighteous authority?

_____11) Believe it is "Christian" to be "patriotic," "support our troops," send your children to fight and die in political wars for the interests of the Luciferian global elite?

_____12) Consider the police, politicians, lawyers, judges as "True Christian brethren"?

_____13) Watch television, videos, go to movies which do not honor God?

_____14) Allow your children to watch TV, videos, go to movies which do not honor God?

_____15) Watch pornography?

_____16) Smoke or chew tobacco? Become intoxicated from drinking alcohol?

_____17) Get vaccinated or allow your children to be vaccinated?

_____18) Use prescription or nonprescription drugs – legal or illegal?

_____19) Except in a sudden dire life and death emergency, seek medical assistance from a doctor or any other government-approved health care provider?

_____20) Enroll your children in today's public or private schools?

_____21) Home school your children?

_____22) Affiliate and join in a spirit of affirmation with people who reject the Word of God and that have no concern for the truth of the Bible?

_____23) Celebrate or participate in pagan holidays? (e.g. Christmas, Easter, Halloween.)

_____24) Oppose or dislike those who strive to observe God's Commandments and who instruct and reprove others to do likewise?

_____25) Seek or acquire spiritual counsel from a pastor, priest, minister, rabbi, counselor, psychologist, friend, books, movies, religious celebrities, members of your church, or anyone or anything that does not counsel exclusively from the true and correct version of the Bible?

_____26) Believe that a pastor, priest, minister, rabbi, or any other ward of a government-approved church has the God-ordained authority to forgive your sins? (Ezekiel 13:22).

_____27) Think it Scriptural for a woman to pastor a church, be an Elder, teach men, or usurp authority over a man?

_____28) Acknowledge or pray to saints, angels, dead people, the Pope, "Virgin Mother Mary," Buddha, Allah, or any other religious or spiritual figure?

_____29) Seek spiritual inspiration, material benefit, or pray, using statues, icons, beads (e.g. rosary), pictures or images?

_____30) Believe that once you have verbally accepted Jesus Christ as your personal Lord and Savior (made a confession of faith), you are thereafter Saved and going to heaven?

_____31) Believe you can willfully transgress God's Commandments, precepts and ordinances, and still be Saved?

_____32) Engage in or believe that homosexuality is a lifestyle acceptable to God?

_____33) Live with or marry someone who is not your original spouse, or who has been previously married?

_____34) Believe that Jesus Christ is God, God in human form, Who died for the sins of *His Elect*, rose on the third day, and now sits at the right hand of the triune Father God in heaven?

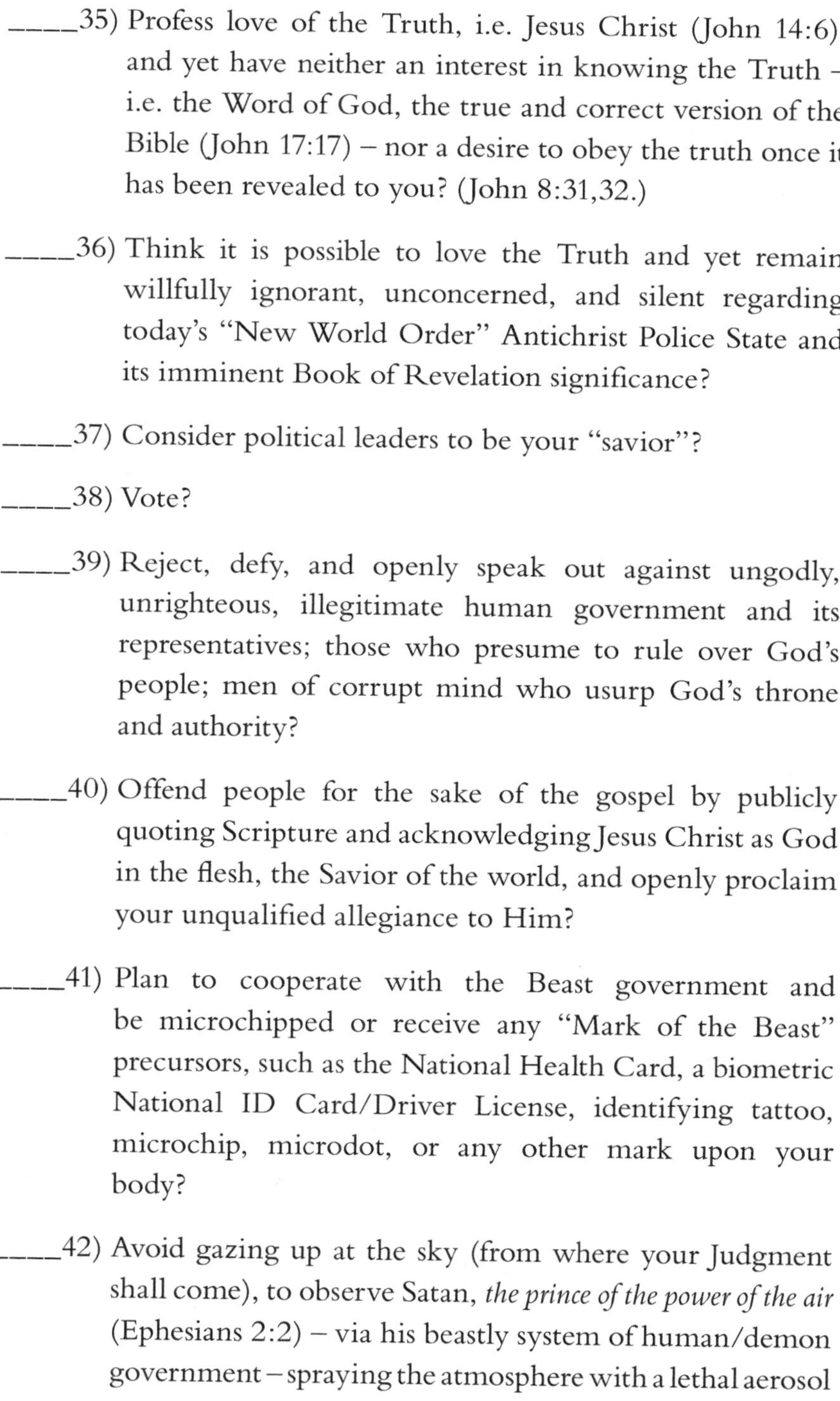

____35) Profess love of the Truth, i.e. Jesus Christ (John 14:6), and yet have neither an interest in knowing the Truth – i.e. the Word of God, the true and correct version of the Bible (John 17:17) – nor a desire to obey the truth once it has been revealed to you? (John 8:31,32.)

____36) Think it is possible to love the Truth and yet remain willfully ignorant, unconcerned, and silent regarding today's "New World Order" Antichrist Police State and its imminent Book of Revelation significance?

____37) Consider political leaders to be your "savior"?

____38) Vote?

____39) Reject, defy, and openly speak out against ungodly, unrighteous, illegitimate human government and its representatives; those who presume to rule over God's people; men of corrupt mind who usurp God's throne and authority?

____40) Offend people for the sake of the gospel by publicly quoting Scripture and acknowledging Jesus Christ as God in the flesh, the Savior of the world, and openly proclaim your unqualified allegiance to Him?

____41) Plan to cooperate with the Beast government and be microchipped or receive any "Mark of the Beast" precursors, such as the National Health Card, a biometric National ID Card/Driver License, identifying tattoo, microchip, microdot, or any other mark upon your body?

____42) Avoid gazing up at the sky (from where your Judgment shall come), to observe Satan, *the prince of the power of the air* (Ephesians 2:2) – via his beastly system of human/demon government – spraying the atmosphere with a lethal aerosol mixture of viral, bacterial, fungal pathogens; polymer nanofibers and toxic metals, known as "Chemtrails"?

____43) Believe Dan Rather, Barbara Walters, Rush Limbaugh, Bill O'Reilly, Barack Obama, and the National Academy of Sciences when they tell you that vaccines are safe and do not cause Autism; and that packaged processed food and Fluoride and Lithium in the drinking water is not harmful, and is even beneficial for your health?

A True Christian will have answered all of the above questions without error. Professing Christians, pseudo-Christians, and other neopagans will have answered one or more of the questions incorrectly. *Enter ye in at the strait gate: for wide is the gate, and broad is the way that leadeth to destruction, and many there be which go in thereat: Because strait is the gate, and narrow is the way, which leadeth unto life, and few there be that find it* (Matthew 7:13,14).

Such individuals need to *repent, and believe the gospel* (Mark 1:15; Luke 13:3). *For I say unto you, That except your righteousness shall exceed the righteousness of the scribes and Pharisees, ye shall in no case enter into the kingdom of heaven* (Matthew 5:20).

Your "good deeds" cannot Save you. Matthew 7:22-23: *Many will say to me in that day, Lord, Lord, have we not prophesied in thy name? and in thy name have cast out devils? And in thy name done many wonderful works? And then will I profess unto them, I never knew you: depart from me, ye that work iniquity.*

God looks at the heart, not the pretentious outward appearance. *The LORD is nigh unto them that are of a broken heart; and saveth such as be of a contrite spirit* (Psalm 34:18).... *but to this man will I look, even to him that is poor and of a contrite spirit, and trembleth at my word* (Isaiah 66:2). *Even so ye also outwardly appear righteous unto men, but within ye are full of hypocrisy and iniquity* (Matthew 23:28).

The Scripturally correct answers are provided at the bottom of the Book Ordering page.

Is Your Church a True Christian Church?

Because with lies ye have made the heart of the righteous sad, whom I have not made sad; and strengthened the hands of the wicked, that he should not return from his wicked way, by promising him life. – Ezekiel 13:22

THE WORLD-FRIENDLY "CHURCH" WELCOMES YOU TO ... *THE SOCIAL CLUB!*

It is a considerable challenge to locate a True Christian Church in today's neopagan revival American culture. The True Church is the "Body of Christ" (1 Corinthians 12:27); Jesus Christ is the head of the Body (Colossians 1:18). Few churches today have Jesus Christ as the Head, but rather, formally acknowledge the government State Attorney General as their 501(c)3 administrative authority. These "churches" are merely *buildings* peopled with individuals who care nothing for the truth – beyond what they have been told by their pastor – which is "another gospel" (Galatians 1:8,9). They also have "another Jesus," the "Jesus of the Social Gospel" (2 Corinthians 11:4). Isaiah 30:9-11: ... *this is a rebellious people, lying children, children that will not hear the law of the LORD: Which say to the seers, See not; and to the prophets, Prophesy not unto us right things, speak unto us smooth things, prophesy deceits: Get you out of the way, turn aside out of the path, cause the Holy One of Israel to cease from before us.* Welcome to the *Social Club* that calls itself "The Church."

Today's Social Club Church is the primary reason why the Globalist's Agenda was able to come into power and continues to proliferate. In the Social Club Church there is no need to speak out against evil; no need to take a stand against wickedness in high places; no need to defend the poor in spirit, Godly widows and the fatherless (James 1:27). All that is required is to just sit there and listen to a weak and diluted version of the Gospel that is intended to make you feel good about yourself and not convict you of your sins. You will not be told to repent of your unrighteous ways, but instead will be affirmed that you are a "good person" who is "going to heaven." You will be encouraged to strive for prosperity in the things of this world, for it is assumed as a foregone conclusion that by your mere presence in the church building you are "Saved" and immune from the righteous wrath of God's Judgment. There will be lots of fun things to do in the meantime: parties and luncheons and bowling and basketball and baseball leagues; and happy times celebrating pagan holidays like Christmas and Easter. In disobedience to Jeremiah 10:1-4, there will be a beautiful Christmas tree in the church lobby and a government flag in the sanctuary, proving how righteous and law-abiding you all must be. During Bible Study on Sundays and Wednesdays, your children will be instructed in subtle witchcraft doctrines taught by women who rule over men (Isaiah 3:12; 1 Timothy 2:12). There will be movies in the church, films of quasi-Christianity, like those of JRR Toilken and C.S. Lewis, offering even more reinforcement of the paganized Christian message. Nothing more will be required of you except to make regular donations to finance the salaries of the church Board of Directors, and maybe blacktop the parking lot. Do this, and you are "guaranteed" a free entry into the Kingdom of God during "The Rapture," which – as your 501(c)3 pastor has assured you – could happen at any minute. (But he neglected to tell you to ignore the fact that the prerequisite prophesies have not yet been fulfilled, or that no where in the Bible is there taught a Pre-Tribulation "secret rapture doctrine.") For your sheep-like acquiesce you will experience no persecution by the criminal government, no testing of your faith. Just keep your mouth shut and your eyes on the prize; nobody will be the wiser. You can have your cake and eat it too; enjoy your Burger King Religion – have it *your* way: find your life and not lose it for the sake of Jesus Christ. Matthew 10:39: *He that findeth his life shall lose it: and he that loseth his life for my sake shall find it. Ye are the salt of the earth: but if the salt have lost his savor, wherewith shall it be salted? it is thenceforth good for nothing, but to be cast out, and to be trodden under foot of men* (Matthew 5:13).

God's people hate evil (Psalm 97:10) and are willing to lay down their life to oppose it and defend the truth (Hebrews 11:33,34).

Satan's people just want to "obey the government," be safe, and compromise.

Which are you?

Does your Church obey God or the Beast?

The Bible commands in Psalm 82:3,4: *Defend the poor and fatherless: do justice to the afflicted and needy. Deliver the poor and needy: rid them out of the hand of the wicked.*

Proverb 24:10-12 warns: *If thou faint in the day of adversity, thy strength is small. If thou forebear to deliver them that are drawn unto death, and those that are ready to be slain; If thou sayest, Behold, we knew it not; doth not he that pondereth the heart consider it? and he that keepeth thy soul, doth not he know it? and shall not he render to every man according to his works?*

In Psalm 94:16 God asks: *Who will rise up for me against the evildoers? or who will stand up for me against the workers of iniquity?*

Ephesians 5:11 counsels: *And have no fellowship with the unfruitful works of darkness, but rather reprove them.*

Galatians 1:18 advises: *But though we, or an angel from heaven, preach any other gospel unto you than that which we have preached unto you, let him be accursed.*

Revelation 20:4 states: ... *and I saw the souls of them that were beheaded for the witness of Jesus, and for the word of God, and which had not worshipped the beast, neither his image* ...

Human civil government is the image of the beast (Revelation 13:14,15; 14:9-11). To worship is to obey (Romans 6:16). The True Church of Jesus Christ is in obedience to God, not to Satan's beastly government. Matthew 6:24: *No man can serve two masters.* Does the "church" which you attend obey God, or does it obey (worship) the government Beast? One way to determine the answer to that question is by your response to the following example:

Vaccines are a global government eugenics operation targeting new born infants and children (the image of God) who are being deliberately transferred diseases and cognitively impaired by their own body's autoimmune response to heavy metal toxicity and the neurotoxins produced by bacterial components present in all vaccines. The True Church of Jesus Christ is in obedience to God, Who said, *If ye love me, keep my commandments* (John 14:15). The above list of Scriptures are not suggestions, but *commandments.* Hence, the True Body of Christ will do as God has commanded. Those who fail to obey God are part of the corporate abomination known as organized religion, the Whore of Babylon (Revelation 17), which includes the modern Protestant denominational Christian Churches. (There exists many religions claiming to be "Christian," but which are, in fact, neopaganism – e.g. Catholicism and some denominational Protestant sects.)

List below all that your church is doing in obedience to God to oppose the perpetrators of this abomination known as *vaccines,* in accordance with Psalm 82:3,4 … *Deliver the poor and needy: rid them out of the hand of the wicked,* and Ephesians 5:11: … *reprove the unfruitful works of darkness* ("reprove" means "to rebuke, express disapproval") and Psalm 94:16: … *rise up against the evildoers and stand up against the workers of iniquity.* Feel free to extend this list should the page capacity be exceeded by the sheer volume of your good works:

1)

2)

3)

4)

5)

6)

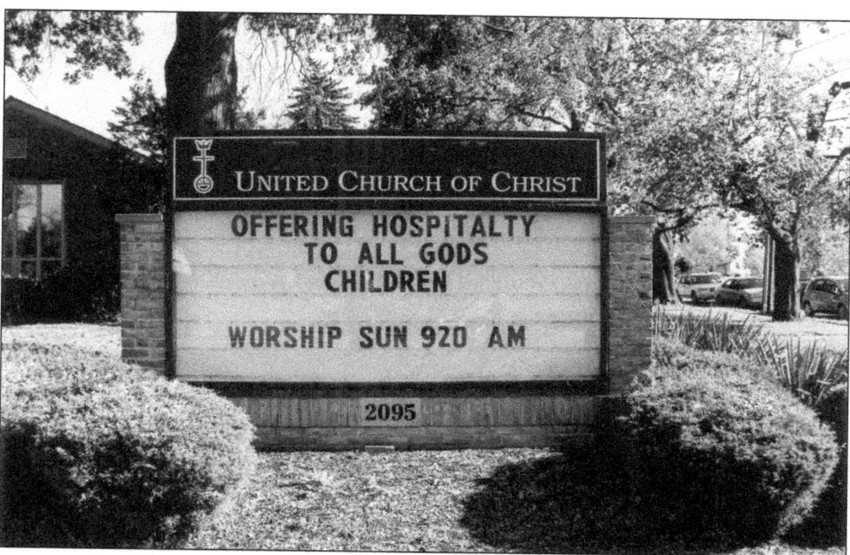

Today's Professing Christianity is an amalgamation of ancient pantheism (i.e. "All Gods"), Biblical Christianity, and modern neopagan American culture.

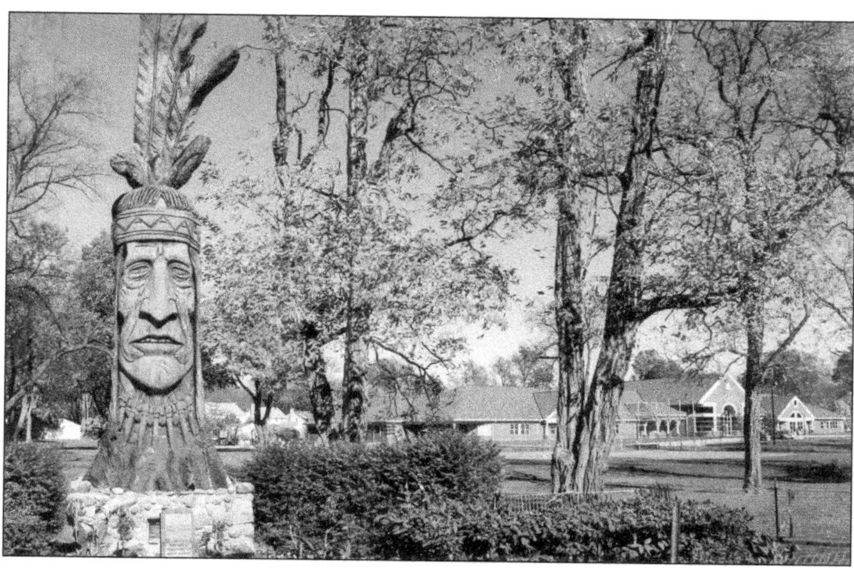

And here is one of their "gods." Idols, *carved images* like this, serve as *focus points* for territorial demons claiming jurisdiction over a geographic locale. Strategically situated next to the above cited "Christian" church, notice the elementary school in the background.

The True Church of Jesus Christ is *persecuted*. True Christians throughout the world are presently experiencing persecution to the point of death. In the Philippines, China, India, Pakistan, Sudan, the Middle East and elsewhere, underground "Home Churches" are the only refuge from the scourge of government death squads patrolling the land in search of those considered by the Beast government to be "a threat" to the state – i.e. True Christians and their 1611 King James Bibles. Death, sudden or by meticulous torture, is often the end for hunted and faithful servants of the Lord Jesus Christ.

Romans 11:22: *Behold therefore the goodness and severity of God: on them which fell, severity; but toward thee, goodness, if thou continue in his goodness: otherwise thou also shall be cut off.* The false church, the world-friendly church, does not preach or teach about the severity (judgment) of God – calling people to repentance – but only preaches on His goodness ("... you're Saved and on your way to heaven"). The false teachings of "Pre-Tribulation Rapture" and "Once Saved Always Saved" are doctrinal errors resulting from omission of this vital Scripture. The deceit is so pervasive that modern churches have become synagogues of Satan (Rev 2:9;3:9).

U.S. flag in front of a 501(c)3 Professing Christian Church. "Government Worship," like "Flag Worship" (i.e. sacred pole worship or the above pagan obelisk) is yet another form of pantheistic idolatry. *No man can serve two masters ... to whom ye yield yourselves servants to obey, his servants ye are to whom ye obey ...* (Matthew 6:24; Romans 6:16). Tax-exempt churches obey Satan's government – the unholy "image of the beast" (Revelation 13:14,15; 14:9-11; 15:2; 16:2; 19:20; 20:4) – not the righteous government of Jesus Christ.

Who Can Be Saved?

Salvation is by grace through faith (Ephesians 2:8). But not everyone is Saved into the Kingdom of Heaven (Revelation 9:20-21; John 8:21,24). In fact, the Word of God affirms that the vast majority of people are condemned to an eternity in hell (Matthew 7:13). Furthermore, the Holy Bible also states they were *never* intended by God to be Saved (Psalm 58:3; John 8:44). Is this a contradiction of the concept of free will? No, it is not. The reason why is because God *preordained* whom He would and would not Save (Jeremiah 1:5; Roman 8:29-30; Ephesians 1:5,11). He predetermined before the beginning of time that certain individuals would not be advancing to a higher state of being in the presence of Almighty God, but would, by virtue of their own decision, invariably denigrate to the status of demons condemned to a burning fire for the purpose of purifying their soul from iniquity and sin. Yet, a belated attempt for purification is to no avail, since they are *beyond* redemption.

Those who are not Saved into the Kingdom of God made that decision in the realm of infinity *before* they were born. Like the fallen angels who rebelled, they are not Saved, and cannot be Saved, because they committed the only unforgivable sin unto death – blasphemy against the Holy Ghost (Matthew 12:31-33; 1 John 5:16). They blasphemed God in their spirit, even before He had given them a physical body, as in the case of a material human being; or an eternal soul, if an angelic being that fell from grace during the mutiny that occurred in heaven at the time of the creation of Earth and its newly formed human inhabitants in the Garden of Eden.

Who are the unsaved? Specifically, who are these people? They are the ones who decided to exercise their free will in favor of rejecting the Truth and believing the Lie. This is the very definition of the Illuminati and their rank and file Criminal Fraternity. They, as well as all those who are not directly implicated, but nonetheless are intimately associated in a kindred spirit, are sympathetic with their father, Lucifer, with whom they desire to spend eternity, having rejected a much better fate long before they ever walked the earth. There is no redemption, no eternal hope for these creatures. They are fulfilling the role which God intended for them to play: *acting as resistance to the righteous.* Their presence on this earth serves no other larger purpose than to be in opposition to the holy saints of God. That is their only true purpose for existing. Without evil to oppose good, what value or virtue would there be in living righteously? *Anyone* could do it! No special exercise of will would be necessary. Therefore, the wicked are fulfilling a necessary function.

It is not coincidental that governments – i.e. people who occupy positions within government – spend the greater part of their time opposing those who are righteous. The highest percentage concentration of unsaved are found in political office and those in sympathetic support of them. (Anyone who takes politics seriously is either a simpleton or is in like-minded collusion with the depraved and unjust. Voting is the definition of insanity: "Repeating the same action over and over again, and expecting a different result.") In the end, God will purge the earth of their tainted spiritual bloodline and establish His kingdom that will be populated by a pure spiritual genetic strain known in Scripture as the *Remnant Elect* (Titus 1:1; Matthew 24:22,24,31; 1 Peter 1:2; Revelation 12:17; 19:21).

There was in a city a judge, which feared not God, neither regarded man: and there was a widow in that city; and she came unto him saying, Avenge me of mine adversary. And he would not for a while: but afterward he said within himself, Though I fear not God, nor regard man; yet this widow troubleth me, I will avenge her, lest by her continual coming she weary me. And the Lord said, Hear what the unjust judge saith. And shall not God avenge his own elect, which cry day and night unto him, though he bear long with them? I tell you that he will avenge them speedily. Nevertheless when the Son of man cometh, shall he find faith on the earth? (Luke 18:2-8). During this time of imminent persecution by the Criminal Fraternity New World Order government, cry out to God in the name of the Lord Jesus Christ. Perhaps He will have mercy and Save you and avenge you of your adversary, the Illuminati Global Hierarchy, Criminal Fraternity, and their fallen angel overlords and rebellious leader.

And they shall go into the holes of the rocks, and into the caves of the earth, for fear of the LORD, and for the glory of his majesty, when he ariseth to shake terribly the earth. In that day a man shall cast his idols of silver, and his idols of gold, which they made each one for himself to worship, to the moles and to the bats; To go into the clefts of the rocks, and into the tops of the ragged rocks, for fear of the LORD, and for the glory of his majesty, when he ariseth to shake terribly the earth. – Isaiah 2:19-21

And it shall come to pass in that day, that the LORD shall punish the host of the high ones that are on high, and the kings of the earth upon the earth … And your covenant with death shall be disannulled, and your agreement with hell shall not stand; when the overflowing scourge shall pass through, then ye shall be trodden down by it. – Isaiah 24:21; 28:18

… and they shall take them captives, whose captives they were; and they shall rule over their oppressors. – Isaiah 14:2

Therefore all they that devour thee shall be devoured; and all thine adversaries, every one of them, shall go into captivity; and they that spoil thee shall be a spoil, and all that prey upon thee will I give for a prey. For I will restore health unto thee, and I will heal thee of thy wounds, saith the LORD; because they called thee an Outcast, saying, This is Zion, whom no man seeketh after. – Jeremiah 30:16,17

And it shall come to pass in the day that the LORD shall give thee rest from thy sorrow, and from thy fear, and from the hard bondage wherein thou wast made to serve … Arise, shine; for thy light is come, and the glory of the LORD is risen upon thee. For, behold, the darkness shall cover the earth, and gross darkness the people: but the LORD shall arise upon thee, and his glory shall be seen upon thee. – Isaiah 14:3;60:1,2

Come, my people, enter thou into thy chambers, and shut thy doors about thee: hide thyself as it were for a little moment, until the indignation be overpast. For, behold, the LORD cometh out of his place to punish the inhabitants of the earth for their iniquity: the earth also shall disclose her blood, and shall no more cover her slain. – Isaiah 26:20-21

Wisdom crieth without; she uttereth her voice in the streets: She crieth in the chief place of concourse, in the openings of the gates: in the city she uttereth her words, saying, How long, ye simple ones, will ye love simplicity? and the scorners delight in their scorning, and fools hate knowledge? Turn you at my reproof: behold, I will pour out my spirit unto you, I will make known my words unto you. Because I have called, and ye refused; I have stretched out my hand, and no man regarded; But ye have set at nought all my counsel, and would none of my reproof: I also will laugh at your calamity; I will mock when your fear cometh; When your fear cometh as desolation, and your destruction cometh as a whirlwind; when distress and anguish cometh upon you. Then shall they call upon me, but I will not answer; they shall seek me early, but they shall not find me: For that they hated knowledge, and did not choose the fear of the LORD: They would none of my counsel: they despised all my reproof. Therefore shall they eat of the fruit of their own way, and be filled with their own devices. For the turning away of the simple shall slay them, and the prosperity of fools shall destroy them. But whoso hearkeneth unto me shall dwell safely, and shall be quiet from fear of evil.

– Proverb 1:20-33

And this is the condemnation, that light is come into the world, and men loved darkness rather than light, because their deeds were evil. For every one that doeth evil hateth the light, neither cometh to the light, lest his deeds should be reproved. But he that doeth truth cometh to the light, that his deeds may be made manifest, that they are wrought in God.

–John 3:19-21

Many shall be purified, and made white, and tried; but the wicked shall do wickedly: and none of the wicked shall understand; but the wise shall understand. – Daniel 12:10

And I saw the dead, small and great, stand before God; and the books were opened: and another book was opened, which is the book of life: and the dead were judged out of those things which were written in the books, according to their works. – Revelation 20:12

Because ye have said, we have made a covenant with death, and with hell are we at agreement; when the overflowing scourge shall pass through, it shall not come unto us: for we have made lies our refuge, and under falsehood have we hid ourselves; ... And your covenant with death shall be disannulled, and your agreement with hell shall not stand; when the overflowing scourge shall pass thorough, then ye shall be trodden down by it.
– Isaiah 28:15,18

Woe to thee that spoilest, and thou wast not spoiled; and dealest treacherously, and they dealt not treacherously with thee! When thou shalt cease to spoil, thou shalt be spoiled; and when thou shalt make an end to deal treacherously, they shall deal treacherously with thee. – Isaiah 33:1

The triumphing of the wicked is short, and the joy of the hypocrite but for a moment. – Job 20:5

I beheld till the thrones were cast down, and the Ancient of days did sit, whose garment was white as snow, and the hair of his head like the pure wool: his throne was like the fiery flame, and his wheels as burning fire. A fiery stream issued and came forth from before him: thousand thousands ministered unto him, and ten thousand times ten thousand stood before him: the judgment was set, and the books were opened. – Daniel 7:9-10

And I saw a great white throne, and him that sat on it, from whose face the earth and the heaven fled away; and there was found no place for them.

And I saw the dead, small and great, stand before God; and the books were opened: and another book was opened, which is the book of life: and the dead were judged out of those things which were written in the books, according to their works.... and whosoever was not found written in the book of life was cast into the lake of fire. – Revelation 20:11-12,15

But the saints of the most High shall take the kingdom, and possess the kingdom for ever, even for ever and ever. – Daniel 7:18

APPENDIX H

Other Books by Soul Esprit

The initial impetus for writing *The Great Deception*, and its sequel, *The Coming of Wisdom,* occurred in 1991, when the author was given a promotion by God and transitioned to writing books. When the words, *The Great Deception and The Coming of Wisdom* were impressed upon his mind from an external source, he said to himself, "That would make a good title for a book." Five years later, over 1000 single-spaced pages were produced as a direct result of that one prophetic communication.

When reading *Fools Paradise: The Spiritual Implications of Gambling*, you walk through the silvery mirror of material illusion to encounter what the author experienced in a seemingly commonplace setting, where apparent reality is stripped away to reveal what controls the game from behind the curtain.

Seven Who Dared is cutting edge spiritual exposé. Upon learning what takes place at a certain Castle in Europe, the author's righteous indignation was stirred to such a degree that he immediately wanted to go there. But, lacking funds, he wrote the book instead. First he imagined it, then his research confirmed it. The details were *that* real.

The Criminal Fraternity: Servants of the Lie was a book that had to be written. Elizabethan masks are pulled off smiling character façades to expose their true identity and reveal the ugly truth of their real face. The Bible affirms in Psalm 62:9: ... *men of high degree are a lie.*

Never was flawless health and freedom from disease so easily obtained than by following the best prescription in the universe. *Genesis 1:29 Diet: Perfect Health without Doctors, Hospitals, or Pharmaceutical Drugs* was written to explain what nearly everyone has wrong when it comes to their physical, psychological and spiritual well being.

Fractal Trading: Analyzing Financial Markets using Fractal Geometry and the Golden Ratio was written as a practical guide for investors. A companion book to *When Will the Illuminati Crash the Stock Market?,* it outlines the methodology the author used to forecast the stock market crashes, and which provided the framework for integrating the present historical period with the Biblical Timeline counting down the future history of mankind.

The Globalist's Agenda forewarns of a time fast approaching, when America has become the vassal of an international government that rules by dictatorial decrees. This is not a book about "Conspiracy Theories," it is a book about Conspiracy Facts. Representatives of the government of the United States of America have committed treason by disregarding the Constitution and have thereby declared war on their own citizenry. The globalist's Luciferian New World Order has finally arrived.

At some point during an ongoing 20 year struggle to merely survive, the author realized that more was at stake than meaningless suffering. Suddenly, vicious enemies and homelessness for ten freezing cold winters and sweltering hot summers began to make sense. In retrospect, he was doing "field research" that resulted in writing *Everything is a Test: How God Delivered Me from "Impossible" Situations.* All the more amazing because it is true.

Fractal Trading:

Analyzing Financial Markets Using
Fractal Geometry and the Golden Ratio

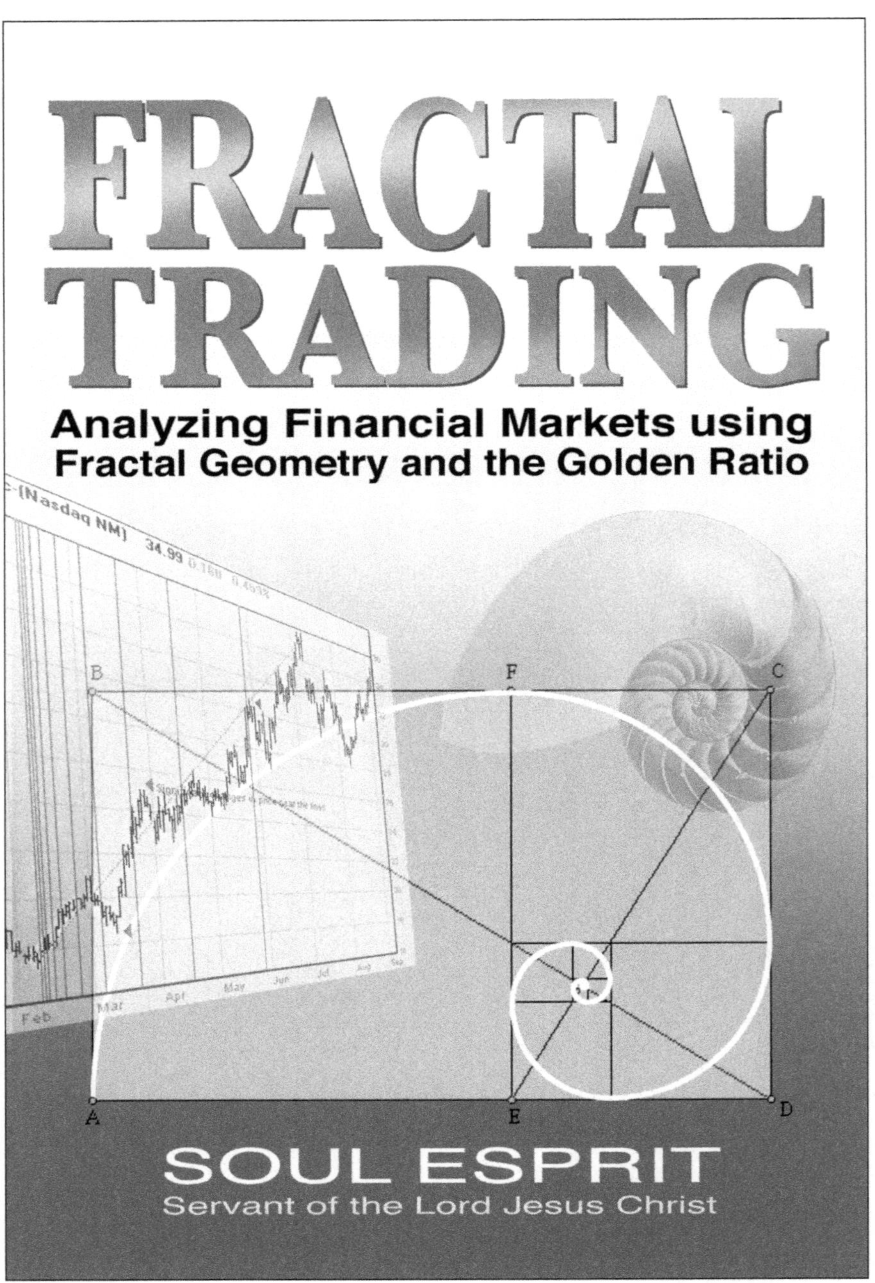

Whether you are a novice trader or experienced investor, this book provides valuable instruction on how to:

- Know *when to sell*
- Objectively determine precision entries and exits
- Position for advancing or declining markets
- Trade for the short-term or invest long-term
- Know when to be fully invested and when to be in cash
- Safely trade leveraged markets for maximizing returns
- Calculate key turning points and establish market positions *before* the trend changes direction

You have read all the books and seen all the videos, bought all the software, went to the seminars offering hope for learning how to trade. You spent thousands of dollars and as many hours laboring over an endeavor that has befuddled many a dedicated mind. But in the end, you still lost money. The financial landscape is strewn with frustrated hopes and depleted bank accounts.

Legally acquire the *advance information* of an "Insider Trader"

This is the definitive guide for a time-tested approach used by the author to achieve a published economic forecast record unparalleled in recent stock market history. Presented in a concise format, he instructs the aspiring trader or professional analyst in how to identify the current location of a market's price in relation to its past history and projected future. Implementing this same methodology, he correctly anticipated the precision timeline for the collapse of the U.S. and global economies.

Soul Esprit, Servant of the Lord Jesus Christ, is the author of nine books and is the only person on record to document by publication – prior to the event – every major advance and decline in the DJIA economic barometer since 2003. One of the nation's top market analysts on predicting the rise and fall of financial markets over the last decade, and utilizing geometric and mathematical relationships to precisely forecast the coming U.S. and global monetary crash, his technical studies actually precede political events, proving that the politico-economic future can be known in advance.

NarrowGate Publishing
www.getperfectwisdom.org

Genesis 1:29 Diet:

Perfect Health Without Doctors, Hospitals, or Pharmaceutical Drugs

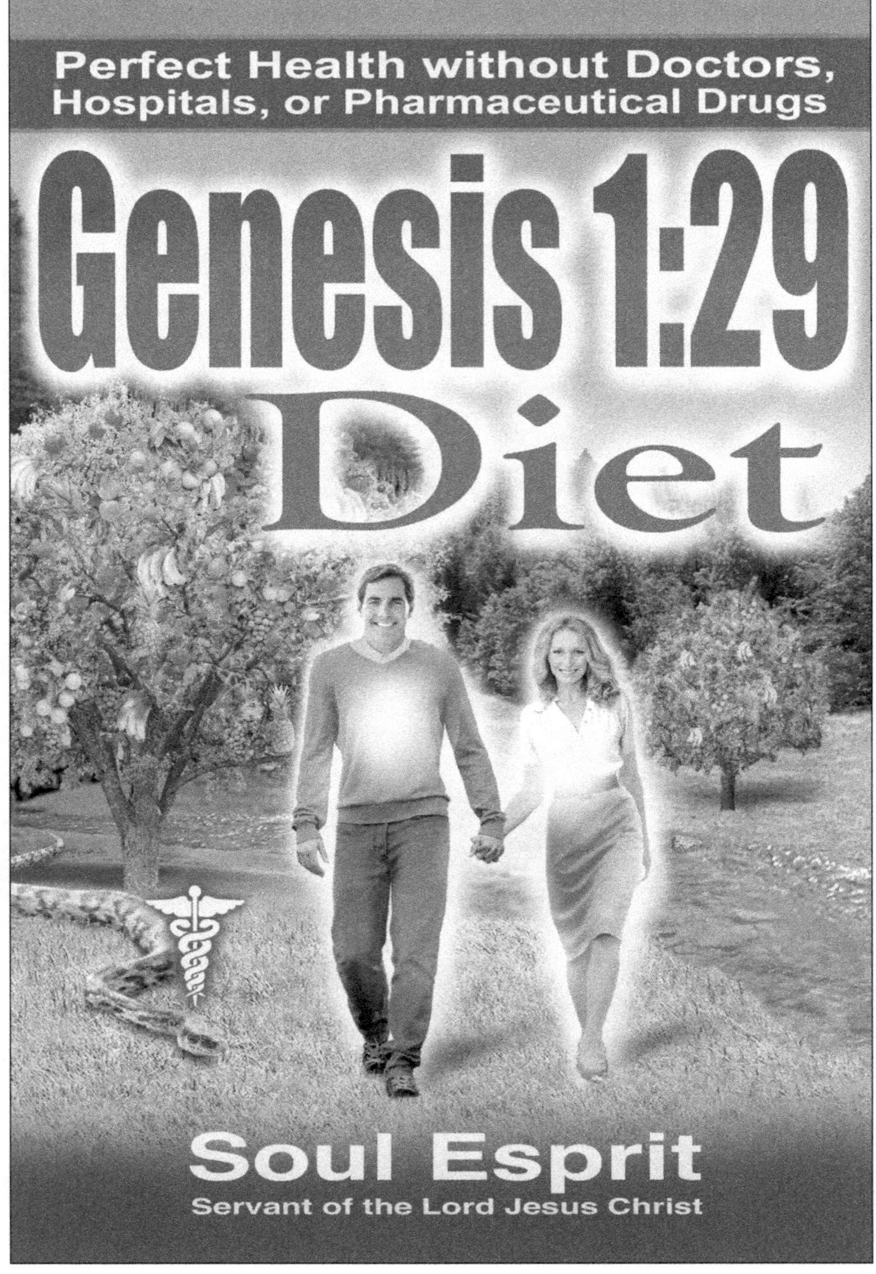

Who Are You Going To Believe... Man or God?

Did you ever wonder why ...

- Most people today are overweight?
- Almost everyone is afflicted with an acute or chronic debilitating disease?
- You never seem to get well, but only weaker and more ill?
- Doctors, hospitals, pharmaceutical drugs and vaccines perpetuate your illness?

Read this book and discover the answer to these questions, and more, that your doctor cannot give you, because he doesn't know! (Or is afraid to tell you.)

Purveyors of snake oil and other witchcraft lotions and potions have changed little over the centuries. With few exceptions, yesterday's traveling "Dr. Good" has been replaced by today's version of the village witchdoctor, identified by the sage initials "MD". The New Medicine is merely the Old Sorcery from ages past; modern health care has become a cult of worshipping doctors.

The way of man inevitably leads to death; God's way leads to health and eternal life

Today, there is available to the general public literally hundreds of approaches claiming to provide optimum good health – by observing the latest "fad diet", ingesting a "miracle" food item, or by taking a pharmaceutical "wonder" drug. However, none of these are efficacious unless entirely based upon the Word of God. Few people believe God and what He teaches in His Holy Scriptures. The spirit of man is hostile to the truth; an individual will not receive the truth unless his spirit has been regenerated, Born Again (John 3:3) by the indwelling Spirit of God. Those trusting in the deceit of man invariably fall prey to the consequences of their rejection of The Truth: Jesus Christ.

Genesis 1:29 Diet is not a diet in the conventional sense of the word, but is an overall lifestyle in obedience to God. Do what He says and you will stop financing your illnesses and premature death ... then you will lose your dependence on the world's *second* oldest profession.

Soul Esprit, Servant of the Lord Jesus Christ, is the author of nine books and an expert in the fields of health, nutrition, and exposing today's fraudulent medical health care industry.

NarrowGate Publishing

www.getperfectwisdom.net

Seven Who Dared

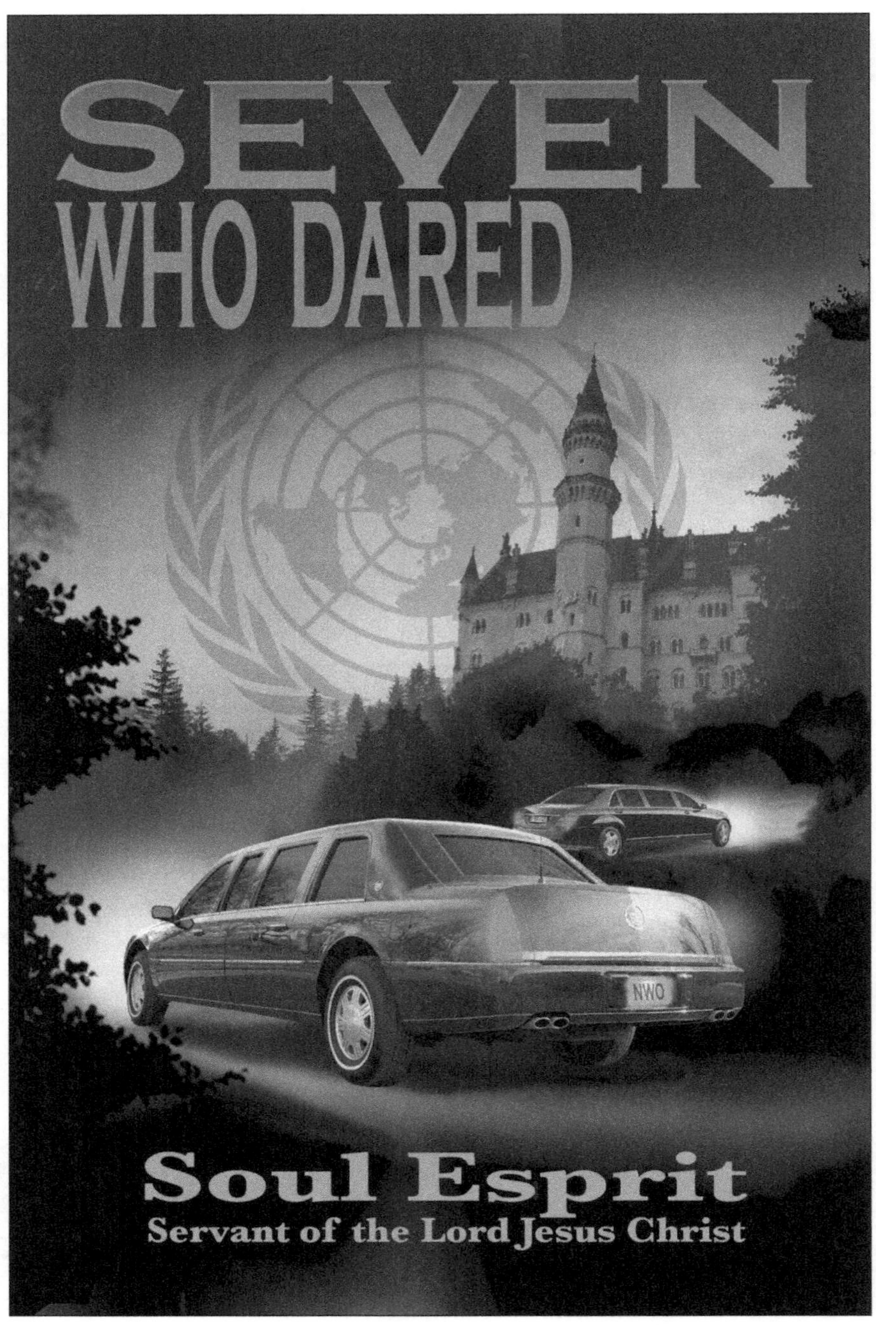

Is this book based on

FICTION OR **FACT ?**

Learn the truth about ...

- The Luciferian Hierarchy that rules the world
- What the super rich global elite do for "recreation"
- Who the major players are for the New World Order
- Their terrorist plans for enslaving you and your children
- What you can do about it

WHO ARE THE SEVEN WHO DARED?

God's mighty warriors are raised up and ready to engage the enemy in battle. There's a chess master and genius strategist, a young man who accepted a challenge that could easily get him killed. Then, there's the world's undefeated kickboxing champion; lethal as a tiger, gentle as a kitten. And a renowned author, researcher and expert authority in diverse fields, including CIA mind-control programming and the occult. And a street preacher and Bible scholar who defies the unrighteous authority of corrupt men. Also, a multimillionaire financier who risks everything in defense of the truth. And a decorated war veteran, demolition and weapons expert that understands the true meaning of God's righteous judgment. Finally, a Godly visionary with the ability to perceive beyond space and time; a man who rejected the myth of the American Dream, and determined instead to live by God's principles, even if it cost him his life.

Together, these seven, in bold defense of a righteous cause that would make most men's blood run cold, give new meaning to the word – courage.

Soul Esprit, Servant of the Lord Jesus Christ, is the author of nine books and is a financial market analyst and economic forecaster.

NarrowGate Publishing

www.getperfectwisdom.com

ISBN 0-978-9841279-8-6

90000

0 978984 127986

Fools Paradise:

The Spiritual Implications
of Gambling

Within these pages you will discover:

- The shocking truth about casino gambling
- The real reason why all "gamblers" ultimately lose
- The true meaning of the words "Luck", "Chance", "Coincidence"
- There exists another level of reality beyond the apparent world of cause and effect

READ THE BOOK THAT HAS TURNED THE GAMBLING INDUSTRY UPSIDE DOWN!

Increasing numbers of people are being lured by the promise of easy riches offered by casinos that have sprung up all across America, drawing the unwary masses like a glittering beacon signaling the way to Mecca.

Much more than just a book about gambling, ***Fools Paradise: The Spiritual Implications of Gambling***, is a spiritual exposé, a rare glimpse into the world of casinos and gambling that will not only edify your spiritual understanding, but will make you pause, question, and even challenge the very meaning of apparent reality itself. This is not a book that instructs how to gamble, but counsels not to gamble, with temporal money, or your eternal soul.

Fools Paradise is an unique one-of-a-kind work of nonfiction. There has never before been a book written on this subject. The recounting of events has not been embellished; that would be unnecessary, because the absolute reality of the spiritual realm is often more incredible than even the most creative fiction. In the pages to follow you will perhaps come to realize that it is not simply the casino odds that defeat a player – just as, often times in life, it is not merely "circumstances" or "bad luck" that beats us down – but rather, it's something else....

Soul Esprit, Servant of the Lord Jesus Christ, is the author of nine books and a top financial market analyst and economic forecaster. His lucid insights into the world of the unseen explains why he is one of today's foremost spiritual exposé writers.

NarrowGate Publishing

www.getperfectwisdom.com

The Criminal Fraternity:

Servants of the Lie

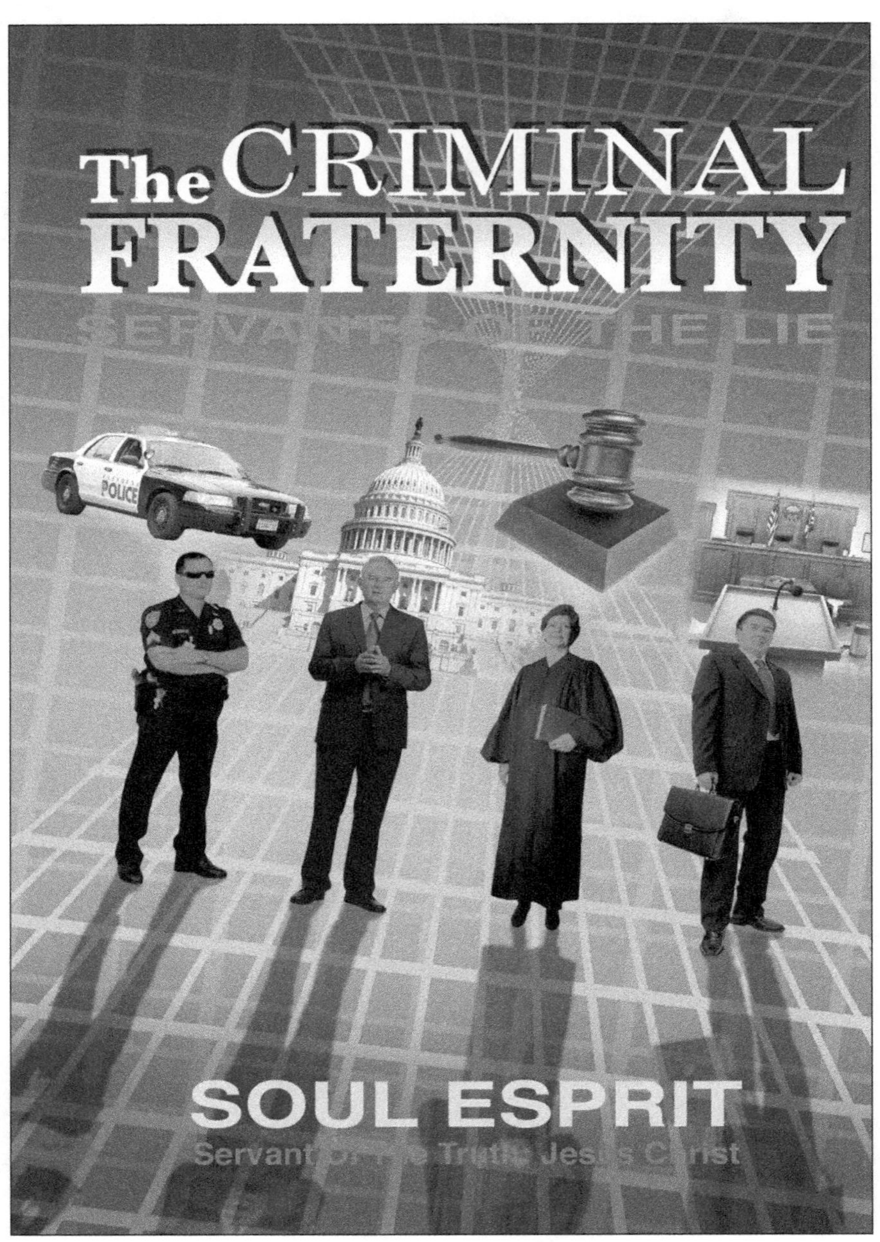

WHO are the *REAL* CRIMINALS?

They masquerade as your friend, but are your deadly enemies:

- *Police*
- *Politicians*
- *Judges*
- *Attorneys*

LEARN THE TRUTH THAT *THE CRIMINAL FRATERNITY* HOPES YOU WILL *NEVER* DISCOVER

Here's the book that exposes the *real* Organized Crime network. After reading *The Criminal Fraternity* you will never again naively assume that civil government exists for the public good. Within these pages you will learn exactly who it is that represents a menace to society and are the greatest threat to you and your family, intending injury: physically, mentally, financially, but most of all, spiritually. Armed with this vital information, you will be informed and prepared for the life threatening times that are imminently upon us. Quoting from Orwell's insightful book, 1984: "If you want a picture of the future, imagine a boot stamping on a human face – forever." And *that* is what The Criminal Fraternity intend to do – to YOU.

The Criminal Fraternity is a landmark volume that challenges some of our culture's most cherished and widely held beliefs. A frankly bold exposé, it reveals the nemesis of the Truth, naming and identifying the mortal enemies of all who are righteous in Jesus Christ. Ultimately, it is He that will bring them to justice. Psalm 63:11: ... the mouth of them that speak lies shall be stopped.

Soul Esprit, Servant of the Lord Jesus Christ, is the author of nine books and has written extensively on the coming global Police State and dictatorial world government.

NarrowGate Publishing
www.getperfectwisdom.com

ISBN 978-0-9841281-2-9
90000
9 780984 128129

Everything is a Test:

How God Delivered Me
from "Impossible" Situations

ONE OF THE WORLD'S TOP MARKET ANALYSTS... *LIVED IN A VAN!*

The spiritual warfare didn't become fully evident until the author began writing spiritual exposé books in the early 1990's. Then, as the expression goes, "All hell broke loose." For the next 20 years he experienced more conflict than most people could encounter in several lifetimes.

That Satan wants to destroy this author's True Christian witness is clearly evident. The Great Deceiver tried everything imaginable: financial devastation, long-term poverty, homelessness, betrayal by family and false friends, imprisoned for standing against evil and defending the truth. Between several extended interludes of living without a home and not having a warm and secure place in which to write, the author researched and composed 9 books, over 3000 single-spaced pages of text, edited 7 times.

Everything is a Test: How God Delivered Me from "Impossible" Situations, is a truly amazing account of what the author had to endure in order to get his manuscripts into print. Timely significant, and often dealing with subject matter of historical proportions, due to his dire circumstances and chronic lack of funds to publish, most of the volumes remained dormant on computer disc for nearly two decades!

WHAT WOULD YOU DO IF SUDDENLY YOU LOST ALL YOUR MONEY, BUSINESS, HOME, CAR, AND THEN IT GOT WORSE?

Reading this book will convince you that there is most certainly God in Heaven, Who intimately knows your circumstances and is patiently watching and waiting to see what you will do next. Remember: Don't give up. Hope in God Jesus Christ. Your troubles are only, *a Test.*

Soul Esprit, Servant of the Lord Jesus Christ, is the author of nine books and a top financial market analyst and economic forecaster. His lucid insights into the world of the unseen explains why he is one of today's foremost spiritual exposé writers.

NarrowGate Publishing
www.getperfectwisdom.com

ISBN 978-0-9841281-1-2
90000
9 780984 128112

The Great Deception

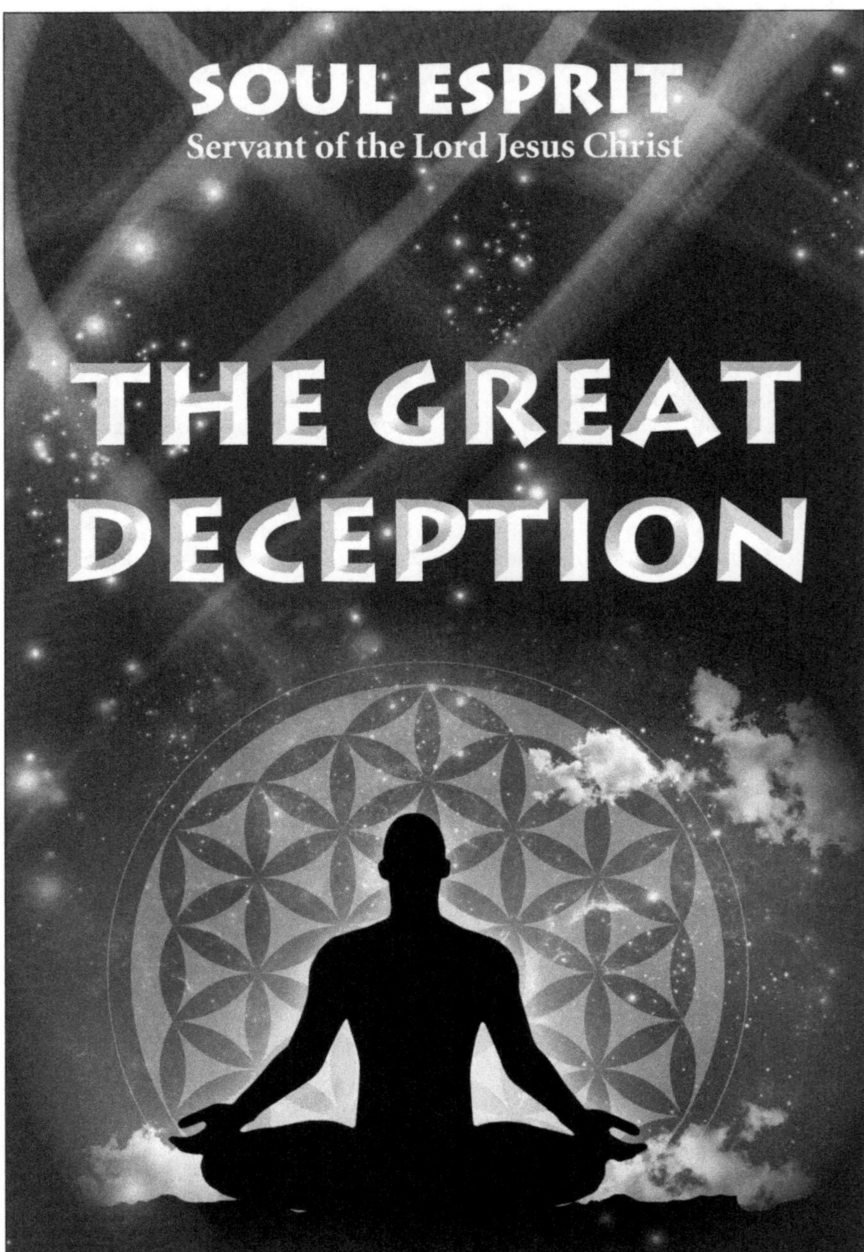

ARE YOU BEING DECEIVED?

How do you know if what you think and believe is true? It could all be a deception. Question what you assume to be right as if your life depends on it, because . . . it does.

Kay Harris has it all – mother of two children, wife of a Wall Street executive, money, a magnificent country club estate, elite social life – yet, something is missing. Confronted by life's major questions, she embarks on a quest for answers that leads her on a labyrinth journey riddled with lost broken lives, dead end streets, and forks in the road leading to nowhere. It is a journey that each and every one of us must make – alone.

WHAT YOU DON'T KNOW *CAN* HURT YOU

A tour de force, *The Great Deception* takes a renewed look at the old cultural paradigms of the 1980's that resulted in today's spiritually bankrupt America. This book presents a more in-depth understanding of the New Age "New Spirituality" (Sorcery) that spawned the present New World Order "New Freedom" (Slavery). A hard-hitting futuristic glimpse of our emergent spiritual and technetronic mind-manipulated world, this volume explodes many of the societal myths that you once took for granted. It will challenge what you hold to be true, open your eyes, and perhaps even change your perception of the world in which you live. This stunning exposé is essential reading to prepare you for the coming mass mind control and spiritual counterfeits characteristic of the modern Age of Deception.

Be forewarned. You are about to pass through a door that is a portal to another world, another reality: *The Great Deception*. Without a special kind of Wisdom, you *will* be deceived.

Soul Esprit, Servant of the Lord Jesus Christ, is the author of ten books and has written on a broad range of topics including globalism, medical and political corruption, the U.S. and global economy, and exposé of spiritual and religious deception.

www.soulesprit.com

ISBN 978-0-9841279-4-8

NarrowGate Publishing
www.getperfectwisdom.com

The Coming of Wisdom

sequel to

The Great Deception

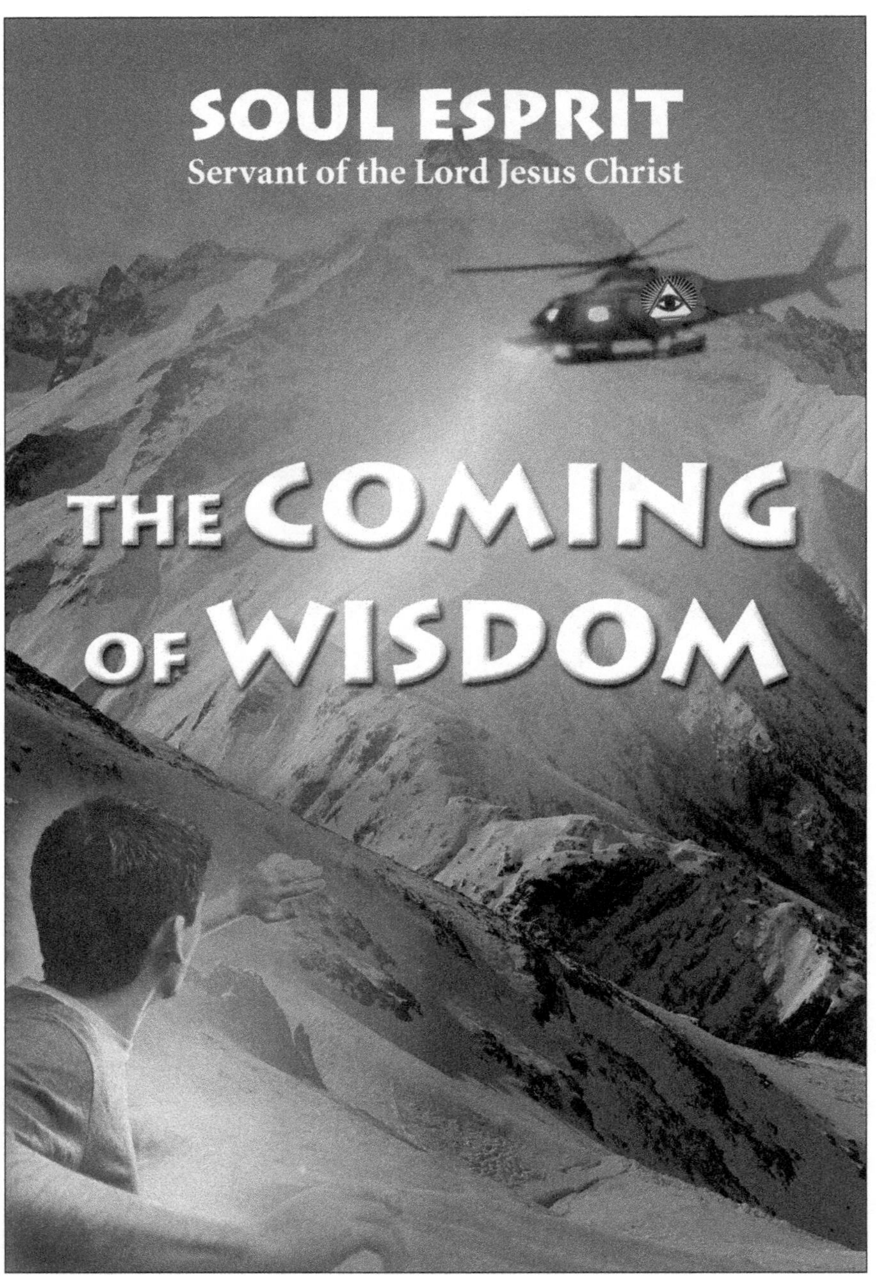

IF THE TRUTH DISTURBS YOU ...
BURN THIS BOOK!

(but if it stirs you, read on)

The end is now upon us, and the ongoing drama is as real as it gets. *The Coming of Wisdom* picks up where *The Great Deception* left off – in the year 2027 – the world gasping in the final death throes of the Illuminati's New World Order dictatorial global government. Written 30 years before the story date, this is an insightful and realistic portrayal of the future that reads like today's headlines. The second novel, spanning over 5,000 years of human history, brings together the key elements of globalism – political, religious, economic, social and scientific – that are fulfilling Revelation prophesy at this present time.

The Coming of Wisdom is a sobering antidote for false teachings of pseudo-Christianity, such as a secret "Pre-Tribulation Rapture" and "obeying unrighteous government." This volume demonstrates the Scriptural mandate that if you are not openly proclaiming your allegiance to Jesus Christ – and suffering persecution for it – you are not of His Elect.

Will **YOU** be taking the *Mark of the Beast?* ...
What about your *children?*

The Police State is now fully operational, and they're closing in ... *Fast!* What will you do on that fateful day when they come for YOU? Who will you go to for help? Who can you trust? Get an up close and personal look at what life will be like for those who are willing to die for the truth, and THE TRUTH is the *Lord Jesus Christ.*

Soul Esprit, Servant of the Lord Jesus Christ, is the author of ten books and has written on a broad range of topics including globalism, medical and political corruption, the U.S. and global economy, and exposé of spiritual and religious deception.

ISBN 978-0-9841279-6-2

NarrowGate Publishing
www.getperfectwisdom.com

The Globalist's Agenda:
Design for a New World Order

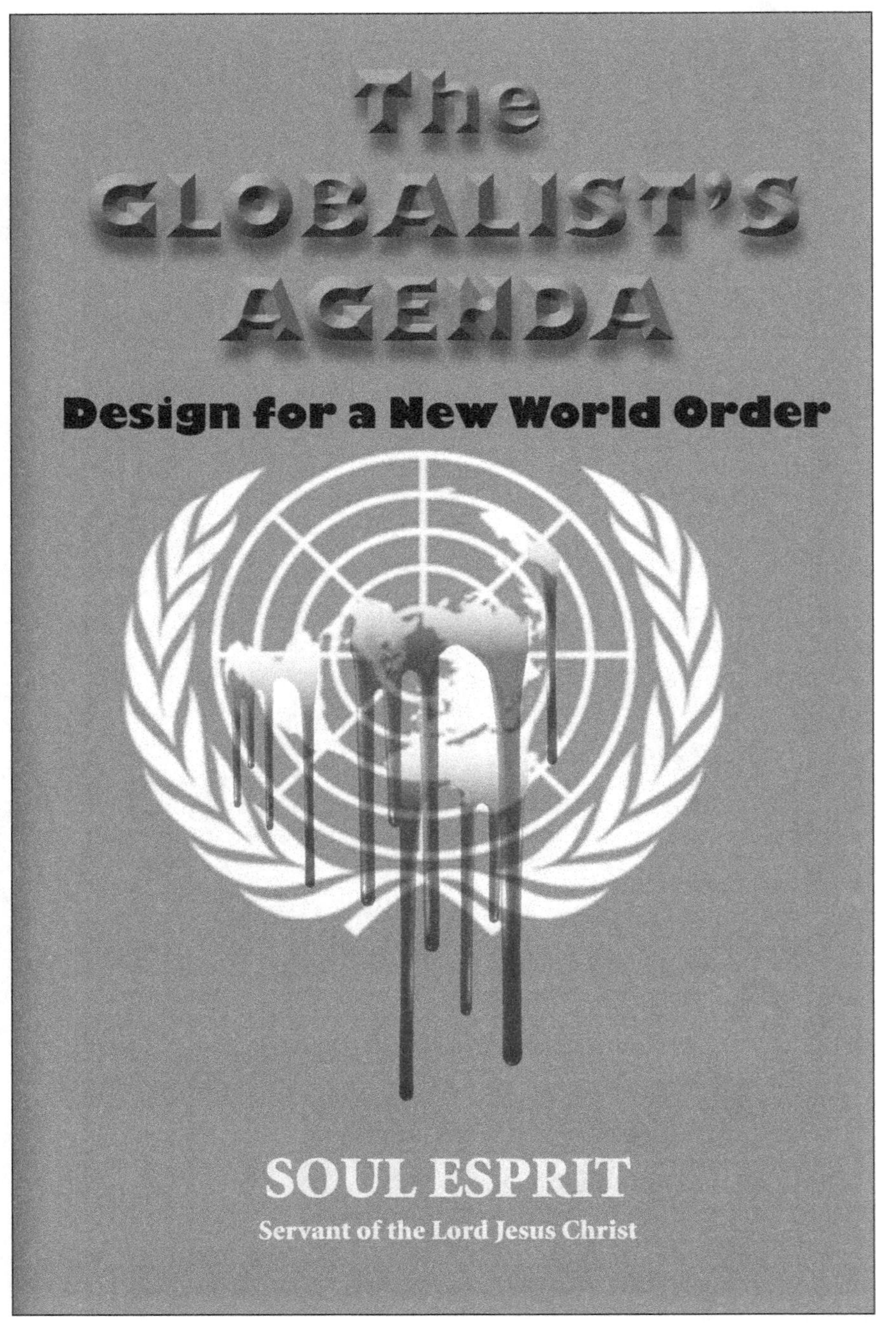

"Conspiracy Theories" are no longer *just theories*, they are **published facts!**

Did you know that:

◊ There are over 800 FEMA Concentration Camps already built in the U.S. for incarcerating Americans?

◊ You could be arrested and imprisoned without probable cause, Due Process, legal representation and Habeas Corpus – indefinitely?

◊ 95% of all supermarket food has been weaponized by genetic modification that causes sterility, infertility, and chronic illnesses?

◊ Vaccines are being used for transferring diseases to children and for global depopulation, especially third world countries?

◊ Millions of plastic disposable "FEMA coffins" are stored in preparation for civil revolt?

◊ Communities all across America have been for decades mass medicated to make them docile using fluoride and lithium added to the drinking water supply?

◊ Senate Bill S18 – already passed in the State of Massachusetts – gives police authorization to enter private residences to conduct warrantless searches and quarantine peaceful citizens?

◊ The U.S. imprison rate is 8 times higher than any other nation, including Russia?

◊ You will not be permitted to buy or sell in the new commerce without receiving in your right hand an injected Verichip RFID human implantable microchip?

◊ The "War on Terror" is being used as a pretense to set up a Police State Surveillance network consisting of Digital Fingerprints, Iris Scans, Facial Recognition Cameras, Highway Checkpoints and Government ID Cards?

THE GOVERNMENT HAS DECLARED WAR ON ITS OWN CITIZENRY!

The turning point in American and world history occurred on September 11, 2011. The pretext was "terrorism by a foreign enemy," but the truth is planned Martial Law in America and microchipping of the world population. The Globalist's Agenda is a Spiritual Agenda working behind the scenes to enslave everyone in an Orwellian surveillance network that will soon be the worst oppressive tyranny the world has ever known. The stage is set. The plan is in place. The time for their End Game ***is now***.

Soul Esprit, Servant of the Lord Jesus Christ, is the author of ten books and has written extensively on the emerging police state and dictatorial world government.

ISBN 978-0-9841281-8-1

NarrowGate Publishing
www.getperfectwisdom.com

APPENDIX I

Relevant Topics of Interest

Agent Provocateur and CointelPro:

These are terms that can be applied to government agents planted among the opposition – i.e. unsuspecting public. The role they play in fomenting political, religious and racial strife is of crucial importance for the Luciferian Brotherhood, especially when their actions create panic, confusion and chaos among the masses. Typically, Agents Provocateur and CointelPro government agents are present among crowds of protesters, and are responsible for inciting police to indiscriminately attack a group of otherwise peaceful demonstrators (controlled-media camera crews are positioned and ready to film coverage of the "government resisters"). Installed as leaders of popular social movements, such as Political Patriotism, these decoys infiltrate and take over key resistance organizations to destroy them from within. In provocateuring social unrest, they are often facilitator "change agents" used by the upper level CF to synthesize a semblance of order out of the chaos which they have played an instrumental role to incite (Ordo ab Chao; Hegelian Dialectic: Problem-Reaction-Solution). From the smoldering ruins caused by the ruling elite, there emerges a new paradigm more conducive to their global Police State agenda. Agents Provocateur and CointelPro are often the means by which this is accomplished. All members of the Criminal Fraternity – high level government officials, their Wards (attorneys and judges), and other functionaries (e.g. police), are strategically positioned to potentially assume the role of a government facilitator.

Mind-controlled Agents Provocateur and CointelPro are known to function within the Patriot movement. Quoting a former agent: "They've been using too many of us to do this dirty work for them, especially through the Patriot Community."

Bewitched:

Who hath bewitched you …? the apostle Paul asked in Galatians 3:1. This telling question is answered in depth throughout the 1611 King James Bible. The final stage for the commencement of the NWO was set when CF Luciferians, occupying the very pinnacle of the Satanic Pyramid of power, placed some of the world's top-ranking devil worshippers in the highest office in the land. Typically, the Illuminati employs the services of U.S. Presidents to bewitch the undiscerning masses into thinking they have nothing to fear from Satan's system of totalitarian rule. In modern history the Luciferian takeover of America began in earnest with the reign of Franklin Delano Roosevelt, and was followed in quick succession by other Illuminati Presidential shills – Gerald Ford, Jimmy Carter, Ronald Reagan, George H. W. Bush, Bill Clinton, and George W. Bush Jr., all of whom were merely *figureheads* without any real power except for the illusion their higher ranking cult superiors created to make it appear as if they had decision-making authority. Bewitched, the unsaved populace admire and honor such reprehensible parodies in the manner of a pagan idol. (Since the time of Roosevelt to this current day, the only real President with decision-making power was John F. Kennedy.)

Respect for human rulers is an affront to the sovereignty of God. Proverb 24:23: *These things also belong to the wise. It is not good to have respect of persons in judgment.* In their demand for a king to rule over them the spiritually dead affirm their rejection of Jesus Christ as KING of kings and LORD of lords, the master of their lives (1 Samuel 8:7-8). Further prophesied in verses 9-18, for refusing to acknowledge the Lord of Hosts as their sovereign leader, America and the rest of the world will bear the inevitable Tribulation consequences when led into captivity by the Criminal Fraternity's conspiracy against God.

Bohemian Grove:

A secluded locale in northern California, near San Francisco and located on the Russian River, where more than 2000 high level LCF Luciferians and select underlings gather every July 15th to offer *human sacrifices* to a 40 foot tall statue of the pagan deity, Molech, symbolically represented by the occult symbol of an owl. For 133 years, it is here that political figures engage in satanic rituals, acts of sodomy, pedophilia, and other perversions indicative of their perverse nature. While "partying" at "the Grove," the goal of the Luciferian elite is to blaspheme God in accordance with Deuteronomy 16:21,22: *Thou shalt not plant thee a grove of any trees near unto the altar of the LORD thy God, which thou shalt make thee. Neither shalt thou set thee up any image; which the LORD thy God hateth.* American Presidents and various other high-ranking political savants, business moguls, and some key Hollywood celebrities (e.g. Ronald Reagan, Arnold Swartzenegger) calmly stand by to observe a live human being sacrificed upon a stone cold altar. Eyewitness reports describe the snuff murders of MKUltra mind-controlled slaves and perverted sexual acts performed with children and among the Luciferians themselves (ref: *Trance: Formation of America).* Ladies and Gentlemen, I present to you ... America's government leaders.

It is at the Grove that Illuminati-appointees are announced to be the next U.S. President or State governor (It was at their yearly satanic bacchanal that Reagan and Swartzenegger received confirmation of their appointments to high LCF office.) A talk show host, Alex Jones, infiltrated the infamous Grove in the year 2000 and secretly filmed video footage of a ritual human sacrifice.

Catholicism (Religious Criminal Fraternity):

As the religious component of the Criminal Fraternity, the RCF is spearheaded by the Roman Catholic Church, with NWO political ties via the Jesuit priesthood, the so-called "Society of Jesus." The Vatican is the driving force behind today's Ecumenical Movement to unite all the world's religions into the endtime Harlot Babylon described in Revelation 17-19. The term, "Babylon," has historically been a code word for *Rome.* The Pope is the False Prophet spoken of in Revelation 13:11-16. Further proof that the Vatican is the leader of the last days apostate church is provided in Revelation 17:18, which specifies *a City,* and also 17:9, delineating the location: *sits on seven hills.* The city of Rome is situated on seven hills. These identifying verses support the conclusion that the Roman Catholic Church is the entity referred to in these Revelation prophesies. The Beast upon which the Harlot Catholic Church sits is the Antichrist's NWO global government (Revelation 13;17:3,8,11). The final fall of Rome as the epicenter of revived Hellenistic paganism – further detailed in Chapter 18 – will, ironically, be at the hands of its former enabler, the Antichrist's LCF Beast system (17:16,17).

The true *Church* of Jesus Christ is "the called out ones," those few that have separated themselves from the world. The word "Catholic" means "universal," hence, the phrase, "Catholic *Church,*" is a contradiction in terms. Needless to say, Roman Catholicism is *not* the *True* Church of Jesus Christ, and neither does it proclaim the true gospel (Romans 1:16,17). The great whore Catholic Church (Revelation 17:1;19:2) is intimately associated with the Luciferian's drive to create a political, economic and religious worldwide system. The Catholic Jesuits – the Vatican information-gathering equivalent of the CIA/FBI – were instrumental in forming a link between European Freemasonry, Knights Templar (which, for Catholics, later became the Knights of Malta, and then the Knights of Columbus), and the early Holy Roman Empire. During the world wars, as today, the Jesuits are the Illuminati intelligence branch for the globally powerful Pope of Rome. It was via the

Jesuit *rat lines* that Nazi war criminals were granted safe passage for escaping to South America after W.W.II.

Catholicism is *not* Christianity. It is pagan idolatry, goddess worship and witchcraft all rolled into one God-blaspheming cult. Idolatry and goddess worship are the oldest forms of venerating demons known to mankind. Because of their rejection of the truth of God's Word – the 1611 KJV Bible – the more than 1 billion Catholics in the world today are Spiritually Blind; God has given them over to a spirit of *strong delusion* (2 Thessalonians 2:9-12). Devoid of Godly wisdom and spiritual discernment, while propagandized and brainwashed by the decrees of demonized men – i.e. the Pope, cardinals, bishops, priests – those professing an allegiance to Catholic idol worship are easy prey to the most ridiculous and unscriptural doctrines and spiritual counterfeits. Embracing New Age philosophy, Catholics are a synthesis of pagan beliefs and Protestant Christianity. Foremost among these pagan beliefs is their veneration of the image of "Virgin Mary," whom the True Christian Elect realize is merely a demon that calls itself "Mary." Offering prayers, personal sacrifices and pleas for eternal salvation to this masquerading demon, as well as to dead "saints" and other deceased people (necromancy), Catholics unwittingly invoke demon spirits, rather than the true spirit of Jesus Christ. ("Marian Apparitions" have manifested since 1531, most notably in geographic regions where *wars, suffering, death and immorality* are rampant. Hence, the presence of "Mary" is indicative of demonic strongholds in these troubled areas of the world.) For all this, Catholicism – as one of the most Sripturally-resistant religions in the world – is cursed by God. Proverb 21:16: *The man that wandereth out of the way of understanding shall remain in the congregation of the dead.* Wise in their own conceit, confident in their ignorance, the followers of Catholicism's unscriptural man-made doctrines have for centuries been duped by lies and deceits.

The Catholic Church, with its occult-based pageantry and pagan rituals, demonstrates *rebellion* against God by a rejection of the Holy Bible as the standard of doctrinal authority. The Bible states that rebellion is witchcraft (1 Samuel 15:23). Thus, Catholicism's rejection of God's Word *is* witchcraft. Modern day neowitches coined a name for their pagan practices, calling them the *Old Religion.* The Catholic Church is actually a form of the Old Religion. 1 Corinthians 10:20: ... *the things which the Gentiles sacrifice, they sacrifice to devils, and not to God.* That Catholicism is a religion of idolatry and witchcraft externally cloaked with a thin veneer of Christianity is obvious to anyone with Godly discernment. Its goddess worshipping practices and pagan rituals are blasphemy of the Holy Spirit. Contrary to what most Catholics profess, Roman Catholicism's essential theology was never part of the first century Church doctrines that Jesus Christ established through his disciples at Pentecost. The Catholic Church claims their doctrines to be derived from the traditions handed down by the apostles, however, in the centuries since the resurrection of Jesus Christ this so-called "Apostolic Succession" has never existed. Catholicism was never the gospel message preached by any of the apostles (Galatians 1:8,9).

Historically, the global spread of Catholicism was the primary vehicle by which Satan has throughout Western Civilization promulgated a form of witchcraft disguised as Christianity. Although the "church" of Rome lays claim to being the "true Church," it rejects the Bible's authority and instead teaches *the doctrines of fallen man* to its masses of biblically illiterate followers. Galatians 1:8 forewarns of God's condemnation of the Catholic Church in today's apostate Laodicean church age: *But though we, or an angel from heaven, preach any other gospel unto you than that which we have preached unto you, let him be accursed.* And Matthew 15:8,9: *This people draweth nigh unto me with their mouth, and honoreth me with their lips; but their heart is far from me. But in vain they do worship me, teaching for doctrines the commandments of men.*

All forms of Catholicism (e.g. Roman, Russian Orthodox, Marian) are steeped in occultism, masking covert witchcraft and Satanism with double-meaning symbolism. During the Dark Ages,

Catholic congregations were *forbidden to read the Bible*, and consequently, were kept *in the dark* concerning the truth about their paganized religious beliefs and practices. It required God's intervention, through the work of Godly men such as Martin Luther, to protest (hence the word, *Protestant*) the Catholic corruption of the true Word of God. Throughout much of Roman Catholic history the Catholic Mass was read in Latin, thus rendering the religious occult ceremonies meaningless to the unlearned common people. So disguised, Catholic church services allowed for open demonstrations of occult power. (The term, "Mass," borrowed from the ancient occult lexicon, is a word used by *pagans* in reference to their *blood sacrifice satanic rituals.*) Beginning in 1962, Pope Paul VI introduced open *black magic witchcraft* into Catholic theology via the outward expression of wearing the *Twisted Cross*, a satanic symbol that blasphemes the crucified Jesus Christ.

The true nature of Catholicism is further demonstrated by a long series of heresies incorporated into its theological doctrine throughout its bloody history. (The rampaging Inquisitions were the *Catholic Crusades* of the Middle Ages led by *Freemasonry's* Catholic Knights Templar in hot pursuit of persecuted *True Christians.*) The following is a list of unscriptural pagan practices and the dates of their incorporation into Catholic teachings. The entries not only prove that the Roman Catholic Church is *not* True Christianity, but also show the character of its neopagan idolatry and witchcraft practices:

1) Prayers for the dead – necromancy: 300 AD
2) Making the sign of the cross – idolatry: 300 AD
3) Veneration of angels and dead saints; images used in worship – idolatry: 375 AD
4) The Mass as a daily celebration – blasphemy of Jesus Christ's death as not being sufficient for forgiveness of sins and salvation (Hebrews 7:27): 394 AD

5) Exaltation of Mary as the "Mother of God" – Goddess worship. The real Mary was not the mother of God. God has no mother; He is a Spirit, and must be worshipped in spirit and truth (John 4:24): 431 AD

6) Extreme Unction, Last Rites – pagan ritual for the dead: 526 AD

7) Doctrine of Purgatory – pagan doctrine: 593 AD

8) Prayers to Mary and dead saints – goddess worship, necromancy, idolatry: 600 AD

9) Worship of cross, images and relics – idolatry: 786 AD

10) Canonization of dead saints – idolatry, especially as pertains to statues and relics of such "saints": 995 AD

11) Celibacy of priesthood – pagan ritual (1 Timothy 4:3): 1079

12) The Rosary – prayer beads used in pagan cultures; vain repetition of prayers (Matthew 6:7)): 1090

13) Indulgences: 1190

14) Transubstantiation – repeated sacrifice of Jesus Christ (Hebrews 7:27): 1215

15) Confession of sins to a priest: 1215

16) Adoration of the wafer (Host) as the actual flesh of Jesus Christ. How could God be present in a stale piece of bread when He is in heaven and sits at the right hand of the Father? (Colossians 3:1): 1220

17) Purgatory proclaimed as a dogma (Hebrews 9:27): 1439

18) Doctrine of "Seven Sacraments": 1439

19) Catholic Church *tradition* declared an equal authority to the Bible Blasphemy of the Holy Ghost, the only unforgivable sin (Mark 3:29): 1545

20) Apocryphal Books added to Bible: 1546

21) Immaculate Conception of Mary (Romans 3:23; 5:12): 1854

22) Infallibility of Pope in matters of faith and morals: 1870

23) The world consecrated to the Immaculate Heart of Mary: 1942

24) Mary proclaimed "Queen of the World": 1946

25) Assumption of the Virgin Mary into heaven. Mary died in the same manner as any other human being; God never intended her to be deified: 1950

26) Russia consecrated to Mary: 1952

27) Vatican II declared ecumenical council for the universal church: 1962

28) Mary proclaimed the Mother of the Roman Catholic Church: 1965

29) Pope John Paul II announces "The Year of Mary": 1987

30) Mary proclaimed to be "Advocate", "Ark of the Covenant," "Mediatrix" and "Co-Redeemer" with Jesus Christ (Jeremiah 7:18-19; 44:15-29): This is the so-called "Fifth Marian Doctrine. As of this writing, not yet *officially* announced, but planned to be declared soon.

Notice the acceleration in Rome's emphasis upon "Mary" since 1942, a time of the world's bloodiest war. Expect to see in the years ahead an increase in the occurrence of "Marian apparitions" (masquerading demons), the integration of apostate Christianity with all the world's major religions (Ecumenicalism), and an acceleration of demonic manifestations wrought by the Catholic Charismatic movement (outpouring of the spirit of antichrist). Headed by the False Prophet – the Pope – the Catholic Church will continue to play an integral role in organizing the NWO end times One World Church. Because sin originally came into the world through a woman deceived by Satan, (masquerading as a serpent), so too in these endtimes it is once again through the deceptions of a woman (androgynous Satan disguised as "Mary") that significant numbers of people are being misled to their own destruction.

When speaking to Christians and Muslims in Brussels, Belgium, Pope John Paul II stated: "Christians and Moslems, we meet one another in faith in the one God ... and strive to put into practice the teaching of our respective holy books." (The God of Christians and Muslims are diametrically opposed. Catholicism does not consider the Bible to be its primary source of doctrine, but instead believes its "church tradition" is the ultimate authority.) Inspired by the Pope's ecumenical efforts to unite the world, *Interfaith Councils* subsequently sprung up all across America, assemblies where Christians met for prayer and to plan social action with the followers of all religions. "We must yolk together with Rome," is the battle cry heard at enthusiastic rallies. "Together, we must fight the evil in our society." Through the ecumenical leadership of the Vatican, the Roman Catholic Church is fast becoming the bridge uniting all the religions of the world.

In 1986, in Assisi, Italy, John Paul II organized the gathering together of 130 leaders from the 12 major world religions. Praying for world peace were Hindus, Muslims, Buddhists, Catholics, Protestants, African and North American witch doctors, spiritists, animists, Wiccan witches and various other sorcerers, as well as sun and snake worshippers. The Pope announced: "We need to respect one another's religious beliefs. We all have the same message. We pray to the same God." The Roman Catholic potentate permitted the Dalai Lama to replace the cross on St. Peter's Church altar with a statue of Buddha, and allowed him and his monks to perform worship services in the cathedral. The Buddhist was given a standing ovation after proclaiming to a capacity crowd: "All the world's major religions are basically the same."

The Catholic Church changed the Ten Commandments! In order to reconcile their practice of idolatry and make it appear quasi-Christian, the most powerful city on earth – the Vatican – attempted to correct God. The Commandment given to Moses by

God in Exodus 20:3-5, and again in Deuteronomy 5:7-9, warning against the practice of idolatry, was deleted from the *Catholic version* of the Bible (New American Standard). The original Scripture that was deleted, reads: *Thou shalt have no other gods before me. Thou shalt not make unto thee any graven image, or any likeness of anything that is in heaven above, or that is in the earth beneath, or that is in the water under the earth: Thou shalt not bow down thyself to them, or serve them: for I the LORD thy God am a jealous God.* To fill the void left by the Catholic Church's deliberate omission of this Commandment that God decreed from Mount Sinai, the Popes of Rome divided another Commandment to make it into two Commandments. This slight of hand was performed in the following manner: The Exodus/Deuteronomy Commandment that was divided is: *Thou shalt not covet thy neighbor's house, thou shalt not covet thy neighbor's wife, nor his manservant, nor his maidservant, nor his ox, nor his ass, nor any thing that is thy neighbor's.* The *Catholic version*, consisting of two separate Commandments, reads: *Thou shalt not covet thy neighbor's wife. Thou shalt not covet thy neighbor's goods.* Thus, one Commandment was changed into two. Fait accompli.

Although Roman Catholicism is one of the largest and most widespread religions in the world (second only to Islam), it is merely one among many forms of counterfeit Christianity that exists today. Its alternative gospel makes it appealing to the biblically-illiterate who hope that membership or faith in the theology of a man-made institution will somehow secure their eternal future. It is unscriptural for anyone to believe they can attain eternal salvation through an association with a system of human traditions (Matthew 15:8,9; 2 Corinthians 6:16-17; Revelation 18:4). Idolatry, goddess worship, blaspheming of the Holy Spirit, rejection of the Word of God – these are only some of the pagan practices and delusional doctrines which make Catholicism a dangerous cultic belief system having little or no relevance to True Christianity. Isaiah 66:3,4: … *Yea, they have chosen their own ways, and their soul delighteth in their abominations. I also will choose their delusions.* Tragically, those many who are well-meaning – but deceived by Roman

Catholic doctrines – will not realize their fatal error until *after* the Day of Judgment, when they suddenly awaken in the burning Lake of Fire.

Catholicism is pure Satanism. All who are entrapped in this man-made system are under demonic mind control. Referring to child sacrifices in the basement catacombs of the Vatican, a Rothschild Illuminati defector said that the Roman Catholic Vatican was "the most evil place on earth."

"Christian" Celebrities:

Whether televangelists, best-selling book authors, or radio talk show hosts, these RCF "Christian" leaders promote NWO religious and political doctrines while masquerading as *ministers of righteousness* (2 Corinthians 11:15). Most people are familiar with the more conspicuous charlatans who traded Jesus Christ for a Mercedes Benz – individuals such as Billy Graham, Benny Hinn, Paul and Jan Crouse, Jimmy Swaggert, Oral Roberts, Jack Van Eppy, Jim and Tammy Baker, Tim LaHaye, John Hagee, Hal Lindsey, Pat Robertson, Robert Schuller – most of whom are 33 degree Freemasons. These false *teachers, having itching ears* (2 Timothy 4:3), have turned many away from the truth of the gospel and to fables (ref. v.4). Billy Graham announced to a world audience on TV that "Jesus Christ is not necessary for salvation." The "second team Hall of Eternal Shame" is populated with such *false apostles, deceitful workers* (2 Corinthians 11:13) as: Kenneth Copeland, TK Jakes, and Chuck Colson (of Watergate repute), who are working to establish worldwide Ecumenicalism. Hank Hanegraaff is a radio talk show host and an apologist for pagan Roman Catholicism, the false Pre-Tribulation Rapture doctrine, Satanic Ritual Abuse, and Satanism in America. James Dobson, a "Christian" *psychologist* (psychology is witchcraft, hence, this phrase is an oxymoron), is another example of a Professing Christian who turned away from the truth for personal gain. He publicly endorses the Harry Potter witchcraft book series, as do many of his RCF brethren.

Philippians 3:2: *Beware of dogs, beware of evil workers, beware of the concision.* Today, the apostasy is everywhere. Just as tragic is the virtual nonexistence of any True Christian opposition to apostate Christianity. Isaiah 56:10,11 affirms: *His watchmen are blind, they are all ignorant, they are all dumb dogs, they cannot bark; sleeping, lying down, loving to slumber. Yea, they are greedy dogs which can never have enough, and they are shepards that cannot understand: they all look to their own way, every one for his gain, from his quarter.* Today, the only public media resource available for hearing the true Word of God is select Internet and short wave radio broadcasts – sources that reach less than 1 percent of the world population. Yet, the Lord has reserved 7000 that have not bowed to the image of the New World Order Beast government (ref. 1 Kings 19:18; Romans 11:4). Therefore, God's people are still "out there," but they are so vastly outnumbered by the majority unrighteous – especially those many professing Christianity – as to make their presence practically invisible. Psalm 53:2,3: *God looked down from heaven upon the children of men, to see if there were any that did understand, that did seek God. Every one of them has gone back: they are altogether become filthy; there is none that doeth good, no, not one.*

The gospel of Jesus Christ has been replaced by the pseudo-Christian "Prosperity gospel," the "Purpose Driven Life/Purpose Driven Church gospel," and the "NIV Bible gospel." False Christian leaders will not warn and educate their following to oppose the LCF's antichrist socialist doctrines, laws and decrees, and neither will they risk the loss of their 501(c)3 tax-exempt status by speaking out against the Luciferian policies of an illegitimate Criminal Fraternity government. John 10:12,13: *But he that is a hireling, and not the shepard, whose own the sheep are not, seeth the wolf coming, and leaveth the sheep, and fleeth: and the wolf catches them, and scattereth the sheep. The hireling fleeth, because he is an hireling, and careth not for the sheep.* The end for Christian celebrities will be according to their works (2 Corinthians 11:15; Romans 2:6). It is the Lake of Fire.

"Christian" front groups:

Front groups, such as the Clergy Response Team, Christian Coalition, and Christian Identity (White Supremists), are CIA operations planted among the general population and Christian communities in order to further the globalist's Luciferian agenda of world religious unity and ethnic and religious strife (Hegelian Dialectic). Some key leaders of Pat Robertson's Christian Coalition, for example, are members in good standing with the Luciferian elite (e.g. Former spokesman Ralph Reed attends Bilderberger global conferences). Christian Identity/Ayrian groups claim to be the literal physical descendants of "Israel, God's chosen people," even though it is a genetic impossibility for white-skinned Europeans to have descended from a dark skin Middle Eastern race. The neo-Nazi philosophy of white supremacy can be traced back to ancient Egyptian Isis cults from which it evolved into its present form via the following British Freemasonry secret societies: The Order of St. John of Jerusalem (1070), Knights of Malta, Knights Templar, Theosophical Society, Hitler and Nazi Germany's Thule Society, Aleister Crowley and Aldous Huxley's Vril Society, and several other intermediate linkages. Aryan Nation Supremacists promote the same basic thesis as did Hitler, Stalin and Lenin: self exaltation, exclusion and hatred of all nonwhite races, eugenics, and racial supremacy.

Government-sponsored "Christian" front groups may superficially appear to be Christian, or profess some biblical doctrines, yet, they are actually political-religious cults. The World Council of Churches – perhaps the largest of the RCF front groups – while superficially Christian, promotes globalist doctrines in support of world unity. Examples of the more conspicuous religious cults professing Christianity today are Catholicism, and the following *Masonic* derivatives: Mormonism, Jehovah Witness, Christian Science. Examples of some *Protestant* denominations that have incorporated false doctrine into their theology are: Episcopalian, Methodist, Presbyterian, Lutheran, Baptist, Southern Baptist.

"Christian" Political Patriot Movement:

Much like the phrases, *"Christian"* Police Officer, *"Christian"* Politician, *"Christian"* Judge, *"Christian"* Attorney; the phrase, "*Christian"* Political Patriot is a contradiction in terms since no such individual exists. This is so because it is not possible to serve two masters (Matthew 6:24; Luke 16:13), and therefore, it is impossible to serve *both* God and Country. When a "Christian" Political Patriot claims to love his "country" and to also love "God," he has either redefined God to be other than the God of the King James Bible, or, he loves the LCF and hates God. Anyone who claims to serve both the Lord *and* Caesar, is lying, and is therefore a hypocrite. Political Patriots who profess Christianity are not Christians at all, but merely, LCF Patriots.

The Political Patriot fails to realize that the term "country" is synonymous with "government." In other words, whenever he says he loves his country, what he really means is that he loves his *government*, which is the very entity he professes to oppose. Since he is allied with his sworn enemy – Satan's human government – he is therefore neither a Patriot in the Constitutional sense of the word, nor is he a True Christian. Rather, he is *double minded, and unstable in all his ways* (James 1:8).

In addition to Agents Provocateur, the Political Patriot community is manned by former military personnel who, as a result of psychological trauma incurred during their military experience, have been passively mind-controlled to retain allegiance to their *handler* – the United States Federal Government. Since intense military brainwashing occurred when they were young and impressionable (having been recruited or volunteered for military service in their late teens or early twenties, when their personal identity was not yet fully formed), the psychological reprogramming that is part of a military recruit's standard basic training conditions them to identify with the "government" (America no longer exists in its original 1776 form, and is now a UN state). Their intense military brainwashing leaves permanent psychological scars. Givernment becomes their mind control "handler." For the remainder of their life many ex-GI's maintain allegiance to the military, an association which they consider to be synonymous with the vague notion of "love of country." Consequently, some of the best examples of mind control programmed subjects are former military personnel. (ref. Chapter 5 for more on Political Patriotism).

CIA Trauma-Based Mind Control:

In the context of the NWO Luciferian takeover, this is a psychological conditioning program used by the CIA/FBI and other "Black Budget" government agencies to create government operatives that are either knowingly or unwittingly acting as double agents for the LCF Luciferian globalists. If unwitting, they have been mind-controlled and are being directed by their *handlers* – government agents skilled in the application of psychological manipulation and trauma-based physical torture. Most politically active victims of trauma-based mind control, after having been abducted by government agents, tortured and psychologically programmed, carry on their normal routine of posing as the people's advocate, yet, their fractured mind has been programmed with several compartmentalized personalities created by the intensive trauma. In many instances, such individuals are completely unaware they are mind-controlled and are acting under the supervision of their LCF handlers. Consequently, they may appear to be quite normal, but are plagued with logical inconsistencies and contradictions, having separate identities that act antagonistic to their public persona. An example of this is Billy Graham, world renowned spokesperson for Christianity. He is a 33rd degree Mason, promoter of the worldwide Ecumenical Movement for unifying all the world's religions to form the endtimes church of the Antichrist, and international ambassador to global leaders of both the Legal Criminal Fraternity and the Religious Criminal Fraternity (most notable of which is the Vatican). Presumably, at some early point in Graham's career as a religious celebrity, he underwent mind control psychological conditioning to program him for catering to the interests of the Luciferian globalists. Simultaneous, he appeared not to compromise his Christian values. For decades, his crusades have been funded by various Illuminati families, most notable of which are Rockefeller and Van Duyn. Further causalities of mind control programming can be found among other well known televangelists and Christian celebrities.

As "Manchurian Candidates," the creation of programmed political personalities is a tactic used by governments for planting their own people among the opposition. The target candidate is rigorously mind-controlled to be unaware of having been mind-controlled. Their subconscious alter ego psychologically restructured, the duplicity can be very deceptive – their public persona convincing to the unsuspecting masses who believe their scripted propaganda.

Citizen Surveillance:

The LCF wants to know everything *about you.* The following are only some of the ways in which they are able to accomplish that: Social Security Number, insurance policy, bank accounts, utility bills, medical records, school records, unemployment insurance, workers compensation, welfare funds, mortgage payments, drivers license, marriage license, passport, post office and mail delivery persons, Internet web sites visited, phoning toll free 800 number listener "Call In" lines, direct mail correspondence, surveys, newspaper and magazine public opinion polls, census; querying neighbors, business associates, friends, etc. By disengaging from "the system," you, the peaceable citizen, can become transparent to the watchful all-seeing eye of the Beast. Enemies of the New World Order (e.g. those who uphold the Constitution, True Christians, etc.) are baited and drawn out into the open so they can be identified and their personal information maintained in a government dossier data bank. At the appropriate time (e.g. declaration of

Martial Law) they will be efficiently located or hunted down and exterminated. When a concerned "Patriot" makes his identity or location known by accessing a web site or calling the police, for example, the LCF instantly traces his whereabouts and creates a file to begin their surveillance and compile personal information. Soon to follow will be chronic harassment and torment by the Beast's servants. (The author once made the mistake of contacting Christian Patriot talk show hosts via the telephone and e-mail. The mad CF dogs immediately began sniffing him; a concerted campaign of terror ensued, consisting of incessant telephone harassment – multiple calls every day, characterized by mysterious silence on the other end – government planes and helicopters flown close overhead and employing infrared detectors to scan the contents of his residence. Ultimately, a rabid SWAT team suddenly burst through the front door, shouting and brandishing military assault weapons. Lesson: Keep to yourself. Trust *no one*, except the Lord Jesus Christ. Never, *never interact with the government in any manner whatsoever.* In these end times of the Luciferian takeover of America and the world, with victims of CIA mind control posing as "Christians" and "Patriots," trust no *human being.* Absolutely *none.*

Common Law Citizen Legal Defense:

This is a small and unusual niche of sincerely deluded individuals who steadfastly believe they can beat the LCF at their own game. Regardless of results to the contrary, they yet retain the belief that they can force hardened legal criminals to abide by their own unjust laws. Amazingly naive, these wannabe-lawyers purport to advise maligned citizens in such matters as not paying income or property taxes, nullifying a social security number, operating a motor vehicle without a drivers license, beating traffic tickets, and many other gray areas of man's corrupt laws. For a fee, they may put on entertaining seminars instructing people in how to sort through the maze of paperwork necessary to file affidavits, law suits, motions, etc, ad nauseum. Although their basic understanding of "the system" is often correct and may be motivated by a righteous concern, nevertheless, the Beast feels no obligation to honor its own laws or to provide justification for its felonious actions against victimized citizens. Because they have the guns and the full force of the Beast behind them, the LCF ignores those who typically spend more time in jail than they do conducting seminars and promoting their unrealistic appeals to "get justice." Little do they realize that, after all is said and done – well-reasoned arguments notwithstanding – the Masonic judge will still find guilty all those who oppose his Masonic Brotherhood, and will extract from his dazed victims the usual tribute money and loss of freedom. No amount of truth – short of Jesus Christ Himself – can persuade legal criminals to voluntarily come clean of their criminality. They will always *do whatever they want.*

The more deeply a practitioner of citizen legal defense becomes involved with Satan's corrupt system of "justice," the more they metamorphose into a legal criminal, adopting the same jargon, mannerisms, arrogant attitude and criminal mindset of police, attorneys, judges and politicians. Ultimately, they become merely an extension of the LCF.

Any thinking person would not bother to waste their time attempting to reason with a criminal that has a gun; and neither would they volunteer themselves to be practice for a common law citizen defender/pretender. Spare yourself the aggravation and just simply ignore, evade, or resist the Beast, and it will flee from you (James 4:7).

Congressional Record 94554:

This is an LCF official public document which states: "People are the enemy of the state." When one finally arrives at the understanding that man's civil government and its attendant LCF Servants of the Lie are *terrorists*, then and only then do their depraved actions begin to make rational sense. As so often has occurred throughout man's history, the present ruling elite in America has declared war upon its on citizenry. Violent acts of war are currently being staged by the various Illuminati witchcraft families in an effort to incite among the people of the modern world patriotic sentiments in support of a dictatorial world government. The objective is to bring the entire population of planet Earth under subjugation to a single individual whom Scripture identifies as the Antichrist. As the consummate legal criminal he will further the Beast's agenda expressed by CR 94554. Micro-chipping of the world's people will be his ultimate goal.

Containment Agent:

Once damaging truth has leaked out to the general public, the CF will assign Containment Agents to control the flow of information to the public. This is called *Damage Control.* Appearing to act in the public interest, a Containment Agent creates disinformation to serve as a cover-up story, or simply generate a patriotic following who will inadvertently reveal their identity and location to the police and federal agents. Criminal Fraternity operatives posing as citizen advocates act as Containment Agents to buffer the release of vital information, and also to effectively *discredit* those exposing the falsehoods of the Criminal Fraternity. An illustration of this can be seen in the occult phenomenon of Satanic Ritual Abuse (SRA) – generational cult ritual child sacrifice, pedophilia, pornography and white slavery. The national and global network of Satanists (mostly LCF) attempt to discredit the courtroom testimony of ritually abused children by means of the invented scientific-sounding term, *False Memory Syndrome.* Traumatized victims of organized Satanism or CIA mind control experimentation (conducted from the 1950's to the present) may later come forward to expose the Satanic cult and reveal the identity of individual legal criminals who abused them. Cathy O'Brien, co-author of the book, *Trance: Formation of America*, as a result of her intensive trauma programming, acquired a photographic memory that retained a perfect record of the words and horrifying deeds of her persecutors. Named in her book are several prominent Luciferians: George H.W. Bush, serial killer, pedophile, international narcotics dealer, and Level 4 Illuminati; Dick Cheney: sociopath, rapist, serial killer; Gerald Ford: pedophile, child rapist, pornography kingpin; Ronald Reagan: Illuminati puppet. These are only some examples of high-level CF Containment Agents. (For more names and supporting documentation, see *References.*)

Election:

The Legal Criminal Fraternity, rather than striving to be part of the Remnant Elect, merely want to be elected. They seek the approval of men; they want "the vote." Narrow in their perspective, petty and shortsighted, their all-consuming desire is to climb to the top of the heap of rotting garbage known as human civil government. These, the children of disobedience, have no desire to serve God, but only to serve themselves. For them, attaining to heaven is not a high priority. In fact, it is not a priority at all, since they do *not like to retain God in their knowledge* (Romans 1:28). They function best in a structured institutionalized context, preferably one that oppresses other people: the greater the oppression, the greater their sense of personal and spiritual fulfillment. They are most comfortable occupying government offices, functioning as Wards of the state – politicians, judges, attorneys, police, jailers – punitive representatives of Satan's kingdom on earth. They enjoy being in close proximity to the Beast, where they can intermingle among their own kindred-spirited ilk. Typical of the Criminal Fraternity – as the spiritual offspring of Satan – is their drive to mimic the things of God. Recall that Lucifer desires to *be like the most High* (Isaiah 14:12-15). Thus, so does the Criminal Fraternity. Yet *they too* shall one day *be brought down to hell, to the sides of the pit.*

The evil perpetrated by the Criminal Fraternity is so profound that they *not only do the same, but have pleasure in them that do them* (Romans 1:32). Their conscious seared, minds reprobate, the LCF has no awareness or desire to repent of their wickedness, but only to be appointed or elected to hold a government public office.

In contrast, God's Elect are those who have received a love of the truth that they might be Saved (ref. 2 Thessalonians 2:9-12). They are among the *few*, not the many. ... *for wide is the gate, and broad is the way, that leadeth to destruction, and many there be which go in thereat: Because strait is the gate, and narrow is the way, which leadeth unto life, and few there be that find it* (Matthew 7:13,14). Those who are of *God's election* are known by the "fruit" of their good works (Matthew 7:16-27); they have a genuine concern for the poor and disadvantaged, orphans, widows, children in general, and others who are True Christians (James 1:27; Matthew 25:31-46; Luke 10:29-37; Matthew 10:13-16; 1 John 3:14); and they hate evil (Psalm 97:10; 139:21-24; Proverb 8:13; Amos 5:15). Above all, they love God (Luke 10:39-42), have repented of their sins and believe the gospel (Mark 1:15), and obey and serve Jesus Christ of the 1611 King James Bible. Only True Christians are of *God's election*.

Federal Reserve/IRS/Income Tax:

In perhaps the greatest Ponzi Scheme of all time, the Federal Reserve – which is neither "Federal" (i.e. a governmental body) nor a "Reserve" – is a privately owned *corporation* with share holders and a board of directors, most of whom are not U.S. citizens. "The Fed" was created in 1913 by international CF bankers, the Rothschilds, as a means to seize control of American politics by dictating domestic and international policy to Washington government officials. The Federal Reserve is a *Centralized Bank*, one of the key planks of the Communist Manifesto. At the time of its establishment the European globalists also created the Internal Revenue Service as a means by which the Rothschild/Rockefeller crime families could be guaranteed repayment of their fiat currency loaned to the U.S. federal government. The IRS, a fraudulent Criminal Fraternity enterprise, is a *collection agency for the Federal Reserve Bank*. It has nothing to do with funding government for the betterment of the American way of life. Citizen's extorted income tax payments go toward funding projects to bring about Satan's New World Order.

The Internal Revenue Service is an unconstitutional entity that was created by the European Rothschild dynasty to generate a steady cash flow into their New World Order coffers. These extorted funds from U.S. citizens are then used to finance their world terrorist activities and to further the agenda of Satan's global fascist government. Although there exists *no* Constitutional law requiring U.S. citizens to pay income taxes, yet, by fraud, intimidation and deceit, the LCF has managed to brainwash and frighten the stupid American public into believing that it is their "patriotic duty" to "support the government" by "paying their fair share of taxes." According to the Federal Revised Tax Code (the LCF's own corrupt law book) *only federal employees working in Washington DC* are required to pay taxes on their earned income. In other words, the only individuals mandated by law to pay tribute money to the Beast are Washington's own *Criminal Fraternity* – the elitist mob who typically pay no income taxes whatsoever! Proclaiming themselves to be a privileged class not subject to their own unrighteous laws, upper-level Servants of the Lie profiteer from the sweat and blood of those who *actually work* for a living. Anyone who pays income taxes to the rich is cursed by God. Proverb 22:16: *He that oppresseth the poor to increase his riches, and he that giveth to the rich, shall surely come to want.*

Income tax is a *voluntary* tax. Irwin Schiff of Las Vegas Nevada offered a training course that provided instruction on how to legally avoid paying taxes. The LCF, in violation of their own laws, denied Schiff's First Amendment right to free speech when banning circulation of one of his books exposing their fraudulent income tax racketeering swindle. Under penalty of imprisonment, the Beast has prohibited him from distributing his literature exposing the Federal Mafia tax fraud. (Appropriately named, one of his books banned from public distribution is titled *The Federal Mafia.*) Although what he and several other Constitutional advocates have to say may be true and correct from a legal and moral standpoint, anyone who actively declines to participate in the embezzlement income tax scam may perhaps one day encounter legal terrorists that will imprison him just the same (ref. this section: *Newspapers and TV – Propaganda, USA, (3)*). Irwin Schiff is presently serving a long prison term in a Federal BOP facility.

There are many Constitutionally-based income tax objectors whose lives have been ruined, and who are forgotten and wasting away in one of the Beast's penal institutions. Therefore, heed the advice of the informed: *Don't protest,* but instead, simply *don't pay.* Do not attract any attention to yourself by informing the LCF of your intentions, and neither advise them that you are opposed to its extortion racket of fraudulent taxation. Just simply, and quietly, withdraw your support. Obey God rather than man. If the LCF insists on you handing over your money, truthfully tell it that you do not have any money belonging to them to hand over, and that you pay all the taxes that you owe (i.e. none). Once the Beast realizes there is no money for its legal terrorists to steal, they'll probably leave you alone ... for a while. (Of course, you will not want to leave a paper trail which the government dogs in heat can sniff back to you. Therefore, while you still can, deal in cash only.)

American IRS agents are neither trained by, nor are they on the bankroll of, the U.S. Treasury Department. Rather, they are employees paid by the Treasury of the *United Nations.* The Internal Revenue Service is a member of a multi-national pact called the International Criminal Police Organization (INTERPOL). Its mission is two fold:

a) Finance NWO genocidal programs

b) Collect and compile information on citizens for use by the international Luciferians. The U.S. Attorney General and the Secretary of the Treasury are *INTERPOL representatives.* As required by INTERPOL's Constitution, these Federal public servants must *expatriate their allegiance to America.* Therefore, they have no loyalty to American interests, but only to the globalists. Funds which the IRS extorts from U.S. citizens are deposited into the International Monetary Fund (IMF), a non-U.S. government *international bank* (World Bank). Hence, not a penny of your so-called *federal* income taxes have ever gone toward building a road or bridge, but instead, went directly to build and maintain the Luciferian's many-headed New World Order monster. Citizen's tax dollars are used to create the political and military machinery that enslaves them. The blood supply of the Beast is absconded funds from citizens. Cut off the head of the Beast by withdrawing your support.

In summary, on behalf of a private bank – the Federal Reserve – a non-U.S. government entity – the IRS – extorts payments in the form of "taxes" from cowered citizens, then deposits these extorted funds into the international Treasury of the internationalist's World Bank. These annual billions of dollars are spent on NWO propaganda and global projects designed to create the infrastructure of the Antichrist's political-religious-economic kingdom. The IRS does not collect taxes for the Treasury of the United States of America, but for the Treasury of the *United Nations.* The LCF takes the money they steal from you by intimidation and force, then uses these same funds to further their global Police State agenda: wars, abortion, population control through vaccines and doping the food supply; promotion of homosexuality, witchcraft and other occult teachings in schools; food, water and atmospheric sabotage (Chemtrails/HAARP); mass public disinformation and brainwashing by their scripted media; as well as the other means discussed throughout this volume to control the citizenry and exterminate mankind.

Render unto God that which is God's – and it's *all* God's – *nothing* belongs to Caesar that does not belong to God. It is an act of disobedience to God to pay tithes to Satan/Caesar/the LCF Beast government. Matthew 17:25-27 explains that, as subjects of the King of kings – Jesus Christ – True Christians *are exempt* from paying taxes to human governments. Those submitting to income taxation are *helping* the enemies of God, Satan's kingdom on earth, which is human civil government. Doing so confers a curse: 2 Chronicles 19:2: ... *Shouldest thou help the ungodly, and love them that hate the LORD? therefore is wrath upon thee from before the LORD.*

Do not support a system designed to destroy you and your children. Any money that you hand over to the LCF terrorists is used for global NWO programs and CF terrorism directed *against you.* It would be far better to utilize your hard earned funds to furnish yourself with surpluses of storable food and provisions, military arms, alternative shelters and emergency life support systems (e.g. water distillers – both electric and non-electric; solar panels, seeds for growing food, etc.). Use your money to make yourself invisible to the Beast. And be prepared for the worst.

Freemasonry - FOP Connection:

The Freemasonry – Fraternal Order of Police connection ties together the LCF Freemasonry Brotherhood fraternity of Police, Judges, Attorneys and Politicians. The emblem of the Fraternal Order of Police (FOP) openly reveals its affiliation with Freemasonry, a satanic religious cult. In addition to the blatantly displayed five-pointed satanic pentagram, there is information on the fraternal badge that reveals insight to their carefully guarded secret. A lodge number and the name of a Grandmaster is often inscribed, as well as the Latin words: *Jus-Fidus-Libertatum.* Typical of the Servants of the Lie, they prefer to hide their true identity and intentions from outsiders by the use of coded words and phrases written in an archaic language. (Luciferians seem to prefer Latin.) Realizing that the dumbed-down masses are not likely to know a foreign language, nor to have the initiative to discover the meaning of unfamiliar terms, the LCF is thus able to employ the use of obscure words, phrases and slogans to symbolically conceal the true intentions behind their criminality (e.g. There is no letter "J" in Latin, thus further obscuring transliteration of the word, *Jus*)

The above cryptic motto demonstrates *reverse meaning*, a common practice employed among Luciferians. The translation provided by FOP disinformation is: "Law is the safeguard of freedom," but the *true and correct* translation is: "Real faith makes men free." Since all members of the Criminal Fraternity are pathological liars from birth (Psalm 58:3), in further decoding the true meaning of this

FOP motto, the following can be discerned by the Holy Spirit: The phrase, "Real faith makes men free," has a religious connotation. According to a Luciferian, "Real faith" is faith in *their* god, the god of Freemasonry – i.e. Lucifer/Satan. It is this blind trust which they believe makes men free from adherence to the absolute standard of truth established by the Laws of God. Freemasonry's former exalted leader and highpriest, Albert Pike, authored a key occult text, *Morals and Dogma,* in which he stated, "Do what thou wilt is the whole of the law." Note his use of Old English terminology, mocking the King James translation. Clearly, the desired "freedom" cryptically referred to by FOP Masons is a freedom from the moral constraints imposed by a supremely holy God Who executes righteous judgments upon His enemies. Pike went on to state in his book that the "God" of Freemasonry is Lucifer.

Genesis Chapter 6 - implications:

From verses 2 and 4 it is evident that the fallen angels, otherwise known as *demons,* fathered children from human females. These offspring were the Greek/Roman "mythological gods" of antiquity: Zeus/Jupiter; Aphrodite/Venus, Hercules, Mars, etc., who were actual real beings and did exist as human-demon hybrids. These were the giants referred to in verse 4, and they were called "Titans," which in the Hebrew transliterates to "Satans." Hence, these *mighty men ... of renown* were the literal sons of Belial, the Devil. Ancient cultures of that time recorded similar super-human creatures. For example, the Scandinavian Norsemen spoke of Thor, Wooden and other extraordinary human beings, which are the same father god figures as the Greek Zeus and Roman Jupiter. Verse 4 also states that these giants were present *in the earth,* signifying their spiritual genetic origin as the pit of hell. Further, the same verse states they were physically present *after* the great flood, which is confirmed in several later books of the Bible, such as the Book of Joshua, referencing Rephim, Anakim, Nephilim, all of which were exceptional for their large physical size and unusual anatomical characteristics (e.g. King Og of Bashan was over 10 feet tall and had six fingers and six toes). The "im" ending denotes "angelic," but in this context is referring to "fallen angels," which are not to be confused with the holy angels of God. This distinction is a point of contention for the upper echelon Criminal Fraternity, who think of themselves as "gods," or as directly descended from "the gods." However, their spiritual lineage is traceable to these *fallen* angels, otherwise known as demons or devils.

The Illuminati generational Satanists – the trillionaire crime families of the world, as the driving force behind globalism and the push to establish a worldwide Police State for their master, Satan – are striving to eradicate all human beings from the Earth. It is in their Luciferian doctrines where they find justification to subjugate all the peoples of the world. Believing themselves to be "gods" or "extraterrestrial aliens," they think they are special and superior to "mere" human mortals. Yet, the offspring of Satan are not entirely incorrect in their assumed identity, since, in a way, they truly *are* aliens from another world, beings fallen to earth, "extraterrestrials" in the same sense that the little space people ("greys," demons masquerading as human "saviors") claim to be ET's. Chapter 3 of this volume affirms Genesis 6 – i.e. the LCF elite are the *spiritual progeny* of a union between demons and humans. They are the cursed recipients of a transfer of generational occult power resulting from the wicked deeds of their ancestors. Just like their distant progenitors (Genesis 6:4), these quasi-human men and women are supremely evil (v.5), and in biblical times, when they further inbred with the rest of the human race, were the primary reason that God regretted having made mankind. With the exception of the 8 member family of Noah, there were no other humans on earth at that time that did not have a tainted genetic bloodline. In God's righteous wrath He therefore summarily destroyed all of quasi-humanity.

As in the days of Noe (Matthew 24:37), the human bloodline today has been contaminated with demonic blood that is concentrated in the multi-generational progeny of world leaders and the very rich and politically influential. These families, all of which are blood-related, are aware they are not fully human, as confirmed by the fact that some of them are capable of shape-shifting into 8 foot tall reptiles during their child sacrificing rituals. It is by virtue of this and other *subhuman* occult abilities (manifestations of their indwelling demons) that they mistakenly believe they have "evolved" into superior beings, thinking themselves "advanced" in a spiritual/biological genetic sense. Yet, as demonstrated by the depravity of their wicked deeds, nothing could be further from the truth.

The lower tier members of the Criminal Fraternity – judges, attorneys, police – share a common demonic blood lineage with their more socially elevated Luciferian cousins, but to a lesser degree. Their genealogical parentage was insufficiently cursed by God (Exodus 20:5; 34:7) to allow for their promotion to high-ranking positions within the international Illuminati Brotherhood witchcraft coven. Although subordinates in the hierarchy may not be able to physically transmutate into a reptilian form like their blue-blooded brethren, nevertheless, they too are capable of committing horrendously evil acts, and especially against the children of God.

Gun Confiscation:

It was on July 9th, 2001 that the United Nations proposed legislation for disarming all non-governmental U.S. citizens. Since the 1998 start of the Illuminati's global Chemtrail pathogenic inoculation of the world's lower atmosphere, weather modification and HAARP global mind control campaign, unconstitutional gun confiscation laws represent yet another loss of American freedom and liberty. With the media censored to insure there was no print or televised coverage of the citizen disarmament event, and with their propaganda machine in high gear, the Criminal Fraternity's UN third party legislation met no opposition from sleepy-eyed Americans. In response to the disinformation preceding the event,

Hollywood and citizen groups such as *Mothers Against Guns*, effectively lobbied for gathering national support in favor of taking guns out of the hands of citizens and placing them in the clutches of legal criminals. Over 600,000 Medical Criminal Fraternity physicians supported the fascist decree to take away citizens' guns when requiring their patients to complete a form revealing whether they own any handguns or other weapons, or if they know of anyone who does. This information, effectively serving as *gun registration*, is fed back to the FBI/BATF/CIA/DHS citizen surveillance Matrix computer files for later access in locating the owner of the "illegal firearm." Whenever the LCF says, "Gun Control," what they really mean is "Gun Confiscation."

Hollywood:

A plant species formerly used by medieval witches and sorcerers to cast spells on people. Beginning in the latter half of the twentieth century, and up until the present time, the Hollywood film industry continues a tradition of mesmerizing the public with magical incantations commonly known as "movies." The Luciferian globalists effectively use this powerful mind-controlling visual medium as a tool for programming and conditioning the masses to uncritically accept NWO propaganda as truth. By incremental degrees, the masses are desensitized and hypnotically induced to the present consensus belief that evil is good and good is evil (Isaiah 5:20). Hollywood movies are frequently used to broadcast the Luciferian globalist agenda, give advance notice of their planned acts of terrorism, promote the false "benevolent" image of the LCF, indoctrinate the youth into witchcraft beliefs and lifestyle, promote the homosexual agenda, discredit Bible truths, and to prepare the masses for acceptance of a world culture based on satanic doctrines and practices.

Homeland Security:

Like the "War on Terrorism" and "War on Drugs" (see below), this is yet another fraud put forth by the snickering LCF fiends under the direction of their supra-government Illuminati masters. Intended to instill fear into the hearts of the citizenry of America, "Homeland Security" legislation serves as yet another straight jacket for worldwide enslavement. The Luciferians planned far in advance how they would induce Americans and citizens in the rest of the world to freely submit to their demands for a global dictatorship. "The Plan" calls for instigating acts of terrorism on a scale that will immediately bring the people of the United States to their knees, bowing before the Beast, pleading for their lives when offering their freedom in exchange for Big Brother to protect them from *the terrorists*! And the Criminal Fraternity terrorists are only too happy to oblige.

Homosexuality/Lesbianism and the gay NWO agenda:

All gays are demon-possessed. Like witches, they are in rebellion against God, Who made them male and female for the express purpose of a lifelong solitary partnership with the opposing sex (ref. Genesis 1:27; 2:24). The Bible defines *rebellion* as *witchcraft* (ref. 1 Samuel 15:23). It therefore follows that homosexuals are modern day witches in rebellion to God. The converse is also true – i.e. *all* witches are gay, and/or bisexual, which is essentially the same.

A much overlooked aspect of the rampant spread of homosexuality/lesbianism in today's American and world culture is the fact that during the physical act of sodomy there is a transference of demon spirits between sexual partners. This is especially alarming when considering the present teaching in elementary schools that "alternative lifestyles" are an acceptable choice for children and teenagers. This preconditions them to the predatory attacks of pedophile mature men and women. The transference of deadly AIDS between sodomites is the physical corollary of the transference of spiritually deadly demons.

Newspapers and TV - Propaganda, USA:

The Illuminati controls all the forums of mainstream media and some alternative media. As a vital component of the Criminal

Fraternity organized crime network, the disinformation news reported to the public is largely falsehoods with just enough truth so that most people will uncritically accept it as "fact." This is *thought control.* Today, those hoping to discern the truth must realize that *all* members of the Criminal Fraternity are pathological liars from birth; they were born to lie. Psalm 58:3: *The wicked are estranged from the womb: they go astray as soon as they be born, speaking lies.* The media molds public opinion by controlling thoughts through repetition and promulgation of a belief or an ideology that serves the purpose of government interests. Mind control is a subtle process of changing perceptions and opinions. Watching television, reading the newspapers, viewing movies and secular videos alters cognitive perceptions until your thoughts are not fully your own, but are those of the Beast's programmers. The Luciferians have a saying: "You are what you read."

Fulfillment of Revelation prophesy is progressing at an accelerated rate that renders impossible the reporting of current events in a static medium such as a book. Each year there is more freedom-eroding New World Order legislation than the previous year. Presently, the time interval between key political events is getting shorter, sometimes measured in terms of weeks, or even days. Consequently, today's U.S. citizenry is an easy target for absorbing further NWO lies and deception via the world controller's preferred source – the controlled media.

True Christians, having been given a different spirit than that of the willfully deceived, rely only upon the 1611 King James Bible as their source of unchanging truth. A true servant of God would never read a newspaper or watch television news in order to "stay informed about what's going on in the world." Those few who love the Truth are adverse to lies. Reading the newspaper or listening to the spun version of world events on TV is antagonistic to their truth-loving spirit.

To demonstrate the pervasiveness of the CF Beast's group-think rhetoric, this author one day randomly picked up a copy of the local newspaper and began reading articles reprinted from national news services. The following accounts – titled as they appeared in the newspaper and including this author's clarifying comments – were obtained from just *one section* of a *small community newspaper*:

1) **Cops don disguises to collar speeders**
   by Louise Story, The Wall Street Journal

   Printed on the front page, this propaganda piece was intended to portray the police as righteous public servants "just doing their job," and also to subtly intimidate the citizenry to obey the Beast. The news article speaks of increasing police surveillance of "traffic offenders" who speed or fail to make complete stops at traffic lights and stop signs. A statistic was cited that the use of *surveillance cameras* has increased *50 percent* since the previous year! An example of the news article disinformation reads: "... these new tactics present a more effective way to curb aggressive driving and make the roads safer." The focus of the story was to report that "Police are increasingly teaming up with officers from other towns to blanket a particular area [revenue-collecting ticket-writing legal criminals]. Also discussed are newly popularized '*blitzes,*' where "police from several departments team up on [drivers] in one town with an unusually high number of cops." Discerning individuals will instantly recognize the preceding statements as Orwellian doublespeak. A True Christian is able to see through the cover story and will laugh and say: "It's a New World Order Police State drill for conditioning the apathetic public to accept Martial Law!" The same paragraph ended with: "... allows towns that are too small to have dedicated traffic officers set up major speed traps." For the doublespeak phrase, "speed traps", read "check points." It's all about conditioning you to accept tyranny as "normal."

   This article demonstrated the *incremental* nature of the encroaching Police State when describing the *militarized guerrilla police tactics* increasingly being implemented by police to spy on and arrest citizens. The article mentions that the cops are now *wearing disguises* which enable them to move undetected among peaceful citizens who wish only to go about their business without being molested by legal criminals. "Dressed up as golfers looking for their ball at the edge of a golf course, and disguising themselves as construction workers fixing street lights, [or adopting] the look of a homeless person, wearing a bandana, old Army jacket, and jeans with the knees cut out, a beat-up duffle bag at their side.... State police in Pennsylvania last month also started disguising some officers, dressing them in camouflage and deploying them in wooded areas alongside state roads." These CF Servants of the Lie surreptitiously radio back license plate numbers to a nearby uniformed officer who makes the arrest. Someday soon, when the police decoy reads *your* license plate number and instantly passes *your* identity on to the cop just up the road, it will not be for "speeding," but for "terrorism." You are going to a FEMA camp.

2) **Prisons cost too much**
by Jabari Asim, Washington Post Writers Group

This article was not so much intentional propaganda as it was confirming facts and details related throughout this book. The author, an Afro-American, indicated concern over the statistics that "... in some cities, more than half the young African-American men are under the supervision of the criminal justice system ... more than 2 million Americans are behind bars [and 6 million more are on probation or parole under the watchful eye of the Big Brother Beast] ... and a six fold increase in the federal and state [jail/prison] populations between 1974 and 2002: from 216,000 to 1,355,748." These figures, daunting as they are, confirm that the NWO prison system is a thriving economy; Satan is alive and well. Asim further writes: "The economic *costs* have been huge. Between 1982 and 1999, direct expenditures on corrections by federal, state and local governments increased from $9 billion to $49 billion." Substitute for the words, "costs" and "expenditures" the word, "profits," then read the previous sentence again. *That* is the true meaning of what the article writer was trying to express, but was unable to convey, perhaps because he feared the LCF. If he were a True Christian that did not fear man, but God, he would have stated the truth that Luciferian globalists are major stock holders in America's burgeoning prison industry that has increased nearly 600 percent in only 16 years. Trafficking in human souls is a significant source of revenue for the LCF, who generate profits from extortion at the point of a gun.

Also cited was a reference to "... our justice system's glaring failure to rehabilitate those whom it has chosen to punish." Again, one can only speculate that the journalist is either ignorant of the facts or simply concerned about losing his job. The spirit of truth declares that black men and others in prison on drug charges are *not incarcerated to be rehabilitated*; they are locked away, given 10 to 30 year prison sentences – their young lives ruined – in order to put them out of commission so they *will no longer be drug running competition for the CIA and other LCF crime syndicates.*

3) IRS beginning to win the war against tax protesters
by Albert B. Crenshaw, The Washington Post

The article writer, obviously a NWO parrot (notice that, like the previous journalist, he too is employed by the Washington District of Criminals propaganda news agency), used emotionally-charged words and phrases like "tax evaders" and "protesters" to denigrate righteously outraged citizens that publicly challenged the *Federal* Reserve's extortion racket as an illegitimate unconstitutional corporation of the globalist's IMF World Bank. Unlike the first article, no attempt was made to conceal overt propaganda presented as fact, and which has no supporting basis in truth. By a subtle process of thought conditioning, Crenshaw – a sycophant servant of the state – reinforced LCF terror-tactics to induce citizens reading the article to "pay up or else." He felt it unnecessary to provide documentation – such as a full name – when authoritatively stating that "a 26 year old man who had been resisting the IRS and making typical tax-protester-type arguments in the US Tax Court to try to stave off collection of more than $3,000 in taxes and penalties, suddenly recanted all and promised to pay his tax, interest and penalties and never to 'make these arguments in the future or appear in the (Tax) Court again,' according to the Tax Court ruling. The man's about-face, in which he quickly signed all required documents, persuaded the court to drop an additional penalty – as much as $25,000 – for making frivolous arguments or using a court case as a delaying tactic. Instead, he got off with a warning." Observing the Constitution and Bill of Rights is not a "frivolous argument" or a "delaying tactic." The Beast slackens its larceny and considers it a virtuous concession not to abscond with even more extorted funds.

Only someone that has been mind-controlled all their life would believe a word of the Tax Court's ruling. In stating that the man "had been resisting the IRS and making typical tax-protestor-type arguments" is a clear admission on the part of the Beast that it fears anyone who stands on Constitutional Law. Using such phrases as "promised to pay his taxes" assumes an unproven assertion that any taxes are in fact due. The U.S. Constitution says that no taxes are due; nowhere in the law is there a provision requiring citizens to pay income taxes. Therefore, all the pejorative statements made in the above article are proven to be false and misleading.

The writer of this propaganda piece further went on to make much adieu about the notion that the "Tax Court is getting tougher." So, therefore, Mr. and Mrs. terrified American citizen, you must hand over to the illegal illegitimate unconstitutional IRS as much of your hard-earned income as they demand, or else the Beast will come and stomp it's Orwellian boot on your face – forever.

The Sixteenth Amendment, which created the Income Tax Law in 1913, is *unconstitutional.* For anyone who is not a federal government employee working in the Washington District of Columbia, the paying of federal or other government income taxes is expressly *prohibited* by Article 1, Section 2, Clause 3; Section 8; and Section 9, Clause 4. By the LCF's own admission, only Satan's servants must pay tribute money to Satan.

Imagine the audacity of a government that was originally created to be the *servant of the people*, now unilaterally declaring (according to political parrot, Crenshaw): "Serious sanctions necessary to deter him and others similarly situated." That sounds like what Bill Clinton once said in reference to the Branch Dividians at Waco after he had authorized torching to death dozens of Christian men, women and their small children in a flaming inferno – i.e.: "... and we may have to do it again." Same phraseology; same antichrist spirit.

Was this Washington reporter trying to frighten the citizens of America into paying their unconstitutional taxes when stating: "The Tax Court ... is showing an increased willingness to hand out real pain to those it regards as abusers of the system." Government by the people, of the people, for the people? Real pain? That's a telling choice of words. It means: "Give us your money or we will take it from you by force." The LCF will *do whatever it wants.*

After proudly relating an account of an engineer and his wife who "failed to file tax returns from 1987 to 1997," and how the Florida court added $20,000 to the pirated man's already more than $300,000 in taxes and penalties, the DC sycophant recited, "The Tax Court determined that the IRS had met its burden of proving fraud and upheld the agency's assessment of back taxes and penalties. Then it added its own penalty." The journalist failed to mention that the Tax Court and the IRS are one and the same entity, and also that a fraudulent enterprise such as the IRS labeling fraudulent the actions of a righteously indignant innocent man is a classic example of *1984* doublespeak: Slavery is Freedom, War is Peace (*Woe unto them that call evil good, and good evil.* Isaiah 5:20). The name of the "engineer" was conspicuously missing from this account, and therefore, this story too is an undocumented fiction to induce fear and trembling among the terrorized citizenry.

Finally, when attacking Irwin Schiff, who, "for many years ... counseled through books and a Web site that paying taxes is voluntary... " and who is "now liable for more than $2 million in taxes and penalties," the NWO media puppet flippantly professed that "The court victories are good news for the IRS, which has sometimes struggled to convince the public that tax protesters' arguments are not valid." Correction: It is the IRS and the Beast's civil government arguments that are not valid. In portraying Irwin Schiff as a "promoter of frivolous tax evasion excuses," federal agent Crenshaw failed to recognize the righteous character of those few who stand up and are heard; *who call evil, evil.* (Schiff has for many years offered a $5,000 reward to anyone who can show him the law stating that paying income taxes is mandatory for U.S. citizens. To date, no one has yet come forward to claim the prize – it's not mandatory, but voluntary.)

The last word on paying "mandatory income taxes" is that – like the Federal Reserve centralized banking system in America – income taxes are *unconstitutional*, and therefore, *illegal.* Anyone who submits to paying tribute money to the Beast government becomes a servant of the same. *Know ye not, that to whom ye yield yourselves servants to obey, his servants ye are to whom ye obey; whether of sin unto death, or of obedience unto righteousness?* (Romans 6:16). Servants of Jesus Christ do not serve the Beast, nor do they submit to the Beast's demands to pay tribute money. The battle cry of the early American colonists was "Millions for defense, but not one cent for tribute." If only today's cowardly dumbed-down U.S. citizenry could remember that glorious past when truth was something worth fighting for.

Irwin Schiff understood it. He should be a national hero. But instead, he's in a federal prison.

During the time this author was perusing the newspaper from which the above three articles were obtained, he did not find anything written that was not Police State propaganda intended to condition the readers not to resist the NWO terrorists. After reading a short propaganda story about yet another unnamed "enemy of the state"– this time, a man who shot ten rounds at the police (who reportedly did not return gun fire) – the writer noted that the "right-wing extremist" was taken into police custody and given a 30 year prison sentence. The message to the reader was: "Don't resist tyranny, or you're going to jail." Finally, there was a story about a veteran police detective who raped his stepdaughter at her 22nd birthday party celebration – and probably would not have to spend a day in jail for it. Lest this author would become nauseated, he settled for reading the comic section, but *even that* was spun to support the LCF's Police State propaganda!

Pre-Tribulation Rapture:

This is the unscriptural belief held by Professing Christians hoping they won't have to suffer persecution for the sake of Jesus Christ. It is their hope that they will be spared physical pain when bodily taken from the earth *prior to* the commencement of God's wrath during the Great Tribulation. They believe this, even though in the King James Bible there is no Scriptural support for such a false assumption. There is, however, much Scripture to prove that all those who love the Truth (Jesus Christ) will suffer persecution (2 Timothy 3:12); and, except those *accounted worthy to escape all these things that shall come to pass* (Luke 21:36), everyone will go through the Tribulation (Matthew 24:29-31). Typical of a Satanic doctrine and the utterances of the spiritually deceived, the Pre-Tribulation "Rapture" doctrine is a cultic belief that is in opposition to the truth of the Bible.

Proverb 10:30: *The righteous shall never be removed: but the wicked shall not inhabit the earth.* Therefore, the "Pre-Trib" believers will indeed be taken away because they are unrighteous in believing a false doctrine. Consequently, their eternal destiny will not be in heaven but a burning future in hell. Those who eagerly hope to be taken up bodily into Paradise, without having their faith tested; those who believe the fictional Tim LaHaye *Left Behind* novel series, give evidence of their rejection of the Word of God. The 1611 KJV provides assurance that such individuals will not enter into His eternal rest. The True Christian Elect who are still alive *immediately after* the Tribulation is over (Matthew 24:29), *will* physically meet Jesus Christ in the air. It is *only these* who will not have to experience physical death, but they will likely be persecuted by the Antichrist LCF Beast. Prior to that single event, there *is no* "Pre-Tribulation Rapture."

Pseudo-Christianity:

These are the Professing Christians, those many who profess to be Christian, but are merely deceiving themselves. Frequently condemned throughout the Holy Scriptures, they are proof that *the heart is deceitful above all things, and desperately wicked: who can know it?* (Jeremiah 17:9). Titus 1:16 speaks of them in these terms: *They profess that they know God; but in works they deny him, being abominable, and disobedient, and unto every good work reprobate.* In today's Jesus Christ rejecting world, if someone claims to be "a Christian," that is often the first indication they are not a Scripturally-approved True Christian. The unqualified proclamation of being "Christian" fails to impart any substantive meaning in today's neopagan culture. Even hardened legal criminals (Presidents and Masonic members of Congress) lay claim to the distinction of being "a Christian." An individual's spiritual identity must be defined in terms of their relationship to the spoken and written Word of God – i.e. Jesus Christ and His 1611 King James Bible. Today, instead of acknowledging their fallen nature by realizing they are inherently evil, and repenting of their sins, many insist they are "Christian." Yet, it is not an individual's opinion which determines if they are a Christian, but rather, what *God says* is a Christian. The Lord Jesus Christ declared in Matthew 7:16: *Ye shall know them by their fruits.* Professing Christians are *goats;* they bear the *fruit* of goats. Differentiation of True Christians, Matthew 25:31-46 makes a clear distinction between goats and sheep and mentions what some of those fruits are.

Likewise confusing is what pseudo-Christianity terms, "The Church." To them, it means a building, a physical location were like-minded people profess to be "Christian." This is Scripturally incorrect. The True Church, like True Christians, is not part of the world system of organized religion. The True Church of Jesus Christ, which was first established on Pentecost about 2000 years ago, consists of all those *throughout world history* who did not deny Jesus Christ. The Church itself is not a building, but rather, a select few individuals – the Remnant Elect –who pass through the narrow gate that leads to life everlasting, not through the broadway that leads to death (Matthew 7:13,14). Therefore, in order to avoid further terminology confusion, True Christians should specify exactly what they mean whenever using the phrase: *The Church.* For instance, instead of the unqualified term, "Church," they should substitute the Greek definition of Church – "the called out ones." This will serve to clarify contemporary word meanings and thus avoid mistaking the True Church with the *Apostate* Church.

The following is a partial list of some characteristics typifying a pseudo-Christian *Apostate Church.* For a more complete list, ref. "Are you a True Christian?" at back of this book.

1) The church is registered with the Beast government; the pastor has signed a 501(c)3 tax exempt document affirming that the head of his/her "church" is the State's Attorney General, not Jesus Christ. Also, as a Ward of the State, the Apostate Church agrees not to speak out against abortion, homosexuality and the Police State NWO Luciferian government. Such a "Church" is antichrist (1 John 2:22,23).

2) The church members believe in a "Pre-Tribulation Rapture."

3) The church is thought of in terms of being a physical construct – a building, a place of worship, etc.

4) The church members believe that "God is love," and that He will therefore not send anyone to hell who "believes in Jesus." The church members believe "once saved, always saved," and that the grace of God is a license to sin. They believe that divorce is "OK," and that "Christians" should "love everyone."

5) Their "Jesus" is different from the Jesus of the 1611 Authorized King James Bible.

6) The church members do not use KJV Scripture to support their beliefs. Often they present no Scripture of any kind in defense of their own personal opinions.

7) Their Bible version is the NIV, or any other version among numerous versions antithetical to the Authorized 1611 King James.

8) When church members are asked about Chemtrails, their dull delayed response is invariably: "Huh? Whater' chemtrails?" When further information is provided them, they indicate feigned interest or no interest.

9) The pastor does not publicly speak out against government tyranny.

10) The pastor is involved in politics, or expresses an interest in the political process (e.g. voting), or is sympathetic toward the Criminal Fraternity (e.g. "We should pray for our President and elected officials").

11) The pastor draws a guaranteed salary, plays golf or does yard work on Sundays, watches television, drives an SUV, and is a Freemason.

12) The pastor is a woman; or, if ostensibly a man, exhibits feminine mannerisms. The pastor is sympathetic toward gays and homosexuality ("We should hate the sin and love the sinner").

Rex 84:

Illuminati code for CF legislation that, when enacted, will officially suspend, then abolish, the Constitution and Bill of Rights. It is also the document which allows for the establishment of concentration camps in America. Recently discovered cargo on board a trans-oceanic ship docked in a San Diego California port were 3000 crates containing ... guillotines. Revelation 20:4: *... and I saw the souls of them that were beheaded for the witness of Jesus, and for the word of God, and which had not worshipped the beast, neither his image, neither had received his mark upon their foreheads, or in their hands....* These implements will one day separate not only heads from bodies, but also, True Christians from pseudo-Christians.

Rockefellers, Rothschilds and other Illuminists:

The name says it all: Feller: one who destroys, brings down, or fells – formerly used in the context of timber cutting – and "Rock," obviously intended to mean The Rock of our salvation, God Jesus Christ. Hence, the hope of the Luciferian Rockefellers is to "bring down" God Himself. Their European equivalent and mentor, the Rothschilds, have been avid Satan worshippers for many generations. They are 1st Level Luciferians; the Rockefellers are 2nd Level Luciferians. It is said that one of the earlier Rothschilds, Amschel, routinely set a place at his dinner table for Satan to manifest physically, and who would later play cards with the family. Such intimate association with the demonic is what gave these European bankers the financial clout to orchestrate a Federal Reserve banking system in Europe and later, in America. The satanic patriarch, John D. Rockefeller, passed the Luciferian torch on to his brood of offspring, including his son, David, who is one of today's top Illuminatus behind the creation of a worldwide dictatorial Police State. In the convoluted inter-familial relationships among the global elite, practically every high government official in a position of world influence was birthed by *planned breeding* to insure transfer of generational occult power and maximum expression of their demonic genetic heritage.

Satanic Ritual Abuse (SRA):

There exists a national and international network of child abductors, child prostitution and pornography – including bestiality, snuff films (ritual murder) and human sacrifice. Well documented in the literature, confirmed by independent accounts and testimonials, SRA is commonly practiced throughout the world, and has been steadily growing in America, especially over the last 50 years. (Over 1 million children are missing in the U.S. yearly; 8 million worldwide.) The nearly exponential increase in this, the most heinous of all crimes against humanity, can be attributed to the devastation that Satan's Criminal Fraternity has wreaked upon modern society, replacing the Word of God with Luciferian occult doctrines. Today, people have been indoctrinated through the Illuminati-controlled media, culture, and occult-based school curriculum to have no Scripturally-based sense of right and wrong, and therefore, no moral conscience. Spiritually anesthetized, people today are incapable of righteous indignation; they do not become angry at an injustice and experience no outrage at what the CF has done and is presently doing to them and their children. The skyrocketing divorce rate and fractured family is proof of the damage that has been planned by the globalists in destroying the basic unit of society.

Children raised by dysfunctional adults – one or both of which are often not their true biological parent – increases the probability for the occurrence of child abuse. In a world where sodomites are given special legal privileges, it is becoming ever more typical for children to be raised by demon-possessed homosexuals. Mass media indoctrination – television, the Hollywood film and music industry – conditions children at a young age to accept a satanic belief system in place of their *grandparent's* former Christian values.

Disinformation and denial of the existence of SRA has done much to perpetuate it, especially among apostate "Christianity." Religious Criminal Fraternity spokespersons and eminent pseudo-Christian highpriests are either strangely silent on the matter of SRA, or adamantly speak out *in defense of its nonexistence*! Some of these celebrity religionists and radio and television personalities have themselves been SRA mind-controlled and programmed. They were groomed by their occult handlers to become government operatives that function to confuse and obfuscate the SRA issue. For example, national radio talk show host, Hank Hanegraaff, billing himself as "The Bible Answer Man" and "President of the Christian Research Institute (CRI)," is a classic example of a mind-controlled pseudo-Christian programmed to be an SRA apologist. (He is also an apologist for the false "Pre-Tribulation Rapture" doctrine and the *unChristian* Catholic Church.) As a popular "Christian celebrity" offering a toll-free 800 Call-in number, Hanegraaff appeals to a biblically illiterate audience while acting as an apologist for Satanists and witches. (This author has taped broadcasts documenting his adamant public denials of the existence of Satanic Ritual Abuse.) In defending child-sacrificing Luciferians, he therefore betrays his own allegiance. Hanegraaff's associates, Gretchen and Bob Passantino, are authors of a work on Satanism and the occult. While posing as Christian researchers within the CRI, they are *advisors* to the "Bible Answer Man," and are affiliated with anti-Christian front groups identifying themselves as Wiccan witches and Satanists. Such is the level of deceit among the leadership of today's end time apostate Religious Criminal Fraternity.

A disinformation ploy known as False Memory Syndrome (FMS) is often promulgated by the Satanist's network of the Legal and Medical Criminal Fraternity in an attempt to deny the existence of SRA. Emergency treatment medical doctors, psychologists, psychiatrists, social workers and other mental health workers cooperate to legitimatize the FMS ruse. In attempting to discredit the reality of SRA, their severely traumatized patients are told they have merely *imagined* they were forced to participate in child-sacrificing blood rituals. Felony charges brought against CF members – most of whom are respectable citizens within the community – are typically not successfully prosecuted by the Freemasonry courts: the police, judges and attorneys, who are often *themselves* practicing witches, Satanists, sexual predators and child molesters.

Independent unrelated sources (ref. *References*) have documented the existence of organized Satanism within virtually every police department in America. Likewise, the medical community is well supplied with Luciferians in key positions that can *discredit* the reports and *cover up* the aftermath of child sacrifices that routinely take place in communities all across America. From police chiefs to coroners, judges to hospital trauma surgeons, the local covens have operatives in place for insuring that knowledge of their heinous criminal activities never leaks out to the mainstream media. Web sites offering help for traumatized SRA victims are soon disabled; legitimate organizations providing victim assistance are quickly disbanded or infiltrated and in their place are spurious SRA organizations and groups run by Satanists who apprehend runaway "defectors" and bring them back into the coven. Children and women attempting to escape the web of the Satanic ritual network are usually caught and traumatized still further. The international SRA cult is like a spider web that receives vibrations from crisis centers, children services organizations and government social services programs; any ritual abuse survivor who calls into an SRA hot line, or checks into a hospital, Trauma Clinic, or Crisis Center, will fall into a trap set for catching ritually abused escapees.

The local news media is controlled by key members of the SRA network. Ritual cult murderers are never named in the press because they are shielded by layers of collusion within the vast Criminal Fraternity organization. There is not an editor of *any* large newspaper in the country who will print a story exposing the existence or prevalence of SRA ritual abuse and murder, or who will name the influential LCF Masons responsible for such horrendous crimes.

Ritualized abuse can be perpetrated by anyone, and especially by those that have government-sanctioned positional authority. Police, politicians, attorneys, judges, doctors, are common within the SRA network. They seek power, spiritual power, and will kill to get it. The global SRA organization can be traced all the way to the key Illuminati families who rule the world. The Satanic hierarchy is multi-generational and extends its power and influence throughout all strata of society. High-ranking members of Freemasonry secret and semisecret societies are prolific ritual child abusers.

Shadow Government:

As Illuminati-sponsored front men, figurehead Presidents offer a convincing image that the American public can pin their hopes for a New Age of prosperity. But little do they realize that those occupying high political offices are placed into power by the Illuminati supra-government.

The Luciferian Council of 13 is in control of the world, irrespective of who occupies the titular office of "U.S. President." The Illuminati correctly calculates that the truth-hating American public will rally around an individual with low moral standards and who exhibits characteristics of compulsive lying and treason.
Simplistic trust in government officials demonstrates the amazing degree of ignorance, spiritual blindness, unrepentant sin and sheer stupidity of the American people.

"Snipers" and School Shootings:

Like 9/11, "snipers" are simply another example of *planned terrorism* by the CF globalists. The Luciferians calculate to convince the masses that their children are not safe from the many threats which Luciferians sponsor and create. The human-demon hybrids that run the world understand the mentality of the sheeple – they *should,* since it was *they* who incrementally programmed the people to become sheeple – and therefore they realize that a global government will become a reality when the 325 million duped citizens of America *beg them* to be protected from "the terrorists" (i.e. *them*). Rather than rise up against the Beast that oppresses them, instead, the spiritually timid forfeit their God-given rights to the government Devil. Spiritually Blind and twice dead (Jude 12), they love the chains that bind them.

The adolescent perpetrators of school shootings have been mind-controlled by CIA trauma-based conditioning that fragments their mind into discrete compartmentalized personalities. Some of these "Delta Slaves" are programmed as efficient killers. Young adults are selected from families of generational Satanists; these are children raised in a home environment where, since infancy, they were emotionally, physically and sexually abused by their parents, guardians and relatives. This lifelong history of trauma preconditions them for more intensified programming and mind fragmentation by psychological trauma techniques implemented by government mind control specialists (handlers). Microchips implanted into these "experimental subjects" allows for remote control of their actions via electronic signaling directly to their brain. In this manner the Luciferians can create a monster, without conscious or will; an emotionless child or young adult programmed to stage a mass murder, blow up a building, incite a riot, or any number of other acts for promoting chaos according to the NWO "Problem-Reaction-Solution" Hegelian Dialectic. For example, school shootings by mind-controlled micro-chipped teenagers is calculated to create a public outcry for *more gun control laws*, which are actually *gun confiscation laws* to disarm the public. Thus, the "solution": No citizen armaments means a *resistance-free NWO takeover of America.*

The Government's "War on Drugs":

There *is no* government War on Drugs. The reasons are as follows: The governments of the world, especially England and the United States, are the largest and most extensively organized dope dealers in the world. The United States Federal government's primary source of revenue is derived from trafficking in illicit narcotics. By means of interlocking corporate directorates – most of which are nonexistent shell companies – and the cooperation of the foreign-owned Federal Reserve centralized banking system, several hundred billion dollars per year in drug money profits taken from American streets and school playgrounds are laundered and then used to promote the Luciferian NWO agenda. Drugs (both "legal" pharmaceutical drugs and illegal street drugs) are the world's largest and most profitable business enterprise. Dominated and controlled by the Beast government, global trafficking in narcotics is operated by the very same Criminal Fraternity that strives to criminalize drug usage among its citizenry. The FBI, CIA and Justice Department are the chief vehicle through which drugs are efficiently imported into America. These LCF government agencies act as a *protection racket* for the underworld drug cartels, and also fund and promote international terrorists groups, most of which are involved in drug transport and distribution for the U.S. federal government.

An even greater hypocrisy is the manner in which the CF *eliminates their competition,* entrapping the small-time dope dealer, then declaring possession or distribution a felony offense punishable by a minimum of 8 years in a federal prison. (The *conspiratorial* LCF has the audacity to label the drug offense a "conspiracy." Meanwhile, socially-acceptable legal criminals are the middlemen in a drug conspiracy industry they pretend to police!) Above suspicion, the LCF has the favor and protection of the worldwide shadow government – the supremely wicked and wealthy men positioned within the Illuminati crime cartel who rule over governments and generate enormous profits from inflicting human misery on a global scale (e.g. instigating and financing wars, staging terrorist events). Over the last 100 years, drug trafficking has exponentially multiplied their wealth.

The book, *Dope, Inc.,* reveals that the U.S. economy and Federal Reserve banking system are supported and maintained by the international drug trade. Even so, financial gain is only one objective among the international Luciferian Brotherhood's larger agenda of propagating drug usage as a means of social mind control and physical and psychological destruction, especially among children and adolescent young adults. International drug smuggling is an *open conspiracy* requiring the cooperation of governments, big business and financial institutions. Today's large banks throughout the world are essentially drug laundering facilities. Bankers and politicians work together with seedy third world drug smugglers and dope traffickers to bring their *cash crop* to the marketplace. Ruthless drug lords, by virtue of their political influence and vast wealth gained from the drug trade, are sometimes promoted to respectable positions of power within government. This is a further reason why Capital Hill's rally cry of a "*War on Drugs*" is such a laughable farce. A true war on drugs is impossible because the financial and social control interests of the CF drug politicians would be severely compromised.

The LCF's so-called "War on Drugs" assumes an even greater depth of perversity in consideration of the fact that those incarcerated for "drug violations" are supplied with a steady flow of street contraband from prison guards, the government's own agents.

UFO's and "extraterrestrials":

There is very little that needs to be said about this subject. Lacking spiritual discernment, all speculation is merely indoctrination into an occult-based theology. From the message conveyed by the "greys" – in one of their many deceptive manifestations – it is clear that all UFO-related phenomenon are strictly of a non-material spiritual nature. Further, while the content of their communications is antagonistic to biblical principles and to the Christian God, it is highly supportive of occult theology and the NWO Luciferian agenda. From these cursory observation alone – and there are many more – it can be deduced that the abode of these cosmic impostors is none other than the realm of the "prince of the power of the air (Ephesians 2:2). In conclusion, the UFO's are nonmaterial manifestations of evil spirits; they are the Genesis 6:4 fallen angels. For all the interest among the Spiritually Blind that are perishing, these beings of light (2 Corinthians 11:14) are nothing more than *masquerading demons.*

An alien "savior" will draw millions of Professing Christians and others away from Jesus Christ. And *that* will be The Greatest Deception (ref. *The Great Deception* and *The Coming of Wisdom*).

501(c)3 tax exempt government "Christian" churches:

The pastors of these State incorporated churches are agents of the Criminal Fraternity. The head of their church is not Jesus Christ (Colossians 1:18; Ephesians 1:22; 4:5), but the State's Attorney General. Nearly 100 percent of today's churches claiming to be Christian are 501(c)3 tax exempt corporations. Having committed spiritual fornication with the Luciferian world system, these apostate *Professing Christian* churches are not True Christian Churches, but rather, *government churches,* where misguided pastors and their congregations attempt to serve two masters (Matthew 6:24). In having been deceived into taking the name of the government Beast (Revelation 13:17), because they do not love the truth, God has sent them *strong delusion, that they should believe a lie* (2 Thessalonians 2:9-12). The CIA has recruited over 100,000 Christian pastors in America into their "Clergy Response Team" which swares allegiance to the Antichrist Beast government (ref. pp. 152-153). The spirit of antichrist (1 John 2:18,19) reigns in today's Whore of Babylon (Revelation 17:5) that serves the interests of ungodly government while calling itself "Christian." True Christians are to *come out of her, my people, that ye be not partakers of her sins, and that ye receive not of her plagues* (Revelation 18:4). In these final days, True Christians should gather in their homes for mutual fellowship and to read the 1611 King James Bible. *That* is the True Christian Church.

What the Illuminati Globalists **FEAR** the most ...

THE AUTHORIZED 1611 KING JAMES BIBLE IS THE ONLY WORD OF GOD.

There is one body, and one Spirit, even as ye are called in one hope of your calling; One Lord, one faith, one baptism, One God and Father of all ... (Ephesians 4:4-6).

THERE IS ONLY ONE WORD OF GOD ... JESUS CHRIST,

his name is called the Word of God (Revelation 19:13), *the way, the truth, and the life* (John 14:6), *the sword of the Spirit* (Ephesians 6:17), *quick, and powerful, and sharper than any twoedged sword* (Hebrews 4:12). *In the beginning was the Word, and the Word was with God, and the Word was God. The same was in the beginning with God. All things were made by him; and without him was not any thing made that was made. In him was life; and the life was the light of men. And the light shineth in darkness; and the darkness comprehended it not* (John 1:1-5).

Jesus Christ is God, One God, the *spoken* **Word of God**; His 1611 King James Bible is One Word, the *written* **Word of God**, Jesus Christ.

Sanctify them through thy truth: thy word is truth (John 17:17).

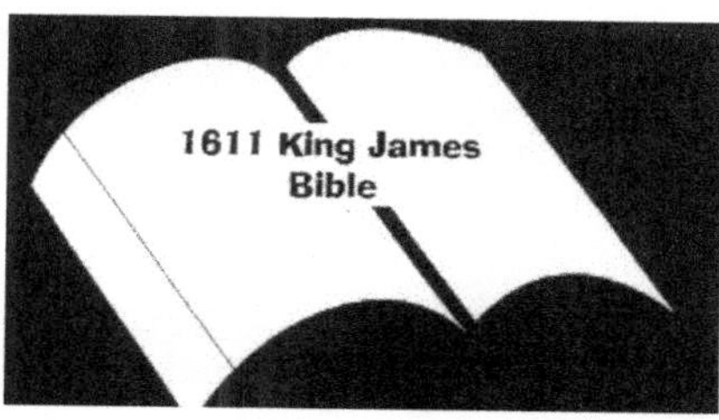

For I testify unto every man that heareth the words of the prophecy of this book, If any man shall add unto these things, God shall add unto him the plagues that are written in this book. And if any man shall take away from the words of the book of this prophecy, God shall take away his part out of the book of life, and out of the holy city, and from the things which are written in this book (Revelation 22:18,19).

Book Ordering

The following books can be ordered online from
bn.com or *amazon.com*

Any other websites are unapproved and unauthorized.
These titles can also be purchased direct from retail bookstores.

__ The Great Deception

__ The Coming of Wisdom (sequel to The Great Deception)

__ Fools Paradise: The Spiritual Implications of Gambling

__ Seven Who Dared

__ The Criminal Fraternity: Servants of the Lie

__ *When* Will the Illuminati Crash the Stock Market? An Insider's Look at the Elite Satanic Luciferians Who Dictate the Rise and Fall of Global Economies

__ Genesis 1:29 Diet: Perfect Health Without Doctors, Hospitals, or Pharmaceutical Drugs

__ Fractal Trading: Analyzing Financial Markets using Fractal Geometry and the Golden Ratio

__ The Globalist's Agenda: Design for a New World Order

__ Everything is a Test: How God Delivered Me from "Impossible" Situations

soulesprit.com

Answers to Questionnaire: 1, 2, 21, 34, 39, 40: "Yes"
All other answers: "No"